The Principal's Quick-Reference Guide to School Law

Second Edition

SECOND EDITION

THE PRINCIPAL'S QUICK-REFERENCE GUIDE TO SCHOOL LAW

Reducing Liability, Litigation, and Other Potential Legal Tangles

DENNIS R. DUNKLEE   ROBERT J. SHOOP

FOREWORD BY CHARLES J. RUSSO

CORWIN PRESS
A SAGE Publications Company
Thousand Oaks, California

For information:

Corwin Press
A Sage Publications Company
2455 Teller Road
Thousand Oaks, California 91320
www.corwinpress.com

Sage Publications Ltd.
1 Oliver's Yard
55 City Road
London EC1Y 1SP
United Kingdom

Sage Publications India Pvt. Ltd.
B-42, Panchsheel Enclave
Post Box 4109
New Delhi 110 017 India

Printed in the United States of America

Library of Congress Cataloging-in-Publication Data

Dunklee, Dennis R.
The principal's quick-reference guide to school law: Reducing liability, litigation, and other potential legal tangles/Dennis R. Dunklee, Robert J. Shoop.—2nd ed.
        p. cm.
Includes bibliographical references and index.
ISBN 978-1-4129-2593-8 (cloth)—ISBN 978-1-4129-2594-5 (pbk.)
  1. Educational law and legislation—United States—Popular works. 2. School management and organization—United States—Popular works. I. Shoop, Robert J. II. Title.
KF4119.6.D86 2006
344.73'07—dc22   2005031689

This book is printed on acid-free paper.

10   9   8   7   6   5   4   3

Acquisitions Editor:	Elizabeth Brenkus
Editorial Assistant:	Desirée Enayati
Production Editor:	Beth A. Bernstein
Copy Editor:	Barbara Coster
Typesetter:	C&M Digitals (P) Ltd.
Proofreader:	Christine Dahlin
Indexer:	Sylvia Coates
Cover Designer:	Lisa Miller

Brief Contents

Detailed Contents

Foreword

The Supreme Court's monumental 1954 ruling in *Brown v. Board of Education* raised the consciousness of school officials in K–12 settings about their duty to provide equal education opportunities for all children. *Brown* not only opened an era of equal educational opportunity for all students but also heightened the awareness of educational leaders to comply with the many legal obligations that arise as a result of the evolution of the field that is today known as School (or Education) Law.

In fact, when asked, most principals will readily admit that School Law and related legal issues occupy a great deal of time in their daily activities. The centrality of School Law for educational leaders is reflected in a comprehensive study conducted on behalf of the University Council for Educational Administration (UCEA), a consortium of doctoral degree granting institutions in the United States and overseas. This study revealed that with 87.5% of UCEA's members offering courses in education law, it is the second most commonly taught subject in leadership programs. Moreover, insofar as many universities offer a variety of graduate and undergraduate classes in School Law, it remains a crucial element in the preparation of professional educators, clearly indicating that as an applied, rather than purely theoretical discipline, it is essential for educators at all levels.

Aware of the crucial role that School Law plays in the day-to-day professional lives of educators, *The Principal's Quick-Reference Guide to School Law: Reducing Liability, Litigation, and Other Potential Legal Tangles* concisely and accurately accomplishes the goal that its title proclaims. Written in easy-to-read straightforward language, *The Principal's Quick-Reference Guide* neatly addresses long-standing and emerging issues that impact on daily school operations. Whether examining such legal staples of the field as negligence and the adequate supervision of students, the constitutional rights of students and teachers, discipline, search and seizure, and sexual harassment or emerging concerns as represented by the No Child Left Behind Act, *The Principal's Quick-Reference Guide* is replete with practical examples and useful advice on dealing with legal matters as they emerge. In so doing, *The Principal's Quick-Reference Guide* recognizes that School Law is a dynamic, intellectually stimulating discipline that is constantly evolving to meet the needs of educational leaders as they direct the daily activities in their schools.

In enhancing its usefulness, each chapter in *The Principal's Quick-Reference Guide* includes focus points that bring home the practical dimensions of their topics. *The Principal's Quick-Reference Guide* also focuses on such basic concepts as due process and equal protection, essential elements in the development of sound policies and best practices. In other words, as important as abstract legal principles or theories may be, *The Principal's Quick-Reference Guide* is a useful resource for practitioners who need to understand and apply basic legal principles, rather than memorize case holdings apart from their applications in day-to-day, real life situations.

At the heart of *The Principal's Quick-Reference Guide* is the authors' awareness of the need to help educators to become proactive rather than reactive so that they can use the law as a tool to help ensure that they can meet the needs of all of their constituents, ranging from students and parents to faculty, staff, and the local community. Yet, as the goal of making the law proactive becomes complicated due to the ever-changing nature of School Law, *The Principal's Quick-Reference Guide* teaches educators to think like lawyers but not to become lawyers. Put another way, rather than trying to turn educators into lawyers who are equipped to deal with such technical and procedural matters as jurisdiction and statutes of limitation, this book provides principals of a broad understanding of the law that will allow them to accomplish two important goals.

First, *The Principal's Quick-Reference Guide* provides principals with awareness of the legal dimensions of a wide array of topics so they can better frame questions for their attorneys to answer, performing a kind of triage to limit problems when a legal controversy arises. To this end, it teaches principals to recognize the great value in making their attorneys equal partners not only in problem-solving after the fact, but also in developing responsive, proactive policies before difficulties can arise. Such a proactive approach is consistent with the notion of preventative law wherein knowledgeable educators can identify potential problems in advance and in concert with an attorney can work to ensure they do not develop into crises. Moreover, when educational leaders select attorneys for their boards, for example, they would be well-advised to hire individuals with specialized practices in education law, thereby avoiding potential lapses in critical knowledge and ensuring their advice has the most up-to-date perspectives on legal matters.

Second, *The Principal's Quick-Reference Guide* helps principals to rely upon their substantive knowledge of the law by providing a handy, user-friendly guide that affords them the opportunity to update their knowledge so they can develop sound policies to enhance the day-to-day operations of schools.

In sum, given the breadth of coverage and the ease with which principals, and others, can access vital information about schools, the second edition of *The Principal's Quick-Reference Guide* will continue to remain an essential resource that sits on the desks of principals.

—Charles J. Russo, JD, EdD
Panzer Chair in Education and
Adjunct Professor of Law, University of Dayton

Preface and Advisement

In the first edition of this book we stated that

> *Once upon a time there was order in our schools and change occurred so benevo-lently that it was called progress. There was a place and a time for everything. There were authorities, too. The principal spoke without hesitation about what was appropriate behavior. Dad and Mom told their children to go to school and "mind the teacher," and students listened and learned and behaved themselves. Teachers and school administrators worked in harmony with each other. Parents left edu-cational decisions up to the schools. The courts rarely got involved with schools, and when they were asked to make a decision, they tended to side with schools.*
>
> *Then something happened. Some say parents failed in their responsibility. Some say schools lost their direction and control. Some say society became too permissive. Some say the courts started to get involved where they did not belong.* (p. xxx)

We couldn't say then, and we still can't say definitively what happened (societal changes, court rulings, etc.), but we know that much that was nailed down suddenly came loose. We know that the job of school principal is vastly different today from what it was 20 years ago, 10 years ago—or even yesterday. Today's principals grapple with a sea of conflicting demands from their school boards, central office administrators, students, teachers, parents, and commu-nity pressure groups. Principals' jobs are further complicated by the seemingly endless and often contradictory statutes, court decisions, and attorney generals' opinions that directly affect the operation of their schools. As a result of these pressures, principals often feel insecure and, at times, powerless when it comes to balancing the pressure to do something, on the one hand, against legal restraints, on the other. Today's principals face an additional dilemma as they address the task of balancing the need for order with the need to respect the legal rights of students, teachers, and parents.

Although a number of good books are available on education law, few focus directly on the specific needs of the principal. *The Principal's Quick-Reference Guide,* First edition, was written exclusively for preservice and inservice princi-pals, vice principals, and other building-level administrators, to provide basic information on the current status of law and site-based risk management as it relates to the legal rights and responsibilities inherent in managing and leading schools. The second edition follows the same blueprint and has the same essential goals. In addition, the second edition provides programmatic guidance for other school district personnel, for example, directors of student services, human resources, special education, support services, and risk managers.

Nearly all school administrators have had a course in school law. They know that the law affects almost every facet of education. However, most school law courses end without helping the principal translate school law and policy into education procedures and practice. This book helps close that gap and places principals in a better position to maintain a safe school and to be on the offensive in litigation avoidance and conflict resolution.

Most legal actions brought against school principals are not based on the areas of education leadership or knowledge of curriculum. Principals who find themselves defendants in court often got there because they didn't know the relevant law or didn't practice sound management based on an understanding of existing court decisions. This book helps principals understand and gives them a stronger foundation for the management of risk.

As we did in the first edition, we designed this book to be a desk reference in which a school administrator can quickly find and identify important legal points to consider during decision-making processes when such decisions may have legal consequences. This second edition retains that design. To further assist in that process, we continue to use straightforward, nontechnical language and follow a standard format in presenting pertinent information.

WHAT'S NEW OR DIFFERENT IN THE SECOND EDITION?

This second edition, while retaining the reader-friendly format we introduced in the first edition, demonstrates the inevitable introduction of new precedents that continue to shape education law. It would be redundant to list all of those changes here; however, a few are particularly significant.

- Each chapter, including the Management Cues and Risk Management Guidelines, has been carefully updated to ensure primacy of precedence.
- A comprehensive index is included at the close of the book.
- Additional references to important U.S. Supreme Court and other landmark cases are cited in many chapters for those interested in further research and analysis.
- Two new chapters that address significant and expanding issues under the law have been added: "The No Child Left Behind Act: Implications of NCLB on Local Schools" (Chapter 3) and "State-Created Danger and Deliberate Indifference" (Chapter 14).
- Chapter 8, "The Principal's Responsibilities in Providing Special Education Services," has been completely edited to reflect the most current trends and laws affecting this ever-changing area of legal complexities.

Learned Hand noted in an address to the Association of the Bar of the City of New York in 1921: "After now some dozen years of experience [as a judge] I must say that as a litigant I should dread a lawsuit beyond almost anything else short of sickness and death" (Association of the Bar, 1926, p. 87). The operative word in 1921 was *dread*. The operative word in the second edition of this book is *prevention*, and as was true in the first edition, this practitioner's guide to education law is designed to reduce ex post facto decision making (applying law or making rules after the fact) in real-life, school-based risk management and incident resolution. If Latin were a living language, perhaps we could coin a new phrase, *pre facto decision making*, to describe this book's proactive approach to avoiding litigation and managing risk. We hope that by continuing to equip principals and other school leaders to act with both knowledge and understanding of education law, we will help them to be able to make wise, safe, and legally defensible decisions in the best interests of students, teachers, and parents. We hope that this book might make the daunting job of being an effective school leader a bit easier.

Please be advised that this book and the statements of the authors represent an attempt to respond to the professional needs of the reader. The case law interpretation and the presentation of scenarios are not designed as statements of final authority. Only a court of law, guided by individual case facts, can be considered as an authority on a specific issue. That issue may be treated differently from court to court, state to state. This book serves a purpose for the education profession and provides only suggested guidelines for the avoidance of litigation. This book should not be considered a forecaster of impending or future litigation. It should also be noted that any guidelines suggested should be treated with caution in light of the specific subject matter examined and the expected level of personal involvement. There are those administrative and teaching responsibilities that transcend the norm, requiring a higher degree of duty and care, supervision, instruction, and maintenance. This book is designed to provide accurate and authoritative information in regard to the subject matter covered. In publishing this book, neither the authors nor the publisher is engaged in rendering legal service. If legal advice or assistance is required, the services of a competent attorney should be sought. Although the Management Cues used as examples in this book are loosely based on actual or common events, such examples should be considered fictitious or hypothetical, and any resemblance to real people or to specific incidents is coincidental.

ACKNOWLEDGMENTS

The authors wish to acknowledge the hard work of and thank the SGD Writing Center, especially Sandy, for the exemplary editing, proofing, and support for us as we developed this second edition. As always, when we were lost for just the right word, phrase, or direction, Sandy was there with the "best" answer, and inevitably the "right" answer. And, of course, here's to Bucky—little known, but still remembered.

Corwin Press gratefully acknowledges the contributions of the following reviewers:

Dana Trevethan
Principal
Turlock High School
Turlock, CA

Michelle Kocar
Principal
Liberty Elementary School
North Ridgeville, OH

Stephen Handley
Principal
Terry High School
Terry, MS

John Casper
Supervisor of Secondary Instruction
Nelson County Public Schools
Bardstown, KY

REFERENCE

Association of the Bar of the City of New York. (1926). *Lectures on Legal Topics*. New York: Author.

About the Authors

 **Dr. Dennis R. Dunklee** is Associate Professor in the Education Leadership Department in the Graduate School of Education at George Mason University. He teaches courses in education law and school leadership and serves as an advisor and chair for master's and doctoral candidates in school leadership. Because of his expertise and practical experience, he is frequently called on to consult in the areas of effective schools, school law, administrator evaluation, instructional supervision, school-community relations, problem solving, and conflict resolution. In addition, he has been involved as a consultant and expert witness in numerous school-related lawsuits nationwide. During his 25 years in public schools, he served as a teacher, elementary school principal, junior high and middle school principal, high school principal, and central office administrator. As a university scholar and researcher, he has published eight textbooks, two monographs, and more than 100 articles on issues in the fields of school law, business management, administrative practice, and leadership theory. He is active in a number of professional organizations, has presented papers at international, national, regional, state, and local conferences, and is a widely sought after clinician for inservice workshops. He was an invited participant and presenter in the 2005 Oxford (University) Round Table on Education Law: Individual Rights and Freedoms.

He received his PhD in school administration and foundations from Kansas State University. His major area of research was in the field of education law, and his dissertation was on tort liability for negligence. He holds a master's degree in elementary and secondary school administration from Washburn University.

This is Dr. Dunklee's sixth book for Corwin Press. His other Corwin books are *Anatomy of a Lawsuit: What Every Education Leader Should Know about Legal Actions* (2006) (with Robert J. Shoop), *Strategic Listening for School Leaders* (2005) (with Jeannine Tate), *The Principal's Quick-Reference Guide to School Law* (2002) (with Robert J. Shoop), *If You Want to Lead, Not Just Manage* (2000), and *You Sound Taller on the Telephone: A Practitioner's View of the Principalship* (1999).

Dr. Robert J. Shoop is Professor of Education Law and Senior Scholar in the Leadership Studies Program at Kansas State University. He is a nationally recognized expert in the area of school law, with a focus on sexual harassment and abuse prevention, and risk management. He is the coproducer of a number of video programs on eliminating sexual harassment. These productions have received national and international recognition, including First Place Award, 1996 National Council of Family Relations Annual Media Competition; 1996 Gold Award of Merit, Houston Film Festival; and 1995 Golden Camera Award, International Film and Video Festival. He is the 1996 recipient of the Michael C. Holen Excellence in Graduate Teaching Award, a past recipient of Kansas State University's Outstanding Undergraduate Teacher Award, and a past member of the board of directors of the Educational Law Association. He has served as a teacher, community education director, and principal, and he was the Ohio State Evaluator of Student Rights and Responsibilities. He has consulted with national associations, community colleges, universities, governmental agencies, and businesses and educational organizations throughout the United States and in several foreign countries. He has appeared as a guest on CNN, *The Today Show* with both Katie Couric and Matt Lauer, ABC's *20/20*, *MSNBC with Lester Holt, Day and Date, The Jim Bohannon Show, The Oliver North Show, The Mark Furman Show, The Mark Walberg Show,* and *Outside the Lines with Bob Ley.*

He is the author or coauthor of over 100 journal articles, 15 books, and several monographs and book chapters on various legal issues. His most recent books are *Virtuous Leadership* (2004), *Sexual Exploitation of Students: How to Spot It, and Stop It* (2003), *Leadership Lessons from Bill Snyder* (1998), *Sexual Harassment Prevention* (1997), *Sexual Harassment on Campus: A Guide for Administrators, Faculty Members, and Students* (1996) (coedited with Dr. Bernice Sandler), and *How to Stop Sexual Harassment in Our Schools* (1994).

This is the sixth law-related book written by the team of Shoop and Dunklee. Their other books are *Anatomy of a Lawsuit: What Every Education Leader Should Know about Legal Actions* (2006), *The Principal's Quick-Reference Guide to School Law* (2002), *The Legal Manual for Programming Professionals* (1994), *A Primer for School Risk Management* (1993), and *School Law for the Principal* (1992).

Introduction

Laws reflect the society that develops them. Similarly, judges and juries operate within a social context that influences the outcome of litigation concerning particular issues. Consequently, laws and judicial decisions reflect the political trends, philosophical attitudes, ethical viewpoints, and even the tendency toward compassion that prevail when legislatures enact them and courts interpret them. Beyond constitutional law, which is more focused because of the actions of the Supreme Court, school principals have to deal with an expanse of law that includes contracts, property, torts, general administrative law, legal relationships, civil rights, risk management, and so forth—all affecting the operation and administration of schools. Because education in the United States is controlled by each of the fifty states, it is sometimes difficult to identify or summarize any single interpretation of law that prevails in all states, much less all school districts.

So what is a principal to do when trying to become knowledgeable about school law to be effective in leading and managing a school? With differing statutory bases from state to state, with widely varying perspectives and philosophies influencing how judges and juries decide school litigation cases, and with schools often being the frontline arenas for conflicting social and political agendas, where can a principal obtain helpful and reliable guidance concerning decision making within the confines of the law? Consulting the school district's general counsel is certainly necessary and appropriate at times, but not regarding every single day-to-day decision that has legal ramifications. School principals need to understand the legal concepts and framework on which pertinent education law rests, so they can act decisively—and legally—to manage effective schools.

The authors of this book believe that the avoidance of education litigation requires more than just knowledge of the law. The determination to prevent disputes, avoid litigation, and manage risk is an effective administrative mind-set—a mind-set referred to as preventive law, which increases the prospect of a "safe school" as well as the prospects for court rulings that are favorable to school districts and to the education enterprise in total.

In addition, the authors recognize that certain legal concepts affecting school law remain unchanged regardless of state legislative actions or court decisions. In this book, principals will find clear and simple explanations of these concepts. The most critical and the knotty legal issues facing schools will be presented, and points for school administrators to consider in making decisions regarding those issues will be suggested. This book, then, offers principals easy-to-understand guidelines for making decisions that minimize risk and avoid litigation.

However, readers of this book should keep in mind that the precedents identified by the authors may not neatly fit the numerous peculiarities and conditions of any single incident. The authors present concepts of law so that school administrators can apply such concepts to real-life school-based situations as they arise and can use the book in the decision-making processes before final decisions are made. It is important to understand that the facts of an individual situation are of utmost importance and that small variations in facts often result in large differences in appropriate decision making and, ultimately, in how a court might view the situation under the law.

This book represents an attempt by the authors to respond to the professional needs of school principals regarding school law. However, this book should not be considered as a statement of final authority but, rather, as a resource providing suggested guidelines for the avoidance of litigation. As stated in the preface, only a court of law guided by individual case facts can be considered as an authority on a specific issue—and remember, that issue may be treated differently from court to court, state to state. Also note that any risk management guidelines suggested should be viewed in light of the specific subject matter taught and the expected level of duty and standard of care.

School administrators are expected to know the law. The courts will not accept ignorance of the law as a defense. As stated in the preface, the majority of legal actions brought against school districts and school administrators are not based on their education leadership or knowledge of curriculum but, rather, on their failure to know the relevant law and to practice sound management based on an understanding of existing court decisions. Effective school administrators do not want to win lawsuits; they want to avoid them altogether. Understanding the basic concepts of law adds significant strength to the effective principal's decision-making abilities and catalogue of information.

The chapters in this book contain basic principles and guidelines for numerous legal issues. After an explanatory introduction, each chapter and section is presented in a template format. The use of a template makes the following possible:

- The authors have been able to condense a significant amount of information, resulting in a comprehensive yet compact desk reference.
- The reader can find answers quickly and easily to questions that arise in a particular situation.

The template includes an explanation of relevant law, Examples of Management Cues, and Guidelines for Risk Management.

- Cases cited to support relevant legal principles in each chapter have been selected on a precedent-setting or best-example basis regardless of jurisdiction or date of adjudication. They provide a baseline for decision making. In choosing this approach, the authors ensure that the book is not out of precedent today or even tomorrow.
- The Examples of Management Cues (triggering events) illustrate those kinds of events that should trigger action by school administrators. They represent red flags for which the basic text and Guidelines suggest decision-making strategies.
- The Guidelines for Risk Management are recommended strategies or actions that assist school administrators in making sound policy and procedural decisions.

In selecting material to be covered in this book from the vast quantity of existing legal precedent and law, as well as in choosing the legal concepts to discuss, the authors centered their focus on the daily activities of a typical school principal. Specifically, they attempted to answer the question, What does a school principal need to know about the laws affecting schools to make wise decisions? The book, therefore, does not claim to explore or even touch on all areas of school law but, rather, concentrates on those areas that are consistently troublesome for school administrative personnel and, as a result, often end in litigation.

The function of law is to regulate human conduct to ensure a harmonious and safe society. School administrators are constantly challenged to achieve a balance that allows students, teachers, other school employees, and parents as much freedom as possible and, at the same time, allows the school to function effectively without unreasonable interference from the conduct of any individuals. This book is designed to assist school administrators in maintaining such a balance.

▌ FOCUS POINT: Understanding Judicial Decisions

This second edition book, as was true with the first edition, does not require students or practitioners to analyze case law. The authors have done that for the reader and present a general overview of the outcomes of cases that directly impact the everyday professional responsibilities of school leaders. We include this Focus Point to assist you if you wish to research an issue by examining a specific case firsthand.

When researching referenced cases to read or analyze, in order to determine why a case is decided in the way it was, it's necessary to find the *ratio decidendi* ("reason for deciding")—the point on which the judgment balances. This is accomplished, for the most part, by carefully analyzing the "facts of the case" that were treated as "material" by the judge. In other words, "material facts" are the *ratio decidendi*. Conclusions or statements by a judge that depart from the *ratio decidendi* are not binding as precedents and are referred to as *orbiter dicta* ("other statements of the court that are not necessary for its decision"). This type of dicta is evident when

1. A statement of law is based on "immaterial" facts.

2. A statement of law, although based on established facts in the case, does not shape the rationale for the decision in the case. For example, when a judge makes a statement leading to one conclusion but makes a contrary decision on the facts for a different reason.

Llewellyn (1989) explains what to look for when reading and interpreting case law. He noted that

[f]or all our cases are decided, all our opinions are written, all our predictions, all our arguments are made, on certain four assumptions. . . . :

1. The court must decide the dispute that is before it.

2. The court can decide only the particular dispute which is before it.

3. The court can decide the particular dispute only according to a general rule that covers a whole class of like disputes.

4. Everything, everything, everything, big or small, a judge may say in an opinion is to be read with primary reference to the particular dispute, the particular question before him. (p. 286)

STATE WEB SITES

The authors recognize that a desk reference that will be useful to principals across the nation must by nature cover certain topics only in general terms and that in certain areas (such as special education) ongoing legislation and litigation continue to supersede and outdate established precedent as soon as it can be written down. They also realize that principals need access to their own specific state's laws and regulations to act in compliance with such legal directives. While we've not attempted to include these in this book, we call your attention to the fact that individual state Web sites can be accessed by practitioners to supplement the general discussion of certain topics and help readers gain information about education-specific laws and regulations particular to their own states.

LOCATING CASE-SPECIFIC INFORMATION AND LATEST PRECEDENT

There are a number of law-based Web sites available for practitioners to access. Because case law is extremely fluid, the authors recommend seeking current updates/court rulings on specific subjects by utilizing the availability and services of the World Wide Web.

CHAPTER RESOURCE

Llewellyn, K. N. (1989). *The case law system in America*. Chicago: University of Chicago Press.

1

Preventive Law

Developing Risk and Crisis Management Programs

Accidents, incidents, or transgressions are organizational and managerial problems, not always, as we tend to think, people problems. Regardless of the root cause of problems that may lead to litigation, such events are too often dealt with ex post facto rather than through a well-planned, active program of risk anticipation and litigation prevention. Risk factors diminish with a well-defined, proactive program of preventive law. The function of preventive law is to regulate or manage human conduct to ensure a harmonious society while attempting to strike a balance that allows individuals as much freedom as possible—at the same time, allowing society to function without unreasonable interference from the conduct of individuals.

School districts should recognize liability as a high priority in daily operations. In many school districts, responsibility for preventing litigious actions or inaction and loss is relegated to middle- and low-level staff members. The long-standing misperception is that safety and loss programs involve minor personnel matters and relatively insignificant details. Yet when a major incident, accident, or loss occurs, it requires significant top-level time and energy. A senior manager should be assigned the responsibility for a district's risk management prerogatives. In the development and implementation of policies and procedures, school districts, in cooperation with their legal counsel, should include the concepts and practice of preventive law as a major component of their overall risk management program. A tendency in many school districts is to temporize and downplay the significance of legal problems, seeking answers to such problems at the operational level rather than at the organizational level, and school districts often rely on legal counsel only after they have gotten in trouble. That said, despite district initiatives, principals can significantly reduce their exposure to liability by incorporating and practicing preventive law as outlined below.

FOCUS POINT: Tenets of Preventive Law and Risk Management

The concepts of preventive law and the management of risk, which are interwoven through the chapters of this book, are illustrated by six general beliefs or tenets:

1. *An understanding of the substance of law limits an education organization's culpability and exposure.* Effective principals base their day-to-day decision making on the substance of law, which consists of both an understanding of the basic tenets of law and knowledge of current education litigation decisions.

2. *The proper application of procedures, informed decision making, and foreseeability reduces liability and environmental and organizational loss.* Effective principals adhere to procedures and precedents established by law, exercise reasonable and prudent judgment in situations not directly addressed by the law, and integrate foreseeability (the art or science of intuitively knowing what might happen) when practicing preventive law, thus minimizing exposure to liability and loss.

3. *Working with counsel reduces budget loss.* When they have questions about legal issues that are not directly addressed in established laws and procedures, effective principals consult legal counsel.

4. *Flexibility endangers system stability but enhances conflict resolution.* Although principals must strictly adhere to, enforce, and monitor all policies and procedures, effective principals demonstrate flexibility and reduce conflict (and avoid litigation) by fostering a school climate in which divergent ideas may be presented, respected, permitted to flourish, and channeled into productive results for the school.

5. *Knowledge of precedent, constitutional compliance, and public information needs enhances crisis and motivational management and monitoring.* Effective principals understand the legal ramifications of precedent-setting cases and consider the significant protections provided to students, teachers, and others under various interpretations of the Constitution when making decisions. They also know that it is often up to them to educate parents and others about how court actions influence the daily operations of the school.

6. *Leadership in the education enterprise must be coupled with leadership in preventive law.* Effective education leadership sometimes involves taking calculated risks when complicated situations warrant decisive action; however, such risks must be legal and must demonstrate a commonsense commitment to preventive law.

I FOCUS POINT: What Is Preventive Law?

Preventive law is generally defined as a program, supported by policies, procedures, and regulations, that endeavors to minimize the risk of litigation or to secure, with more certainty, legal rights and duties. Preventive law emphasizes the importance of *pre facto* planning to avoid legal problems and their consequences should litigation ensue. The components of preventive law include four basic tenets—all of which should be put into everyday practice at the building level by respective principals:

1. The *anticipation* of legal challenges (foreseeability)

2. The *evaluation* of the legal merits of such potential challenges

3. A *consideration* of the policies (in effect or proposed) affected by such potential challenges

4. *Implementation or modification*, where appropriate, in response to the first three steps

I FOCUS POINT: Identifying Potential Risks

To the extent that human behavior and the law are reasonably foreseeable, informed school principals practicing preventive law and common risk management methods can predict certain legal risks and reduce their scope through policy, procedure, and practice. In those areas in which the law is less certain, principals can at least *identify* and *analyze* risk and choose courses of action that are less precarious than others. *Risk identification* focuses on the question, What losses can happen? whereas *risk analysis* goes further, asking, How likely is it that the loss will happen; and, if the loss happens, how serious will it be, and how often might it occur? Thus consideration is given to both frequency and severity probabilities. Figure 1.1 provides a simple tool to analyze foreseeable risks. The figure presents a formula that integrates the three key factors of preventive law: (1) how *likely* an event is to occur, (2) the *frequency* with which the opportunity exists for such an occurrence, and (3) the *potential consequences* of such an event. The formula provides numerical ratings for each factor that, when multiplied together, produce a risk score. In other words, *likelihood* times *exposure* times *potential consequences* equals the level of *potential risk* ($L \times E \times PC = R$).

Figure 1.1

Risk Analysis Model

Likelihood Scale	Exposure Scale	Potential Consequences Scale	Risk Scale
Probable — 10 Might well — 9 be expected Quite possible, — 8 could happen — 7 — 6 Unusual, — 5 but possible — 4 Remotely — 3 possible Conceivable, — 2 but unlikely Practically — 1 impossible	Continuous — 10 — 9 Frequent — 8 (daily) — 7 — 6 Regular — 5 (once a week) — 4 Occasional — 3 (monthly) Minimal — 2 (a few times a year) Rare — 1 (once a year or less)	Catastrophe — 10 (many fatalities, critical financial loss, critical public — 9 relations problem) Disaster — 8 (multiple fatalities, critical financial loss, critical public relations problem) — 7 Very serious (fatality, significant financial loss, significant — 6 public relations problem) Serious — 5 (disability results, serious financial loss, serious public — 4 relations problem) Important — 3 (serious injury, serious financial loss, serious public relations problem) — 2 Noticeable (minor injury, potential — 1 financial loss, minimal public relations problem)	1000 — Very high risk Consider discontinuing operation 750 — High risk Immediate correction required 500 450 — Substantial risk Timely correction 250 — required Possible risk 200 — Nonroutine attention required 100 — Known risk Routine attention recommended
Likelihood ×	**Exposure** ×	**Potential Consequences** =	**Risk**

The following example shows how the formula can be used to support districtwide or site-based risk management. Examples that principals can apply to their own buildings and operations follow.

A newspaper reports the explosion of a water heater in a local office building. There were several fatalities, severe injuries, and significant structural damage to the building. Your school district records indicate that the water heaters in most of your buildings are more than 10 years old and have not been inspected for 7 years. Should your district allocate resources for a full inspection of its facilities' water heaters? If yes, when should this be done? First, the *likelihood* of an explosion needs to be identified. Most people would probably rate the likelihood as 5 (unusual but possible). The *exposure* rating usually depends on how frequently the piece of equipment is in use.

In the case of a water heater, that rating would normally be a 10 (continuous). However, school officials might be concerned with how frequently people are in the vicinity of the operating water heater and might rate the exposure as 8 (frequent, daily). In this example, a school official might use a composite rating of 9. The third factor is an estimate of the *potential consequences* of an explosion. The potential consequence scale suggests three interrelated types of consequences: physical injury, financial loss, and public relations problems. In this example, the school official assumed that the potential consequences range between 7 (very serious) and 8 (disaster), for a composite rating of 7.5. *To estimate the risk, the school official multiplied 5 times 9 times 7.5, which produced a risk score of 337.5.* This score indicates that a *substantial* risk exists and *timely correction* (inspection) is advised.

Although the risk analysis model presented here is clearly subjective in nature, it provides at least a *consistent* way of thinking about risk and preventive law, as well as a simplified way of reporting. Finally, and perhaps most important, the model aids in the process of forecasting, an important element or concept in the law—commonly called *foreseeability*. Foreseeability is discussed in detail in Chapter 15.

The usefulness of the model in both scope and diversity is further demonstrated in the following selected examples derived during field testing.

Example 1. A school principal calculated the school's risk regarding injuries related to slippery entry areas during inclement weather as follows:

> *Likelihood* = 10 (Probable)
> *Exposure* = 3 (Occasional)
> *Potential consequences* = 1 (Noticeable)

The resultant risk score of 30 indicates a *known risk*, with routine attention recommended.

Example 2. A school principal calculated the school's risk regarding injuries related to children falling over the sides of a playground slide as follows:

> *Likelihood* = 3 (Remotely possible)
> *Exposure* = 10 (Continuous)
> *Potential consequences* = 4 (Serious)

The resultant risk score of 120 indicates a *possible risk*, with nonroutine or focused attention advised.

Example 3. A school principal calculated the school's risk regarding injuries related to students traveling on field trips in school-owned vehicles as follows:

> *Likelihood* = 6.75 (average of 3–8, from Remotely possible to Quite possible, could happen)
> *Exposure* = 5 (Regular)
> *Potential consequences* = 6 (average of 4–7, from Serious to Very serious)

The resultant risk score of 202 indicates a *possible risk*, with nonroutine or focused attention advised.

Example 4. A school principal calculated the school's risk regarding injuries related to a disturbance in a high school in a mid-Atlantic state, resulting from a group of students displaying a Confederate flag, as follows:

Likelihood = 6 (average of 5–7, from Unusual but possible, to Could happen)
Exposure = 8 (Frequent)
Potential consequences = 1 (Noticeable)

The resultant risk score of 48 indicates a *known risk*, with routine or focused attention advised.

Example 5. A school principal in an urban environment calculated the school's risk regarding the sexual molestation of a student during the school day by an outsider as follows:

Likelihood = 8 (Quite possible)
Exposure = 8 (Frequent)
Potential consequences = 5 (average of 3–7, from Important to Very serious)

The resultant risk score of 320 indicates a *substantial risk*, with timely correction required.

A rural school principal, on the other hand, calculated this same example as follows:

Likelihood = 3 (Remotely possible)
Exposure = 8 (Frequent)
Potential consequences = 5 (average of 3–7, from Important to Very serious)

This official's risk score of 120 indicates a *possible risk*, with nonroutine attention advised.

FOCUS POINT: Affirmative Duty of School-Based Personnel in Risk Management and Prevention

Duty of Building Administrator (Principal, Headmaster, Headmistress) to Students and Parents (at a minimum)

- Ensure compliance with applicable federal, state, and local laws and regulations; enforce established school policies, procedures, and rules; and establish additional rules, as necessary and appropriate in the particular education environment, to ensure the safety and well-being of students while under the care of the school.
- Provide effective supervision of the education program (including the development, oversight, and evaluation of appropriate curricular, intracurricular, and extracurricular activities).

- Promote the hiring of competent administrative, teaching, and support staff appropriately trained in specific disciplines.
- Provide effective supervision of staff (including the appropriate delegation of authority, formalization and assignment of specific responsibilities, direction of daily work activities, and observation and evaluation of performance).
- Manage the school's physical facilities and material and financial resources to ensure the maintenance of a safe and productive learning environment.
- Develop and maintain communication channels and media that promote effective two-way communication about school-related issues (including student progress) between administrators and parents, administrators and teachers, administrators and students, teachers and parents, teachers and students.

Duty of Education Administrator (Associate or Assistant Principal, Dean, Supervisor, Department Chair, et al.) to Students and Parents (at a minimum)

- Adhere to applicable federal, state, and local laws and regulations; adhere to and enforce established school policies, procedures, and rules in the performance of assigned duties and responsibilities; and recommend additional policies, procedures, and rules, as appropriate, within the scope of delegated authority.
- Provide effective supervision of the instructional activities presented by staff members of programs within the scope of delegated authority.
- Provide effective supervision of all staff members assigned to, or working with, programs within the scope of delegated authority.
- Facilitate effective two-way communication about school-related issues (including student progress) in programs within the scope of delegated authority, between administrators and parents, administrators and teachers, administrators and students, teachers and parents, teachers and students.

Duty of Teacher to Students and Parents (at a minimum)

- Adhere to applicable federal, state, and local laws and regulations; adhere to and enforce established school policies, procedures, and rules in the performance of assigned duties and responsibilities.
- Develop and present instructional activities that are appropriate to and consistent with the approved education program and specifically designed to increase students' knowledge; facilitate the development of learning skills, life skills, and appropriate social behavior; and prepare students to interact effectively in general society.
- Provide effective supervision of students participating in instructional activities that are within the scope of assigned responsibility to ensure students' safety and general well-being.

- Facilitate effective two-way communication about school-related issues (including student progress) in programs within the scope of assigned responsibility, between administrators and parents, administrators and teachers, administrators and students, teachers and parents, teachers and students.

▌ FOCUS POINT: Adopting a Preventive Law Mind-Set

During the preceding century, changes in American culture created numerous conflicts in society. These conflicts led to new issues. New issues required new laws. Needless to say, for effective principals to practice preventive law and risk management, it is imperative that they seek out current updates on laws that affect education. All too often, unfortunately, the need to know is considered ex post facto. Effective principals do not wait for legal counsel to provide preservice—they take the time to read, listen, and actively apply what they know to their schools to avoid harm to students and others and to short-circuit incidents that might lead to litigation. Although it's not suggested that principals walk around with Figure 1.1 in their hands, the model presented here gives principals a framework for a mind-set in practicing preventive law—an effective way for principals to think about risk and liability prevention as they go about business as usual.

Crisis Management

A crisis or emergency is a situation that occurs unpredictably, requires immediate action, and poses a threat of injury, loss of life, or significant damage to property (Dunklee & Shoop, 1993). In the past few years, an unprecedented number of crisis situations have been reported in our nation's schools. Some of these emergencies were caused by natural disasters, others were the result of accidents, and still others the result of violence and malicious or suicidal acts. School districts and individual school administrators are accountable and can be held legally liable for the safety and well-being of students, district employees, and visitors to the district's facilities. The direct and indirect costs when losses occur can be great. Creating and maintaining a safe environment requires both an active risk management program—to prevent foreseeable dangers—and an effective crisis management program—to manage the emergency and limit the damage once crisis occurs.

A key element in crisis management is preparedness. Effective response in emergency situations requires structure, order, discipline, and linear thinking and action on the part of crisis managers.

When a crisis appears or is impending, a school district's response is critical. To safeguard resources, certain actions must be preplanned so that responses to crises are prompt and effective. Effective crisis management protects the integrity of the *in loco parentis* responsibilities to students that are inherent in the education enterprise. Effective crisis planning [also] integrates and coordinates school procedures with similar crisis plans at the [district,] municipal, county, and state levels. (Dunklee & Shoop, 1993)

Examples of Management Cues

The range of potential types of emergencies is long, and schools should have plans in place to address, at a minimum, all the following:

- Bomb threat
- Chemical spill or biohazard
- Death or suicide
- Fire or explosion
- Gun or other weapon on campus
- Hostage situation
- Kidnapping, childnapping, or missing student
- Major student disruption
- Medical emergency
- Natural gas or other toxic odor
- Public demonstration
- Sexual assault
- Shooting or stabbing
- Tornado, hurricane, or other severe weather
- Violent visitor or staff member

Once an emergency occurs, the goal is to "save lives and to preserve property—to minimize the organization's actual losses of physical and human resources—so that normal activity can be restored promptly" (Dunklee & Shoop, 1993).

Suggested Risk Management Guidelines

As stated previously (Dunklee & Shoop, 1993), all schools should have a written crisis management plan that includes the specific procedures to be followed in emergencies. The following information is often included in crisis management procedure manuals:

- The purpose, scope, and organization of the manual
- The structure of the crisis management organization, including key contact personnel (most important—who's in charge!)
- Evacuation instructions, including explanations of alarm signals and diagrams of exit routes
- Communication procedures to be followed during and after the emergency
- Sites of potential emergencies
- Appropriate responses to emergencies

- Arrangements for obtaining assistance from emergency service organizations and local government agencies
- Procedures for coordinating use of district resources and personnel during emergencies
- Available district resources
- A system for informing the district of the emergency and for notifying parents or guardians
- Plans for taking the following actions, if appropriate:
  - School cancellation
  - Early dismissal
  - Evacuation
  - Sheltering

In addition,

- Develop, disseminate, and implement a comprehensive crisis management plan that clearly identifies and communicates the procedures to be followed in the event of emergencies.
- Provide training to appropriate personnel to ensure that they will be able to respond promptly and effectively in a crisis.
- Coordinate crisis planning with appropriate district, municipal, and county agencies.

I FOCUS POINT: Working With the Media

During and after a crisis, schools need effective communications with the media, employees, students, parents, and the community at large. Postcrisis communications should inform employees and patrons as soon as possible of the extent of the losses caused by the crisis and describe the school district's or school site's short- and long-term recovery plan.

The following "Working with the Media" section is included in the Fairfax County (VA) Public Schools *Crisis Management Handbook* (2004). It has been reformatted by the authors to fit Suggested Risk Management Guidelines.

Suggested Risk Management Guidelines

- Although schools are public buildings, administrators do not have to allow the media on campus.
- Permission must be granted by the administration for members of the press to be on campus.
- Police answer questions regarding criminal investigations. Administrators should focus on what the school is doing to secure student safety and maintain student welfare.

- Identify one school spokesperson.
- Identify and maintain a media staging area. (This should be coordinated with police.)
- Don't let reporters wander.
- Direct all media to the school spokesperson to maintain consistency.
- Prepare factual written statements for the press in cooperation with the police and the Office of Community Relations. Provide updates.
- Be certain that every media member receives the same information.
- Be accurate. If uncertain, don't speculate. When appropriate, refer media to other agencies, such as the police or the health department.
- Set limits for time and location.
- When giving an interview:
  - Ask in advance what specific questions will be asked.
  - Don't say, "No comment." If an answer is not known, offer to get information and to get back to the reporter. Don't speak off the record.
  - Keep answers brief and to the point.
  - Emphasize positive action being taken. Turn negative questions into simple positive statements.

- Ensure that the sensitivities of those who are touched by the crisis are respected by the reporters.
- Before agreeing to let staff members be interviewed, obtain their consent.
- Students under the age of 18 may not be interviewed on campus without parental permission.
- Yearbook and school newspaper photographs are public documents. Access to them must be provided.

CHAPTER RESOURCES

Dunklee, D. R., & Shoop, R. J. (1993). *A primer for school risk management: Creating and maintaining district and site-based liability prevention programs.* Needham Heights, MA: Allyn & Bacon.

Fairfax County (VA) Public Schools. (2004). *Crisis management handbook.* Fairfax, VA: Fairfax County Public Schools, Office of Security and Risk Management Services & Office of Community Relations.

2

The School and the Legal Environment

The U.S. Constitution provides particular protections of individual rights. Various state and federal statutes protect the general welfare of society and implement the constitutional rights of individuals. School districts develop policies, procedures, and regulations that ensure that necessary steps are taken to provide a safe place for employees to work, students to learn, parents to interact, and visitors to feel welcome. With such *district* policies, procedures, and regulations in place, principals should ask three questions:

1. Am I implementing the regulations?

2. Am I monitoring the regulations?

3. Am I practicing foreseeability when it comes to preventing the violation of regulations?

This chapter is presented simply as a reminder to principals that, although it's next to impossible to keep up with the day-to-day changes in the law, it's important to remember the foundations on which laws are made and how such laws affect the decision-making processes of the courts and school district counsel.

AUTHORS' NOTE: Cases cited throughout this chapter have been selected on a precedent-setting or best-example basis regardless of jurisdiction or date of adjudication. (See Introduction for more information.)

SECTION A: FOUNDATIONS OF THE SCHOOL'S RELATIONSHIP TO THE LEGAL ENVIRONMENT

This section reviews several sources of law and their relationship to the structure and operation of schools and school districts. This review of the structure of law and operation of the state and federal courts provides the foundation for understanding the manner in which our legal system monitors the education enterprise.

When school districts and schools fail to provide a safe place—a place that not only observes the rights of individuals but also protects those rights—the courts will intervene. Our nation's court system provides the structure that determines the exact relationship between the individual and the law in question. In other words, if schools don't do it, the courts will.

I FOCUS POINT: Basic Principles of Our Legal System

- Our system of government provides a structure of laws that protects individual rights and guarantees freedom of religion, speech, press, assembly, and the right of each individual to call on the courts or government to correct injustices.
- A law is a rule of civil conduct prescribed by local, state, or federal mandates commanding what is right and prohibiting what is wrong. Laws, then, are simply collections of those rules and principles of conduct that the federal, state, and local communities recognize and enforce.
- There are separate legal systems for each of the 50 states, the District of Columbia, and the federal government. For the most part, each of these systems applies its own body of law.
- All laws are based on the assumption that for each action, there is an expected consequence. Laws are society's attempts to ensure that there are consequences that ought to result if certain prohibited acts are committed. Our system of laws is based on the assumptions that all citizens should be judged by the same standards of behavior, and for every wrong, an inescapable penalty follows.
- In our legal system, the principle of due process of law allows people who have been accused of breaking a law, been harmed by other individuals, or been accused of harming another person to bring their side of the issue before a court for a decision as to whether they must submit to the force of government or will be protected by it.
- Our government is based on the consent of the governed, and the Bill of Rights denies those in power any legal opportunity to coerce that consent. Authority is to be controlled by public opinion, not public opinion by authority. This is the social contract theory of government; consequently, law is not a static set of printed documents but is, rather, a living and changing set of precepts that depend on the courts for interpretation.

FOCUS POINT: Constitutional Law, Common Law, Statutory Law, and Administrative Law

- **Constitutional Law.** Whether at the federal or state level, a constitution is the basic source of law for the jurisdiction. A constitution specifies the structure of the government and outlines the powers and duties of its principal officers and subdivisions. It also designates the allocation of power between levels of government—between the federal government and the states in the U.S. Constitution and between state and local governmental bodies in state constitutions. In addition, constitutions spell out the exact limitations of governmental power. In both the U.S. Constitution and state constitutions, these proscriptions are contained in a bill of rights.

- Constitutions are broad philosophical statements of general beliefs. The U.S. Constitution is written in such broad and general language that it has been amended only 26 times in over 200 years. State constitutions are more detailed and specific, with the result that most are frequently amended. Just as the U.S. Constitution is the supreme law in the United States, state constitutions are the supreme law within each state. State constitutions may not contain provisions, however, that conflict with the U.S. Constitution.

- Because the U.S. Constitution contains no mention of education, Congress is not authorized to provide a system of education. The Tenth Amendment to the U.S. Constitution stipulates that "the powers not delegated to the United States by the Constitution, nor prohibited by it to the states, are reserved to the states respectively, or to the people." The U.S. Supreme Court has repeatedly and consistently confirmed the authority of states to provide for the general welfare of their residents, including the establishment and control of their public schools. However, the U.S. Supreme Court has applied various provisions of the U.S. Constitution to jurisdictions to ensure compliance.

- **Common Law.** Many legal experts believe statutes are not law until they are actually tested and adjudicated in a court of law. A court, when confronted with a problem that cannot be solved by reference to pertinent legislation (statutory law), decides that case according to common law. The English common law is defined as those principles, procedures, and rules of action, enforced by courts, that are based on history or custom, with modifications as required by circumstances and conditions over time. Common law is not automatic but must be applied by a court. Courts decide specific disputes by examining constitutional, statutory, or administrative law. The court determines the facts of the case and then examines prior judicial decisions to identify legal precedents (if any). This process illustrates *stare decisis* or "let the decision stand."

- **Statutory and Administrative Law.** Statutory laws are laws passed by a legislative body. These laws may alter the common law by adding to, deleting from, or eliminating the law. The courts under our system of government are the final interpreters of legislative provisions. Administrative laws are regulations promulgated by administrative agencies. An administrative agency is a governmental authority, other than a court or legislative body, that affects the rights of private parties through adjudication or rule making. In many cases, the operations of schools are affected more by the administrative process than by the judicial process. It is not uncommon for a state to have several hundred agencies with powers of adjudication, rule making, or both.

▌ FOCUS POINT: How Laws Are Made and Enforced

It is the American ideal that the power to control the conduct of people by the use of public will is inherent in the people. By adopting a constitution, the people delegate certain power to the state. Constitutions divide this power and assign it to three branches of government. Although no one branch performs only one function, each has a generally defined area of influence. The responsibilities belong to three separate but equal branches of government. The legislative branch makes the laws. The judicial branch interprets the law. The executive branch enforces the law.

   • **The Legislative Branch.** The primary function of the legislative branch is making laws. It is limited in its function only by the state and federal constitutions. Each state legislature has the absolute power to make laws governing education. It is important to understand that this state-held power makes education a state function, makes school funds state funds, and makes school buildings state property. Although it is an accepted principle of law that the state legislature cannot delegate its law-making powers, it can delegate to subordinate agencies the authority to make the rules and regulations necessary to implement these laws. One such subordinate agency is the state board of education. State boards of education are the policy-making and planning bodies for the public school systems in most states. They have specific responsibility for adopting policies, enacting regulations, and establishing general rules for carrying out the duties placed on them by state legislatures. Local school districts and local boards are created by the state legislature and have only those powers that are specifically delegated by the legislature or that can be reasonably implied.

   • **The Executive Branch.** Although each state has a unique governmental structure, the typical executive branch includes a governor, a lieutenant governor, a secretary of state, a treasurer, and an attorney general. The governor is the chief executive officer of the state and is responsible for the enforcement of the laws of the state. The attorney general is a member of the executive branch of government who often has a significant impact on the operation of schools in the state. This person represents the state in all suits and pleas to which the state is a party, gives legal advice to the governor and other executive officers on request, and performs such other duties as required by law. The attorney general acts as both the defender and the prosecutor of the state's interest. The attorney general acts on behalf of the state, much as a private attorney acts on behalf of a private client, and renders opinions on questions of interest to the state submitted by state officials. In such opinions, the attorney general identifies the laws applicable to the question and the set of facts presented. These opinions are not laws or court decisions; they are interpretations of state law that are enforceable in the absence of a contrary court ruling.

• **The Judicial Branch**. Courts interpret law and settle disputes by applying the law. However, a court can decide a controversy only when it has authority to hear and adjudicate the case. The appropriate jurisdiction emanates directly from the law. Court names vary from state to state. For example, trial courts are called supreme courts in New York, circuit courts in Missouri, and district courts in Kansas. The principal function of the courts is to decide specific cases in light of the constitution and the laws.

In each state, two judicial systems operate simultaneously: the federal court system and the state courts. Courts in both systems are classified as having either original or appellate jurisdiction. Original jurisdiction refers to the right of a court to hear a case for the first time. A trial on the facts occurs in a court of original jurisdiction. Once the initial trial is over and a judgment rendered, the appellate process may begin. Appellate jurisdiction refers to the right of a court to hear cases on appeal from courts of original jurisdiction. In appellate courts, matters of fact are no longer in dispute; instead, questions of law or proceedings from the lower courts serve as the basis for review. The appellate process can proceed to the state's highest court and, under certain circumstances, to the U.S. Supreme Court.

The federal court system of the United States includes district courts, special federal courts, courts of appeal, and the U.S. Supreme Court. There are 97 federal district courts, with at least 1 in each state, including the District of Columbia, the Virgin Islands, and Puerto Rico. Each district court has a chief judge and other federal judges appointed by the president of the United States. These courts have original jurisdiction in cases between citizens of different states in which an amount of money over $10,000 is in dispute and in cases involving litigation under federal statutes or the U.S. Constitution. The district courts have no appellate function. Appeals from the district courts are made to the courts of appeal in the respective circuits. In some limited circumstances, a special three-judge district court can be convened to decide a controversy. This type of tribunal would be used when a state statute is being challenged under the U.S. Constitution. A special application must be made to the district court, and if granted, the chief judge and at least one other judge must be from the court of appeals. The importance of this type of tribunal lies in the fact that an appeal of its decision goes directly to the U.S. Supreme Court.

The first level of appeal in the federal court system is in the courts of appeal. These courts provide an intermediate level of appeal between the district courts and the Supreme Court. These courts have only appellate jurisdiction and review the record of the trial court for violations of legal proceedings or questions of law rather than questions of fact. The courts of appeal operate with several judges. There is no jury; a panel of three or more judges decide the cases before them. In some cases, the judges may sit *en banc* (together) to decide the case. There are 12 federal circuits in the United States, each with a court of appeals. A 13th federal circuit exists to hear appeals regarding certain types of cases (those regarding copyrights, customs, and other matters mostly pertaining to commerce).

The U.S. Supreme Court, alone among the federal courts, was created directly by the Constitution rather than by congressional legislation. This court consists of the Chief Justice and eight Associate Justices. Six justices constitute a quorum. The Supreme Court meets for an annual term beginning the first Monday in October. It has limited original jurisdiction and exercises appellate jurisdiction to review cases by appeal of right and *writ of certiorari* (an appellate proceeding directing that the record from an inferior court be moved to a superior court for review) over federal district courts, federal courts of appeal, and the state supreme courts. The Supreme Court is the nation's highest court. It is often referred to as "the court of last resort" in that there are no appeals to its decisions. A constitutional amendment ultimately could be used to reverse this court's decision; however, this has occurred in only four instances. Because more than 5,000 cases are appealed to the Supreme Court each year, the Court most frequently will deny *certiorari* and refuse to review the decisions of the lower courts. The denial of *certiorari* has the effect of sustaining the decisions of the lower courts.

▌ FOCUS POINT: Court Functions

A court is an organizational structure that assembles at an appointed time and place to administer law judicially. The primary purpose of courts is to ensure that every person has a fair and unbiased trial before an impartial arbiter. It is assumed that there are always conflicting interests and that the courts must weigh one against the other. Often, the decision is not between good and bad but the choice of selecting the greater good or the lesser evil. The courts seek to determine legal liability. For liability to exist, there must be a law and a set of facts that the law defines as illegal. Courts have three general functions: deciding controversies, interpreting enacted law, and performing judicial review.

- **Deciding controversies** consists of determining the facts of the dispute and applying the applicable law. One or more statutes or regulations may apply. If none do, the court must decide the controversy based on previous decisions of the appellate courts of the state in similar situations. If the case presents a new situation, the court's job is more difficult. When a court does not wait for legislative action and makes a decision, it has in fact made a new law. In this process, *stare decisis*, or the adherence to precedent, creates a new foundational common law.

- **Interpretation of enacted law** occurs when a statute does not provide a clear answer to the question before the court. Because it is not always possible to draft legislation that is unambiguous when applied to specific controversies, the court may be forced to strike down a statute that it feels is vague, ambiguous, or contradictory. The courts tend to use the following four approaches or a combination of these approaches in interpreting legislation and making their decisions:

1. *Literal*: The courts look to the ordinary interpretation of words to determine their meaning.

2. *Purposive*: The courts attempt to ascertain what the legislature intended the law to mean.

3. *Precedent based*: The courts look to past, similar cases and laws to find support for one interpretation of the law.

4. *Policy based*: The courts interpret the law in relationship to the courts' own views of what is best for society.

- **Judicial review** is a supreme court's power to declare that a statute is unconstitutional. However, this power is not without its limits. Judges at all levels are expected to base their decisions on precedents under the legal doctrine of *stare decisis*. In other words, the court must look to other decisions in similar cases to find direction in dealing with new cases.

SECTION B: CLAUSES OF AND AMENDMENTS TO THE U.S. CONSTITUTION THAT AFFECT EDUCATION PRACTICE

Certain clauses and amendments to the U.S. Constitution repeatedly appear as the basis for court decisions regarding specific education issues. Any examination of school law needs to begin, at a minimum, with a solid grounding in these constitutional elements that form the legal environment in which schools operate. Although we can find issues that relate to the education enterprise throughout the U.S. Constitution, the following are the most commonly cited.

▌FOCUS POINT: General Welfare Clause

Under Article I, Section 8, of the Constitution, Congress has the power to "lay and collect taxes, duties, imports and excises, to pay the debts and provide for the common defense and general welfare of the United States." Congress has often used the general welfare clause as the rationale for the enactment of legislation that directly affects the operation of public schools.

▌ FOCUS POINT: First Amendment

The First Amendment states that

> Congress shall make no law respecting an establishment of religion, or prohibiting the free exercise thereof; or abridging the freedom of speech, or of the press; or the right of the people peaceably to assemble, and to petition the Government for a redress of grievances.

This amendment affords pervasive personal freedom to the citizens of this country. It has been used as the basis for litigation involving the use of public funds to aid nonpublic school students, separation of church and state in curriculum matters, students' and teachers' freedom of speech, press censorship, and academic freedom issues.

▌ FOCUS POINT: Fourth Amendment

The Fourth Amendment protects the rights of citizens "to be secure in their persons, houses, papers and effects against unreasonable search or seizure." This amendment emerged in the late 1960s as the basis for litigation concerning the search of students' lockers and personal belongings.

▌ FOCUS POINT: Fifth Amendment

The Fifth Amendment protects citizens from being compelled in any criminal case to be a witness against themselves. Although most due process litigation concerns the Fourteenth Amendment, several self-incrimination issues have been raised in cases concerning teachers being questioned by superiors regarding their activities outside the classroom.

▌ FOCUS POINT: Fourteenth Amendment

The Fourteenth Amendment provides that no state shall "deny to any person within its jurisdiction the equal protection of the laws." This amendment is frequently cited in education cases that deal with race, gender, or ethnic background issues.

Recent cases regarding individuals with disabilities and school finance issues also have been based on this amendment. As a corollary, this amendment guarantees the right of citizens to due process under the law and thus has been used to support school employees' claims of wrongful discharge and parents' claims of unfair treatment of their children by school officials.

OTHER PROVISIONS OF THE U.S. CONSTITUTION OF INTEREST TO EDUCATORS

Article II

Section 1. The executive Power shall be vested in a President of the United States of America.

Article III

Section 1. The judicial Power of the United States, shall be vested in one supreme Court, and in such inferior Courts as the Congress may from time to time ordain and establish. The Judges, both of the supreme and inferior Courts, shall hold their Offices during good Behaviour, and shall, at stated Times, receive for their Services a Compensation, which shall not be diminished during their Continuance in Office.

Section 2. The judicial Power shall extend to all Cases, in Law and Equity, arising under this Constitution, the Laws of the United States, and Treaties made, or which shall be made, under their Authority;—to all Cases affecting Ambassadors, other public Ministers and Consuls;—to all Cases of admiralty and maritime Jurisdiction;—to Controversies to which the United States shall be a Party;—to Controversies between two or more States;—between a State and Citizens of another State;—between Citizens of different States;—between Citizens of the same State claiming Lands under the Grants of different States, and between a State, or the Citizens thereof, and foreign States, Citizens or Subjects.

Article IV

Section 1. Full Faith and Credit shall be given in each State to the public Acts, Records, and judicial Proceedings of every other State.

Section 2. The Citizens of each State shall be entitled to all Privileges and Immunities of Citizens in the several States.

Section 4. The United States shall guarantee to every State in this Union a Republican Form of Government, and shall protect each of them against Invasion; and on Application of the Legislature, or of the Executive (when the Legislature cannot be convened) against domestic Violence.

Article V

The Congress, whenever two thirds of both Houses shall deem it necessary, shall propose Amendments to this Constitution, or, on the Application of the Legislatures of two thirds of the several States, shall call a Convention for proposing Amendments, which, in either Case, shall be valid to all Intents and Purposes, as part of this Constitution, when ratified by the Legislatures of three fourths of the several States, or by Conventions in three fourths thereof, as the one or the other Mode of Ratification may be proposed by the Congress; Provided that no Amendment which may be made prior to the Year One thousand eight hundred and eight shall in any Manner affect the first and fourth Clauses in the Ninth Section of the first Article; and that no State, without its Consent, shall be deprived of its equal Suffrage in the Senate.

Article VI

This Constitution, and the Laws of the United States which shall be made in Pursuance thereof; and all Treaties made, or which shall be made, under the Authority of the United States, shall be the supreme Law of the Land; and the Judges in every State shall be bound thereby, any Thing in the Constitution or Laws of any State to the Contrary notwithstanding.

The Senators and Representatives before mentioned, and the Members of the several State Legislatures, and all executive and judicial Officers, both of the United States and of the several States, shall be bound by Oath or Affirmation, to support this Constitution; but no religious Test shall ever be required as a Qualification to any Office or public Trust under the United States.

Amendment VI

In all criminal prosecutions, the accused shall enjoy the right to a speedy and public trial, by an impartial jury of the State and district wherein the crime shall have been committed, which district shall have been previously ascertained by law, and to be informed of the nature and cause of the accusation; to be confronted with the witnesses against him; to have compulsory process for obtaining witnesses in his favor, and to have the Assistance of Counsel for his defence.

Amendment VII

In Suits at common law, where the value in controversy shall exceed twenty dollars, the right of trial by jury shall be preserved, and no fact tried by jury, shall be otherwise re-examined in any Court of the United States, than according to the rules of the common law.

Amendment VIII

Excessive bail shall not be required, nor excessive fines imposed, nor cruel and unusual punishments inflicted.

Amendment IX

The enumeration in the Constitution, of certain rights, shall not be construed to deny or disparage others retained by the people.

Amendment X

The powers not delegated to the United States by the Constitution, nor prohibited by it to the States, are reserved to the States respectively, or to the people.

Amendment XI

The Judicial power of the United States shall not be construed to extend to any suit in law or equity, commenced or prosecuted against one of the United States by Citizens of another State, or by Citizens or Subjects of any Foreign State.

Amendment XIII

Section 1. Neither slavery nor involuntary servitude, except as a punishment for crime whereof the party shall have been duly convicted, shall exist within the United States, or any place subject to their jurisdiction.

Section 2. Congress shall have power to enforce this article by appropriate legislation.

SECTION C: LANDMARK SUPREME COURT RULINGS THAT AFFECT EDUCATION PRACTICE

Desegregation, school finance, student and teacher rights, special education, and the separation of church and state emerged as the notable issues defining elementary and secondary education law for the 21st century.

▌ FOCUS POINT: Desegregation

"Separate but equal" was the rule as the century began under the dictates of *Plessy v. Ferguson* (1896). However, separate and unequal was the reality for the next half of the century for all but white public schoolchildren, as isolated but ineffective attempts were made to change the rule. In *Gong Lum v. Rice* (1927), the Supreme Court rejected a Chinese student's equal protection claim, observing that the plaintiff could have attended a public school for minority children that was state supported and equal to that available to majority children.

It was not until the late 1930s and 1940s that courts concluded that higher education segregation practices were not equal. With that finding, African American plaintiffs directly challenged the K–12 separate but equal standards in Kansas, South Carolina, Virginia, and Delaware starting in 1951. In *Brown v. Board of Education of Topeka* (1954), the Supreme Court agreed with the plaintiffs and rejected the separate but equal doctrine, stipulating that racially segregated public schools were "inherently unequal." A year later in *Brown v. Board of Education of Topeka (Brown II)* (1955), the Court ordered that the transformation from segregated dual systems to unitary systems must occur "with all deliberate speed."

However, due to the Court's abstract ruling on desegregation, noncompliance remained. In *Cooper v. Aaron* (1958), the Court ruled that desegregation of the schools could not be postponed.

When Virginia repealed its compulsory attendance laws, making school attendance a matter of local option, Prince Edward County closed its public schools, and private citizens formed a foundation that funded private "academy schools." The Supreme Court directed the county to levy taxes in order to raise funds to reopen and to operate a nondiscriminatory public school system like those in other counties in Virginia *(Griffin v. County School Board of Prince Edward County,* 1964).

The case of *Green v. County School Board of New Kent County, Virginia* (1968) centered on a freedom-of-choice plan under which students were permitted to choose either of the district's two schools. In this case, the Court held that the freedom-of-choice plan was unsatisfactory and ruled that school authorities must eliminate racial identification of schools in several areas: the composition of the student body, faculty, and staff; transportation; extracurricular activities; and facilities.

The Court continued its active role in desegregation by defining, in *Swann v. Charlotte-Mecklenburg Board of Education* (1971), the scope of the duty to desegregate. Because assigning students to neighborhood schools would have left the district's schools racially segregated, the federal district court required the creation of noncontiguous attendance zones accompanied by the busing of students between city and suburban neighborhoods. In upholding the district court's remedy, the Supreme Court asserted that the dismantling of the dual school system could be accomplished by

- Assigning teachers to achieve a particular degree of faculty desegregation
- Ensuring that future school construction or closings would not perpetuate a dual school system
- Scrutinizing one-race schools to ensure that the racial composition did not result from discriminatory action
- Altering attendance zones and employing pairing and grouping of noncontiguous zones to counteract past segregation, and
- Employing bus transportation as a constitutionally permissible method of dismantling the dual system

Examined together, *Green* and *Swann* created a comprehensive framework for desegregation remedies.

In *Milliken v. Bradley* (1974), the Court considered whether the Constitution required school districts near Detroit to participate in remedying discrimination even though (a) a formerly *de jure* segregated school district in the city (racially separate schools created by statute) contained a high percentage of African

Americans and (b) meaningful racial mixing was impossible because of the low percentage of white inhabitants. The Court determined that outlying districts may not be required to participate in remediation as long as they were not practicing discriminatory acts. However, because Detroit was practicing *de jure* segregation, the lower courts were instructed to formulate a decree to eliminate the practice within that school district.

On remand, in *Milliken v. Bradley (Milliken II)* (1977), the Court upheld a desegregation plan that included educational components in the areas of reading, inservice teacher training, new testing programs, and expanded counseling and career guidance programs, with costs to be shared by the school district and the state. With this decision, the Court created a politically attractive alternative to mandatory integration as a remedy for past discrimination. As a result, the federal judiciary became less aggressive in requiring massive student reassignment plans to integrate schools, and no Supreme Court decisions on desegregation were issued in the 1980s.

Three Supreme Court decisions on desegregation in the 1990s strongly suggest that court activism in desegregation has ended. *Board of Education of Oklahoma Public Schools v. Dowell* (1991) addressed the termination of an injunction and disclosed the Court's views regarding the use of the term *unitary* and the importance of local control. In *Freeman v. Pitts* (1992), the Court held that federal district courts have the discretion to withdraw their supervision over formally segregated school systems incrementally and are not responsible for segregation based on demographic changes in student population.

Finally, in *Missouri v. Jenkins* (1995), the Court evaluated Kansas City's 18-year history of desegregation orders. Over this period, the district court had ordered $1.5 billion in compensatory programs as well as a tax increase to fund the initiatives. In 1994, the State of Missouri challenged the continuation of teacher salary increases and moved for a finding of partially unitary status. The Supreme Court granted the requested relief, invalidating the court-ordered tax increase and noting that racial imbalance within a school district does not violate the U.S. Constitution.

I FOCUS POINT: School Finance

The Supreme Court's active role in school desegregation encouraged school funding proponents to seek redress in the courts. A series of lawsuits filed in the early 1970s argued that disparities in educational opportunity produced by traditional public school financing structures violated the equal protection clauses of the federal and state constitution. In *San Antonio Independent School District v. Rodriguez* (1973), the Court determined that (a) although education is one of the most important services performed by the state, it is not within the limited category of fundamental rights guaranteed by the U.S. Constitution and (b) any educational disadvantage resulting from disparities in wealth among school districts does not create a suspect class deserving of heightened constitutional protection. The two key aspects of the Court's reasoning were deference to state's rights and judicial noninterference with legislative action.

Because proponents of school finance reform viewed *Rodriguez* as conclusively disposing of federal constitutional claims, litigation shifted to state courts under state constitutional provisions requiring public education to be "uniform," "adequate," or "thorough and efficient." State court rulings on the issue have been almost evenly divided, with the opinions reflecting disagreement on two interrelated issues: (1) whether to define the education right in terms of "equity" or "adequacy" and (2) whether to measure legislative compliance in terms of inputs such as money per student, program offerings, and school physical facilities, or outputs such as levels of student academic performance. Also disputed is whether public education is a political problem to be resolved by the legislature or whether it is a matter properly within accepted bounds of judicial review.

The seminal case for state-based school finance litigation is *Serrano v. Priest* (1971). Finding for the plaintiffs under the federal and state constitutions' equal protection clauses, the California State Supreme Court held that the quality of a child's educational opportunity could not be conditioned by the happenstance of residence (i.e., the presence or absence of taxable wealth). Although the federal claim in *Serrano* was subsequently negated by *Rodriguez*, the successful state claim served as a model for generations of subsequent constitutional litigation over wealth-based issues and generated an explosion of litigation that continues to the present time. *Serrano* led the way by securing the legitimacy of fiscal equity claims (inequality of resource inputs) and laid the first steps to eventual litigation that expanded the claim to include fiscal adequacy, a concept that has come to be defined in terms of equality of educational outcomes, rather than focusing solely on equality of front-end opportunity.

Between 1972 and 1989, state school finance cases were bitter battles over equality of fiscal inputs. A watershed case occurred in 1989 in *Rose v. Council for Better Education, Inc.*, however, when the Kentucky State Supreme Court overturned that state's school funding system under the state constitution's thorough and efficient (T&E) clause. Although not the first state to have ruled for the plaintiffs based on a T&E clause, *Rose* represented a watershed event through the court's close scrutiny of what is meant by a thorough education. Evidencing the fact that the history of school finance litigation has been one of ever-increasing sophistication and combinations of concepts, the Supreme Court of Kentucky found that the quality of education in poorer local school districts was "substantially less in most, if not all the following categories: teacher's pay, provision of basic educational materials, student-teacher ratio, curriculum, quality of basic management, size, adequacy, and condition of school physical plants, and per year expenditure per student." The court imposed on the state legislature "an absolute duty . . . to recreate, reestablish a new system of common schools" according to the standards expressed by the court. In *Rose* the court literally abolished the system of schooling and demanded that it be replaced by one that took into account both the principle and detail of what is meant by an adequate education. It required that the system provide not only equal inputs but also equality in all uses of money, implying that opportunity is defined by more than the mere distributional attributes of a state aid formula, but also how money is spent on behalf of each child.

As time has gone by, the shift signaled in *Rose* has become even more pronounced. Multiple iterations of lawsuits such as *Abbott v. Burke* (1990)—a continuation of *Robinson v. Cahill* (1972)—in New Jersey have returned to court to test new issues and to force compliance with extant rulings. While exhaustive tracing of the development of sophistication in claims is beyond this section, it is accurate to say that plaintiffs have experienced periods of success and setbacks, that the current wave of litigation at the start of the 21st century has highly favored plaintiffs' claims, and that modern claims are zeroing in on adequacy issues in the context of the recently accelerated demands by states for educational accountability and the stringent outcomes requirements of the federal No Child Left Behind Act (NCLB) (Pub. L. No. 107-110, 2001). If claims now focus on inadequate resources to meet increased student achievement standards, it is certain that such claims will only accelerate as state legislatures heighten their demands for fiscal accountability for tax dollars and as the requirements of NCLB hit full force by 2010. (For a comprehensive analysis of school finance see D. C. Thompson and R. Wood, 2005.)

I FOCUS POINT: Student and Teacher Rights

It was not until a century after its passage that Section 1983 of the Civil Rights Act of 1871 discernibly affected public elementary and secondary education law. Its first effect was in the arena of free speech rights. In the landmark 1968 decision, *Pickering v. Board of Education of Township High School District 205*, the Court held that absent proof of false statements knowingly or recklessly made, teachers' exercise of their right to speak out on issues of public concern cannot be used as the basis for dismissal from public employment. This right was subsequently modified in *Mount Healthy City School District Board of Education v. Doyle* (1977), in which the Court determined that even if a teacher's expression is constitutionally protected, school officials are not precluded from disciplining or discharging the employee if sufficient cause exists independent of the protected speech. Two years later, in *Givhan v. Western Line Consolidated School District* (1979), the Court concluded that as long as a teacher's expression pertains to matters of public concern in contrast to personal grievances, statements made in private or through a public medium are constitutionally protected.

In the area of procedural due process, the Court determined that a school system is not required to establish cause for the nonrenewal of a probationary teacher's contract (*Board of Regents of State Colleges v. Roth*, 1972).

The advent of collective bargaining in the middle of the 20th century had a significant impact in defining other teacher rights. However, because union authority is largely defined by state statute, the Supreme Court has played a minimal role in this area.

The landmark decision for student free speech rights is *Tinker v. Des Moines Independent Community School District* (1969), in which the Court upheld the students' right to wear black armbands in silent protest of American involvement in the Vietnam war. The Court ruled that students may express opinions even on controversial subjects if they do so without "materially and substantially interfere[ing] with the requirements of appropriate discipline in the operation of the school and without colliding with the rights of others." In *Bethel School District No. 403 v. Fraser* (1986), the Court held that the First Amendment free speech clause does not prevent a school district from disciplining a high school student for giving a lewd speech at a school assembly. The Court further modified a student's free speech rights in *Hazelwood School District v. Kuhlmeier* (1988), when it determined that

> educators do not offend the First Amendment by exercising editorial control over the style and content of student speech in school-sponsored expressive activities as long as their actions are reasonably related to legitimate pedagogical concerns.

The Equal Access Act of 1984, 20 U.S.C. § 4071, affords First Amendment protections to students' rights to form groups. Under the act, if a school allows any noncurricular clubs to meet, the school cannot prohibit student groups from meeting, regardless of the religious, political, philosophical, or other content of the group's activities. However, the *Tinker* principle applies, and school officials may prohibit meetings that may be harmful or may pose a threat of material and substantial disruption.

Due process rights for students were addressed in *Goss v. Lopez* (1975), in which the Court held that for a suspension from school of 10 days or less, due process merely requires that students be given oral or written notice of the charges, and if a student denies them, school officials must provide an explanation of the evidence and provide an opportunity for students to present their side of the story.

In *New Jersey v. T.L.O.* (1985), the Court addressed the application of the Fourth Amendment protection from unreasonable search and seizure, as it applies to public school students, and held that the legality of a search of a student depends on the reasonableness under all the circumstances of the search. Determining the reasonableness of a search involves a two-step process: first, whether the action was justified at its inception, and second, whether the search, as actually conducted, was reasonably related in scope to the circumstances that justified the search in the first place.

It is clear from this brief overview of the Supreme Court's rulings in the areas of student and teacher rights that as long as educators act reasonably and within the parameters established by the Court, their actions will be upheld.

FOCUS POINT: Special Education

Under the Education for All Handicapped Children Act of 1975, and now under the Individuals with Disabilities Education Act (IDEA) that was reauthorized in 1997, children eligible for IDEA services have a right to a free, appropriate, public education, including special education and related services, in the least restrictive environment. IDEA includes extensive procedural safeguards to protect parent and student rights and to ensure that appropriate placement decisions are made. Under *Honig v. Doe* (1988), and as clarified in the 1997 amendments to IDEA, certain procedural and placement protections also apply when a child with a disability is disciplined for behavior that was a manifestation of the student's disability. In addition, reasonable attorneys' fees may be awarded to parents who prevail in court review, under IDEA (20 U.S.C. § 1415[i][3][B]).

In 1982, in *Board of Education of the Hendrick Hudson Central School District v. Rowley*, the Court established the standard of review to be applied in determining the appropriateness of an eligible child's educational program. The standard is used to determine whether the school has complied with the procedures identified in IDEA, and whether the student's individualized education program (IEP) is reasonably calculated to enable the student to receive educational benefit from the special education and related services provided as specified in the IEP.

Special education litigation is especially common in the arena of related health services. In 1984, the Court ruled, in *Irving Independent School District v. Tatro*, that services provided by a physician other than for diagnostic and evaluation purposes are subject to the medical services exclusion; the services that can be provided by a nurse or qualified layperson are not excluded under IDEA. This holding was restated in 1999 in *Cedar Rapids Community School District v. Garret F.*, 1999 WL 104410 (U.S.).

FOCUS POINT: Church and State

By far the most unsettled legal question in public education is the relationship between church and state. To withstand scrutiny under the establishment clause, governmental action must have a secular purpose, must have a primary effect that neither advances nor impedes religion, and must avoid excessive governmental entanglement with religion (*Lemon v. Kurtzman*, 1971).

In 1985, in *School District of the City of Grand Rapids et al. v. Ball*, the Court applied the *Lemon* test to invalidate an extensive "shared-time" program under which a Michigan school district rented space from 40 parochial schools and one independent private school to offer a variety of enrichment and remedial courses to private school students. In *Aguilar v. Felton* (1985), the Court invalidated New York City's use of federal funds to provide services for private school students under Chapter 1 of the Elementary and Secondary Education

Act of 1965 because the program advanced religion and created an excessive governmental entanglement between church and state. However, in *Agostini v. Felton* (1997), with six new justices, the Court overruled *Aguilar* and *Ball*, holding that New York City's Title I program does not run contrary to any of the three *Lemon* criteria.

In the area of school prayer, in *Lee v. Weisman* (1992), the Court ruled that prayers organized by public school officials at graduation exercises were unconstitutional. The lead opinion has been interpreted by the Fifth Circuit, in *Jones v. Clear Creek Independent School District* (1992), to allow public high school seniors to choose student volunteers to deliver nonsectarian, nonproselytizing invocations at their graduation ceremonies. The position taken by the Fifth Circuit, however, has been specifically rejected by the Ninth Circuit, in *Harris v. Joint School District 241* (1994), and by the Third Circuit, in *ACLU of New Jersey v. Black Horse Pike Regional Board of Education* (1996).

The debate on the separation of church and state will continue during upcoming sessions of the Supreme Court with cases such as *Santa Fe Independent School District v. Doe* (Case No. 99-062), regarding whether students may lead group prayers prior to the beginning of high school football games, and *Mitchell v. Helms* (Case No. 98-1648), in which Louisiana parents have challenged a federal program providing computers, televisions, and other supplies to parochial schools. Another probable review is in the area of the constitutionality of vouchers for religious schools. Several states currently have voucher programs; others offer tax deductions or credits for private school tuition.

SECTION D: HIGHLIGHTS OF SELECTED PORTIONS OF FEDERAL STATUTES THAT AFFECT EDUCATION PRACTICE

State legislatures have plenary power to make laws that direct how education shall be provided within their states. However, Congress also enacts statutes that guarantee certain rights and protections to students, parents, and school personnel. This section highlights some of that federal legislation that dictates certain practices and protections in the education enterprise.

> ### FOCUS POINT: Civil Rights Acts of 1866, 1870—42 U.S.C. §§ 1981 and 1988; Civil Rights Acts of 1871—42 U.S.C. §§ 1983, 1985, and 1986; Civil Rights Acts of 1964, Titles IV and VII—42 U.S.C. §§ 2000d, 2000e-2

These acts that mandate equal employment opportunities are discussed in Chapters 4 and 5.

FOCUS POINT: Title IX of the Education Amendments of 1972 and the Title IX Regulations 34 C.F.R. § 106-1 et seq.

Title IX and its administrative regulations prohibit an education program or activity that receives federal funds from denying any individual admission to, participation in, or the benefits of any academic, extracurricular, research, occupational training, aid, service, or other education program or activity on the basis of gender. Programs that receive federal funds are specifically prohibited from

- Preferentially ranking applicants by gender
- Applying numerical quotas based on gender
- Administering any preadmission tests that have a disproportionately adverse effect on persons on the basis of gender unless the test is a valid predictor of success in the program and alternative tests are unavailable
- Applying any rule concerning parental, family, or marital status or making any preadmission inquiry regarding the marital status of an applicant
- Subjecting any person to separate or different rules of behavior, sanctions, or other treatment on the basis of gender
- Measuring skill or progress in a physical education class in any manner that has an adverse effect on members of one sex

In addition, programs that receive federal funds may not exclude any student from any class or extracurricular activity on the basis of pregnancy, childbirth, termination of pregnancy, or recovery therefrom unless the student requests to participate in a separate program or activity and the separate program is comparable to that offered to other students. It is permissible to require a doctor's certification that the student is physically and emotionally able to participate in the normal program or activity. Furthermore, the program or activity must treat the pregnancy, childbirth, or termination of pregnancy in the same manner that it treats any other temporary disability under its medical or hospital benefit, service, plan, or policy.

Title IX does not prohibit an education program or activity from

- Grouping students in physical education classes by ability as assessed by objective standards
- Separating students by gender within physical education classes or other activities that involve body contact
- Conducting classes in elementary and secondary schools that deal with human sexuality in separate sections for boys and girls
- Making requirements based on vocal range or quality that result in a chorus of one or predominately one gender

FOCUS POINT: Family Educational Rights and Privacy Act of 1974 (FERPA), 20 U.S.C. § 1232G

FERPA (see also in Chapter 9), also referred to as the Buckley Amendment, requires educational agencies and institutions to provide parents of students attending a school of the agency or institution the right to inspect and review the education records of their children. Each educational agency or institution may establish its own procedures for granting parents' requests for access to the education records of their children but must make the records available within a maximum of 45 days after the parent request is made. Agencies and institutions that fail to provide parental access to records will lose federal funding for their programs.

The law further provides that educational agencies or institutions must provide the parents with an opportunity for a hearing to challenge the content of a student's education records to

- Ensure that the records are not inaccurate, misleading, or otherwise in violation of the privacy or other rights of students
- Provide an opportunity to correct or delete any inaccurate, misleading, or otherwise inappropriate data contained therein
- Insert into the records a written explanation from the parents regarding the content of the records

The law prohibits the release of education records (or personally identifiable information contained therein other than directory information) of students without the written consent of their parents to any individual, agency, or organization, other than to the following:

- Other school officials, including teachers who have legitimate educational interests
- Officials of other schools or school systems in which the student seeks to or intends to enroll, on condition that the student's parents be notified of the transfer, receive a copy of the record if desired, and have an opportunity for a hearing to challenge the content of the record
- Authorized representatives of the federal, state, or local government
- Officials in connection with a student's application for, or receipt of, financial aid
- Organizations conducting studies for, or on behalf of, educational agencies or institutions for the purpose of developing, validating, or administering predictive tests, administering student aid programs, and improving instruction, if the studies are conducted in a manner that will not permit the personal identification of students and their parents by persons other than representatives of the organizations and if the information will be destroyed when no longer needed
- Accrediting organizations to carry out their accrediting functions

- Appropriate persons, in connection with an emergency, if the knowledge of the information is necessary to protect the health or safety of the student or other persons
- Parents who have given written consent that specifies records to be released, the reasons for such release, and to whom—with a copy of the records to be released for the student's parents and the student if desired by the parents, or
- Information is furnished in compliance with judicial order or lawfully issued subpoena, and the parents and the students are notified of the orders or subpoenas in advance of the compliance by the educational institution or agency

FERPA limits the information that can be provided to persons other than parents to directory information unless

- Parents have given written consent that specifies records to be released, the reasons for such release, and to whom—with a copy of the records to be released for the student's parents and the student, if desired by the parents, or
- Information is furnished in compliance with judicial order or lawfully issued subpoena, and the parents and the students are notified of the orders or subpoenas in advance of the compliance by the educational institution or agency

The transfer of information is made on the condition that the third party will not provide the information to any other party without the written consent of the parents. Other provisions of FERPA follow:

- If a student is 18 years of age (or older) or is attending an institution of postsecondary education, the permission or consent required of and the rights accorded to the parents of the student shall only be required of and accorded to the student.
- All instructional material (e.g., teacher's manuals, films, tapes, or other supplementary material to be used in connection with any research program or project designed to explore or develop new or unproven teaching methods or techniques) must be made available for inspection by the parents or guardians of the children involved.
- No student may be required, as part of any applicable program, to submit to psychiatric or psychological examination, testing, or treatment in which the primary purpose is to reveal information concerning
  - Political affiliations
  - Mental and psychological problems potentially embarrassing to the student or family
  - Sex behavior and attitudes
  - Illegal, antisocial, self-incriminating, and demeaning behavior

- Critical appraisals of other individuals with whom respondents have close family relationships
- Legally recognized privileged and analogous relationships, such as those of lawyers, physicians, and ministers, or
- Income (other than that required by law to determine eligibility for participation in a program or for receiving financial assistance under such program) without the prior consent of the student (if the student is an adult or emancipated minor) or, in the case of a minor, without the prior written consent of the parent.

FOCUS POINT: Americans with Disabilities Act of 1990 (ADA), Pub. L. No. 101-336, 42 U.S.C. §§ 12101–12213

ADA requires educational institutions to make every reasonable accommodation to ensure access to all facilities, programs, and activities by students and employees, without regard to disability. These requirements apply to private schools and institutions that do not receive federal aid as well as to schools and institutions that are recipients of federal funds. In *Raytheon Co. v Hernandez* (2003), the U.S. Supreme Court decided that an employer's decision not to rehire a former employee who had been terminated for failing a routine drug test was not a violation of ADA.

FOCUS POINT: Individuals with Disabilities Education Act (IDEA), as Amended in 1997, Pub. L. No. 105-17, 20 U.S.C. §§ 1400–1485

IDEA guarantees that all children with disabilities receive a free, appropriate, public education consisting of special education and related services designed to meet their individual needs. In addition, IDEA ensures that the rights of children with disabilities and their parents or guardians are protected and directs states and localities to provide for the education of all children with disabilities.

FOCUS POINT: Age Discrimination in Employment Act of 1967 (ADEA), 29 U.S.C. § 621 (§ 623)

ADEA prohibits employers from failing or refusing to hire, discharging, or otherwise discriminating against any individual with respect to compensation, terms, conditions, or privileges of employment because of the individual's age. The law covers all employees who are 40 or older. In *General Dynamics Land Systems, Inc. v. Cline* (2003), the U.S. Supreme Court resolved a split among the federal courts of appeals by deciding that ADEA does not prohibit an employer from favoring older employees over relatively younger employees. The court found that to read ADEA as barring discrimination against younger workers in favor of older employees did "not square with the natural reading of ADEA."

In 2005, the U.S. Supreme Court struck a major blow for age equality in the workplace when it declared that a bulwark of civil rights laws against race and sex discrimination also protects employees who bring suits in federal court under ADEA. Under the Court's ruling in *Smith et al. v. City of Jackson, Mississippi, et al.* (2005) (see also Newman, 2005), plaintiffs can now bypass what was often the hardest-to-prove aspect of their cases—showing that their employers' discrimination was deliberate. Instead, plaintiffs need only show that they were victims of a policy that caused harm to older workers and went beyond "reasonable" business considerations. This decision elevated age discrimination legally closer to the level of race or gender bias. The scope of discrimination based on age will continue to be narrower because ADEA, while generally modeled on race and sex discrimination laws, allows employers to treat older workers differently as long as they do so based on "reasonable factors other than age." The *Smith* decision applies to all employers (private as well as local, state, and federal government) that have 20 or more employees and to labor unions that have 25 or more employees.

Examples of Management Cues

- Your school district implements a policy to hire only teachers with 10 or more years of experience.
- Your school district includes a requirement of computer literacy on job descriptions for positions that do not include computer use.
- The recently announced reduction-in-force policy appears to target high-salaried employees and/or those eligible for retirement.

Suggested Risk Management Guidelines

- Review all employment practices to ensure that they
  - Are age neutral
  - Do not provide special benefits to one age group over another
  - Comply with all ADEA and other state and local age discrimination statutes

FOCUS POINT: Rehabilitation Act of 1973, 29 U.S.C. § 794 (§ 504)

The specific requirements of the Rehabilitation Act of 1973 and, specifically, Section 504 of the act, are discussed in Chapter 4. The principal's responsibilities in providing special education services under this act are discussed in Chapter 8.

FOCUS POINT: Equal Educational Opportunities Act, 20 U.S.C. § 1703

Section 1703 provides that no state shall deny equal educational opportunity to an individual on account of her or his race, color, sex, or national origin, by

- The deliberate segregation of students on the basis of race, color, or national origin among or within schools, or
- The assignment of students to a school other than the one closest to their place of residence within the school district in which they reside if the assignment results in a greater degree of segregation of students on the basis of race, color, sex, or national origin

The law also prohibits

- Discrimination by an educational agency on the basis of race, color, or national origin in the employment, employment conditions, or assignment to schools of its faculty or staff
- The transfer, whether voluntary or otherwise, of a student from one school to another if the purpose and effect of such transfer is to increase segregation of students on the basis of race, color, or national origin among the schools of such agency, and
- The failure of an educational agency to take appropriate action to overcome language barriers that impede equal participation by its students in its instructional programs

FOCUS POINT: The Family and Medical Leave Act of 1993 (FMLA), Pub. L. No. 103-3, 29 C.F.R. § 825

FMLA provides every covered employee with up to 12 work weeks of unpaid leave in any 12-month period in four specific situations: (1) the birth of a child, (2) placement of a child for adoption or foster care, (3) care of a spouse, child, or parent who has a serious health condition, or (4) the serious health condition of the employee. A serious health condition is defined as inpatient care at a hospital, hospice, or residential medical care facility, or continuing care of a doctor of medicine or osteopathy, or other health care provider, identified by the secretary of labor. To be eligible for this unpaid leave, the employee must have worked for the employer for at least 12 months prior to requesting the leave and have worked at least 1,250 hours during the past year. FMLA generally includes the following points:

- An employee who takes leave under the law must be able to return to the same job or a job with equivalent status, pay, and benefits.

- The employer must continue the employee's health benefits during the period of leave as if the employee were still working. If the employee does not return to work, the employer may require the employee to repay the premium for the health care coverage.
- The employer may require a doctor's certification of the health condition.
- The employee may take the 12 weeks of leave in a block of time or, with the prior concurrence of the employer, intermittently (taking a day periodically or using the leave to reduce the hours worked in a week or a day).
- When spouses are employed by the same employer, the aggregate number of weeks of FMLA leave to which they are entitled in any 12-month period is 12 weeks' except when the leave is for their own serious health condition.
- The employee may request or the employer may require that the employee use all accrued paid leave (sick leave, vacation leave, etc.) before taking the unpaid FMLA leave. In addition, prior to the employee's taking any unpaid leave under this act, the employer may require the employee to use up accrued paid leave first and count the paid leave taken toward the total 12 week's leave mandated by this law.
- Special rules apply with regard to staff "employed principally in an instructional capacity" (Section 108[c][1]) in both public and private schools. First, if the instructional employee requests FMLA leave for a planned medical treatment and the leave would be for more than 20 percent of the total number of working days in the period during which the leave would extend, the school may require the employee to take leave for periods of a particular duration or to transfer temporarily to an available alternative position that better accommodates recurring periods of leave. Second, under certain specified conditions, if an instructional employee requests FMLA leave within five weeks of the conclusion of an academic term, the school may require that the leave extend to the end of the term.
- Employers are required to post conspicuous notice of employees' rights under FMLA in all work locations.
- FMLA does not diminish an employer's obligation under more generous state and local statutes, collective bargaining agreements, or employment policies.

FMLA is administered by the U.S. Department of Labor through a complex set of regulations that integrate its provisions with those of the Americans with Disabilities Act of 1990 (Pub. L. No. 101-336, 29 C.F.R. Part 1630) and state workers' compensation laws.

SECTION E: WORKERS' COMPENSATION

Workers' compensation provides benefits to employees who suffer injuries or ailments that arise out of and in the course of employment. Unlike the Americans with Disabilities Act and the Family and Medical Leave Act, workers' compensation insurance is mandated

by state statutes rather than federal law. Texas is the only state that makes workers'
compensation insurance elective.

FOCUS POINT: General Provisions
Regarding Workers' Compensation

Because workers' compensation insurance derives from 53 different statutes
(50 states, the District of Columbia, U.S. Virgin Islands, and Puerto Rico), the
specific provisions that apply can vary widely. However, the basic concepts on
which all workers' compensation laws are founded include the following:

- Workers' compensation benefits for employees who suffer occupational
  injuries or other covered ailments include payment for medical treatment, vocational rehabilitation, time away from work (income protection), and death and burial costs.
- The employer's workers' compensation insurance is responsible for any
  injury or ailment that is directly related to employment regardless of who
  actually caused the accident. However, that liability is limited to the benefits specified in the workers' compensation law.
- Workers' compensation benefits are provided on an exclusive-remedy
  basis. This means that an injured employee who receives benefits under
  the plan gives up the right to sue the employer for damages. The trade-
  off is between guaranteed and timely benefits and the possibility, but not
  assurance, of a larger settlement as the result of litigation at some uncertain future date.
- Depending on the state's statute, workers' compensation insurance may
  be provided by state funds or private insurance carriers or through self-
  insurance by the county or school district.

Principals, like other employers, have a dual interest in workers' compensation claims. The first is to limit the school district's liability for workers' compensation claims by anticipating and avoiding situations that have the potential
to cause employment-related injury. The second is to ensure that when an
employee suffers an employment-related injury, the incident is reported and the
determination regarding workers' compensation benefits is made as soon as
possible. When the school district is liable, workers' compensation benefits are
far less expensive than the potential cost of civil litigation and any resultant
damage awards.

The primary tenet of workers' compensation is that an injury or illness is
compensable when it arises both out of and in the course of employment. The
term *arising out of* describes the accident and its origin, cause, and character;
the term *in the course of* refers to the time, place, and circumstances surrounding
the accident. A claimant must establish both. For example, the custodian who fell
from a ladder while changing a light bulb in the boys' locker room and fractured

his elbow will likely be eligible for benefits under workers' compensation. The job required the custodian to use the ladder to complete an assigned task, and he was doing the assigned task when he fell. A corollary to this primary tenet is that coverage under workers' compensation does not begin until the employee arrives at work and ends when the employee leaves work—that is, injuries incurred during the normal commuting to and from work are generally not covered. (Your school district's attorney has additional information in the area of commuting.)

The distinction between employment-related and nonemployment-related injuries is not always clear, and problems can arise when interpretation is needed to determine whether there is a direct causal relationship between an injury and the employment situation. The following hypothetical scenarios are based on real cases and illustrate legal principles that have been used to determine whether or not an employee's injury is covered by the workers' compensation insurance. (Note: Although *all workers' compensation cases are decided on the facts and the provisions of the applicable statute*, the following examples are designed to help principals better understand the complexities of workers' compensation law and assist them in anticipating and avoiding potentially dangerous situations.)

Scenario 1. As a voluntary member of the district's contract negotiating team, a school principal was required to attend a scheduled board meeting. On the day of the board meeting, the principal assisted PTA members in preparing some backdrops for the upcoming school carnival. He left for home on his motorcycle quite late, intending to eat, shower, and change into a suit before he left for the board meeting. He was injured in a collision halfway between his school and his home.

Workers' compensation would probably cover this injury. Injuries suffered by employees during their regular commutes may be compensable if they were also performing a special mission for their employers. An employee's conduct is *special* if it is extraordinary in its relationship to routine duties and is not outside the scope of employment. Even though this principal was traveling home rather than between places of work, the trip was reasonably undertaken at the request or invitation of the employer and was a special mission.

Scenario 2. A classroom teacher, who also served as the district's supervisor of foreign languages, owned a computer and offered to use it to develop a master schedule for the district's foreign language program. Because her computer was a desk model, she did this work at home. She was killed in an automobile accident while en route from her home to the central district office to deliver the finished schedule.

Hazards encountered while commuting to and from work are normally not connected to employment and not compensable under workers' compensation. There are, however, exceptions to the rule when (a) the employer furnishes the means of transportation or remunerates the employee and (b) the employee performs some duty in connection with employment at home. This teacher's death would probably be compensable under workers' compensation.

Scenario 3. A community educator was injured when he was assaulted in his car immediately after leaving the school parking lot to go home from work. His car had been immobilized by students departing from the evening night school and was blocking traffic.

Although the victim was beginning a normal commute home, his injuries may be compensable because the employment creates a special risk that extends beyond the boundaries of the employment premises, and the injury occurred within the zone of risk.

Scenario 4. While attending an education conference in another state, a principal fractured both of her heels in a fall. A sample of blood was drawn at the hospital. A doctor testified that the blood alcohol content revealed that the teacher was intoxicated at the time of the accident.

Workers' compensation probably would not cover this accident. Courts have ruled that an employee can abandon employment by reaching an advanced state of intoxication. Any injury suffered thereafter is not in the course of employment, as the employee is no longer able to perform his or her job.

Scenario 5. After adjournment of a night meeting held in a high school building, a district music teacher went to the weight room to work out. While attempting to lift a barbell, he seriously injured his back.

Unless he could demonstrate that his activity could reasonably be expected in connection with his duties, the court would probably not grant compensation. If, however, the employee could demonstrate that he regularly exercised at work, which included lifting weights, and the employer was aware of and permitted such activities, the court would likely rule that the injury arose in the course of employment and was compensable.

Scenario 6. A high school teacher was stabbed by a mental patient because the patient had seen the teacher talking with a student, the patient's girlfriend, after school.

Some state workers' compensation acts do not cover injuries caused by the actions of a third person that are intended to injure the employee for personal reasons. However, because the stabbing was incidental to the teacher's duties and it arose out of his employment, the employee would likely be entitled to workers' compensation benefits.

Scenario 7. A school principal attended an out-of-town conference. Following completion of the conference, he and several other conference participants had dinner in a local restaurant. As they left the restaurant, one of his companions was assaulted by someone unconnected with the conference. As he attempted to assist his companion, the principal himself was assaulted and injured.

In this scenario, there is no causal connection between the conditions under which the employee worked and the injury that arose. The employee's voluntary acts were the main cause of the injury, and his claim for workers' compensation benefits would probably be denied.

Scenario 8. An elementary school teacher suffered injuries while she was participating in a softball game at a statewide teachers' association conference. The district had paid her expenses to attend the conference.

This injury occurred during recreational activities rather than during the course of employment. In similar situations, courts have ruled that (a) if the injury did not occur on the employer's premises, (b) the employer did not require or endorse participation in the game, and (c) the employer obtained no tangible benefit, then there is no relationship between the actions and the employer. In such cases, claims are usually denied.

Scenario 9. A school district special education supervisor was on his way to visit a special education center in another city when he encountered a violent and unusual rainstorm with winds up to 100 miles per hour. When a tree fell on his car, his neck was broken, totally disabling him.

This teacher suffered an injury in the course of his employment; however, the accident did not arise out of his employment. The risks the teacher took in driving to the other city were not inherent in the job, but were risks to which the general public was exposed. This claim would likely be denied.

Suggested Risk Management Guidelines

- Principals should make sure they know the major provisions of the workers' compensation law in their states and their districts' procedures for reporting employment-related injuries and filing claims for workers' compensation benefits.
- Principals should clearly communicate to their faculties and staffs the importance both of avoiding accidental injury and of reporting such injuries immediately when they do occur.
- Principals should also establish and enforce policies and procedures designed to reduce the chances of an employee sustaining an employment-related injury.

SECTION F: LEGAL STATUS OF SCHOOL CHOICE

Choice supporters see choice not only as empowering the poor family to do better by its child but also as creating competitive pressures on traditional neighborhood public schools to spur them to improve. They believe that upper- and middle-class families have long enjoyed school choice and frequently exercise their choice by moving to a different school district, quite often in the suburbs, where they believe better schooling is available. Various choice plans are aimed at giving low-income families options within the public school sector that do not require moving their place of residence. The five choice plan models that are most frequently implemented are family choice, interdistrict transfer, specialized school choice, charter schools, and No Child Left Behind schools (Sugarman, 2004).

In a family choice plan, no one has priority rights to any particular neighborhood school, and students are not assigned to a specific school. Instead, families request their first, second, and third choices of schools, and students are then matched to schools based on parental choices and available space. Generally this plan is implemented in order to achieve racial integration. A second model is interdistrict transfers. Under this model, children may request permission to attend a particular school in their own district or in any other nearby school district that has room for them. This model is also frequently implemented either to achieve racial integration or to benefit low-income minority families. Specialized school choice is a third model. In this model, parents may select from a menu of special schools such as magnet schools or other alternative schools. A fourth model is charter schools, which we discuss in some detail below. The fifth model was created in response to No Child Left Behind. Under NCLB, school districts must offer alternative school choices to families when the school their children attend fails to meet the minimum standards required by the law.

| FOCUS POINT: Legislation Governing Charter Schools and Vouchers

Charter Schools

Charter schools are state-sponsored schools created by a charter, or contract, between the state and the individual school. Typically organized with the goal of improving the educational opportunities of at-risk or special-needs children, charter schools frequently enjoy less restrictive requirements than public schools and greater freedom regarding funding sources and financial management.

The statutes that permit the establishment of charter schools vary widely from state to state; however, enabling legislation typically specifies

- Where official oversight and control reside—that is, with the state board of education, a local board of education, or a city or county government—and who is entitled to apply for a charter—that is, a public school district, group of teachers or parents, or an independent nonprofit organization
- The application and approval procedures and the term of the charter grant, renewal requirements, and grounds for the revocation of a charter
- Permissible sources of funding—that is, public (federal, state, and local monies), private donations, or local or regional grants
- Admissions criteria, curriculum, and teacher qualifications
- Whether the charter school or the local school district is responsible for transporting students to and from the charter school

After a mid-1980s debate in California regarding the idea of freeing teachers to create their own public schools, Minnesota passed the nation's first charter school law authorizing schools to operate essentially free from most state regulations. The first charter school opened its doors in St. Paul, Minnesota, in

September 1992. Since then, 40 states have enacted charter legislation. Today California, Florida, Texas, and Michigan have the majority of the 2,700 charter schools, enrolling approximately 750,000 students.

The basic concept of a charter school includes a state giving permission for a group of educators or others to apply for permission to open a school. If approved, the school receives a charter and a budget equal to what a public school would receive for each student enrolled. To gain renewal, the charter school must demonstrate that its students have gained the educational skills specified in its contract. In some states, the charter schools are limited as to number and freedom from state regulation; in other states, there is little state regulation.

Vouchers

Voucher plans offer parents the opportunity to spend their "education tax dollars" to enroll their children in the schools of their choice. Vouchers are a predetermined sum that represents tax dollars already being collected from citizens and budgeted for education. Voucher supporters contend that, because the state pays a specific dollar amount per student to each school, their voucher will not impact the budget amount allocated for education but will simply allow those tax dollars to be allocated to the school of the parent's choice.

Voucher plans have long been a much-discussed proposal for education reform. The primary legal issue is the question of whether such plans are permitted under the establishment clause of the First Amendment. The fact that the Supreme Court continues to accept the neutrality doctrine in establishment clause cases may indicate that a properly designed voucher program that makes funds available for parents would not be rejected by the Court. Cases like *Campbell v. Manchester Board of School Directors* (1994) in Vermont, *Minnesota Federation of Teachers v. Nelson* (1990) in Minnesota, and *Jackson v. Benson* (1998) in Wisconsin indicate a trend toward allowing state funds to be paid to religious schools.

However, in general, voucher plans have not prevailed in court. Florida initiated the nation's first statewide choice program designed to serve children who attended failing schools. In 1999, students in two Florida schools were eligible, and nearly 60 students took advantage of Opportunity Scholarships. It was anticipated that in the year 2000, up to 60,000 Florida children would have this option. However, in 2000, Florida's school voucher law was ruled unconstitutional, in *Holmes v. Bush*. The court ruled that children attending private schools in Pensacola could finish the school year, but the state could take no other action to implement the law. The program allowed students in Florida's worst public schools to receive vouchers of up to $3,389 a year to pay for a private or parochial school education at taxpayer expense. Opponents of the plan argued that vouchers violate the state constitution by spending public dollars on private schools and violate the establishment clause of the U.S. Constitution. The program was challenged by a coalition that included a teachers' union, the National Association for the Advancement of Colored People, the Florida PTA, the League of Women Voters, and a handful of families and educators.

On June 28, 2000, the U.S. Supreme Court handed down a decision that has reopened the debate surrounding vouchers. In *Mitchell v. Helms*, the Court ruled that some federal aid for private and parochial schools is permitted. The question is, how broadly can this decision be applied? Advocates for voucher plans argue that if the government can buy computers, books, and audiovisual equipment for religious schools, as six justices ruled, how about bricks and mortar for buildings? Why not have states pay the salaries of Catholic-school teachers of a secular subject like mathematics? They also argue that this decision implies that public money can be used to offset tuition at schools sponsored by religious organizations. They believe that this decision makes public policy more flexible in terms of aid following students rather than aid to the public school system exclusively.

Although the *Mitchell* case concerns a narrow program providing instructional materials, one justice took the opportunity to write a strong provoucher opinion focused on a neutrality test: whether aid is equally available to students regardless of where they study. Three justices joined his opinion. Two others voted only to uphold the purchase of computers and other equipment. They drew a distinction between direct aid to schools for materials and funneling money through parents in the form of vouchers that are used for religious as well as secular studies.

On June 27, 2002, the U.S. Supreme Court issued its ruling in *Zelman v. Simmons-Harris*, the Cleveland, Ohio, school voucher case. In a 5–4 decision, the justices ruled that the Cleveland program that allowed parents to use publicly funded vouchers to pay tuition at private schools—including religious schools—did not violate the U.S. Constitution's prohibition on governmental establishment of religion. The Court majority held that the program was "neutral in all respects toward religion," that any tax funds flowing to religious schools did so as a result of individual choice, and that the program provided genuine secular schooling options.

On January 22, 2004, Congress passed the first federally funded school voucher program, allocating $14 million to establish a program for low-income students in the District of Columbia. This will likely renew the national debate over school choice issues, including controversy about public money going to religiously affiliated schools as noted by the Pew Forum on Religion and Public Life (2005).

The questions surrounding school vouchers and choice will continue to be a subject of public debate over the next few years, as states and other localities wrestle with ways to improve education and whether school vouchers add to, or help resolve, school choice issues.

Examples of Management Cues

- In a public meeting, a number of parents ask the school principal to explain the charter school movement.
- At a community forum, a group of parents ask the school principal why they have to pay taxes when they send their children to a private school.

Suggested Risk Management Guideline

- Issues relating to charter schools and vouchers are unlikely to directly impact the daily operation of public schools at the building level; however, competent educational leaders should be able to provide accurate and current information regarding both charter schools and vouchers.

SECTION G: STATUTE OF LIMITATIONS FOR FEDERAL CASES

Prior to 1990, when federal cases did not contain their own statute of limitations, the federal courts applied the "most analogous state statute of limitations" to those cases. In 1990, the U.S. Congress enacted a "catchall" four-year statute of limitations. This law was affirmed by the U.S. Supreme Court in the case of *Jones v. R. R. Donnelley & Sons* (2004). This decision may subject school districts to a longer period of legal exposure than might have been the case when shorter limitation periods were possible.

EXAMPLES OF LEADING U.S. SUPREME COURT CASES ON EDUCATION

Desegregation—Separate, but Equal, Facilities

Plessy v. Ferguson

Desegregation—Racial Desegregation Mandated

Bolling v. Sharpe

Brown v. Board of Education of Topeka (Brown I)

Desegregation—Implementation

Brown v. Board of Education of Topeka (Brown II)

Brown v. Board of Education of Topeka (Brown III)

Desegregation—Challenges to Segregation

Alexander v. Holmes County Board of Education

Carter v. West Feliciana School Board

Columbus Board of Education v. Penick

Cooper v. Aaron

Dandridge v. Jefferson Parish School Board

Gomperts v. Chase

Griffin v. County School Board

Guey Heung Lee v. Johnson

Northcross v. Board of Education

Desegregation—Free Transfers and "Freedom of Choice" Programs

Goss v. Board of Education

Green v. County School Board of New Kent County, Virginia

Monroe v. Board of Commissioners

Raney v. Board of Education

Desegregation—Attendance Zones

Dowell v. Board of Education

McDaniel v. Barresi

Pasadena City Board of Education v. Spangler

Vetterli v. U.S. District Court

Desegregation—Busing

Board of Education of City of Los Angeles v. Superior Court

Bustop Inc. v. Board of Education of City of Los Angeles

North Carolina State Board of Education v. Swann

Washington v. Seattle School District Number I

Desegregation—Faculty Desegregation

Bradley v. School Board (Bradley I)

Bradley v. School Board (Bradley II)

Davis v. Board of School Commissioners

Rogers v. Paul

U.S. v. Montgomery Board of Education

Desegregation in Other Facilities

Evans v. Newton

Gilmore v. City of Montgomery

Hills v. Gautreaux

Federal District Court Authority

Bush v. Orleans School Board

Crawford v. Board of Education

Dayton Board of Education v. Brinkman (Dayton I)

Dayton Board of Education v. Brinkman (Dayton II)

Keyes v. School District No. 1, Denver, Colorado

Milliken v. Bradley (Milliken I)

Milliken v. Bradley (Milliken II)

Swann v. Charlotte-Mecklenburg Board of Education

United States v. Scotland Neck Board of Education

Winston-Salem/Forsyth Board of Education v. Scott

Wright v. Council of City of Emporia

Private Schools and the Constitution—Formulation of the Rules

Board of Education v. Allen

Cochran v. Louisiana State Board of Education

Everson v. Board of Education

Farrington v. Tokushige

McCollum v. Board of Education

Meyer v. Nebraska

Pierce v. Society of Sisters

Zorach v. Clauson

Taxpayer Standing—Challenges to State Support of Private Schools

Flast v. Cohen

Valley Forge Christian College v. Americans United for Separation of Church and State

Private Schools—Government Regulation

Allen v. Wright

Bob Jones University v. U.S.

Grove City College v. Bell

Mueller v. Allen

Norwood v. Harrison

Runyon v. McCrary

St. Martin's Evangelical Lutheran Church v. South Dakota

Wheeler v. Barrera

School District Operations—School District Budget and Finance

Askew v. Hargrave

Bell v. New Jersey & Pennsylvania

Bennett v. Kentucky Department of Education

Bennett v. New Jersey

Board of Education v. Harris

Gordon v. Lance

Kadrmas v. Dickinson Public Schools

San Antonio Independent School District v. Rodriguez

Schmidt v. Oakland Unified School District

Volt Information Sciences v. Board of Trustees of Leland Stanford Junior University

School District Operations—School Elections

East Carroll Parish School Board v. Marshall

Hadley v. Junior College District

Kramer v. Union School District

Mayor v. Educational Equality League

Sailors v. Board of Education

School District Operations—Access to School Buildings

Ellis v. Dixon

ADDITIONAL CASES OF INTEREST TO EDUCATORS

Duty of the Legislature

Jami McDuffy et al. v. Secretary of the Executive Office of Education et al., 615 N.E.2d 516, 415 Mass. 545 (1993). "Duty" of the legislature "to cherish" public schools.

Common Schools

Commonwealth v. Hartman, 17 Pa. 118 (Pa. 1851). The legislature is not prohibited from creating common schools by expanding on the pauper school provision in the state constitution.

Rose v. The Council for Better Education, Inc., 790 S.W.2d 186 (Ky. 1989). "To provide an efficient system of common schools throughout the state."

State ex rel. Clark v. Haworth, 122 Ind. 462, 23 N.E. 946 (Ind. 1890). The regulation of common schools is within the power of the legislature.

Charter Schools

Council of Organizations and Others for Education about Parochiaid v. Governor, 455 Mich. 557, 566 N.W.2d 208 (Mich. 1997). The definition of "public school" includes "charter school" and does not constitute parochial aid to religious schools.

Textbook Fees/Free Public Education

Cardiff v. Bismarck Public School District, 263 N.W.2d 105 (N.D. 1978). A textbook fee in elementary schools violates the state constitution.

Hartzell v. Connell, 35 Cal.3d 899, 201 Cal.Rptr. 601, 679, P.2d 35 (1984). State constitutional provision for free public education prohibits fees for regular or extracurricular programs.

Randolph County Board of Education v. Adams, 467 S.E.2d 150 (W. Va. 1995). A fee for textbooks and other materials violates the free public schools provision of the state constitution.

Article VI, Clause 2, of the U.S. Constitution Supremacy Clause

Wheeler v. Barrera, 417 U.S. 402, 94 S.Ct. 2274 (1974); 422 U.S. 1004, 95 S.Ct. 2625 (1975). States are not obligated to expend federal funds for purposes that violate the state constitution.

CHAPTER RESOURCES

Abbott v. Burke, 693 A.2d 417 (N.J. 1990).

ACLU of New Jersey v. Black Horse Pike Regional Board of Education, 84 F.3d, 1471 (1996).

Agostini v. Felton, 521 U.S. 203 (1997).

Aguilar v. Felton, 473 U.S. 402 (1985).

Bethel School District No. 403 v. Fraser, 478 U.S. 675 (1986).

Board of Education of the Hendrick Hudson Central School District v. Rowley, 457 U.S. 176 (1982).

Board of Education of Oklahoma Public Schools v. Dowell, 498 U.S. 237 (1991).

Board of Regents of State Colleges v. Roth, 408 U.S. 564 (1972).

Brown v. Board of Education of Topeka (Brown I), 347 U.S. 483 (1954).

Brown v. Board of Education of Topeka (Brown II), 349 U.S. 294 (1955).

Campbell v. Manchester Board of School Directors., 641 A.2d 352 (Vt. 1994).

Cedar Rapids Community School District v. Garret F., 1999 WL 104410 (U.S.).

Cooper v. Aaron, 358 U.S. 1 (1958).

Freeman v. Pitts, 503 U.S. 467 (1992).

General Dynamics Land Systems, Inc. v. Cline (20-1080) 540 U.S. 581 (2004).

Givhan v. Western Line Consolidated School District, 439 U.S. 410 (1979).

Gong Lum v. Rice, 275 U.S. 78 (1927).

Goss v. Lopez, 419 U.S. 565 (1975).

Green v. County School Board of New Kent County, Virginia, 391 U.S. 430 (1968).

Griffin v. County School Board of Prince Edward County, 377 U.S. 218 (1964).

Harris v. Joint School District 241, 41 F.3d 447 (1994).

Hazelwood School District v. Kuhlmeier, 484 U.S. 260 (1988).

Holmes v. Bush, CV 99-3370, Fla. 2d DCA (2000).

Honig v. Doe, 484 U.S. 305 (1988).

Irving Independent School District v. Tatro, 468 U.S. 883 (1984).

Jackson v. Benson, 578 N.W.2d 973 (1998).

Jones v. Clear Creek Independent School District, 977 F.2d 963 (5th Cir. 1992).

Jones v. R. R. Donnelley & Sons Co., 123 S.Ct. 1836 (2004).

Lee v. Weisman, 505 U.S. 577 (1992).

Lemon v. Kurtzman, 403 U.S. 602 (1971).

Milliken v. Bradley (Milliken I), 418 U.S. 717 (1974).

Milliken v. Bradley (Milliken II), 433 U.S. 267 (1977).

Minnesota Federation of Teachers v. Nelson, 740 F. Supp. 694 (D. Minn. 1990).

Missouri v. Jenkins, 515 U.S. 70 (1995).

Mitchell v. Helms (98-1648) 530 U.S. 793 (2000).

Mount Healthy City School District Board of Education v. Doyle, 427 U.S. 274 (1977).

New Jersey v. T.L.O., 469 U.S. 325 (1985).

Newman, D. (2005). Breakthrough: A landmark Supreme Court decision is being hailed as "the Emancipation Proclamation for older workers." *AARP Bulletin, 46*(5), 10–12.

No Child Left Behind Act, Pub. L. No. 107-110 (2001).

Pew Forum on Religion and Public Life. (2005). Retrieved May 6, 2005, from http://pewforum.org

Pickering v. Board of Education of Township High School District 205, 391 U.S. 563 (1968).

Plessy v. Ferguson, 163 U.S. 537 (1896).

Raytheon Co. v. Hernandez, 540 U.S. 44 (2003).

Robinson v. Cahill, 287 A.2d 187 (1972).

Rose v. Council for Better Education, Inc., 790 S.W.2d 186 (1989).

San Antonio Independent School District v. Rodriguez, 411 U.S. 1 (1973).

Santa Fe Independent School District v. Doe (99-062) 530 U.S. 290 (2000).

School District of the City of Grand Rapids et al. v. Ball, 473 U.S. 373 (1989).

Serrano v. Priest, 487 P.2d 1241 (1971).

Smith et al. v. City of Jackson, Mississippi, et al., 125 S. Ct. 1536 (2005).

Sugarman, S. D. (2004). *The promise of school choice for improving the education of low-income minority children.* Paper presented at symposium, Rekindling the Spirit of Brown v. Board of Education. 6 AFR AM L and Pol'y Rep., 202, 11 Asian L.J. 284, 15 Berkeley La Raza L.J. 75, 19 Berkeley Women's L.J. 403, Calif. L. Rev. (2004).

Swann v. Charlotte-Mecklenburg Board of Education, 402 U.S. 1 (1971).

Thompson, D. C., & Wood, R. (2005). *Money and schools* (3rd ed.). Larchmont, NY: Eye on Education.

Tinker v. Des Moines Independent Community School District, 393 U.S. 503 (1969).

Zelman v. Simmons-Harris (00-1751) 536 U.S. 639 (2002).

3

The No Child Left Behind Act: Implications of NCLB on Local Schools

The No Child Left Behind Act (NCLB) of 2001 was signed into law on January 8, 2002. NCLB reauthorized and amended the Elementary and Secondary Education Act of 1965, which established a system of federal support for school districts based on the congressionally established proportion of school-age children from families living below the poverty line. Since first enacted, programs included under the umbrella of the Elementary and Secondary Education Act multiplied, and as a result, Congress used its power under Article I, Section 8, of the U.S. Constitution—that is, the spending clause that requires recipients of funds under the law to comply with certain obligations— to increase the scope and amount of state and local accountability for federal funds. The enactment of NCLB further extended federal expectations for

AUTHORS' NOTE: This chapter was written by Penelope M. Early, PhD, and Gary R. Galluzzo, PhD, professors in the College of Education and Human Development at George Mason University. Penny is the Director of the Center for Education Policy, and Gary is a former Dean of the College and former Executive Vice President of the National Board for Professional Teaching Standards.

schools by requiring each state to implement a plan to raise student achievement in general, close the achievement gaps in student achievement, raise the standards for teacher quality, and prepare a plan for allowing parents in schools that are not making *adequate yearly progress* (AYP) to transfer their children to schools *not failing*. Most notably, the law requires that all children will reach the state's standards for student achievement by the 2013–2014 school year.

With the passage of NCLB, the involvement of the federal government in local school improvement efforts reached a new level. The goal of the act is to "close the achievement gap with accountability, flexibility, and choice, so that no child is left behind" (NCLB, January 8, 2002). Thus, this act altered accountability in schools by changing its focus from equal opportunity to learn to the expectation of equal outcomes, primarily as measured on standardized tests. The U.S. Department of Education continues to provide more guidance for schools on implementation of the law. Because this information is expansive, it is useful to go to the department's Web site (www.ed.gov) and use the agency's search engine to find information on specific questions. It is important to note, however, that many details of NCLB implementation are determined by individual states, and you can consult the Web site for the state education agency or state board of education.

NCLB also impacts the manner in which schools use federal funds to support education of English language learners (ELLs), and created uncertainty about testing of special education students and the qualifications of special education teachers. These issues are addressed in Chapters 8 and 12.

SECTION A: MAJOR PROVISIONS OF NCLB OF INTEREST TO PRINCIPALS

I FOCUS POINT: Highly Qualified Teachers

NCLB includes definitions of highly qualified new elementary-level teachers, highly qualified veteran elementary-level teachers, highly qualified new secondary-level teachers, and highly qualified veteran secondary-level teachers (NCLB, § 1119). By the end of the 2005–2006 school year, all public school teachers in core academic subjects must be certified by the school district and state as highly qualified. Because states traditionally have established criteria for teacher qualifications through certification or licensure requirements, many states found that the federal requirements were at odds with state law or regulation. A provision in the NCLB report language (No Child Left Behind Act of 2001, Conference Report to Accompany H.R. 1, December 13, 2001) allows states to create alternative ways to meet the highly qualified standards. Referred to as HOUSSE (high, objective, uniform, state, standards of evaluation), each state must submit these alternative standards to the U.S. Department of Education for approval. The HOUSSE provisions are unique to each state and should be available on each state education agency's Web site.

Examples of Management Cues

- In a small high school, the one science teacher has a college major in biology but also teaches chemistry and physics under a general science license offered by the state. NCLB language suggests that this teacher will have to have the equivalent of an academic major in both chemistry and physics to meet the law's definition of highly qualified. The teacher has said she will resign if she has to complete two additional college majors.
- A rural school has 12 teachers, each of whom must teach multiple subjects, for example, art, English, and music; history, physical education, and math; and general science, Spanish, and band. How will these teachers meet the highly qualified standard?
- A large suburban school includes both middle and secondary programs (Grades 5–12). Some of the teachers hold K–6 certification and others 7–12. Which of the NCLB definitions apply?

Suggested Risk Management Guidelines

- Teachers are required to be highly qualified if they teach even one class in a core academic subject as defined by NCLB (English, reading or language arts, mathematics, science, foreign languages, civics and government, economics, arts, history, and geography). Know the academic preparation for all teachers so their qualification status can be determined and made available on demand.
- NCLB applies the definition of a highly qualified secondary school teacher to individuals teaching seventh and eighth grades. Know how your state's HOUSSE provisions align the highly qualified teacher requirements with middle school teaching requirements.
- The U.S. Department of Education has determined that special provisions apply to teachers in rural schools teaching science or teaching multiple subjects. In all cases, it is important to know the details of the state's HOUSSE provisions for meeting the highly qualified standards. This should be available on the section of the state department of education's Web site related to NCLB. In addition, the U.S. Department of Education's Web site (http://www.ed.gov/nclb/methods/teachers/hqtflexibility.html) details the general flexibility offered to states on this issue.

I FOCUS POINT: NCLB and Annual Testing

NCLB requires annual testing in Grades 3 through 8 and at least once in high school. This has presented a problem for those states that had previously mandated a different testing schedule. In addition, NCLB requires each state to report annually its progress toward making AYP as measured by student achievement. That is, each state must inform the federal government as well as the general public how well the students are performing on its achievement tests. Moreover, the data must be disaggregated such that five kinds of subgroups of students can be tracked as well. Those five groups are (1) minority students, (2) students on free or reduced lunch, (3) students who have individualized education programs (IEPs), (4) students for whom English is a new language, and (5) a comparison of girls and boys.

From these data, educators, citizens, and policymakers can directly conclude whether the school's general academic performance is meeting AYP targets, as well as the existence and amount of achievement variance among children in the different subgroups. Under the requirements of NCLB, a school as a total entity can be making AYP, but it can be found to be in need of improvement if any of the subgroups in the disaggregated data are not. In essence, a school is now being held accountable for how well it "raises the floor" in terms of student achievement, as much as it is held accountable for the overall progress of its student body.

▌ FOCUS POINT: NCLB and ELLs

The education of immigrant students for whom English is a new language poses another problem to the complete implementation of NCLB. In many ways, it is similar to the education of exceptional needs students in that NCLB expects schools to close the achievement gap between ELLs and regular education students. Once again, standard practice has been to work diligently to educate all children while simultaneously accepting that some who do not speak English will not perform as well as those who do. NCLB wants to see that achievement gap closed, and the act gives the state the power to declare a school failing that does not close that gap.

Example of a Management Cue

- There is a persistent gap in standardized test scores between ELLs and regular students.

Suggested Risk Management Guidelines

- Principals need to know where the gaps are in student achievement.
- Use student achievement data to make decisions about resource allocation.
- Consider the trade-offs between support programs and classroom instruction in light of the demands of NCLB.

▌ FOCUS POINT: Public School Choice

Title I schools that have been identified as (a) in the first or second year of school improvement, (b) in corrective action, or (c) undergoing restructuring because they have not met AYP goals for one or more years must notify parents of students in the school that their students are eligible to transfer to another public school. Parents must be advised that the school district will pay all or a portion of the transportation for students to attend their new schools. The U.S. Department of Education has established guidelines to determine how much money (and from what source) can be used for transporting students to a new school. If a school is in corrective action or restructuring, parents may request the provision of supplemental services (discussed later in this chapter), such as tutoring, for the student.

Examples of Management Cues

- In late September, a school receives information that it did not meet its AYP goals for the previous year. Rather than cause disruption to the schedule, the school board wants to wait until spring to notify parents and offer them the option of transferring their students to a different school. The transfer would take effect the following fall.
- A school was identified as in need of improvement for one year, and about 3 percent of the students transferred to a new school. The school met its AYP goals the following year. Are those students now requesting to return to their home school?
- A school in a remote area is identified as in need of improvement, but the nearest eligible school to receive transfer students is nearly 100 miles away.

Suggested Risk Management Guidelines

- Become familiar with federal guidelines on school choice and supplemental services and state or local policies to implement these guidelines. Have this information available for parents in a form they can understand (this might include providing it in languages other than English).
- As soon as a school learns it has been placed in need of improvement status, it must notify parents and allow students to transfer even though the school year has begun. The choice option may not be delayed because of the academic calendar.
- Once a school has made AYP for two years and no longer is identified as in need of improvement, it is not obligated to offer choice provisions to students enrolled in it. Students who elected to transfer to a new school may remain there until they have completed the highest grade in the school regardless of the change in status of the students' original home school. However, the school district is no longer required to provide transportation for that student.
- In some situations, such as in rural areas, choice within a district or even extending to another school district is not an option. In this case, other alternatives might be explored, such as online instruction.
- It is important to keep current on changing regulations and guidelines on choice options offered by the U.S. Department of Education. Because the

department may adjust how new information is arrayed on its Web site, the best resource is to bookmark www.ed.gov and use the agency's search engine to find answers to specific questions.

▌FOCUS POINT: Unsafe Schools and Choice

NCLB allows students who have been victims of a violent crime while in or on the grounds of a public elementary or secondary school or who attend a school that has been designated as persistently dangerous to transfer to a safe school within their district.

Examples of Management Cues

- The number of students expelled from a school for bringing weapons or dangerous items onto school grounds has increased from the previous year.
- Although there have been no incidents in the school, gang activity has increased in the neighborhood, and some incidents have been reported on school grounds.
- Parents have come to the school requesting transfers for their students and citing NCLB's safe school provision as the rationale.

Suggested Risk Management Guidelines

- Each state must implement a system to track incidents of school violence. From these data, the state determines at what point a school is identified as persistently unsafe. Only a student who was a crime victim or who is attending a school identified in this way may request a transfer under NCLB choice provisions. Find out the state process for identifying unsafe schools and the district policy for allowing transfers for students who are victims of violent crime on school grounds.
- Have information on this provision and the status of the school as safe or not safe available for parents.

▌FOCUS POINT: Supplemental Educational Services

Under NCLB, supplemental services means tutoring and other supplemental academic enrichment services to help students enrolled in a school in its second year of needing improvement or in corrective action or restructuring status. Parents must be notified of the supplemental services option and how to access this assistance.

Examples of Management Cues

- The issue of tutoring services for students was raised at a PTA meeting. The school has met its AYP goals each year, but some parents want additional tutoring made available for their children.
- A school is in its second year of needing improvement and may slip into corrective action if test scores do not improve. No parents have contacted the school about supplemental academic services, possibly because they are concerned about the cost of these services.

Suggested Risk Management Guidelines

- Prepare information for parents explaining under what conditions the school must offer services like tutoring to students. Include information on the school district's obligation to pay for all or part of these services. (Note: Schools that consistently meet their AYP goals are not required to offer supplemental educational services such as tutoring. This provision applies only to schools that have not met AYP for two or more years.)
- Find out if your state has compiled a list of supplemental service providers, and from that have available for parents a list of providers in your area.
- Make time to meet with parents and the supplemental service provider to establish clear academic goals for the student who is being tutored and a deadline by which these goals will be met.
- Find out the district's procedure for paying for supplemental services. Check the U.S. Department of Education's Web site (www.ed.gov) for detailed information on what federal funds can be used to pay for supplemental services.

❙ FOCUS POINT: NCLB and Military Recruiters

NCLB includes a provision allowing military recruiters access to contact information for secondary school students. Although some school districts generally do not release this information, citing compliance with the Family Educational Rights and Privacy Act (FERPA), if a military recruiter requests student contact information, the local school district is obligated to provide it. However, this does not mean that information on students is automatically made available to recruiters. Parents must be notified and given the opportunity to have their child's name removed from any such contact directory or list.

Examples of Management Cues

- Local army recruiters asked for the names and contact information for all secondary students in your high school. They also want to have information on the army as a career available in the school.

- An organization in the community that opposes war in general and federal support for the military objects to any contact between military recruiters and secondary school students on the basis of violation of student privacy rights. They propose a system whereby parents must agree in advance to have contact information on their child given to military recruiters.

Suggested Risk Management Guidelines

- Know your school district's policies and procedures regarding the placement of materials from military recruiters in the schools, such as in the counseling office or career center.
- NCLB requires secondary schools to make contact information available to military recruiters; however, parents must be notified of this and given the information to opt out. If the school does not have either a form or process for parents to exert the opt-out option, these should be created and made public.
- Understand the difference between opt in and opt out. A policy that requires parents to opt in, that is, sign a form agreeing that contact information may be given to recruiters, is not allowed under NCLB. See the U.S. Department of Education's guidelines on this at www.ed.gov/policy/gen/guid/fpco/hottopics/ht10–09–02.html.

SECTION B: CURRENT LEGAL CHALLENGES TO NCLB

FOCUS POINT: State Standards More Rigorous Than NCLB Mandates

Most states' plans for meeting the expectations of NCLB were approved by the U.S. Department of Education between calendar years 2002 and 2004, and many states began to comply with the federal law during the 2003–2004 school year. There are exceptions, however. Connecticut, Texas, and Virginia, for example, were three of the nation's leading states in the implementation of state-legislated standards-based education. That is, these three states wrote academic content standards and adopted statewide testing protocols prior to the passage of NCLB. When the federal law was passed, decision makers in these states adjusted existing school improvement plans in an attempt to meet the requirements of the law without losing their own remedies for school improvement. When the U.S. Department of Education was unwilling to waive certain

---

AUTHORS' NOTE: Regardless of whether the cases discussed below are adjudicated, the premise of each is important to understand.

NCLB requirements, decision makers in these states objected in a variety of ways: by threatening litigation, asking members of their congressional delegations to mount efforts to amend the law, or essentially ignoring troublesome provisions. Information on each state's plan to comply with NCLB should be available on each state's department of education Web site. In addition, approved state plans are posted on the U.S. Department of Education's Web site (http://www.ed.gov/about/contacts/state/index.html).

FOCUS POINT: Conflicts Between NCLB and Federal Special Education Law

Although NCLB and the Individuals with Disabilities Education Act (IDEA) have different conceptual approaches to the education of children with disabilities (see also Chapter 8), only one issue has generated litigation to date. This relates to the intersection of NCLB and the IDEA, which was last signed into law in 1997 and amended as the Individuals with Disabilities Education Improvement Act in 2004. In a complaint filed in the U.S. District Court, Northern District of Illinois, by the Board of Education of Ottawa High School District et al. in Ottawa, Illinois, plaintiffs sought to have two components of NCLB invalidated (*Ottawa High School District v. Spellings*, 2005).

The first was the definition of AYP and the second was the penalties for schools that do not reach their AYP targets. The plaintiffs contend that NCLB and IDEA are incompatible in their expectations. They argued that IDEA requires schools to create IEPs for students with disabilities that allow them to work at the most appropriate pace, while NCLB tracks their progress toward achieving AYP annually. Under the provisions of NCLB, a school or school district would be penalized by the withholding of federal funds for failing to meet AYP. The U.S. District Court, Northern District of Illinois, dismissed the Ottawa lawsuit, finding that the plaintiffs failed to satisfy the legal elements of "standing." To have standing, plaintiffs filing suit in federal courts must demonstrate three things: (1) an injury in fact, (2) a causal relationship between the injury and the challenged conduct, and (3) a likelihood that the injury will be redressed by a favorable decision. In the Court's July 20, 2005, decision, it found that the plaintiffs had met none of the three elements of standing.

At least for now, the tension between AYP and students with disabilities' IEPs will not be resolved by the courts. However, as all principals know, the achievement of students with exceptional needs is a historic problem, heretofore accepted as part of the way schools work. Exceptional needs students, even in spite of the legislation for a "least restrictive environment" or "inclusion," generally have not been held to the same standards for performance as regular education students. At the intersection of NCLB and IDEA, much more is at stake. It introduces the likelihood that a generally high-performing school will be declared a failing school because of the test performance of its exceptional needs students. It also raises the possibility that children with disabilities will be blamed if a school does not meet AYP.

FOCUS POINT: Unfunded Mandate—States and Schools Have Insufficient Funds to Comply With NCLB Mandates

Concerns and litigation over funding for NCLB programs and requirements have emerged in both federal and state courts. The former involves the unfunded mandate argument, and the latter finance equalization among school districts.

States and localities have objected that the federal government has not provided adequate funding to assist them in meeting the letter and spirit of the law. An unfunded mandate is a law that comes with high-stakes requirements but no funding or inadequate funding to accomplish its goals locally. In *Reading School District v. Pennsylvania Department of Education* (2004), the Reading School District in Pennsylvania became the first school district in the country to file suit over NCLB, claiming that the Pennsylvania Department of Education failed to fulfill its mandate under NCLB to provide the school district with the resources and technical assistance it needed to meet its obligations of AYP.

In April 2005, the U.S. District Court for the Eastern District received a complaint from seven school districts and the National Education Association and some of its state and local affiliates (*School District of the City of Pontiac et al. v. Spellings*) challenging the government's failure to fund NCLB adequately. The plaintiffs were clear that they were not trying to have NCLB found unconstitutional. Rather, their suit contends that the federal funding to support the law's implementation at the state and local level is not equal to the federal government's expectations. Specifically, the plaintiffs in *Pontiac* identified Section 9527(a) of the No Child Left Behind law, which reads:

GENERAL PROHIBITION. Nothing in this Act shall be construed to authorize an officer or employee of the Federal Government to mandate, direct, or control a State, local education agency, or school's curriculum, program of instruction, or allocation of State or local resources, or mandate a State or any subdivision thereof to spend any funds or incur any costs not paid for under this Act. [20 U.S.C. § 7907(a)]

The plaintiffs submit that Secretary of Education Margaret Spellings violated this unfunded mandate language in the law. Further, they contend that to meet the requirements of the law, they must spend money from state and local budgets and take those funds from other priorities. In this way, these local school districts incur costs not paid for under the act, and the plaintiffs seek injunctive relief so they will not be penalized by the federal government by withholding other federal funds should they not comply with NCLB. This particular case is supported by research conducted by the National Conference of State Legislatures and the Congressional Research Service, which concluded that states are spending millions of dollars annually from their own budgets to meet federal requirements.

Rather than responding to the plaintiffs' brief in this case, the U.S. Department of Education filed its own motion arguing that (a) the plaintiffs in this case lack legal standing and (b) they are wrong in their interpretation of the unfunded mandate provision. The matter of legal standing generally limits successful challenges to federal law because of the difficulty in meeting the legal standard noted previously. In addition, there are many examples of federal education law that were never funded at an adequate level. Principals who find that the cost of NCLB requirements exceed available resources may not find resolution of the problem in the courts.

The argument of insufficient funds to support all of the requirements of NCLB has also emerged in finance equalization litigation. If a local school district feels that funding from the state is inadequate, then the additional expectations of meeting NCLB standards add power to the district's complaint. With approximately half the states involved in some form of educational funding litigation, the argument that more state funds are needed to give children a reasonable chance to pass NCLB required tests is likely to be found in plaintiffs' briefs.

Examples of Management Cues

- A principal may find she cannot hire both a teacher for students with exceptional needs and a math teacher because there are not enough district funds to support both needs.
- The school may need to eliminate popular afterschool activities for students to use those district funds to make sure all teachers are highly qualified to meet the provisions of NCLB.
- For a number of years, the school system has provided in-depth professional development for new teachers based on the state's curricular standards and examinations. However, under NCLB, there are different assessment expectations, and now all teachers will need additional training, but there are only resources to offer professional development to new personnel.

Suggested Risk Management Guidelines

- Create a school planning team that keeps abreast of the needs of the school and assists in identifying the areas most in need of additional discretionary funding.

- Plan the discretionary budget around those dimensions of NCLB on which the school has yet to measure up.
- Understand that the issues appearing in legal challenges to NCLB are a useful barometer for potential amendments to the law when it is next reauthorized by the U.S. Congress.

CHAPTER RESOURCES

Individuals with Disabilities Education Improvement Act of 2004, Pub. L. No. 108-446, 118 Stat. 2651.

No Child Left Behind Act of 2001, Pub. L. No. 107-110, H.R. 1 (2001).

Ottawa High School District v. Spellings, No. 05-C-0655 (N.D. Ill. Feb. 3, 2005).

Reading School District v. Pennsylvania Department of Education, No. 2278 (Pa. Commw. Aug. 6, 2004).

School District of the City of Pontiac et al. v. Spellings, No. 05-71535 (E.D. Mich. Apr. 20, 2005).

U.S. Department of Education Web site: www.ed.gov

4

Constitutional and Statutory Foundations of Staff Selection, Contracting, and Evaluation

While principals' authority to hire and fire personnel is usually limited to recommendation, principals have major responsibilities in human resources management and are continuously involved with employee relations. Principals recommend teachers and support personnel for employment, evaluate personnel, and document cases for dismissal or nonrenewal. In this pursuit, principals operate in accordance with often confusing federal and state constitutional provisions, statutes, regulations, and local school board policies.

Discrimination in selection and hiring is a dangerous error for any school district. Principals need to be aware of their vulnerability in litigation when they act as agents of the board in any preemployment matters.

AUTHORS' NOTE: Cases cited throughout this chapter have been selected on a precedent-setting or best-example basis regardless of jurisdiction or date of adjudication. (See Introduction for more information.)

This chapter examines the problems that school districts and principals must avoid in the recruitment, selection, hiring, and evaluation of qualified personnel. The areas examined and the points stressed emanate from legislation and litigation.

SECTION A: EQUAL EMPLOYMENT

Failure to recognize and implement nondiscriminatory and appropriate procedures is among the most common sources of liability in human resources management. In a litigious society, principals are wise to consider every employment situation as a source of potential litigation and to conduct personnel business in such a way that legal defense will not be needed.

School employment decisions are the ultimate responsibility of school boards, who, by law, select and contract with all school district personnel. However, school principals must be aware of the legal constraints on employment practices, because they are actively involved in recruiting, interviewing, and recommending teachers and support staff for employment.

The growing complexity of employment relationships can be traced primarily to the enactment of Title VII of the Civil Rights Act of 1964. Title VII established the fundamental concept of equal employment opportunity, which has become the guiding principle of employment practices in the United States today. Subsequent amendment of Title VII and the enactment of other federal laws governing employment practices have broadened the scope of protection for employees and have restricted discriminatory employment practices by employers, including school boards and their administrative staffs.

Federal laws prohibiting discrimination in employment are based on both the Thirteenth and Fourteenth Amendments to the U.S. Constitution. These post–Civil War amendments served as the basis for the Civil Rights Acts of 1866, 1870, and 1871, which were enacted by Congress during the Reconstruction Period to define and protect the newly established rights of freedmen. These civil rights acts are identified as Sections 1981, 1982, and 1983 of Title 42 of the U.S. Code, commonly cited as 42 U.S.C. 1981.

The following brief descriptions of major federal laws that affect faculty and staff selection and management highlight areas in which principals need to exercise knowledge and caution.

▎ FOCUS POINT: Title VII of the Civil Rights Act of 1964

Title VII of the Civil Rights Act of 1964 prohibits discrimination in employment by employers or employment agencies, and in membership by unions, on the basis of race, color, religion, gender, or national origin. Probably the most pervasive federal legislation governing employment practices, this law was amended in 1972 to include state and local governments, governmental agencies, and political subdivisions, including school districts. Not only does the law protect employees from discriminatory employment practices, but it also makes it illegal to refuse to hire any individual on the basis of race, color, religion, gender, or national origin. Section 701 of the act was amended to require that women experiencing pregnancy, childbirth, or related medical conditions be treated, for all employment-related purposes (including the receipt of benefits under fringe benefit programs), the same way as other persons not so affected but similar in their ability or inability to work.

Examples of Management Cues

- A high school principal notifies central administration that she needs to replace a resigning social studies teacher who also serves as a football coach. The principal specifically asks to see candidates who are male, ages 25–45, and white (because all the other football coaches are minorities).
- Although the most qualified candidate on paper for a sixth-grade teaching position is a Pakistani woman, when the principal interviews her, he is concerned that the woman's accent would be difficult for children to understand and that the traditional Muslim clothing the woman wears would be a distraction. As a result, the principal recommends that a non-minority candidate, whose qualifications and experience are somewhat less distinguished, be hired.
- A female applicant, during the interview process, requests information concerning maternity leave. She states that she and her husband plan to start their family within the next two to three years. Based on this request for information, the district decides not to hire her.

Suggested Risk Management Guidelines

- Develop policies and procedures to ensure that everyone in every department of the school or school district understands that it is an *unlawful employment practice* to
  - Classify a job by gender of worker or to maintain separate lines of progression or separate seniority lists based on gender, unless gender is a bona fide occupational qualification (BFOQ) for that job.
  - Phrase help-wanted advertisements to indicate a preference, limitation, specification, or discrimination based on gender unless gender is a BFOQ for the particular job. (Note: School districts cannot discriminate in either hiring or employment practices. Title VII and its amendments provide for several exemptions to its coverage, one of which is an exemption where religion, gender, or national origin is a BFOQ reasonably necessary for the normal operation of the particular business or institution—for example, a parochial school. *It is unlikely, however, that public schools will be able to justify any discriminatory employment practice as a BFOQ.*)
  - Forbid or restrict the employment of married women when such restriction is not applicable to married men.

- Discriminate between men and women with regard to fringe benefits, including medical, hospital, accident, life insurance, and retirement benefits; profit-sharing and bonus plans; leave; and other terms, conditions, and privileges of employment.
- Ask questions about pregnancy, childbirth, or related medical conditions that might be used as the basis for excluding any female from employment or promotion opportunities.
- Treat a disability due to pregnancy or childbirth differently from any other disability.
- Fail to make "reasonable accommodations" for the religious practices of employees and job applicants. (Note: Religious practice is defined by the EEOC to include moral or ethical beliefs as to what is right and wrong that are sincerely held with the strength of traditional religious views, whether or not any group espouses such beliefs or the group to which the individual professes to belong accepts such belief. The definition of religious practices includes religious observances. Employers are required to reasonably accommodate the religious practices of an employee or prospective employee, unless they can demonstrate that accommodation would result in undue hardship on the conduct of the business of the employer. When more than one means of accommodation would not cause undue hardship, the employer must offer the alternative that least disadvantages the individual with respect to employment opportunities. The duty to accommodate applies to prospective as well as current employees; therefore, an employer may not permit an applicant's need for a religious accommodation to affect in any way its decision whether to hire the applicant, unless it can demonstrate that it cannot reasonably accommodate the religious practices without undue hardship.)

- Do not require employees to speak only English at all times in the workplace, as presumably that could violate Title VII. However, an employer may have a rule requiring that employees speak only English at certain times where the employer can show that the rule is justified by business necessity.
- Maintain a working environment that is free of harassment on the basis of national origin. Harassment on the basis of national origin is a violation of Title VII. National-origin discrimination includes but is not limited to the denial of equal employment opportunity because of the place of origin of an individual or of the individual's ancestors, or because an individual has the physical, cultural, or linguistic characteristics of an ethnic group.

▌ FOCUS POINT: The Equal Pay Act of 1963

The Equal Pay Act of 1963 is an amendment to the Fair Labor Standards Act of 1938 that governs various labor practices, including minimum wages and overtime. The Equal Pay Act prohibits wage discrimination on the basis of gender among employees who perform equal work in jobs that require equal skill, effort, and responsibility and that are performed under similar working conditions. Legitimate wage rate differences are permissible under certain circumstances—for example, a seniority system or a merit pay plan.

Example of a Management Cue

- Female districtwide grounds care personnel are paid at a lower rate than their male counterparts because "men are expected" to lift "heavier" loads. In addition, overtime opportunities are routinely assigned to men.

Suggested Risk Management Guidelines

- Ensure that all wages and salary schedules treat male and female employees equitably.
- Ensure that *differences* in pay for employees who do equal work, have equal skill requirements, and work under the same conditions are based on a well-defined system of seniority or merit.

FOCUS POINT: The Age Discrimination in Employment Act (ADEA)

The ADEA of 1967 prohibits employment discrimination against individuals 40 years of age or older. Employees as well as job applicants are protected under the terms of the act. The act was amended in 1974 to extend coverage to state and local governments, including school districts. The original law provided coverage up to age 65, but an amendment in 1978 increased the age limit to 70 years, and in 1986, an additional amendment removed any upper age limit, with certain exceptions for collective bargaining agreements and higher education tenure policies.

Under ADEA, school districts may not establish any policies or practices that limit the employment opportunities of people 40 and older, such as identifying a mandatory retirement age. It is also impermissible for a school district to adopt a policy or practice of hiring only beginning teachers, as opposed to those with experience, as part of an effort to control or reduce district expenses.

Example of a Management Cue

- The rigorous schedule of a high school band director in the district is well known. The current "music man," in his mid-50s, is eligible for early retirement. The principal wants to transfer him and replace him with a younger, more vigorous person. This change would help dilute the school's pool of aging teachers, with its average age of 52, and would provide for more eager volunteers for extracurricular sponsorship and supervision. The only opening in the district is for an itinerant, elementary, general music teacher.

Suggested Risk Management Guidelines

- Do not use age as a factor in making employment decisions. School districts are prohibited from hiring, firing, compensating, classifying, or making decisions relative to the terms and conditions of employment based on an individual's age.
- Base employment decisions strictly on the applicant's or employee's capabilities to adequately perform the required work, and clearly document those decisions. In making employment decisions regarding people age 40 and older, principals and others must be certain that their actions are based strictly on an individual's capability and qualifications to perform the job. (Note: From an array of candidates for a position, some of whom may be protected by ADEA, employers can still select the best qualified regardless of age, but they must be sure they can demonstrate the superior qualifications of the hiree. If an employer needs to start due process proceedings against an older employee—that is, one over 40—for cause, the employer has exposure under ADEA and must be sure that the cause of action is based solely on performance and not age.)

❙ FOCUS POINT: The Rehabilitation Act of 1973

The Rehabilitation Act of 1973 is a comprehensive statute designed to aid persons with disabilities in securing rehabilitation training and access to federally funded programs, public buildings, and employment. Section 504 of the act provides, in part, that no otherwise qualified individuals with a disability, solely by reason of their disability, be excluded from participation in, be denied the benefits of, or be subjected to discrimination under any program or activity receiving federal financial assistance.

An employer cannot discriminate against individuals with disabilities who are otherwise qualified for the particular program or activity, that is, those who can perform the job requirements despite their disabling condition. Individuals with disabilities include any person who (a) has a physical or mental impairment that substantially limits one or more of such person's major life activities, (b) has a record of such an impairment, or (c) is regarded as having such an impairment. Section 504's ban on employment discrimination is applicable to any program receiving federal funds. (See Rehabilitation Act of 1973 in Chapter Resources.)

Section 504 covers a wide range of diseases as well as mental and physical conditions. The law protects employees who are active alcoholics or drug abusers only if (a) they are in active rehabilitation and (b) their employment would not constitute a direct threat to property or the safety of others.

Many states and Washington, D.C., through legislative and administrative action, now specifically include HIV, AIDS, or AIDS-related complex (ARC) within the definition of a handicap or a disability in their human rights, civil rights, handicapped rights, or fair employment and housing statutes. Sections 503 and 504 of the act protect employees of government contractors who are "otherwise qualified" and who suffer from, are regarded as suffering from, or have a record of suffering from HIV, ARC, or AIDS. (See Chapter 8 for a discussion of Section 504 of the act as it relates to students with disabilities.)

Examples of Management Cues

- Due to a congenital birth defect, a candidate is legally blind in one eye and has only 20 percent vision in his other eye. He also suffers from seizures that can be only partially controlled by medication. His record in student teaching is exemplary. The principal likes the candidate in the interview session and is impressed by his achievements; however, she feels that the students at her school would take advantage of him and that he would have discipline problems. She recommends a less qualified candidate for the position.
- An itinerant elementary foreign language teacher develops a disability that prevents her from driving. However, she can provide alternate transportation for the same or close to the same mileage reimbursement.

Suggested Risk Management Guidelines

- Make reasonable accommodations for those persons with disabilities who are otherwise qualified for the job. This legal mandate does not mean that employers must make substantial modifications of the job requirements or incur more than minimal costs to reasonably accommodate persons with disabilities. If the district cannot make reasonable accommodations, and if the applicant can't provide a reasonable solution, then a BFOQ might hold up if challenged.
- Consult with your school district's legal counsel if you have questions about what type of accommodations would be considered "reasonable."

FOCUS POINT: The Americans with Disabilities Act of 1990 (ADA)

The ADA incorporates, expands, and intensifies the Rehabilitation Act of 1973. ADA extends comprehensive protection against discrimination in hiring, promotion, discharge, compensation, and training to individuals with disabilities as well as ensuring them access to public buildings, public transportation, and other public services. ADA permits employers to identify essential job responsibilities that are central to the job and need to be more than generally accommodated. If a candidate with a disability is not able to fulfill core essential job responsibilities, this core can be used to disqualify that person.

ADA is one of the most difficult acts for schools and other employers to address. Employers are required to make every "reasonable" accommodation that is not financially unreasonable to accommodate physical disabilities. In the area of mental disabilities, the district must evaluate and be prepared to defend any concerns that a mental disability presents (e.g., foreseeable imminent danger to students, school personnel, or the community).

Examples of Management Cues

- A well-qualified candidate for a position in a school district reveals in an interview that she has a verified mental condition that occasionally causes her to "lose control" when faced with a "confrontational situation."
- A well-qualified candidate for a position in the social studies department is quadriplegic. The social studies department classrooms, equipped with audiovisual equipment and mounted wall maps, are located on the second floor of the school that advertises the vacancy. The building has no elevators, and as a result, the candidate is not hired for the position.
- An experienced and successful third-grade teacher develops asthma and requests that her classroom be equipped with a special air filtration system and that she be excused from playground supervision when air quality conditions are poor.

Suggested Risk Management Guidelines

- Make necessary facility renovations and equipment modifications to reasonably accommodate employees with disabilities. While the employment provisions may not represent significant new challenges for school officials, the "reasonable accommodation" requirements may entail substantial capital expenditures to provide wheelchair ramps, elevators, telephone devices for employees who are hearing impaired, office equipment for employees who are visually impaired, and so forth.
- Do not terminate or discriminate against an applicant or employee with a "mental disability." Employers must "reasonably accommodate" such disabilities, which are explicitly covered by ADA.
- Develop job descriptions that identify essential responsibilities and functions as opposed to those that are desirable but that could easily be assigned to others. Such descriptions should stipulate the working conditions attendant to the essential functions.

FOCUS POINT: The Veterans' Reemployment Rights Act of 1940

The Veterans' Reemployment Rights Act (updated in 1994 through the enactment of the Uniformed Services Employment and Reemployment Rights Act) provides certain protections and benefits to veterans of military service. Individuals who have left employment to serve in the military are guaranteed certain reemployment rights. The law provides that veterans, if still qualified, must be restored to their former position or one of like seniority, status, and pay on their return from military service. If a returning veteran is no longer qualified for the former position by reason of a disability, then the veteran is entitled to an offer of reemployment in a position that will provide similar seniority, status, and pay. Employers are exempted from compliance with the law only when the employer's circumstances have so changed as to make it impossible or unreasonable to reemploy the veteran. The law covers private employers as well as federal and state governments, including school districts.

In 1974, the law was expanded to include Vietnam-era veterans. One provision of the amended law requires that contractors entering into contracts of $10,000 or more with the federal government take affirmative action on behalf of Vietnam-era veterans.

A 1982 amendment to the law established that volunteers who serve as members of the National Guard and Reserve Force of the United States are entitled to various employment rights. Congress requested that employers abide by the provisions of the Veterans' Reemployment Rights law, grant a leave for military training (exclusive of earned vacation), and provide such employees equal consideration for job benefits and promotions as they would any other employees. More recently, under the same act, reservists called to duty in the Persian Gulf not only were entitled to reclaim their old jobs on return from active duty but were also entitled to all the privileges and benefits that would have accrued had they not left.

Example of a Management Cue

- In August, a senior high school English teacher is called up for six to nine months of active duty with his Army Reserve unit. Because the school year has not yet begun, his teaching position is posted as a vacancy, and a middle school teacher in the same district is hired to fill the job. Another person is subsequently hired to fill the vacancy at the middle school created by the transfer. In February, the first teacher is released from active duty. He immediately returns to the district and requests reinstatement in the position to which he had been assigned in August.

Suggested Risk Management Guidelines

- Treat all employees who are called for active duty or training in the armed forces as if they had never left employment with the school district.
- Ensure that any employee returning from active duty as a member of the National Guard or Reserve is rehired into the same job or a similar job, with equal status, pay, and benefits.

FOCUS POINT: The Immigration Reform and Control Act of 1986 (IRCA)

The IRCA of 1986 requires employers to verify the eligibility of every person to work in the United States. The act is designed to protect the employment rights of American citizens and legal aliens (foreign nationals who are authorized to work in this country and possess a valid green card).

Documents that can verify citizenship include a U.S. passport, birth certificate, or driver's license (if a photograph is included). It is not recommended, however, that employers ask applicants to verify their citizenship or that they examine documents prior to hiring. Such documents can reveal information about an applicant that an employer has no right to examine under antidiscrimination laws (for example, race, age, gender).

IRCA's antidiscrimination provisions make it an unfair employment practice for an employer to discriminate against any individual (other than an unauthorized alien) because of national origin or citizenship status.

Examples of Management Cues

- The personnel office hires a teacher to fill an unexpected, midyear vacancy. Because the new hire is a white female, the personnel assistant does not require proof of citizenship or work permit.
- An assistant custodian, who is a Salvadoran immigrant working on a green card, asks the principal to hire his cousin as a custodial aide without going through the normal hiring procedures.

Suggested Risk Management Guidelines

- Make certain that all job offers extended to candidates are understood to be contingent on the candidates' providing proof of their right to work in the United States.
- Require all new employees to prove that they have the right to work in the United States. Do not make the mistake of requiring such proof only for those applicants whom you judge to be foreign looking or to have an accent.

FOCUS POINT: Title IX of the Education Amendments of 1972

Title IX of the Education Amendments of 1972 provides that "no person in the United States shall, on the basis of sex, be excluded from participation in, denied the benefits of, or be subjected to discrimination under any education program or activity receiving federal financial assistance."

In 1975, the Department of Health, Education, and Welfare (HEW) issued regulations governing the operation of federally funded education programs. These regulations were based on HEW's interpretation that the term *person* in Title IX included employees as well as students. Consistent with that interpretation, the regulations included Subpart E covering employment practices.

Although the initial focus of compliance with Title IX was on student access to school activities on a gender-neutral basis, female employees soon began to challenge alleged discriminatory employment practices based on gender, opening a series of contradictory federal court rulings regarding the validity of HEW's regulations and whether employees were, in fact, covered by Title IX.

It was not until 1982 that the U.S. Supreme Court clarified the issue. In *North Haven Board of Education v. Bell*, the Court held that the regulations promulgated by HEW, interpreting *persons* in Section 901(a) of Title IX to encompass employees, were a valid exercise of the department's regulatory authority. However, the Court also ruled that HEW's authority to make regulations and terminate federal funds was limited to the specific programs receiving the financial assistance. It is clear from the *North Haven* case that employees in federally funded education programs are protected from gender discrimination.

In *Grove City College v. Bell* (1984), the U.S. Supreme Court held that the receipt of federal financial assistance by some of the college's students did not trigger institutionwide coverage under Title IX but rather limited coverage to the specific program. Until then, the common interpretation had been that it applied to all the activities at a school that received federal aid for any reason. Congress restored the broader interpretation of Title IX when it passed the Civil Rights Restoration Act in 1988.

The final aspect of Title IX that has direct application to employment practices is the remedies for violation of an individual's rights under the law. The express remedy under Title IX for a violation of its provisions is the termination of federal funds to the specific program. In 1979, the U.S. Supreme Court held, in *Cannon v. University of Chicago*, that a private cause of action, although not explicitly provided in Title IX, was an implied remedy under the law.

Examples of Management Cues

- Noting that the varsity football coaches were provided with team shirts and jackets, the female coaches of the girls' soccer and lacrosse teams requested similar clothing.
- The female head coach of the girls' basketball team demanded a coaching supplementary contract providing for pay equal to that received by the male head coach of the boys' basketball team.

Suggested Risk Management Guideline

- Do not allow gender to be a consideration or a deciding factor in any positions, activities, curricular offerings, sports, other extracurricular activities, or conditions of employment.

SECTION B: STAFF SELECTION

School districts throughout the United States have developed several methods of staff selection, depending on the size and administrative structure of the particular district. The management style of the superintendent determines the degree to which principals are involved in the staffing process. For example, in highly centralized school districts, teachers and support personnel may be assigned to a building with little or no input from the building principal. However, in a decentralized or site-based school district or in a smaller district, the principal is often involved in all phases of teacher and support personnel selection, from recruitment to recommendation for employment. In many districts, the central office maintains a pool of applications and allows principals to review appropriate files and select and interview candidates prior to making a recommendation to the superintendent.

Regardless of the method of staff selection used, it is imperative that school principals have a working knowledge of the legal aspects of employee selection. As indicated in the previous examination of legislation, a number of federal laws and court cases have instituted constraints on employment decisions in an effort to reduce discrimination in the workplace. Employment decisions must be based on nondiscriminatory factors or factors that can be justified as legitimate exemptions under the law. It is important to remember that equal employment opportunity laws apply to both employees and job applicants and that all selection criteria and employment decisions must be based on job-related standards. In other words, any criteria used, information required, or interview questions asked must be directly related to required job performance or be justified as a BFOQ for a particular job. Principals and other interviewers are faced with the three-pronged task of recommending the best qualified teacher or staff person, complying with a multitude of employment laws, and protecting the rights of the prospective hiree.

No one expects to be sued for asking frank questions of a prospective employee. However, litigation in the area of personnel matters continues. This legal activity may be attributed to the public's willingness to go to court but, more likely, is based on an increased awareness of equal employment rights by prospective employees.

Before examining the various facets of the selection process, it is important to note that it is impossible to provide unambiguous guidance as to what inquiries or practices are permissible during the preemployment phase. There are few, if any, categorical rights and wrongs in selection, either legally or professionally. Every employment situation has to be evaluated individually to determine what selection standards are valid and legal. This ambiguity, however, does not relieve school officials of the responsibility for ensuring equal employment opportunities in the school system while legally and ethically securing the services of the best qualified individuals for particular jobs. Equal employment laws have been, and continue to be, enacted specifically to expand employment opportunities for qualified minorities, females, and others in a protected classification who have been at a disadvantage in the labor market and workplace.

❚ FOCUS POINT: Employment Selection

The following information outlines the major steps in the selection process and suggests guidelines that can be used by district-level administrators and school principals to evaluate the process. The material presented has been adapted to fit the education enterprise and was drawn largely from the comprehensive work of Milner and Miner (1978) and Panaro (1990).

Example of a Management Cue

- An informal complaint is filed stating that the school or school district has made an employment decision based on a discriminatory factor or a factor that cannot be justified as a legitimate exemption under the law.

Suggested Risk Management Guidelines

Position Analysis

- When a position becomes available, perform a job analysis to determine the critical work behaviors to be used as criteria for measuring employee performance. Do not overlook the area of supplemental performance needs, such as those for sponsors, coaches, and monitors, for example.
- Develop a job description identifying the skills, knowledge, and abilities needed to perform the job.
- Make sure the job standards identify the requirements for satisfactory performance for a beginner in the job.
- Be able to justify every job standard specified as a valid requirement for the job.
- For nonteaching positions, specify levels of skills or abilities necessary for progressively higher-level positions in the same job family (e.g., Electrician III, II, I).
- Evaluate the qualifications for all positions to ensure that there are no excessive or unnecessary requirements that might disqualify a disproportionate number of minorities, women, or others in a protected classification (disparate impact).

Recruitment

- Include as many potential sources of qualified applicants as possible.
- Use representatives of protected as well as nonprotected classifications of employees as part of the overall recruitment team.
- Add colleges and universities with predominately minority or female populations to contact lists of sources of qualified applicants.
- Maintain records of your various recruiting efforts for documentation and evaluation.

Initial Applications and Screening

- Do not ask preemployment questions that may lead to a charge of discrimination.
    - Ensure that all information required on the application form or asked in an initial interview is job related and designed to give information about the applicant's qualifications for a particular job.
    - Ask all applicants the same questions.
    - Do not use information volunteered by an applicant as a basis for rejecting the applicant if it would be illegal to ask for such information in an interview. Liability for discrimination exists regardless of whether the information was solicited or volunteered.
    - Investigate further to determine whether the applicant can be reasonably accommodated to perform the job if the applicant volunteers information that indicates a problem with the applicant's suitability for the position (e.g., a disability).

- Be sure that notes or summaries of interviews with job applicants
    - Refer only to job-related aspects of the position
    - Use neutral, objective words and language
    - Have no negative inferences (the interviewer should be sensitive to the negative inferences that can be drawn from seemingly harmless written comments)
    - Do not include coded information (e.g., colored-in circle to indicate black applicant, clear circle to indicate white applicant)

Interviews

- Ensure that initial interviews are performed by someone trained in interviewing techniques. (Note: An interviewer may ask of the applicant any questions that the interviewer wishes, provided that the questions are job related and do not address prohibited subjects. Case law has demonstrated that the most dangerous questions, from the perspective of legal liability, are questions that the interviewer regards as the most innocent—the icebreakers or small-talk questions. Comments from the interviewer can also form the legal basis for alleged discrimination.)
- Ensure that the person conducting the initial interview is knowledgeable about the job being filled.
- Conduct initial interviews solely to obtain information that is not provided on the application form and to clarify items on the form that may be difficult to understand. All questions should be limited to those that directly relate to the specified job requirements.
- Document interviews, including the date of the interview, interviewer's name, and the results (e.g., no job available, application processed further).
- Focus only on specific job requirements during subsequent interviews.

- Avoid questions about prohibited, better-not-asked, or suspect areas of information that should not be solicited from prospective applicants unless they can be referenced to a defendable BFOQ. Examples of areas to avoid include, but are not limited to, the following:
  - *In the area of health:* disability, mental illness, whether currently under a doctor's care
  - *In the area of income:* Social Security income, garnishment or bankruptcy record, credit record, alimony or child support paid or received, charge accounts, own or rent home, furniture, car, method of transportation, lowest salary you will accept, spouse's occupation
  - *In the areas of marital status or lifestyle:* married, intent to marry, engaged, gay, living with someone, divorced, prior married name, maiden name, spouse's name
  - *In the areas of race, religion, politics:* race, ancestral origin, nationality or national origin, place of birth, citizenship, parentage, native language, fluency in English, color of eyes, hair, religion, religious holidays observed, belief in the existence of a Supreme Being, available for Saturday or Sunday work; feelings about Equal Rights Amendment, National Organization of Women, various interest groups
  - *In personal areas:* age, date of birth, height, weight, gender
  - *In the area of issues not related to work;* leave job if spouse transferred, friends or relatives working for the district (lawful if pursuant to an antinepotism policy and there is no adverse impact)
  - *In the area of children:* plans to have a family, children under 18, arrangements for care of minor children, intent to become pregnant, time off to have baby, resign or request leave, practice birth control, been pregnant or given birth, abortion, female problems, age (to determine whether of child-bearing age)

Information obtained from questions like the preceding limited examples may not be used as a basis for a selection decision.

Preemployment Testing and Access to Criminal Records

- Do not use preemployment tests that result in a disparate impact on a protected class of individuals. If the use of any preemployment test has an adverse impact on a protected group, the employer must prove that the test is job related and is a valid measure of the skills and abilities it purports to assess, and the test must be validated properly.
- Require physical examinations only where the jobs involved clearly require certain physical standards. All applicants for a job requiring a physical examination must be given the same examination.
- Follow your state's code and your district's policies regarding conducting criminal records checks on prospective employees. (Note: Many states have permitted school boards access to employee criminal records,

and some states require fingerprinting and other personal descriptive information that will be forwarded through the Central Criminal Records Exchange to the FBI to obtain criminal history about the applicant. Usually, such access is limited by state statute but may, as a common example, require conviction information in the following areas: murder, abduction for immoral purposes or sexual assault, failing to secure medical attention for an injured child, neglect of children, pandering, crimes against nature involving children, obscenity, possession or distribution of drugs, arson, and use of a firearm in the commission of a felony.)

Reference Checking

- Ensure that, if certain personal characteristics are known to be important for job performance that might be obtained from references, they are included in the qualifications listed in the job specification. A few examples of such characteristics would include honesty, dependability, and ability to work with others.
- Relate all questions asked in a reference check to the applicant's previous performance. The individual providing the reference should be a person who would have knowledge of the applicant's work performance.
- Comply with any district policy requiring applicants to sign a form authorizing release of the information requested from references. (Applicant consent is a defense to an action of defamation against a former employer or other referencers.) (See discussion of referencing later in this chapter.)
- Follow any district guidelines for evaluating information provided by former employers to make sure that the same information is obtained for all applicants and is used in the same way.

Hiring Decisions

- Make all hiring decisions without regard for race, color, national origin, gender, and religion, and evaluate all hiring decisions to detect any biases that might create an adverse impact on a protected group.
- Document all actions at each stage of the selection process for purposes of evaluation. Any restrictions related to religion, gender, or national origin must be based on a BFOQ necessary to satisfactory performance in the actual job.

Certification (Licensure)

- Ensure that applicants for employment as teachers meet eligibility standards that are set by state certification statutes and administered by state and local agencies. In addition, prospective teachers must satisfy the local board of education's job qualifications that have been designated for a particular position. Noncertificated personnel must meet only job qualifications and, in some cases, licensing requirements (such as those for plumbers and electricians).

- Remember that teachers' eligibility is usually limited to the area of competency that is covered by their certification. Certification, therefore, affects placement and assignment as well as original access to employment as a teacher.

- Keep current in knowing your state's and district's policies regarding hiring noncertificated individuals for teaching positions. In the absence of explicit statutory exception, the prerequisite of certification cannot be waived by local boards of education. At times, however, states have allowed some exceptions when a critical shortage of teachers in a special curricular area has occurred. And in some states, previous experience outside of teaching is considered, and noncertificated teachers have been allowed to teach on a probationary status. (Note: Certification requirements [laws] serve several purposes. They foster adequate professional training to ensure entry-level competence and continued professional development in the licensed area, and they protect certificated teachers, to some degree, against unfair placement or displacement. After certificates are issued to qualified individuals, the law recognizes holders of such certification as competent teachers and places the burden of proof in a termination proceeding on local school boards. The authority of certifying agencies to set the basis for new or renewal certificates includes the power to suspend or revoke certificates for cause, so long as the rationale and regulations are fair in content and fairly applied. Courts will overturn unauthorized and capricious revocation of certificates if the school district that requested the action did not comply with statutory due process procedures.)

SECTION C: NEGLIGENT HIRING, DEFAMATION, AND REFERENCING

This section covers three extremely important areas that can easily expose a principal and school district to liability. The first focus point examines negligent hiring, which, simply defined, is an employer's failure to exercise reasonable care in the selection of applicants relative to the type of position being filled. The second focus point centers on defamation and referencing. A negative reference can harm a person's reputation and limit or preclude employment opportunities, and if a reference contains any alleged facts that are proven to be not true, a person's interest in his or her reputation is protected by laws concerning libel and slander, collectively called defamation.

▌ FOCUS POINT: Negligent Hiring

Most of the litigation in negligent hiring is the result of an employer's failure to screen applicants, conduct thorough background checks, or discover criminal records. With a systematic mechanism in place for checking applicant backgrounds, school districts add three valuable components to the selection process: additional liability prevention, avoidance of the embarrassment of selecting an inappropriate applicant, and protection for students from preventable risk of harm.

Negligent hiring, retention, assignment, and training are all torts that are based on the premise that schools have a common law duty to protect their students. They are expected to use reasonable care to select employees who are competent to do the work assigned to them. Negligent hiring is a doctrine of primary liability, holding the employer liable for its acts, in contrast to the legal theory of *respondeat superior*, which holds the employer liable for acts of its employees.

Liability is generally determined by answering the "but for" causation-in-fact test. In other words, if the district owed a duty to hire a competent person, and if negligence is demonstrated, the next question is, Did the harm occur because of the negligence of the employer? This is often referred to as proximate cause. Was there a natural direct and continuous link between the negligent act and the plaintiff's injury? For example, if a school district hired a person who had been convicted of child molestation and placed a 13-year-old female in his band class, and the teacher molested the child, a case can be made for "but for" causation. On the other hand, if a school district conducts a thorough background check, and the teacher rapes a youngster from another school in the parking lot of the mall, there is probably not a "but for" causation. The issue is whether the school should have been able to anticipate that an employee would cause harm.

Generally, negligent hiring or retention cases involve acts that occurred during working hours while the employee was doing his or her job. However, an employer may be found negligent if it can be shown that the plaintiff and the employee would not have come into contact if not for the employment relationship. For example, extracurricular activities, field trips, and sponsored trips could involve negligent hiring or retention. However, there comes a point when the event is so distant from the employment relationship in time and place that the responsibility for adequate supervision lies with the parents.

Background Checks

Schools, day care centers, sports programs, and other organizations are increasingly using various services to check on the backgrounds of prospective employees as a tool to protect children. For example, the National Alliance for Youth Sport (NAYS) believes that background checks are "critical for ensuring well-being of youngsters participating in youth sports programs" (National Alliance for Youth Sports, n.d.).

A comprehensive system of background checking, consistently followed, not only provides increased protection for the students but also bolsters the district's defense should it face a claim of negligent hiring. The theory of negligent hiring is based on the assumption that an employer whose employees are in contact with the public in the course of their employment must exercise reasonable care in the selection and retention of its employees. In 1982, the Supreme Court of New Jersey explained that a "majority of jurisdictions that have addressed this issue have concluded that an employer who negligently either hires or retains in his employ an individual who is incompetent or unfit for the job, may be liable to a third party whose injury was proximately caused by the employer's negligence" (*DiCosala v. Kay*, 1982).

In order for a determination of negligent hiring to be made, it first must be determined that an employee was unfit and/or caused an injury to another in the course of his or her work. Second, it must be shown that the school was negligent in hiring that individual. A cause of action related to negligent hiring is negligent retention. An allegation of negligent hiring argues that the employer knew or should have known the employee was unfit before he or she was employed, while an allegation of negligent retention argues that during the course of employment, the employer became aware that the employee was unfit. Courts also recognize negligent assignment and negligent training as related causes of action.

Background checks are one tool a school district can use to weed out individuals with criminal backgrounds involving children. School officials should have a clear understanding of the information that will and will not be found when running a background check. For example, a criminal background check will not identify mental disorders.

Although background checks serve a purpose, they are only a supplement to a careful screening process that includes a careful evaluation of all other supporting documents. All applicants should be asked to submit letters of reference. All work experience should be carefully verified. All candidates should be specifically asked if they have ever been charged with child molestation or if they were under any type of investigation when they left any employment.

Screening programs should be integrated into a comprehensive preemployment process. School districts should develop a preemployment questionnaire that asks specific questions about the candidate's involvement in criminal activity. Abusers, like any other criminals, move to locations with the easiest targets. If they know a school district is doing background checks, it is less likely that they will apply.

Fingerprinting

Fingerprinting is increasingly being incorporated into the screening process. "More than half the states now have sexual assault laws covering educators who abuse their positions of trust by having sex with students. In 42 states, applicants for state certification are required to undergo criminal-background screenings that involve fingerprint checks through the Federal Bureau of Investigation and the state police" (Hendrie, 2003).

There is a danger that mandatory fingerprinting is a cosmetic solution to a complex problem. Although some teacher associations resist fingerprinting as a violation of privacy rights, an increasing number of districts believe that background checks help protect children and are not a significant infringement of educator Fourth Amendment rights.

Failure to Warn

Increasingly, plaintiffs are bringing suits against school districts alleging that the district that formerly employed the educator failed to warn the current employer about allegations of abuse. A California case illustrates the current judicial thinking on this matter. The case concerned letters of recommendation that school district officers allegedly wrote. Randi W. claimed that the school district unreservedly recommended an educator for employment without disclosing to prospective employers that they knew complaints of sexual misconduct had been leveled against him. The receiving school district argued that they were induced to hire the educator, who later sexually assaulted Randi W. The Supreme Court concluded that the defendants' letters of recommendation, containing unreserved and unconditional praise for the former employee, despite the defendants' alleged knowledge of complaints of sexual misconduct with students, constituted misleading statements that could form the basis for tort liability for fraud or negligent misrepresentation. Ordinarily, a recommending employer is not held accountable to third persons for failing to disclose negative information regarding a former employee. Nonetheless, liability may be imposed if the recommendation letter amounts to an affirmative misrepresentation presenting a foreseeable and substantial risk of physical harm to a third person. The Supreme Court ruled that the defendants could foresee that, had they not unqualifiedly recommended the former employee, the receiving district would not have hired him. And finally, the defendants could foresee that the former employee might molest or injure a student such as the plaintiff (*Randi W. v. Murdoc Joint Unified School District*, 1997).

Nondisclosure Provisions

It is all too common for a district to allow an employee who is under investigation or has been accused of sexual exploitation to resign and apply for a position in another district or state. In many of these cases, the sending district does not tell the receiving district about the suspicions or allegations. In fact, in some cases there is a negotiated settlement that includes an agreement not to tell future employers about the accusations. This is a classic example of how a "mobile molester" gets passed from one district to another. This all-too-common situation is often referred to as "passing the trash." Generally, nondisclosure agreements contain a provision that allows the employee to resign and prevents the employer from disclosing negative information about the employee. Consequently, future employers considering hiring the former district's employee may be unable to obtain essential information about the employee's fitness to teach. While these agreements may not always be illegal, they are always wrong. Such agreements conceal information from both the local community and prospective employers. In addition, they often violate state child abuse reporting laws.

Examples of Management Cues

- An assistant director of certified personnel has as her primary responsibility the recruitment and placement of elementary school teachers. Candidate A is one of the nearly 200 candidates she interviews one week. Candidate A's credentials generally look very good, but the director notices a two-year gap since the last two employment entries, and the file contains no recommendations from the last two districts in which Candidate A was employed. When questioned about this, Candidate A tells her that he took off some time to travel and study in Europe. In addition, he requested recommendations from his previous employers only very recently, and perhaps the placement office at his university has just not completed processing the paperwork. Before recommending Candidate A for hire, she contacts the two school districts listed on his application to verify Candidate A's employment. Both districts confirm that Candidate A was employed by them and that he voluntarily resigned. They offer no further details, and she asks no additional questions. Two months later, to her shock, Candidate A (now employed as Teacher A) is accused of child molesting by the parents of two of his third-grade students. He is subsequently tried and found guilty. During the trial, evidence is produced that Teacher A was convicted of a similar offense several years earlier and was sentenced to serve two years in prison in another state. The parents of the victims file suit against the assistant director of certified personnel and the school district for the negligent hiring of a convicted child molester.
- Because a specific position becomes available during the winter break, to expedite hiring, the job is awarded to an available candidate without completing the normal procedures of reference and background checking.

Suggested Risk Management Guidelines

- Know your district's policies on criminal background checks. School districts need not conduct criminal background checks on all applicants. The decision should be based on the employee's access to the means or opportunity to commit a crime. *Access* means, among other things, to master keys, money, equipment, drugs or explosives, and most important in the school setting, to potential victims (children).
- Review the employment history of all applicants and require verifiable explanations of inconsistencies or gaps.
- Inform all candidates that there will be a follow-up check on their work history and educational background.

I FOCUS POINT: Defamation and Referencing

Principals are frequently asked to write letters of reference or to provide a telephone reference regarding a former employee's qualifications or performance. Whether done to support a staff member's application for transfer or promotion or for inclusion in a professional credential file, agreeing to provide a written or oral reference is not something that should be done lightly.

This area of tort liability is somewhat confusing because it often involves two competing rights: the referencer's right to freedom of expression and the candidate's right to the protection of reputation. When these two rights come into conflict, the courts are often asked to determine whose right is more compelling. Principals and others in a position to provide references or recommendations may open themselves to potential defamation litigation if they include statements that the candidate might consider damaging.

Defamation is generally defined as any language, spoken or written, that tends to lower an individual in the esteem of any substantial and respectable group. Written defamation is called *libel*; spoken defamation is *slander*. Although the elements that constitute actionable defamation may vary from state to state, the essential elements that apply in the employment context include the following conditions:

- The communication must be defamatory. To understand what makes a communication defamatory, it is useful to keep three principles in mind:

  1. No matter how damaging it may be, no statement of factual truth is defamatory.

  2. A false statement is not defamatory unless it damages the reputation of the person about whom it is made.

  3. A statement of pure opinion is never defamatory. Pure opinion, no matter how outrageous it may be, is neither true nor false.

- The communication must be published, it must reach some third party or parties either by spoken or written word, and it must refer to the plaintiff.
- The third party or parties must understand the communication to be unfavorable to the plaintiff.
- The plaintiff must have been injured by the communication.

Letters of Reference

Writing a letter of reference sometimes places school administrators on the horns of a dilemma. On the one hand, they feel a professional responsibility to prevent incompetent or unfit educators from gaining future employment. On the other hand, they fear being sued for defamation by a former employee who does not get a job because of a negative letter of reference.

Former employees who bring defamation suits argue that the negative reference contained false statements that injured the employee's reputation. These suits allege that the former employer impugned the former employee's ability or fitness to teach. Generally, in order to promote candid and open communication, employers are protected by a form of qualified or conditional privilege. This privilege does not protect the employer who provides information that is known to be false or who acts with reckless disregard for the truth or falsity of the information.

Because of the fear of being sued for defamation, some districts are refusing to provide any substantive information about former employees. Ironically, at the same time some school districts are refusing to provide candid information on employees departing their employ, they are seeking information about prospective employees. In an attempt to foster honest communication and discourage frivolous lawsuits, most states have enacted some form of reference immunity statute.

For a referencer's statement to be defamatory, it must be false and must have a tendency to harm the candidate's reputation. It is not necessary that the statement actually demeaned the plaintiff's reputation; it must simply be shown that if the statement were believed, it would have this effect. Courts usually hold that an untrue statement is defamatory if a significant and *respectable* minority of persons would draw an adverse opinion of the candidate after reading or hearing the statement. If the candidate can demonstrate *actual malice*, in that the referencer knew that the statement was false or that the statement was made with a reckless disregard of the truth, punitive damages would likely be awarded in a typical court action.

Examples of Management Cues

- A marginal employee approaches his principal and requests a letter of reference for a position in another school district. The principal sees an opportunity to help this employee leave her school.
- Principal A in another school district calls the current supervisor (Principal B) of a candidate for a position in Principal A's school. Principal A requests that Principal B "tell him the 'real story' about the candidate."

Suggested Risk Management Guidelines

Prior to Preparing a Reference Letter or Agreeing to Be Identified as a Reference

- Contact the employee to discuss the reference in some detail. Determine to whom the reference information will be given, the specific nature of the position for which the employee is a candidate, and the elements of the employee's work-related qualifications and performance that are relevant to the desired position.

- Discuss the key points your reference will address with the employee. Obtain agreement from the employee regarding her or his strengths and weaknesses and the evidence you intend to cite to support your statements. (While the employee's prior consent to your statement may not protect you from a defamation suit, it can be an important defense against a charge of actual malice.)
- Decline to serve as referencer or offer the employee the opportunity to select another person to provide the reference, if you cannot provide a positive reference for the employee.
- Exercise caution when you are the only person who can provide the necessary recommendation. (For example, when you have supervised a student teacher's classroom experience, be sure that the information you will provide is objective, factual, and precise and that the student teacher has been fully apprised of your evaluation and understands the contents of the recommendation you will provide.)

When Preparing the Reference

- Provide only information that is job related and relevant to the current situation.
- Ensure that the statement of fact is true and provide adequate information to verify its truth, regardless of whether the statement is positive or negative. No matter how damaging it may be, no statement of factual truth is defamatory.
- Clearly label statements of your personal opinion.
- Do not include statements based on rumor or personal hunches.

SECTION D: PERFORMANCE EVALUATION

Although the primary purpose of employee evaluations is to improve the quality of instruction, from a strictly legal point of view, the purpose of employee evaluations is to provide justification (due process) for any action the school district takes in regard to its employees.

Prior to the reform movement in the 1980s, there was little legislation that directly focused on teacher evaluation. Although the stated purpose of every system of teacher evaluation is the improvement of instruction, every educator understands that the evaluation system is going to be used for teacher evaluation. This is appropriate, in that teacher evaluation is one of the primary means of enhancing education. Generally, the responsibility of developing and implementing teacher evaluations is the responsibility of the building administrator. However, this is easier said than done. There is a great degree of disparity in evaluation systems among states and within states.

According to Veir and Dagley (2002), "Presently there is no model statute from which a legally and legislatively sound evaluation system can be developed." They report, "These evaluation systems give the school a means for removing poor or problematic teachers. However, due to regular incongruities in the legislation—its language, structure, procedures, and requirements—the process often cannot be carried out." They conclude that "criteria used to measure teachers must be valid and observable, and the behaviors must be linked to teacher performance."

If done accurately, thoroughly, truthfully, and in a timely manner, evaluations can be a valuable asset to the education profession and the population it serves as well as a definitive defensive instrument for employers in the event that their action regarding a particular employee is challenged. If an evaluation demonstrates contemporaneous and early documentation of deficiencies and misconduct, documents repeated instances or patterns of poor performance, and evidences warning or opportunities to improve, such evaluation can be used to refute allegations that the employer acted arbitrarily, inconsistently, or without warning or that the employer's stated reason for any action was a pretext for discrimination. Thus one important reason for a formal evaluation program is to avoid subjective or arbitrary employment decisions on the part of the school district.

Well-defined evaluation programs benefit employees by providing an opportunity for school district and primary evaluators to formally praise employees for work well done and justify monetary or position advances. At the same time, evaluations provide a warning system by which the employee can be legally advised of any deficiencies and afforded reasonable time and guidance to correct them.

To help ensure accountability and quality teaching, many states, by statute, require periodic appraisal of teaching and principal performance. In states or local districts in which formal evaluation is mandated, principals place their jobs in jeopardy if they fail to satisfactorily evaluate their personnel. Although most professional educators assert that the primary reason for evaluation is improvement or remediation based on a "developmental assessment," the results of evaluations are used in a variety of employment decisions, including retention, tenure, promotion, salary, reassignment, reduction in force, or dismissal based on "personnel rating." When adverse personnel decisions are the result of evaluations, legal concerns often arise regarding issues of procedural fairness and due process. For example: Were established state or local procedures followed? Did school officials employ "equitable standards"? Was sufficient evidence collected to support the decision? Were evaluations conducted in a uniform and consistent manner?

I FOCUS POINT: Evaluation Guidelines and Congruence

Courts are generally reluctant to enter into the teacher evaluation process. Judicial reviews are usually limited to procedural issues of fairness and reasonableness. Two overall objectives are intrinsic in conducting performance evaluations:

1. *Developmental assessment:* The evaluation program must be directed toward the improvement of instruction in the classroom. Developmental assessment is the evaluation of a teacher to help that individual grow professionally. The evaluator does not use distinct evaluative criteria or assign the teacher a formal score or rating. The process spotlights development and improvement. The process is often regarded as a form of clinical supervision.

2. *Personnel rating:* There must be clear strategies for documentation of effectiveness as well as deficiencies in performance that support recommendations for promotion, nonrenewal, or dismissal. Personnel rating is the evaluation of a teacher to make performance-based administrative decisions relative to overall accountability in granting or denying tenure or promotion, renewing contracts, or requesting resignations. This rating process allows for both formative and summative evaluations in helping determine the teacher's professional future.

Principals need to distinguish between these two evaluation objectives and formulate standardized methods of observation, documentation, and conferencing. Successful evaluation programs are clear about the purposes of evaluation and match process to purpose. There must be congruence in the evaluation program between purpose and process.

Teacher evaluation programs must match the educational goals, management style, concept of teaching, and community values of the school district. Evaluation programs must solicit a strong commitment from district-level administrators, principals, and teachers. All participants must believe that the program is useful, valid, and cost effective.

Successful evaluation programs allow for adequate resources, with the two most critical ones being time to conduct evaluations and evaluator-evaluatee training. Principals often complain that time and training are the major obstacles in implementing successful evaluation programs. District-level administrators can assist principals by reducing other demands and helping principals manage their time more effectively. Principals need to be trained in the skills of formal evaluation: helping teachers set goals, making accurate observations, evaluating teachers' plans and tests, coaching teachers in specific skills, and conferencing.

Evaluation Instruments

In past years, an informal discussion between the teacher and the principal near the end of the school year often constituted a teacher's yearly performance evaluation. Usually, such discussions were subjective and focused on behaviors that often did not relate to teaching performance. The most common terms used during such evaluation conferences were *satisfactory* or *no problems noted*. If any problems existed, they were usually not noted in writing but were expressed orally to the teacher by the principal, with corrective comments couched in concern, such as, "I don't want any of my teachers upset or bad-mouthing me to other teachers or to the community."

Today, evaluation instruments are usually formal documents that have been developed through collaborative efforts from the school district, administrators, and teachers. Evaluation programs have greater impact on improved performance when teachers have had viable input into evaluation criteria. A clear mission, coupled with goal-based, results-oriented criteria that are fully understood by teachers, are invaluable factors in the success of the evaluation program. The ideal instrument provides the basis for the assessment of teachers' knowledge, skills, and attitudes and is directly related to effective teaching and professional growth. Such instruments should be periodically validated against actual job requirements and expectations, and personnel subject to formal evaluation should be familiar with the instruments used in the process.

Documentation

The evaluation of teachers must be a continuous process. For tenured teachers, formal evaluations may need only to be conducted the number of times required by state or local policy. However, for some teachers, whether they are new to the profession or experienced, more frequent evaluations may be necessary to help identify inadequate performance and provide a rational basis for any employment decision that might be reached concerning the teacher.

Three difficult areas of documentation are often challenged when questions arise about the kinds of documentation that can be used in the evaluation process. The courts in some jurisdictions have held that third-party documentation, shared with the principal, can be grounds for continuing employment decisions (*In re Feldman*, 1978; see also *Dore v. Dedminster Board of Education*, 1982). Some courts have also ruled that school districts have the right to base continuing employment decisions on matters outside of a teacher's evaluation. In one such case, the court noted that decisions made about the nonrenewal of a nontenured teacher can be made on a "broad basis of input received from a variety of people, including members of the public, parents of students, and a district member's own knowledge of a teacher even if that knowledge is acquired through having a child in the teacher's class" (*Derrickson v. Board of Education*, 1989).

Accurate documentation of evaluation findings is necessary for diagnosing strengths and weaknesses in teacher performance and for specifying any necessary remediation. Such documentation serves as a prerequisite for validating an adverse employment decision during due process proceedings or litigation. It is recommended that several types of written memoranda, in addition to actual evaluation instruments, be used to support the documentation process:

- *Memoranda to the file* should be used to record less significant infractions or deviations by an employee.
- *Specific incident memoranda* should be used to record conferences with an employee concerning a significant event.
- *Summary memoranda* should be used to record conferences with an employee in which several incidents, problems, or deficiencies are discussed.
- *Visitation memoranda* should record observations made of an employee's on-the-job performance.

The use of memoranda, if done appropriately, can provide comprehensive documentation of employee performance and evaluation. Teachers must be informed of the type of documentation that will be made by the principal as evaluator, how it will be used, and the teacher's right of access to the record.

Negative evaluations are never a pleasant experience, particularly when the results will be used to substantiate an adverse employment decision. However, documentation is critical in helping a teacher improve performance as well as in justifying a decision to nonrenew or terminate a contract. When done right, memoranda can make the difference between win or lose in a civil action.

The Evaluation Conference

Evaluation conferences provide the opportunity for the teacher or staff member and the principal to meet professionally to discuss the evaluation. For many principals, this conference often proves to be the most difficult part of the evaluation process because of the direct, personal contact involved. The purposes of the conference are to review the evaluation findings and to discuss any recommendations. The teacher should be invited to review all the evaluation instruments and any memoranda or other notes made during the process. If deficiencies are noted, the evaluator should be prepared to offer both specific steps and a reasonable time frame for improvement. When deficiencies are significant enough that they could lead to a decision to dismiss or nonrenew, the teacher must be advised that failure to demonstrate a specified level of improvement could have such consequences. The teacher must be offered the opportunity to ask questions and seek clarification of all issues discussed during the conference and should be given the opportunity to sign the evaluation report. A signature simply attests to the fact that the teacher has been shown the materials and afforded the opportunity to review the contents of the report, not that the teacher agrees with the conclusions. If the teacher refuses to sign the materials, the evaluator should simply make a file memorandum to the effect that the opportunity was offered but declined by the teacher.

The tone of the conference is important, and the principal as evaluator should maintain a professional demeanor at all times. Demonstrations of anger, threats, or attempts to harass or intimidate the teacher have no place. Private remarks made by a teacher in a principal's office, even though made in a hostile manner, are protected by the First Amendment and cannot be a basis for an adverse employment decision.

Example of a Management Cue

- A teacher claims that his due process rights were ignored in an evaluation and that the current evaluation program lacks equitable standards.

Suggested Risk Management Guidelines

- Define the standards to be used for assessing the effectiveness of teaching and communicate these standards to teachers.

- Apply evaluation standards uniformly and consistently. Treat all employees similarly and fairly throughout the evaluation process.
- Provide opportunity, reasonable time, and support for improvement.
- Follow all procedures specified in state statutes and school board policy.
- Rely on fact when preparing any memoranda; conclusive statements not supported by the facts should be avoided.
- Write any directives given in a memorandum in clear and concise language and avoid educational jargon.
- Write any memoranda in the first person and personalize such documents as much as possible. If others are involved, then use specific names.
- Never write a memorandum when you are angry or have become personally involved. In such circumstances, put aside the memorandum for a day or have an appropriate third party review it prior to sending it to the employee.

CHAPTER RESOURCES

Cannon v. University of Chicago, 99 S.Ct. 1946 (1979).

Derrickson v. Board of Education, 537 F. Supp. (E.D. Mo. 1989. Opinion written after trial, March 31, 1982).

DiCosala v. Kay, 450 A.2d 508 (1982).

Dore v. Dedminster Board of Education, 449 A.2d 547 (N.J. Super. Ct. App. Div. 1982).

Grove City College v. Bell, U.S.L.W. 4283 (1984), 465 U.S. 555 (1984).

Hendrie, C. (2003). States target sexual abuse by educators. *Education Week.* Retrieved April 30, 2003, from http://www.edweek.org

In re Feldman, 395 A.2d 602 (Pa. Commw. Ct. 1978).

Milner, M. G., & Miner, J. B. (1978). *Employee selection within the law.* Washington, DC: Bureau of National Affairs.

National Alliance for Youth Sports. (n.d.). Retrieved December 20, 2003, from http://www.nays.org/fullstory.cfm?articleid=225

North Haven Board of Education v. Bell, 102 S.Ct. 1912 (1982).

Panaro, G. P. (1990). *Employment law manual.* Boston: Warren, Gorham, & Lamont.

Randi W. v. Murdoc Joint Unified School District, 929 P.2d 582 (1997).

Rehabilitation Act of 1973. Sections 501 and 505 of the Rehabilitation Act of 1973 (Rehab. Act) (Pub. L. No. 93-112), as amended, as these sections appear in Volume 29 of the United States Code, beginning at Section 791. Section 501 prohibits employment discrimination against individuals with disabilities in the federal sector. Section 505 contains provisions governing remedies and attorneys' fees under Section 501. Relevant definitions that apply to Sections 501 and 505 precede these sections. Section 512 of the Americans with Disabilities Act of 1990 (ADA) (Pub. L. No. 101-336) amends definitions applicable to the Rehab. Act. The Rehabilitation Act Amendments of 1992 (Pub. L. No. 102-559) further amend the definition of "individual with a disability" and Section 501. In addition, Section 102 of the Civil Rights Act of 1991 (Pub. L. No. 102-166 (CRA) amends the Revised Statutes by adding a new section following Section 1977 (42 U.S.C. 1981), to provide for the recovery of compensatory and punitive damages in cases of intentional violations of Title VII, the Americans with Disabilities Act of 1990, and Section 501 of the Rehabilitation Act of 1973.

Veir, C. C., & Dagley, D. L. (2002). *Legal issues in teacher evaluation legislation: A study of state statutory provisions.* BYU Educ. & L.J. No. 1.

5

Teachers' Constitutional Rights, Terms, and Conditions of Employment

School boards have the statutory authority to make employment decisions for the school system. Because principals often take an active part in the enforcement of contracts, they need to understand the various types of employment documents commonly used by school districts. *It is important to note that any correspondence between the school district and a prospective employee may constitute an implied contract under law.* The same is true of statements made on application forms and job descriptions or in job postings or advertisements. Even selected statements in personnel manuals have been found by the courts to constitute a contract. Section A looks at the issue of teacher licensure and the types of employment contracts most commonly found in the education enterprise.

Education is a state function, and the state has the power to enact statutes that regulate the operation of schools and the activities of school employees. However, these statutes must conform to the significant substantive rights guaranteed under the U.S. Constitution. These rights are absolute and cannot be obstructed by state constitutions or by state or federal statutes except in very limited circumstances. Section B examines teachers' constitutional rights—legitimate situations that often

---

AUTHORS' NOTE: Cases cited throughout this chapter have been selected on a precedent-setting or best-example basis regardless of jurisdiction or date of adjudication. (See Introduction for more information.)

place principals in the difficult position of trying to balance teachers' rights against the rights of students, parents, administrators, and school boards. Section C continues the examination of teachers' rights under the light of their exemplar status.

During the past three decades, school districts have seen a significant increase in teacher activism. Teachers have continuously challenged the right of school boards to control their professional and private lives through contracts, bargaining agreements, evaluation, and monitoring. Many of these challenges have been debated in the courts and form the foundation for this chapter.

SECTION A: LICENSURE AND EMPLOYMENT CONTRACTS

Graduating from college with a teaching degree does not guarantee employment. Generally, state departments of education are responsible for issuing educator licenses, approving teacher education programs in their state, and accrediting the teacher education units at those institutions. An increasing number of states are establishing standardized testing programs for teachers as a criterion for gaining a teaching license. Local school boards may add additional requirements to those of their state.

The term *contract* generally describes a document that has signatures, seals, and witnesses for official notarization. Any written document, however, may serve as a contract between individuals if it is sufficiently definite, extends an offer, solicits acceptance, and denotes consideration. Consideration is defined as something of value that is exchanged by the parties to the contract. In terms of employment contracts, consideration is the salary and other benefits that the school district is willing to pay in exchange for the teaching services of the professional employee. The terms of the consideration must be specific enough to enable all parties to know and understand their obligations under the contract.

Teachers are generally employed under one of two types of contracts: a term/probationary contract or a continuing/tenure contract. Teachers may also hold a supplementary or an *addendum* to contract. Teacher contracts are governed by the laws of contracts, applicable state statutes, and local school board policies and typically include those elements necessary for an enforceable contract: an agreement, including both offer and acceptance, consideration, a description of competent parties, and legal subject matter.

An agreement results from an offer and acceptance between the parties to a contract and refers to the mutual consent by the parties to be bound by the terms specified. When a school district makes an offer to a potential employee, the offer must be made with the intent to enter into a contract and be communicated to the offeree in a form that is definite and certain and not presented as an invitation to negotiate.

The acceptance of an offer to contract can be made only by the person to whom the offer was made and must reflect some tangible evidence, either by word or deed, that the person intends to comply with the terms of the offer. The offer may be accepted anytime before it is withdrawn or expires according to the terms.

Teachers' contracts are usually straightforward agreements drawn on standard forms that specify the basic elements of salary, position, and length of employment. In many states, these standard employment contracts are supplemented by a *master contract* developed through a collective bargaining process and ratified by the school board and teachers' union. In each case, if all the basic elements of the contract are present, then a valid contract exists. The teacher works in accordance with the contract until the contract expires or the school board terminates it for cause.

Although employment contracts have become more specific in terms of responsibilities and duties of the employee, it is not necessary to specify in detail all expectations of employment within the contract document. State laws and regulations, school district policies, and general duties are assumed in the contract. Teachers can be required to perform tasks and duties within their areas of competency and certification even though they are not delineated specifically in the employment contract. Although a teacher's legal rights of employment are derived from the contract, additional rights accrue from any collective bargaining agreement (master contract) in effect at the time of contract issuance.

FOCUS POINT: Probationary Contracts, aka Term Contracts

A probationary or term contract is valid for a specified period of time, after which the employee has no guarantee of reemployment. Both parties are released from the contract's obligations at the end of the term specified. Under such a contract, a probationary period is served during which time school officials determine whether the teacher merits continuing/tenure status. The maximum length of the probationary period varies, although three years is most common. At the end of the probationary term, the school district must either terminate the teacher's employment or employ the teacher under a continuing/tenure contract.

Regulations concerning probationary contracts usually include statements that, at a minimum, clearly specify the following:

- Neither party is entitled to reasons at the expiration of the contract, unless mandated by statute. A school district is only required to provide notice prior to the expiration date of the contract that the contract will not be renewed.
- State statutes or bargaining agreements may require a school district to give notice of its intention to terminate a teacher's probationary contract on or before a specified date during the year the contract expires. If the school district fails to provide such notice, then the teacher may be eligible for continued employment.

Examples of Management Cues

- A prospective teacher refuses to sign a probationary contract without assurance that a continuing or tenure contract is guaranteed.
- On receiving notification that her probationary contract will not be renewed, a teacher insists on knowing why and demands that basic due process procedures be initiated.
- A teacher who completes his first year under probation is found to be unsatisfactory. Because of an error in the district's personnel office, the teacher is not notified of his nonrenewed status and shows up, along with his replacement, for the August back-to-school faculty orientation at his previously assigned school.

Suggested Risk Management Guidelines

- Know and follow your district's policies and practices regarding probationary or term contracts.
- Administer probationary or term contracts strictly and consistently.

▍ FOCUS POINT: Tenure, aka Continuing Contracts

The award of a tenure or continuing contract (hereafter referred to as a tenure contract) requires affirmative acts by both the school district and the teacher (offer and acceptance). Because tenure contracts involve statutory rights, specific procedures and protections vary from state to state. Most tenure statutes specify both the requirements and procedures for obtaining tenure and the causes and procedures for dismissal of tenured personnel.

In interpreting tenure laws, courts have attempted to protect teachers' rights while simultaneously maintaining flexibility for school officials in personnel management.

It is critical that principals understand and convey to teachers the following:

- The authority to grant a tenure contract is a discretionary power of a local school board that cannot be delegated.
- Although a tenure contract provides a certain amount of job security, it does not guarantee permanent employment or the right to teach in a particular school or grade. Teachers may be reassigned to positions for which they are certificated and dismissed for causes specified in tenure law. (A number of states limit the awarding of tenure to teaching positions and exclude administrative and supervisory positions. Where tenure is available for administrative positions, probationary service and other specified statutory terms must be met. Most courts have concluded, however, that continued service as a certificated professional employee, even as an administrator, does not alter tenure right acquired as a teacher.)
- Generally, after a teacher has served the required probationary period and has been reemployed by the school district for the next year, the

district must notify the teacher in writing of its decision to award a tenure contract. The teacher then must notify the school district, in writing or by signing the contract, of acceptance of such tenure. If the teacher fails to accept the contract within a specified length of time, the teacher may forfeit the contract.

- Tenure contracts provide for continued employment unless the school district terminates the service for specified cause following certain procedural due process guidelines.

Examples of Management Cues

- A group of parents disapproves of a tenured teacher's teaching methods and demands her termination.
- Frustrated by a teacher's unwillingness or inability to participate enthusiastically in a schoolwide, multicultural education initiative, an elementary school principal asks the district personnel department to terminate the tenured teacher's employment and hire a replacement teacher who will support the multicultural education program.

Suggested Risk Management Guidelines

- Know and follow your district's policies and practices regarding tenure or continuing contracts.
- Administer tenure or continuing contracts strictly and consistently.

FOCUS POINT: Supplementary Contracts, aka Addendum to Contract, aka Supplemental Duty

In addition to a term/probationary or continuing/tenure contract, a teacher may also hold an addendum to contract, more commonly called a supplemental contract, for services such as coaching, supervising, sponsoring, directing, monitoring, or other similar activities. Generally, when supplemental contracts are issued, the law excludes supplemental contracts from the guarantees inherent in a continuing/tenure contract and from due process requirements.

There is considerable variation in the ways states address supplemental duties, and because courts are bound by the specific facts of the individual situation and their state statutes, there is wide variation in court decisions. Some states view supplemental duties as independent of teaching assignments, some issue a single contract that includes both teaching and supplemental duties, and some states use both single and separate contracts for supplemental duties. For these reasons, it is impossible to recommend or suggest guidelines that fit all jurisdictions. The question of additional pay for supplemental duties is a continuous point of contention between school boards and teacher associations. Typically, school boards want to retain the authority to assign teachers additional duties on an as-needed basis, whereas teachers' associations generally believe that

- Professional employees should have the right to accept or reject cocurricular or extracurricular assignments
- Acceptance or rejection of supplemental assignments should in no way affect the employees' teaching contracts
- Professional services required outside of the students' school day should be compensated through supplemental salary or overtime pay

When disagreements about these issues cannot be resolved at the local level, they frequently result in litigation. As courts have ruled on the issue of supplemental duties and supplemental contracts, three key precedents have emerged.

1. Coaching duties must be performed under supplemental contracts; teachers cannot be required to accept such duties as part of their primary contracts, and teachers can unilaterally terminate or nonrenew their supplemental contracts without affecting their primary contracts. (Note: Prior to 1984, it was generally assumed that primary contracts and supplementary contracts were indivisible and the elimination of one type of duty automatically eliminated the other. Teachers were expected to perform all supplemental duties as a part of their primary contract. This assumption was dispelled by the Kansas Court of Appeals in a 1984 case *Swager v. Board of Education U.S.D. 412*] in which the court ruled in favor of a teacher who claimed his teaching contract was unaffected by the termination of his coaching contract. In 1986, the Kansas Court of Appeals ruled that a negotiated contract does not require a teacher to accept supplemental duties [Ct. App. Kans., No. 58353]. In 1988, the Supreme Court of Kansas ruled that supplemental duties, even when conducted during the school day, are not part of a teacher's primary contract [*Hachiya/Livingston v. U.S.D. 307*].)

2. Teachers employed as coaches are not deprived of property rights when that employment is discontinued. (Note: In *Smith v. Board of Education*, 1983, a school board had offered to continue two teachers' employment as physical education instructors when notification of dismissal from coaching was issued. The teachers argued that they had tenure in their coaching positions and should have been accorded a hearing before being dismissed. The court ruled that the Fourteenth Amendment due process clause does not guarantee a coach continued employment in that capacity.)

3. Extracurricular duty assignments must be nondiscriminatory and related to a teacher's interest and expertise and must not require excessive hours beyond the contractual workday. (Note: In a West Virginia case, a court ruled that "the board of education's power to assign extracurricular duties to teachers is not unlimited and must be exercised in a reasonable manner" [*State ex rel. Hawkins v. Board of Education*, 1980].)

Examples of Management Cues

- A teacher was informed orally by his principal that he would not be retained as head basketball coach for the coming year. The principal implied that if the teacher did not resign from his coaching duties, he would be released. The teacher sent a letter to the board stating, "I hereby resign from duties as head basketball coach, effective the end of this year. I am looking forward, however, to continuing my teaching responsibilities." The board subsequently informed the teacher that resigning from one part of the contract was tantamount to voiding the entire contract.

- An English teacher who for years sponsored the high school drama club and directed the annual school play declined to sign a supplemental contract to continue those duties in the coming school year. The principal told the teacher that in order to maintain her assigned full-time equivalency (FTE), she would have to request his transfer to another school so that she could hire a teacher who would both teach English and sponsor the drama activities.

Suggested Risk Management Guidelines

- Do not require teachers to perform supplemental duties as part of their primary contracts. Teachers who agree to serve as coaches, for example, perform such duties under separate contract (i.e., supplemental contracts).
- Assign extracurricular duty to teachers in a nondiscriminatory and reasonable manner in accordance with their interests and expertise.

I FOCUS POINT: Employment Requirements

School districts possess broad authority in the establishment of job requirements or conditions of employment for school personnel. Many school districts, for example, require teachers to meet continuing education requirements or have regular physical examinations. Some school districts require teachers and administrators to reside within the district, and others prohibit employees from taking other employment during the school year. Courts have generally upheld school districts' rights to establish and enforce such requirements as long as the requirements are reasonable, directly related to the school district's mission, and consistently applied.

The following is an overview of the authority that courts have generally allowed school boards regarding employment requirements:

- Continuing Education Requirements
  - Although states demand minimum certification requirements for professional educators, such requirements do not preclude individual school districts from requiring personnel to seek and acquire higher professional or academic standards, as long as the requirements are applied in a *uniform and nondiscriminatory* manner.
  - The right of school districts to dismiss personnel for failing to satisfy continuing education requirements has been upheld by the courts.

- Health and Physical Requirements
  - School districts may adopt *reasonable* health and physical requirements for professional personnel. The courts have recognized that such requirements are necessary to protect the health and welfare of students and others.
  - Such requirements *must not be applied in an arbitrary manner* and must not contravene any state or federal laws that protect the rights of individuals with disabilities.

- Requirement That Teachers Reside within the School District
  - A school district can require and enforce residency for school district employees if state statutes do not prohibit such a requirement.
  - The policy should be clearly intended to promote and support the school district's primary mission and should be uniformly enforced.

- Prohibition of Outside Work during the School Term
  - A school district may adopt a policy prohibiting outside work by school employees during a school term if the rule is *definite, communicated to the employees, and applied in a uniform and consistent manner* to all employees.

- Nepotism and Conflict of Interest
  - Board policies prohibiting conflict of interest and, as a separate issue, nepotism have been upheld by the courts.
  - Nepotism policies prohibit employment of relatives and family members of employees.
  - Conflict-of-interest policies prohibit employees from entering into a relationship with companies or organizations that conduct business with their school district either directly (direct sales) or indirectly (consulting or contracting for direct sales).

- Requirement That Teachers Be Citizens
  - A state may require an individual to be a citizen or be in the process of seeking citizenship before he or she can receive a teaching license.
  - Aliens who are eligible for U.S. citizenship but refuse to seek naturalization may be excluded from teaching.

Example of a Management Cue

- Prior to the issuance of new contracts, questions are raised by the local teachers' organization regarding the board's *right* to implement and enforce the conditions of contract that are listed below. The teachers' organization wants the board to eliminate all of them but especially targets the third and fourth conditions, claiming that their civil rights are being violated, faculty morale will take a dive, and the recruitment of new and replacement teachers to the district will suffer.

- All teachers employed by the school district are required to take three hours of college credit in their teaching field every three years.
- All teachers employed by the school district are required to provide proof of a current physical examination every three years.
- Effective July 1 of the current year, all newly hired teachers must maintain principal residency within the school district.
- Effective July 1 of the current year, teachers contracted and employed by the school district shall not engage in any other business or profession directly or indirectly, for full or part time, during any term in which their contract is in effect.
- Any employee of the school district who enters into a relationship with companies or organizations that conduct business with the school district, either directly (direct sales) or indirectly (consulting or contracting for direct sales), will be terminated from employment with the school district immediately.
- Effective July 1 of the current year, relatives and family members (including spouses) of any employee of the school district may not be offered a job, hired, or contracted by the school district.

Suggested Risk Management Guidelines

- Be sure to know, understand, and support the conditions of employment required by your board of education.
- Do not circumvent any board policy you disagree with or feel may adversely affect morale or personnel recruitment. When you feel that a proposed board action in the area of any employment requirements may, in fact, adversely affect morale, recruitment, and so forth, you have a professional responsibility to discuss your concerns with superiors.

▌ FOCUS POINT: Collective Bargaining and Contracts

Over the past 30 years, collective bargaining has become a common practice in public school districts. Most states have laws that give teachers the right to join employee organizations, and the courts have held that teachers have a constitutional right to organize. Most state laws outline procedures for identifying which organization will have the right to bargain on behalf of teachers. The laws vary widely from state to state but generally require school boards to bargain with teacher organizations about wages, working hours, and other terms and conditions of employment. About half of the states prohibit strikes by teachers. In situations in which state law prohibits strikes or teachers fail to meet the specified conditions for a strike, courts have upheld a district's right to dismiss striking teachers. In addition, the courts have issued injunctions against teachers who strike and have upheld the board's authority to impose economic sanctions on striking teachers.

In both collective bargaining states and "meet and confer" states, courts have generally held that

- In the absence of a prohibitory statute or regulation, teachers have the right to organize for the purpose of negotiating the conditions of employment.
- There are no federal laws that regulate teachers' unions.
- Teachers have a constitutional right to organize, but there is no constitutional right to bargain collectively.
- State laws determine the procedure by which the exclusive bargaining representative is chosen; typically the representative is selected (elected) by a majority of the teachers.
- Teachers cannot be required to join the organization selected as the bargaining representative but, depending on state law, may be required to pay dues to that organization even if they don't wish to join as members.
- Teachers cannot be required to participate in or support union political activities.

Examples of Management Cues

- A number of teachers are angry that the local teachers' association, which represents teachers at the bargaining table, requires them to pay association dues whether they want to join or not. The teachers' association has asked the board of education to withhold delinquent dues from their paychecks.
- The group of teachers that did not belong to the teachers' association formally requests permission to represent themselves in the upcoming collective bargaining process.

Suggested Risk Management Guidelines

- Find out the status of teachers' rights to organize in your jurisdiction.
- Understand how collective bargaining works in your school district by finding out the answers to the following questions:
  - What are the union's legal responsibilities as the exclusive bargaining representative for teachers?
  - What legal responsibilities does the school board have in the bargaining process?
  - Can the school board bypass the union and make salary agreements with individual teachers?
  - What is the process during collective bargaining?
  - What do the union and board bargain about? Are there limitations? What does a collective bargaining contract include?

– What happens if the union and the board cannot agree on a contract? Do teachers have the right to strike? What penalties can be imposed on teachers who engage in an illegal strike?

SECTION B: TEACHERS' RIGHTS

Although the U.S. Supreme Court has repeatedly emphasized and affirmed the comprehensive authority of states and local school authorities to control the schools, this authority cannot infringe on the constitutional rights of teachers or students. Over the years, judicial interpretation of the U.S. Constitution has expanded individual rights and interests and dramatically reshaped the relationship between the principal and the teacher in employment matters.

The following is an overview of the *major tenets* of law regarding teachers' rights that are the most common and recurring in litigation:

- Employees have constitutionally protected rights that are not surrendered in public employment.
- A constitutionally protected right cannot be the substantial or motivating factor in a school board's decision to dismiss an employee.
- The exercise of a teacher's constitutional rights to free speech or expression can be balanced against the interests of the school district in the operation of an efficient system.
- Most courts recognize that teachers should not be penalized for their private behavior unless it has a clear impact on their effectiveness as educators.
- Comments made by a school district employee, as a citizen, on matters of public concern generally are constitutionally protected. Employee comments about the internal concerns of the school that undermine supervisors' authority are not protected.
- Private comments made by a teacher to a superior are constitutionally protected but may be subject to reasonable time, place, and manner.
- In mixed motives dismissals, plaintiffs have the initial burden of demonstrating that their conduct was constitutionally protected and was a substantial or motivating factor in the decisions to dismiss. If plaintiffs meet this burden, courts will generally enter a judgment in their favor unless the defendant school board proves by a preponderance of evidence that the *same* decision to dismiss would have been reached in the absence of the protected conduct.

Given the legal environment, the principal stands as *the primary arbiter* in problems that require balancing the legal interests of the *public school as an agency of the state*, and *teachers as individuals*. It is important to keep this concept of balance in mind.

The Fifth and Fourteenth Amendments to the U.S. Constitution (the Fifth applying to activities of the federal government and the Fourteenth to those of the states) have been the sources of the greatest volume of constitutionally based education litigation.

The Fourteenth Amendment states that no person shall be deprived of "life, liberty, or property, without due process of law." As courts have interpreted this amendment over time, they have added requirements that procedures must not be arbitrary, unreasonable, or discriminatory in policy or practice. Essentially, then, this amendment demands *fair* procedures.

Courts view due process in two ways: *substantive due process* and *procedural due process*. Substantive due process requires that the policies, rules, or regulations be fair in and of themselves. The basic attributes of substantive due process may be best understood by those features showing its absence. A rule, law, regulation, policy, or action violates substantive due process when it is overly broad or unnecessarily vague, is arbitrary or capricious, invades the protected zone of personal privacy, is unrelated to a valid education objective, or does not use reasonable means to achieve the objective.

Procedural due process means that the policies, rules, and regulations are applied in a fair manner. Procedural due process encompasses such basics as the right to timely, clear notification of charges and their basis and the right to an impartial hearing on the charges in which the accused is given an opportunity to defend against them. As the severity of the potential penalty increases, so does the extent of due process procedural protection.

In determining what process is due, courts apply a balancing-of-interest test that weighs the interests of society, as represented by the school, against the rights of the individual teacher. This test does not have complex technical rules but, rather, is an application of theory about what is fair and just that allows considerable latitude in judicial examination and judgment.

FOCUS POINT: Teachers' Rights to Hearings and Procedural Due Process

The basic elements of procedural due process are the notice of the charges and a hearing. The procedural aspects of a hearing generally are delineated in state statute or school board policy and typically include

- A notice of charges
- Representation by counsel
- Protection against self-incrimination
- Cross-examination of witnesses
- Compulsory attendance of witnesses
- Access to records and reports in the school district's possession
- Record of the hearing
- The right to appeal

Aspects that often cause legal problems are the standard of proof, burden of proof, evidence, and the impartiality of the school board as the hearing body.

The burden of proof in establishing just and sufficient cause for nonrenewal rests with the school district. If an aggrieved party is not satisfied with the results of a hearing and files a lawsuit, the court may reason that because the teaching contract was a property right requiring a due process hearing, the school board has the burden to establish the basis for its adverse decision. In the process of examining the school district's procedures, courts will closely scrutinize any procedural oversight that had the effect of denying a dismissed employee a substantive right.

State statutes or local board policies generally establish professional employees' rights to a hearing and the requirements for notice of nonrenewal or termination, including deadlines for notification, form and content of the notice, and parties designated to issue the notice.

Examples of Management Cues

- A school counselor is accused of touching a student in an inappropriate manner and is immediately sent home. When the formal hearing was held, the accusing student does not appear in person but is represented by her parents.
- Due to anger and extreme frustration over an incident, a principal tells a tenured teacher, "You're fired!" He then requires the teacher to hand in his keys and leave the building immediately. The teacher calls his union representative, who quickly files a grievance on his behalf with the board of education, asserting that the teacher's due process rights to a hearing have been violated.
- A full-time, special education teacher is notified on March 16 that a new program beginning in the fall will employ two part-time teachers. The board is discontinuing the teacher's current position and offering him one of the part-time jobs. The teacher is advised that he is entitled to a hearing if he makes the request within 14 days. The teacher obtains an attorney and, on March 27, requests a hearing. The board receives the request on March 29 and, operating under a state law that requires teacher dismissals to be completed by April 1, sends the teacher and his attorney telegrams setting the hearing date for March 30. The teacher claims he does not have adequate time to prepare for the hearing. The state law that sets the April 1st deadline also requires school districts to give "appropriate and timely" notice.

Suggested Risk Management Guidelines

- Understand and strictly adhere to your district's due process procedures whenever making personnel nonrenewal or termination decisions or other decisions that can adversely affect personnel employment records.
- Be aware of your district's policies regarding proper notice and follow those policies exactly in notifying personnel about nonrenewal and termination decisions.
- Make certain that the process of notifying teachers of nonrenewal or termination ensures that they are provided with the following information,

which assumes that your board of education provides a "right to a hearing" as part of overall personnel policy and that some semblance of the following statements are included in the policy:

- The board, after consideration of the written evaluation and the reasons for the recommendation, will, in its sole discretion, either reject the recommendation or give the teacher written notice of the proposed nonrenewal (or termination) on or before (specific date), preceding the end of the employment term specified in the contract.
- In the event of failure to give notice of proposed nonrenewal (or termination) within the time specified, the board will elect to employ the teacher in the same professional capacity for the succeeding school year.

▌ FOCUS POINT: Teachers' Rights in Evidence and Bias

Whether certain evidence used against a teacher by school officials was proper is often questioned. Although the rules of evidence applicable in court proceedings do not apply in a *strict* sense to dismissal hearings, it is *imperative* that administrators understand that any evidence presented must be substantial, relevant to establish the alleged facts, developed in a constitutionally approved way, documented (which, in its simplest form, means recording time, date, and place, with witnesses listed, if any), and limited to charges made.

In addition, aggrieved employees often charge that school boards serving as hearing bodies are biased and unfair in their actions. The courts have ruled that familiarity with the facts of a case gained by a school district board of education in the performance of its statutory role does not disqualify them as a decision-making body. A board member cannot be disqualified simply because the member has taken a position, even in public, on a policy issue related to the dispute. To bar a school board or a school board member the authority to conduct hearings concerning aggrieved teachers requires convincing proof that the board or member is so corrupt with prejudice and partiality that the board or member is incapable of rendering a fair determination on the evidence presented.

Example of a Management Cue

- The school board fires a teacher for unprofessional conduct. The teacher has refused to attend faculty meetings and complete required routine paperwork. The board grants the teacher's request for a hearing, with his attorney present, in which his termination is upheld. The teacher sues the school district, claiming that his due process rights were violated because the board acted as both "fact finder" and "judge" in the dismissal hearing and that the evidence presented against him was immaterial, irrelevant, and poorly documented.

Suggested Risk Management Guidelines

- Develop procedures that will ensure sufficient documentation of evidence that might be used in a dismissal action.
- Train all administrators who supervise personnel in such procedures. Principals should make sure that their assistant principals are included in such training and are fully versed in the documentation procedures.
- Remember that the chain of evidence, under normal circumstances, starts in the principal's office and that, without convincing evidence (i.e., records, reports, files, notes, times, dates, and names of witnesses, etc.), some of the basic elements of due process in a hearing are missing.

FOCUS POINT: Teachers' Rights in a Reduction in Force (RIF)

The courts have generally recognized the following as reasonable rationales for school districts to implement a reduction in force: enrollment decline; fiscal, economic, or budgetary basis; reorganization or consolidation of school districts; change in the number of teaching positions; curtailment of programs, courses, or services; or other good or just cause. Because staff salaries constitute the major portion of the operating budget, eliminating faculty and administrative positions through an RIF clearly results in reduced school district expenditures. However, RIF actions have also resulted in a proliferation of court actions. Most states have enacted legislation concerning staff reduction; however, the scope and specificity of RIF provisions vary from state to state. (Note: Although *reduction in force* is the standard term used for the public sector, some school districts use private-sector terms such as *downsize* or *right size,* and others use the term *de-staff.*)

Examples of Management Cues

- The tenured teacher with the least amount of seniority in his department finds his position eliminated at the close of the school year. The school district, faced with substantial budget deficits and decreased enrollment, has decided to eliminate certain teaching positions to bring about an RIF. The collective bargaining agreement between the teachers' association and the school district provides that teachers will be placed on unrequested leaves of absence in inverse order of seniority.
- Two tenured business teachers with the same credentials are considered for dismissal or reassignment under an RIF policy. In deciding which teacher to drop from the staff, the principal considers the contribution each has made to the activities program. Even though one teacher has taught for six years, the teacher the principal recommends and the board ultimately chooses to retain has only three years of experience but is a debate coach.

Suggested Risk Management Guideline

- Know and understand the state statutes and the methodology the local board has adopted to implement a legal RIF, so you can explain and counsel teachers if the district determines it must implement an RIF.

FOCUS POINT: Teachers' Rights Regarding Property Interests

Although the U.S. Constitution does not specifically grant a person a right to employment, the courts have derived a right to work from the Fourteenth Amendment. As early as 1923, the Supreme Court declared that the concept of liberty includes the right of the individual "to engage in the common occupations of life" (*Meyer v. Nebraska*). If the state denies a person the right to work, due process must be provided.

It has been established that tenured teachers have both property and liberty interests in their employment contracts and must be afforded due process protection. Property interests are legitimate claims or entitlements to continued employment under contract. Term contract teachers have property interests during the specified period of their contract. The granting of tenure or a continuing contract expands this property interest to include a right to continued employment. In other words, once a teacher earns tenure or a continuing contract, the teacher may not be denied continued employment without due process.

The interpretation of what may be considered a liberty or property interest is particularly compliant to interpretation, allowing for a wide variety of protected conduct in areas considered to be fundamental, such as religion, speech, press, and right to work.

Examples of Management Cues

- A nontenured teacher claims that his ability to secure employment in the teaching profession in another district was ruined by a board member who suggested to others that the teacher has a substance abuse problem and that is the reason his contract was not extended.
- A 59-year-old art teacher with 30 years' tenure in the district is terminated for incompetence. She is not eligible for retirement. She claims that because this is the only job she has ever held and this is the only area she has been trained in, she cannot find another job, at her age and with her limited vocation, that will provide a salary at the level that she has become reliant on. She files a lawsuit demanding her property rights.

Suggested Risk Management Guidelines

- Take care not to compromise the liberty interest for either a tenured or nontenured teacher by taking any action that damages a teacher's reputation in such a way as to interfere with the teacher's future employment opportunities.

- Be able to demonstrate a rational purpose for any action of restraint taken that might be interpreted as interfering with a teacher's liberty or property interest, and be able to prove that such action was justified by a compelling legal or education interest.

FOCUS POINT: Teachers' Rights and the Concept of Vagueness

The vagueness doctrine is well defined in law, and the courts have generally held that when a rule, policy, or statute forbids or requires individuals to do something—using terminology so vague that individuals of common intelligence must guess at its meaning and may differ as to its application—the rule violates due process of law. This doctrine has significant meaning when school districts and principals develop policies, rules, and regulations for the district or individual schools.

Examples of Management Cues

- A tenured teacher is dismissed for not following a board of education policy that states,

  > School employees shall not provide transportation for students in their own personal cars except under the following circumstances: A school-sponsored event to which school or public transportation is not available or in an emergency or otherwise to expedite the process.

  The teacher files a lawsuit against the district, claiming policy vagueness.

- A teacher is reprimanded, and a letter stating this is placed in the teacher's personnel file. The teacher requests that the letter be removed or that she be allowed to place a response in the file. She claims that she "followed the policy to the letter." The policy in dispute states,

  > Building personnel are responsible for the leveling of window shades in their assigned work areas at the close of each school day. Shades are to be generally uniformly configured so as to create a well-kept look. Art projects are not to be displayed in windows except when appropriate.

Suggested Risk Management Guideline

- Do not assume that the written presentation of a rule, regulation, or policy will be understood in the same way by all who will be affected by it.

Before implementation, consider asking a representative group of people who will be affected to review the wording of a new policy or rule to make sure that they generally share an accurate understanding of what the words mean and would respond in the manner intended.

FOCUS POINT: The Student Teacher or Intern—Substitute Teachers

Generally, states permit local school districts to enter into student teacher contracts with colleges and universities for the practical training of prospective teachers. In some states, the state board of education issues student teaching certificates and permits student teachers to assume certain responsibilities as fully certificated teachers. Regardless of how student teachers or interns are assigned, principals need to understand that a potential for liability exists with student teachers just as it does with certificated teachers. Student teachers are ultimately the responsibility of the principal acting in concert with the college or university and the assigned supervising teacher.

The legal problems involving student teachers are generally the same types of problems that affect certificated teachers. Among the most frequently reported are negligence that results in an injury to a student, hitting students or use of corporal punishment, and felony arrest or conviction. In addition, student teachers have been involved with the courts as a result of school district and college or university decisions involving grades in student teaching, discrimination against student teachers, and withdrawal of student teachers from assignments.

One area of continuous concern for principals is determining whether or not student teachers can be used as substitutes for their supervising teachers or other teachers in the school building. Local school district policies often do not address this issue. Principals should not use student teachers in this manner without consulting superiors and the student teacher's college or university supervisor. Principals should approach the use of student teachers as substitutes with caution and in accordance with local school district policies.

Generally, depending on individual state statutes, the courts have held that a student teacher may substitute under the following kinds of circumstances:

- A substitute teacher is not immediately available.
- The student teacher has been in that student teaching assignment for a specified minimum number of school days.
- The supervising teacher, the principal of the school, and the university supervisor agree that the student teacher is capable of successfully handling the teaching responsibilities.
- A certified classroom teacher in an adjacent room or a member of the same teaching team as the student teacher is aware of the absence and agrees to assist the student teacher if needed.

- The principal of the school or the principal's representative is readily available in the building.
- The student teacher is not paid for any substitute service. (This matter is negotiable in some jurisdictions.)

In the area of substitute teachers, it is imperative that schools ensure that any person selected to do substitute work has had a background check. Substitute teachers should be contracted under the same preconditions as a full-time teacher. Substitute teachers are held to the same duty of care as full-time teachers and are liable for foreseeable injuries that are caused by their negligent acts.

Examples of Management Cues

- A graduate student who has been a student teacher for seven weeks is assigned to a cooperating teacher in a sixth-grade classroom. The student teacher is supervising the sixth-grade area of the playground during recess while his cooperating teacher prepares some materials in the classroom. The student teacher decides to join the touch football game his class is having with another class. While he is involved in the game, a student from the class who is not playing football is severely injured in a fall from the top of a swing set.
- Because her student teacher has shown exceptional skills and abilities during the early part of the semester, the cooperating teacher decides to let her teach the next six weeks entirely on her own. To assist the student teacher in her growth and confidence, the cooperating teacher is absent from the classroom most of the time. At the end of the quarter, the cooperating teacher allows the student teacher to assign grades to her students. A parent of a student in the class is irate and wants a grade changed based on the fact that it was assigned by a student teacher. The cooperating teacher refuses the parent's request, and the parent appeals to the principal.
- A student teacher gets exemplary performance reviews from his cooperating teacher. One day, as the principal walks by the teacher's lounge, he smells the distinct odor of burning marijuana. On entering the lounge, he finds the highly touted student teacher smoking what looks like a joint. When he asks what the student teacher is smoking, the student teacher offers the principal a drag and says, "This is really prime stuff."

Suggested Risk Management Guidelines

- Ensure that all parties involved understand and agree that student teachers are expected to comply with the rules, regulations, policies, and procedures of the school and school district and that in the district (if applicable), student teachers may be assigned any duties or responsibilities granted to certificated teachers. This assignment may include the responsibility for student management, curricular goals, proper instruction, and all other duties as assigned by the university supervisor, building principal, or cooperating teacher.

- Develop and implement a brief but comprehensive inservice program for student teachers and interns as they are assigned to your building. Make sure that they understand the preceding suggested guideline and that failure to follow rules, regulations, policies, and procedures may result in termination of their student teaching assignment. Point out that, if a student is injured due to improper actions or inactions on the part of a student teacher, the student teacher can be held liable along with the cooperating teacher, the principal, the district's superintendent, the school board, and the university.

SECTION C: TEACHER BEHAVIORS

The legal obligation that suggests that a teacher serve as an exemplar or role model for students rests in the belief that students, in part, acquire their social attitudes and other important behaviors by replicating those of their teachers. As early as 1885, courts accepted this assumption as "self-evident fact." If it is accepted theory that the examples set by teachers and others in the education enterprise affect students, then a determination must still be made concerning what personal conduct is permissible and what may not be permissible and warrants disciplinary or employment action. Standards of acceptable behavior vary widely from community to community and constantly change over time.

Courts have consistently ruled that when educators subscribe to personal habits or behaviors that may be contrary to currently accepted norms, they can place their positions at risk. The courts have agreed that no amount of standardization of teaching materials or lesson plans can eliminate the *personal qualities* teachers bring to the learning environment. Furthermore, educators serve as *role models* for their students, exerting a subtle but important influence over students' perceptions and values. Through both the presentation of course materials and the examples they set, educators have the opportunity to influence the attitude of students toward government, the political process, and a citizen's social responsibilities. The courts are in agreement that this influence—this exemplar status—is critical to the continued good health of a democracy.

Because public schools are perceived as having the moral development of the child as one of their primary goals, society has historically seen teachers as guardians of community morals and expected them to conduct their personal lives accordingly. Society's desire to ensure the highest level of moral excellence often takes statutory or contractual form.

General cultural values are commonly accepted by the majority of a society. Such values, often referred to as the core value system, are generally well defined, traditional, and relatively stable. Society expects school districts to support and preserve the traditional values inherent in the core of society. However, teachers may, just as other members of society may, elect to adopt patterns, values, and ideals that are considered alternatives to the traditional or core values. In this event, when the issue of individual freedom versus institutional responsibility is in dispute, termination is often the result.

FOCUS POINT: Teacher Behavior—The Concept of Nexus

Due process requires that the dismissal of a teacher or other limitation of property or liberty be justified by demonstration of a rational nexus between the proscribed activity and a serious limitation of the education process. A nexus is commonly defined in teacher employment issues as a connection or link between personal conduct and fitness to teach. Considerations in determining whether or not a nexus exists often include the following:

- The likelihood that the conduct has or may adversely affect students or fellow teachers
- The degree of such adversity now or anticipated
- The proximity or remoteness in time of the conduct
- Extenuating or aggravating circumstances, if any, surrounding the conduct
- The praiseworthiness or blameworthiness of the motives resulting in the conduct
- The extent to which disciplinary action may cause an adverse impact or chilling effect on the constitutional rights of the teacher

Examples of Management Cues

- A teacher is a male stripper in a club in another city almost 60 miles away. A parent of a student finds this out when she and a group of friends go to the club to celebrate a 40th birthday. The parent shares her discovery with some of her neighborhood friends, and the information quickly reaches students in the teacher's class. As a direct result of this incident concerning the teacher's other job, students in his classes start to behave in a way that makes maintaining decorum difficult for the teacher; student grades drop, and a number of parents complain. Some want their children assigned to another teacher as a result of what they have heard.
- A fourth-grade teacher who chooses to live in the community in which she teaches is observed by a parent buying a six-pack of beer along with other groceries at the local grocery store.

Suggested Risk Management Guideline

- Be aware of one's own conduct and remind faculty and staff regularly that, although not usually explicitly outlined in contract form, if their private lives interfere with their professional lives and this results in a classroom or school problem, their jobs may well be jeopardized.

FOCUS POINT: Teacher Behavior—The Concept of Privacy

Teachers have a constitutional right to privacy, and discipline or dismissal for personal conduct outside of the school and in their private life may encroach on that right. Because of the uncertainty concerning the definition and amplitude of privacy rights, as well as their inexplicit constitutional basis, court decisions provide an inconsistent pattern or basis on which to use privacy rights as a defense against violations of a teacher's right to employment.

The courts have, however, tended to agree on several points of law. Courts have ruled that the conduct of an educator's private life must be just that: private. They hold that there exists not only an educator's right to privacy but also an educator's duty of privacy. As a result, it appears that the educator's duty to maintain privacy within the school environment is absolute. If school employees value their privacy and their positions as educators, allowing their private lives to become public is a choice that may bear consequences.

In addition, a nexus must be evident between educators' private acts and their work in the school, in order for these private acts to have any bearing on their employment. If a nexus cannot be shown—that is, that something in the educator's private life has reduced the educator's ability to maintain discipline, present curriculum, or in some other way, perform his or her professional duties—then actions in the educator's private life may not be usable in a disciplinary or termination proceeding.

Courts have also agreed that idle speculation is usually considered to be an infringement on one's private life. Although a school board can inquire into the character, integrity, and personal life of its employees, reprimands or dismissals must be based on supported facts that are neither arbitrary nor capricious.

Example of a Management Cue

- A teacher is dismissed because of off-campus behavior judged to be "conduct unbecoming a teacher." The teacher in question works as a cocktail waitress in a local club that a number of parents patronize. These parents urge her dismissal, noting that her uniform often draws suggestive remarks from some of the club's male patrons. The district is concerned that her conduct will be injurious to her ability to function in the classroom. On the other hand, the teacher believes that the district's conduct toward her is based on idle speculation and that it is arbitrary and capricious and infringes on her private life.

Suggested Risk Management Guideline

- Practice diligence in this area to protect yourself and your faculty and staff. Remind employees often that their private lives must be just that—private. Remind employees how easy it is for their private lives to interfere with their ability to teach and gain the respect of students and parents.

FOCUS POINT: Teacher Behavior—Freedom of Speech in Evaluation and Other Teacher and Principal Matters

In the day-to-day proceedings of school operations and, particularly, during an evaluation conference between a teacher and a principal, it is likely that a variety of comments will be exchanged between the parties. Such private expressions can result in legal problems if they are used as a substantial basis for an adverse employment decision. The U.S. Supreme Court stated, in *Givhan v. Western Line Consolidated School District* (1979), that private expressions of a teacher's views to a principal are constitutionally protected. The Court noted, however, that a teacher's expression of disagreement with superiors may be subject to reasonable time, place, and manner, to prevent the disruption of day-to-day school activities. In addition, the Court held, in *Eckerd v. Indian River School District* (1979), that speech, unless it can be documented as disruptive of day-to-day school activities, cannot be the substantial or motivating factor in a board's decision to terminate a teacher and that the teacher-principal relationship does not require maintenance of personal loyalty and confidence.

Example of a Management Cue

- In a closed-door evaluation conference with his principal, a teacher demonstrates anger at his unsatisfactory evaluation. The teacher states, "I think the superintendent and the board are all dumb bastards, and I think that you are a prostitute to their rules. As a matter of fact," he continues, "you probably slept with all of them to get your job."

Suggested Risk Management Guidelines

- Remember that your staff is not obligated to like you or be loyal to you. They are, however, required to follow your reasonable directions.
- Treat all comments teachers make to you in private conversation with confidentiality, but remind all staff members that although they are entitled to their opinions, they are obligated to follow and support the policies, regulations, and rules set by the board of education, the office of the superintendent, and the principal.

❙ FOCUS POINT: Teacher Behavior—Incompetence

Teachers who continue to perform poorly in the classroom or to demonstrate an inability to follow standard operating procedures after reasonable assistance has been given should be nonrenewed or terminated. However, *incompetence*, the general term used to cover a variety of performance problems, needs clarification before it can safely be used as grounds for dismissal. The courts alone decide what constitutes incompetence after considering all the particular facts of each case. Although the courts have given broad interpretation to the term, incompetence is generally defined as a lack of physical, intellectual, or moral ability; insufficiency; inadequacy; or specific lack of legal qualifications or fitness. School boards have offered a wide variety of reasons to substantiate charges of incompetence, and the courts have generally found that the following conduct is sufficient to sustain dismissals based on incompetence:

- Excessive tardiness and absence during the school year with no excuse
- Lack of classroom management, control, or discipline, including unreasonable discipline
- Failure to provide expected leadership as described in a job description
- Lack of knowledge necessary for competent instruction and inability to convey such knowledge effectively
- Refusal of a teacher to allow supervisory personnel to enter the teacher's classroom
- Willful neglect of duty

Some specific examples may help to clarify the concept of incompetence. In one instance, a school board cancelled the contract of a teacher with 14 years of experience on the basis of incompetence and insubordination. Evidence presented at the hearing showed that the teacher willfully refused to follow reasonable rules and regulations, refused to follow grading procedures, engaged in several heated discussions with the supervisor, and blatantly refused to submit to the supervisor's authority. The court, in *Aaron v. Alabama State Tenure Commission* (1981), found the evidence sufficient to support the conclusion that the teacher was *both* incompetent and insubordinate. Among the reasons used by another school board to dismiss a teacher for incompetence were excessive lateness, negligent conduct that resulted in a minor classroom fire, and instructional deficiencies *(Levyn v. Amback,* 1981).

Some school boards have used the results of student grades or student scores on standardized achievement tests as a means to justify a charge of incompetence on the part of a teacher *(Scheelhasse v. Woodbury Central School District,* 1973). The Eighth Circuit Court of Appeals, in *Karstetter v. Evans* (1971), reversed a federal district court in Iowa and held that the use of student scores on standardized achievement tests was a lawful reason for a school board to consider in making a decision not to renew a teacher. In similar cases, federal courts have ruled that a teacher's procedural due process rights were not violated when the school board introduced the low achievement of the teacher's students as evidence. It is important to note that the courts have consistently held that a teacher's competence or incompetence must be measured by the same standards required of other teachers as demonstrated by yearly evaluations. In other words, a teacher's performance is not measured in a vacuum or against a standard of perfection but is measured against the *standard* required of others performing the same or similar duties.

Examples of Management Cues

- An irate parent confronts a principal with a demand that his son's teacher be fired. The teacher, an experienced and well-liked teacher, accidentally showed an R-rated movie, *Green Meadows*, to his fifth-grade class. When the teacher picked up the movie at a video rental store, he did not see the R rating on the movie's package and assumed that it would be similar to the G-rated *Green Meadows* TV series. The teacher was grading papers while the film was running and did not notice its violence and brief nude scene. (Note: In a common follow-up scenario, the parent demands dismissal for incompetence, and the principal attempts to assure the parent that the teacher will be reprimanded but not fired for his *unintentional* act.)
- A tenured seventh-grade English teacher appeals her termination, claiming that her due process rights were not followed. She is dismissed for incompetence when the school district confronts her with the following facts supported by evidence:
  - She prepared unsatisfactory and illegible daily lesson plans, inadequately evaluated the performance of students, and employed deficient instructional techniques.
  - In the three-year period preceding her dismissal, seven separate and independent classroom observations had been made, with each observer concurring in the identification of her teaching deficiencies and in the need for corrective action.
  - The observers each issued a directive to the teacher requiring improvement in her performance with advisement that her employment could be in jeopardy if she did not succeed in demonstrating improvement in identified areas.
  - Her principal had attempted to provide assistance but the teacher had refused help.

Suggested Risk Management Guidelines

- Develop and follow strict guidelines to document an employee's poor performance. In addition, be able to demonstrate that you gave the employee time, opportunity, and counseling to improve or correct performance.

Aside from creating a favorable impression for the defendant school district, such evidence also demonstrates that the stated rationale for the termination (incompetence) is not a pretext for a hidden, illegal reason.

- Develop and publicize guidelines that clearly delineate incompetence as a part of the formal evaluation procedure and that make clear that incompetence, when documented, is grounds for dismissal.
- Apply the same standards to the evaluation of all teachers and staff.

▌ FOCUS POINT: Teacher Behavior—Insubordination

Insubordination generally refers (a) to the failure of an employee to submit to the reasonable and lawful authority of a superior or (b) to an employee's willful disregard of express or implied directions of the employer and a refusal to obey reasonable orders. This is the most common and simplistic rationale advanced by school officials in dismissal cases based on insubordination. However, insubordination cannot be judged in the abstract. It must be supported by specific facts before a dismissal will be upheld by the courts. As with all other reasons for termination, specific evidence is necessary to substantiate a charge of insubordination. The courts have generally agreed that school employees are insubordinate when they *willfully refuse to obey a reasonable and lawful order given by a superior* or one who has the authority to give such orders.

Charges of insubordination are generally *not supportable* in court actions if

- The alleged conduct was not proved
- The existence of a pertinent school rule or a supervisor's order was not proved
- The pertinent rule or order was not violated
- The teacher or employee tried, although unsuccessfully, to comply with the rule or order
- The teacher's or employee's motive for violating the rule or order was admirable
- No harm resulted from the violation
- The rule or order was unreasonable
- The rule or order was beyond the authority of its maker
- The enforcement of the rule or order revealed possible bias or discrimination against the teacher or employee
- The enforcement of the rule or order violated First Amendment or other constitutional rights
- The rule or order was unlawful

Examples of Management Cues

- A teacher, concerned that she is losing her tan, wants to take a week off in January to go to Jamaica. Although her request for a leave of absence is denied by the principal and the board of education, the teacher goes anyway.

- A principal has been an elementary school principal in the same district for 15 years. Two years ago, his son left on a two-year mission abroad. At that time, the principal and father made a commitment to his son that at the conclusion of his mission, he would join his son in Europe and accompany him home. He planned to use 10 of his 40 accumulated leave days for the trip. Before his scheduled departure, however, the school district changed its leave policy and limited administrators' use of earned leave to "no more than 5 school days per year, or 2 days in succession, except in cases of emergency." The principal's request for leave is denied, but he completes the trip as planned.
- A tenured teacher fails to inform the board whether or not she will accept employment for the next year. The teacher has requested and been granted a one-year leave of absence for the current school year. Prior to the next year, the teacher applied for an extension of leave for the upcoming school year, but her application was denied. School officials set a date for the teacher to inform the district of intentions for the ensuing year. The deadline passes, and the teacher fails to notify the school district whether she will teach in the coming year.

Suggested Risk Management Guideline

- Ensure that specific evidence and documentation collected provide sufficient grounds for termination for insubordination.

| FOCUS POINT: Teacher Behavior—Immoral Conduct

Because it is generally believed that the character of the teacher is of fundamental importance in children's development, school boards feel that they can demand that teachers conform to the boards' interpretations of community values. Teachers who adopt values that conflict with the mores of their communities' school boards are likely to place their teaching positions at risk. The key question is not whether or not teacher actions are immoral but whether or not they negatively affect the education process in a particular school district in a particular location.

Immorality, moral turpitude, unfitness to teach, conduct unbecoming a teacher, teacher misconduct, violation of a code of ethics, and subversive activity are common statutory grounds for the dismissal of a teacher when community values conflict with teacher values or lifestyles.

School districts that attempt to develop guidelines in this area quickly find that court definitions of immorality tend to be left to communities to determine, and the courts' decisions generally reflect core values. To make the development or recommendation of definitive guidelines even more difficult, the courts modify their definitions as societal values change. What was once cause for dismissal as an immoral act may later be seen as acceptable behavior.

Immorality is a value-laden word that is defined in a subjective manner. Behavior that does not conform to the established norm is defined as deviant.

Deviant behavior of school personnel inside or outside of the school may be cited as cause for dismissal.

The following is an overview of legal tenets generally followed by the courts with regard to questions of teacher immorality.

- The conduct of a teacher or any public employee outside the job may be examined, but disciplinary action against the employee based on that conduct is proper *only* where there is a proven rational nexus between the conduct and the duties to be performed.
- Courts have ruled that the conduct of a teacher's private life must be just that: private. They hold that not only do teachers have a right to privacy but they also have a duty to keep their private lives private.
- The conduct of a teacher or any other public employee ceases to be private in at least two circumstances: when the conduct directly affects the performance of the occupational responsibilities of the employee, and when, without contribution on the part of the school officials, the conduct has become the subject of such notoriety as to significantly and reasonably impair the capability of the particular teacher or other employee to discharge the responsibilities of the teaching or other public position.
- The courts demand proof that a teacher's private, personal actions directly affected the teacher's classroom performance, relationship with students, and overall teaching effectiveness. Without such proof, a court would likely say that, at most, the evidence may raise a question regarding the teacher's good judgment in personal affairs.
- The courts have approved inquiries by boards of education into the personal associations of teachers, and school boards may legitimately scrutinize teachers about any matters that might have an adverse effect on students as demonstrated by a direct nexus between the teacher's out-of-school behavior and the teacher's effectiveness in the classroom.
- Unconventional sexual behavior does not, according to judgments in a number of cases nationwide, indicate unfitness to teach, and a clear relationship must be shown between the conduct of a teacher and the teacher's job performance and effectiveness.

Examples of Management Cues

- After an overnight senior class trip, an English teacher at the high school is accused of sexual misconduct by a group of parents who report that she held hands with and hugged a male student in the presence of other students.
- A high school teacher is criticized by a group of parents for "lack of good moral character." The parents allege that this teacher lives with her boyfriend and that this "negatively affects her students." The teacher

admits that during a brief period of time, while her apartment was being renovated, she stayed with a male friend.

- The parent of a 10-year-old fifth-grade girl alleges to the principal that a counselor at the school has taken improper, immoral actions and indecent liberties with her daughter, who was referred to him because she was failing all her subjects and her parents had failed to respond to deficiency notices. The parent is upset with the fact that the counselor allegedly met with her daughter in his office on four occasions, and she accuses the counselor of showing more than professional interest in her daughter.

- Parents complain to a principal about a particular female kindergarten teacher's style of dress, which they consider to be "too masculine." They state that they have "heard rumors about her sexuality" and provide him with an article from a church-related publication that says a school district may use "public reputation in the community" to establish a teacher's homosexuality and that it may dismiss a reputed homosexual teacher for "immorality." Based on the complaints and rumors, the principal decides not to recommend renewal of the teacher's tenure contract.

- Two male teachers in the local school district are fired for immoral conduct after two female students testify at a grand jury hearing that they "smoked pot" at the teachers' apartment. The jury forwards charges against both teachers for unlawful transactions with a minor. The teachers plead guilty to this misdemeanor and are subsequently terminated by the school district. The attorney for the two teachers appeals their dismissal to the board of education, claiming that
  - His clients could not be dismissed for an act committed during off-duty hours in the summer and in the privacy of their own apartment.
  - The board was holding his clients to a higher standard of personal conduct than was warranted under the misdemeanor committed.
  - His clients' misdemeanor act was not likely to leave a harmful impression on their students in the school setting.
  - There is no direct connection (nexus) between his clients' conduct and their work as teachers.

Suggested Risk Management Guidelines

- Before taking any action regarding a question of a teacher's alleged immorality, gather all the available facts and determine whether you can prove that the alleged behavior had a negative effect on the teacher's effectiveness and whether you can demonstrate a nexus between the behavior and the disruption of the education process.
- Remember that a clear relationship *must be shown* between the conduct of a teacher and the teacher's job performance and effectiveness.

FOCUS POINT: Teacher Behavior—Other Causes for Dismissal

In addition to the more common causes for dismissal discussed above, school officials have cited many other reasons to support dismissal actions against their employees. In addition to negligence, incompetence, or insubordination, case law reveals such rationales as failure to attend required institutes, inefficiency, disloyalty, conviction of specified crimes, alcohol or substance abuse, selling drugs, cruelty, public lewdness, and alternative lifestyle choice.

Some state statutes provide for a general category of reasons for dismissal under the cover of *just* or *good cause* or *conduct unbecoming a teacher* (unprofessional conduct). This umbrella approach allows school boards to dismiss employees for a great variety of activities. Because it would be impossible for a state legislature to delineate all possible reasons to justify a dismissal, legislators in such states believe that it is necessary for school boards to have some flexibility in which to apply employment functions. Not all states allow the use of just cause because of its broadness in interpretation. Where applicable, just cause is generally defined as a cause that bears a reasonable relationship to a teacher's unfitness to discharge the duties assigned or is in a reasonable sense detrimental to the students being taught. In states that do not allow this procedure, individual acts and specific causes must be clustered under terms such as *insubordination, incompetence,* or *neglect of duty.* Hypothetical examples include these:

- A teacher is dismissed for failure to administer an individualized education program (IEP) (neglect of duty).
- A teacher is dismissed for use of the words *damn* and *hell* at various times in the classroom, allowing students to play noneducational games, slapping one student and pulling the hair of another, flogging a male student, pulling a female student out of the girls' bathroom and kicking her, and permitting students to settle disputes by fighting. This situation probably finds its best fit under the law in the category of neglect of duty. However, if the teacher has been repeatedly told not to do these things, then insubordination (a willful disregard of express or implied directions) might add weight to the charge of neglect of duty. On the other hand, what about conduct prejudicial to the operation of the school system and incompetent services?
- A teacher is dismissed for excessive lateness (neglect of duty).
- Persistent negligence might be the cause justified by charges that a teacher slept in class, failed to comply with the lesson plan policy, inadequately prepared IEPs, and taught subjects inconsistent with the IEPs the teacher had prepared.
- A teacher is dismissed for failure to cooperate in solving school problems (neglect of duty).

Some dismissal cases take on constitutional dimensions when teachers allege a violation of a protected right. In such cases, the court must balance the constitutional rights of the individual teacher with the needs and interests of school authorities to maintain employee discipline, order, and proper supervision of public schools.

Examples of Management Cues

- A high school industrial arts instructor is a hobbyist gunsmith. He inadvertently leaves a revolver and some ammunition in the pocket of his jacket when he hangs it in his classroom. The jacket is stolen but is later recovered in a restroom. Later the same day, the gun and ammunition are found in the bushes close to the student parking lot.
- A nontenured but well-qualified teacher is plagued by chronic illness. The teacher is nonrenewed; the explanation cites "good cause" for excessive absences. The teacher has missed 21 days during the school year. The principal reports that the absences have a reasonable relationship to his unfitness to discharge the duties assigned and that his absences are detrimental to students.
- A teacher has taught in the same school district and in the same school for 36 years. She knows the board policy that teachers are to administer corporal punishment only by "blows to the child's posterior in the presence of the principal or principal's designee." She has worked with 10 different principals during her years at the school, and she has always tried hard to obey her principal's wishes. During the year in which she is fired for insubordination, her principal is a young man who has been sent there to correct discipline problems that got out of hand under the preceding principal. Her new principal told teachers at the beginning of the school year that if any of them had a discipline problem with children, "bop them in the mouth!" Her principal also prepared and distributed a handbook for teachers that is in conflict with the district's corporal punishment regulation. After the school district receives complaints from parents that the teacher struck students, she is advised that she is being terminated. Her dismissal is based on violation of the board's corporal punishment regulations. Her appeal to the school board contains these two questions: Which regulations should I have followed? If I had refused to follow the principal's regulations, would I have also placed my job in jeopardy?
- A teacher and coach is suspended because he speaks at a public meeting regarding controversy in the athletic department, and he writes to school board members detailing his ideas for restructuring the department. On his return to work after the suspension, the superintendent of his school district advises him that he will not be given further coaching duties because of his failure to submit his suggestions through proper channels.
- A nontenured classroom teacher has been involved in a series of incidents during his employment, including an argument with another teacher that ended with the teacher slapping him and the subsequent suspension of both teachers. He was also involved in an argument with employees of the school cafeteria over the amount of spaghetti that had been served to him, had referred to students as "sons of bitches," and made obscene gestures to students when they failed to obey his commands in his capacity

as cafeteria supervisor. However, the incident that leads to his nonrenewal and the subsequent claim of constitutional infringement that he presents in court is his telephone call to a local radio station during which he conveys the substance of a memorandum concerning teacher dress and appearance that the school principal has circulated to various teachers. The obscene-gesture incident is also listed as a reason for his nonrenewal. (Note: The facts in this situation are illustrative of a *mixed-motive dismissal*, that is, a dismissal based on a *legitimate, school-related reason* [obscene gesture] and, possibly, a *constitutionally impermissible reason* [freedom of speech and expression].)

Suggested Risk Management Guidelines

- Develop a format for anecdotal record keeping that allows for the quick but factual entry of information gathered in day-to-day interaction with faculty and staff. Be careful to record only facts, not opinions, developing information for due process procedures if necessary. Be sure to follow district policy regarding just cause versus specific cause.
- Be wary not to build a case for dismissal based on a reason or reasons that might be protected under the U.S. Constitution.

EXAMPLES OF LEADING U.S. SUPREME COURT CASES ON EDUCATION

Employment—Loyalty Oaths and Academic Freedom

Adler v. Board of Education

Baggett v. Builitt

Beilan v. Board of Education

Connell v. Higginbotham

Cramp v. Board of Public Instruction of Orange County

Elfbrandt v. Russell

Epperson v. Arkansas

Garner v. Los Angeles Board

Keyishian v. Board of Regents

Lochower v. Board of Education

Shelton v. Tucker

Sweezy v. New Hampshire

Whitehill v. Elkins

Wieman v. Updegraff

Employment—Termination and Tenure

Ambach v. Norwick

Carnegie-Mellon University v. Cohill

Cleveland Board of Education v. LaFleur

Cleveland Board of Education v. Loudermill

Corporation of the Presiding Bishop of the Church of Jesus Christ of Latter-Day Saints v. Amos

Delaware State College v. Ricks

Dougherty County Board of Education v. White

Franklin & Marshall College v. EEOC

Givhan v. Western Line Consolidated School District

Harrah Independent School District v. Martin

Hazelwood School District v. U.S.

Indiana ex rel. Anderson v. Brand

Mount Healthy City School District v. Doyle

North Haven Board of Education v. Bell

Ohio Civil Rights Commission v. Dayton Christian Schools

Perry v. Sindermann

Pickering v. Board of Education

Board of Regents v. Roth

Trustees of Keene State College v. Sweeney

University of Tennessee v. Elliot

Employment—Labor Relations

Abood v. Detroit Board of Education

Ansonia Board of Education v. Philbrook

Chicago Teachers Union v. Hudson

Hortonville Joint School District No. I v. Hortonville Education Association

Madison School District v. Wisconsin Employment

Minnesota State Board for Community Colleges v. Knight

NLRB v. Catholic Bishop of Chicago

NLRB v. Yeshiva University

Perry Education Association v. Perry Local Educators' Association Relations Commission

Wygant v. Jackson Board of Education

Employment—Discrimination—§ 1983

Chardon v. Fernandez

Memphis Community School District v. Stachura

Migra v. Warren City School District

Monell v. Department of Social Services

Patsy v. Board of Regents

Rendell-Baker v. Kohn

Springfield Township School District v. Knoll

St. Francis College v. Al-Khazraji

Webb v. Board of Education of Dyer County

ADDITIONAL CASES OF INTEREST TO EDUCATORS

School District Executive Functions

Aldridge v. School District of North Platte, 225 Neb. 580, 407 N.W.2d 495 (1987). Decisions prior to formal meeting.

Fremont RE-1 School District v. Jacobs, 737 P.2d 816 (Colo. 1987). Delegation of authority must be accompanied by specific standards.

Hortonville Joint School District No. 1 v. Hortonville Education Association, 426 U.S. 482, 96 S.Ct. 2308 (U.S. 1976). In the absence of bias, a school board may sit in a quasijudicial capacity in judgment of a case in which it is a party.

McGilva v. Seattle, 113 Wash. 619, 194 P.817 (1921). School districts can exercise only those powers fairly implied or expressly granted by statute.

Smith v. Dorsey, 530 So.2d 5 (Miss. 1988). Constitutional prohibition of nepotism is violated when school board enters into a teaching contract with spouse of board member.

Williams v. Augusta County School Board, 445 S.E.2d 118 (Va. 1994). Conflict of interest statutes are designed to create confidence in public entities.

CHAPTER RESOURCES

Aaron v. Alabama State Tenure Commission, 407 So.2d 136 (Ala. Ct. App. 1981).

Ct. App. Kans., No. 58353, Syllabus by the Court, April 17, 1986.

Eckerd v. Indian River School District, 475 F. Supp. 1350 (D. Del. 1979).

Givhan v. Western Line Consolidated School District, 439 U.S. 410 (1979).

Hachiya/Livingston v. U.S.D. 307, Kan. S.Ct. No. 59594, Syllabus by the Court, February 19, 1988.

Karstetter v. Evans, 3500 F. Supp. 209 (D. Tex. 1971).

Levyn v. Amback, 445 N.Y.S.2d 303 (N.Y. App. Div. 1981).

Meyer v. Nebraska, 262 U.S. 390, 399 (1923).

Scheelhasse v. Woodbury Central School District, 488 F.2d 237 (8th Cir. 1973).

Smith v. Board of Education, 708 F.2d 258 (7th Cir. 1983).

State ex rel. Hawkins v. Board of Education, 275 S.E.2d 908 (W. Va. 1980).

Swager v. Board of Education U.S.D. 412, 9 Kan. App. 648, S.Ct. 412 (1984).

6

Students' Rights

Schools, by their very nature, must encourage free inquiry and free expression of ideas. Such expression should include the personal opinions of students relevant to the subject matter being taught, school activities, services, policies, school personnel, and matters of broad social concern and interest. In expressing themselves on such issues, students have a responsibility to refrain from using defamatory, obscene, or inflammatory language and to conduct themselves in such a way as to allow others to exercise their First Amendment rights as well.

The courts have affirmed that students' free speech rights are protected by the Constitution—so long as they do not present a "clear and present danger" or threaten a "material disruption" of the education process as noted in *Gitlow v. New York* (1925) and in *Tinker v. Des Moines* (1969). In the event that students' activities *threaten the effective operation of the school*, principals are given clear authority to limit or ban students' activities.

SECTION A: STUDENTS' RIGHTS TO SYMBOLIC EXPRESSION

Symbolic expression is nonverbal expression that conveys the personal ideas, feelings, attitudes, or opinions of an individual. People exhibit symbolic expression in a variety of forms: for example, physical gesture, clothing, hairstyle, buttons, jewelry, and tattoos. Symbolic expression contains an element of subjectivity, and in determining whether or

AUTHORS' NOTE: Cases cited throughout this chapter have been selected on a precedent-setting or best-example basis regardless of jurisdiction or date of adjudication. (See Introduction for more information.)

not a form of expression is, in fact, symbolic, some consideration must be given to the intention of the persons who are expressing themselves. In West Virginia Board of Education v. Barnette *(1943), the U.S. Supreme Court heard its first freedom of expression case that involved public schools. The case was brought against a West Virginia public school system by the parents of children who refused to participate in saluting the American flag because they were Jehovah's Witnesses. Although the parents objected to this requirement as a violation of their religious beliefs, the Supreme Court decided this case on free speech grounds. The Court ruled that "the flag salute is a form of utterance. Symbolism is a primitive but effective way of communicating ideas . . . a short cut from mind to mind." Therefore, the students could not be required to salute the American flag.*

During most of the 20th century, students were routinely disciplined for engaging in expression that displeased school authorities. A major turning point in the courts' interpretation of the First Amendment occurred in the landmark case of *Tinker v. Des Moines* (1969). In this case, the U.S. Supreme Court declared that students are "persons," under the Constitution, who must be accorded all its rights and protections, especially the right to freedom of expression, and that the school board's subjective fear of some disruption was not enough to override students' rights to express their political beliefs. The Supreme Court further noted that students possess fundamental rights that schools must respect. However, a controlling principle of *Tinker* was that conduct by a student, in class or out, that for any reason disrupts class work or involves substantial disorder or invasion of the rights of others is not protected by the constitutional guarantee of freedom of speech.

Policy in the area of student expression is difficult to develop and even more difficult to defend. Assuming that rules and regulations regarding student expression have been developed and are maintained as official policy by local boards of education, individual schools may build on these policies and regulations to set standards. Such standards generally will be upheld as long as the rules are in accord with board policy and are reasonable and specific. School officials may restrict freedom of expression where there is evidence of material and substantial disruption, violation of school rules, destruction of school property, or disregard for authority. The key questions to determine whether the rules are reasonable and specific are the following:

- Does the expression targeted cause a health, safety, or disruptive hazard?
- Are the rules based on objective needs?
- Will the rules constitute an arbitrary infringement of constitutionally protected rights? (Unsubstantiated fear and apprehension of disturbance are *not* sufficient grounds to restrict the right to freedom of expression and should not be the basis for the development of standards.)

FOCUS POINT: Symbolic Expression Through Buttons, Jewelry, and So Forth

Students' rights to wear insignia, buttons, jewelry, armbands, and other symbols of political or controversial significance are firmly protected by the

Constitution and the courts. Like other student rights, this right may be forfeited when wearing such symbols causes a material disruption of the education process. A federal appeals court, in *Gusick v. Drebus* (1971), held that school authorities may establish policies regulating these activities when the rule is not arbitrary and is applied, without exception, to all insignia and not just one type of insignia. In situations in which students' insignia is unlikely to cause material disruption of the education process, courts, for example, in *Burnside v. Byars* (1966), have generally ruled that students cannot be deprived of their basic rights to express themselves.

Example of a Management Cue

- In a multicultural school, a group of students start an English Only Spoken Here club, the members of which are wearing "EO" buttons to school. Hispanic students complain to the principal.

Suggested Risk Management Guidelines

- Clearly communicate to students and parents the school policies concerning symbolic expression.
- Ensure that any actions in this area are not arbitrary, capricious, or indefensible. Prohibition of a particular form of expression requires more than a desire to avoid the unpleasantness associated with an unpopular view.
- Buttons, pamphlets, and other insignia may be prohibited if the message they communicate is vulgar, obscene, or ridicules others based on race, origin, color, sex, or religion, or when their content is clearly and defensibly inconsistent with the basic mission of the school.
- School officials may regulate the time and place of the distribution of administratively approved pamphlets, buttons, and insignia.

FOCUS POINT: Symbolic Expression Through Dress and Hairstyle

Many schools have grooming policies intended to improve school discipline and bring order to the classroom environment. Among the items prohibited by various school dress codes have been articles of clothing associated with gang activities, shorts, tight or immodest clothing, undergarments worn outside of clothes, sweat pants and jogging suits, torn clothing, baggy pants, nightclothes, muscle shirts, halter tops, open-back blouses, and fur coats. Although some of these items of dress have been banned as a matter of taste, others have been outlawed to protect the students from becoming the victims of theft or violence. Some school districts, concerned about the expense of the clothing students consider to be "in," adopt uniforms for all students. The courts have not always agreed regarding the authority schools have to control students' appearance. A federal court of appeals, in *Richards v. Thurston* (1970), ruled against a school dress policy, deeming that it was not a justifiable part of the education process. The next year, another federal court, in *Smith v. Tammany Parish School Board* (1971), upheld the right of elementary and secondary schools to promulgate dress codes. The majority of decisions, including *Karr v. Schmidt* (1972), have recognized a constitutional protection for students to regulate their own appearance within the bounds and standards of common decency and modesty. Students have a constitutional right to wear clothing of their own choice, as long as their clothing is neat and clean and does not cause a material disruption of the education process. To be constitutional, a dress code must be reasonably related to the school's responsibility or its curriculum. The courts have tended to distinguish hairstyles from clothing and have indicated that restrictions on hairstyles are more serious invasions of individual freedom than are clothing regulations. However, courts do give schools wide discretion to regulate appearance in the interests of health, safety, order, or discipline.

Examples of Management Cues

- A student who is a member of a punk rock band dyes and spikes his hair. He claims it is part of the band's image—pink and purple. His appearance draws a lot of attention wherever he goes.
- Female students file a petition claiming they are being discriminated against on the basis of their gender because boys may wear cutoff T-shirts to school, but they may not wear tank tops.

Suggested Risk Management Guidelines

- Involve all interested parties, that is, faculty, staff, students, and parents, in the development of school site dress codes.
- In developing and implementing a dress code, keep in mind the following points:
  - Reasonable dress codes will be supported by the courts. Dress codes based solely on taste, style, and fashion rather than health, safety, order, and decency may be considered unreasonable by the courts.
  - Gang-related dress may be banned by school officials.
  - Dress that is considered offensive or that ridicules others on the basis of race, gender, religion, or national origin may be prohibited.

FOCUS POINT: Symbolic Expression Through Physical Gestures

Most people are familiar with a variety of physical gestures used by groups or individuals to express an idea, concept, opinion, or contempt. Although most would agree that obscene, disrespectful, or obviously annoying gestures should be banned from schools, from a policy context they should be viewed on the basis of the degree to which such gestures impinge on the rights of others and their likelihood of creating substantial disruption.

Examples of Management Cues

- A student gives a substitute teacher the finger.
- After being reprimanded by a teacher for a simple infraction, the student flashes the teacher a peace sign.

Suggested Risk Management Guidelines

- Involve faculty, students, parents, and citizens in the formulation of policies regarding physical gestures and obtain the approval of the board of education.
- In developing and implementing such policies, keep in mind that

  - Physical gestures that do not conform to the basics of decency may be regulated.
  - Physical gestures related to gang activity may be banned by school officials.
  - Physical gestures that are considered vulgar or that ridicule others on the basis of race, gender, religion, color, or national origin may be prohibited.

FOCUS POINT: Symbolic Expression Through School Mascots

With the changing awareness of the importance of symbols in communicating values, a number of school districts have found their mascots the targets of community attacks. For example, in *Crosby v. Holsinger* (1988), the principal of a Virginia high school decided to discontinue the use of a cartoon figure named Johnny Reb as the school's mascot because of complaints that it offended black students. A group of students protested the principal's decision as a violation of their First Amendment rights. Although the lower court ruled in favor of the students who wished to retain Johnny Reb as their mascot, a federal appeals court ruled in favor of the principal. The appeals court recognized that school officials need not sponsor or promote all student speech, and that because a school mascot may be interpreted as bearing the school's stamp of approval, the principal was justified in mandating a change that would not offend a segment of the student population.

Example of a Management Cue

- The school's mascot is the Red Raider, and before each athletic event, a student dresses up like an American Indian, paints his face with war paint, and performs a characterization of an Indian war dance. For the past two years, Native American students have protested this characterization, and the American Civil Liberties Union has joined with these students. A poll of the community indicates that 80 percent of the citizens want to keep the Red Raider as the mascot.

Suggested Risk Management Guideline

- Understand that mascots, school symbols, and so forth that target or ridicule a group on the basis of race, gender, religion, or national origin may be prohibited regardless of historic background.

FOCUS POINT: Symbolic Expression Through Gang-Related Regalia and Behaviors—Related Issue: Cults and Satanism

Many communities have seen an increase in gang activity that has caused substantial interference with school programs and activities. Because students announce their membership in a gang by wearing certain colors or emblems, students in some communities in which gang activity has increased have responded by wearing only neutral colors. Many school administrators have revised their student dress code policies to prohibit the wearing of gang colors or emblems. In doing so, these administrators have reraised the legal questions regarding whether students have the right to choose their own dress styles and whether schools can limit that right. Those school districts that have adopted rules prohibiting the wearing of gang symbols and jewelry believe that the presence of gangs and gang activities threaten a substantial disruption of the schools' programs.

In a suit challenging the constitutionality of an antigang policy, a high school student claimed that the policy violated his right of free speech under the First Amendment and his right to equal protection under the Fourteenth Amendment. The court, in *Olsen v. Board of Education of School District 228, Cook County, Illinois* (1987), affirmed the district's right to enforce the dress code, saying that school boards have the responsibility to teach not only academic subjects but also the role of young men and women in a democratic society. It went on to say that students are expected to learn that in our society, individual rights must be balanced with the rights of others. The court's decision indicated that the First Amendment does not necessarily protect an individual's appearance from all regulation. When gang activities endanger the education process and safety of students, schools have the right to regulate students' dress and actions during school hours and on school grounds.

Related Issue—Cults and Satanism

Teachers and parents continue to be concerned about children wearing T-shirts to school that advertise heavy metal music and listening to music groups that, some believe, espouse satanic activity. Many people are concerned that some of this music condones murder, rape, sacrifice to Satan, and suicide, and they have expressed a fear that teenagers may turn these lyrics into a belief system. Others see these activities as simply another fad in the tradition of beatniks, surf bums, flower children, urban cowboys, break-dancers, rappers, and punk rockers. Principals have a dual duty: to protect the rights of the entire student body *and* to protect individual students' rights. These often contradictory roles become increasingly polarized as principals attempt to cope in this area.

In its least objectionable form, teen preoccupation with the occult amounts to little more than a fondness for ripped black T-shirts and heavy metal recordings. At the extreme, however, satanism practiced by teenagers may take on all the trappings of an ancient religion. Some students have become deeply involved in a variety of rituals and perceive themselves as religiously committed to a cult. Still others seem to be passively allowing the influence of their peers to dictate their behavior.

Vagueness

Regulations in the areas of gangs, cults, and so forth must be specific. Courts have found some districts' policies unconstitutionally vague. One court, in *Stephenson v. Davenport Community School District* (1997), held that the absence of important definitions for terms, including *gang*, provided administrators with too much discretion in determining how to *define* a symbol. As a result, the school district's rules did not adequately define those terms that would alert students and others to prohibited symbols.

Examples of Management Cues

- A parent calls the school to express a concern about gang activity at the school. "In fact," he comments, "my daughter won't wear red or blue hair ribbons or clothes because she's afraid she'll be hassled. I gather that one gang wears red neck scarves and the other wears blue. Wearing the wrong color may be enough to invite violence."
- A teacher at the high school reports to the principal that on his drive to school that morning, he noticed that the typical graffiti on the bridges and culverts he passed, such as "Jesus loves you," "Elvis lives," and "Mary loves John," had been replaced by drawings of pentagrams, upside-down crosses, swastikas, hexagrams, and various configurations of the numbers *666* and the letters *fff*. The teacher reports that he recently saw similar drawings on students' notebooks and backpacks.

Suggested Risk Management Guidelines

- Keep current on gang and cult activity in the community and in neighboring schools. Work with local police community liaisons to train faculty and staff to recognize signs of gang and cult activity.
- The *Olsen* court and others have generally suggested the following wording for antigang and anticult policy:

No student on or about school property or at any school activity may

- Wear, possess, distribute, display, or sell any clothing, jewelry, emblem, badge, symbol, sign, or any other item that is evidence of membership or affiliation in a gang or cult
- Commit any act or omission or use any speech, either verbal or non-verbal (gestures, handshakes, etc.), showing membership or affiliation in a gang or cult
- Use any speech or commit any act or omission in furtherance of the interests or activities of any gang or cult, including but not limited to

    o Soliciting others for membership in a gang
    o Requesting any person to pay protection or otherwise intimidating or threatening any person
    o Committing any other illegal act or other violation of school district policies
    o Inciting other students to act with physical violence toward any other person

SECTION B: STUDENTS' RIGHTS TO ORAL AND WRITTEN EXPRESSION

Students' rights to exercise freedom of expression in the school environment have undergone several major transformations. Court decisions upholding schools' rights to set certain limits on student speech reflect a changing interpretation of the First Amendment. Historically, there has been disagreement over the way this amendment should be applied. Some believe that the First Amendment was written primarily to protect citizens from being punished for political dissent. Others take the broader view that the First Amendment extends protection to all expression except overt, antisocial, physical behavior. Oliver Wendell Holmes's "clear and present danger" doctrine, as declared in Gitlow v. New York *(1925), states that speech loses its First Amendment protection when it conflicts with other important social interests. Even proponents of a "full protection" theory of freedom of speech set limits on speech. For example, obscene telephone calls, threatening gestures, disruptive heckling, and sit-ins have been classified as "actions" rather than protected expression.*

| FOCUS POINT: Expression Through Students' Oral Communication

The Supreme Court has relied primarily on two tests to determine whether schools may control freedom of speech or expression. The first is the "clear and present danger" doctrine handed down through *Gitlow*. The second is the "material and substantial disruption" doctrine that derives from the *Tinker* decision. More recent courts have expanded the rationale for schools to limit students' freedom of speech when obscenity is involved. In one case, a student was suspended for delivering a speech nominating another student for elective office and including a graphic sexual metaphor. Two teachers had warned the student not to deliver the speech, but he proceeded to do so anyway. The student brought suit on First and Fourteenth Amendment grounds. The Court, in *Bethel School District No. 403 v. Fraser* (1986), said that although students have the right to advocate unpopular and controversial rules in school, that right must be balanced against the school's interest in teaching socially appropriate behavior. The Court observed that such standards would be difficult to enforce in a school that tolerated the "lewd, indecent and offensive" speech and conduct that the student in this case exhibited.

Examples of Management Cues

- A teacher tells a student to stop "trying to cause trouble," and the student responds by calling him a "Nazi."
- After being told they may not ride the school bus for a week because of a fight they started on the ride home the preceding day, two seventh graders find their bus driver at dismissal time and cuss him out.

Suggested Risk Management Guidelines

- Do not tolerate language that is lewd, indecent, or offensive. Work to balance the values of the community with any policies the school develops toward students' oral expression.
- Ensure that any acts by school officials to censor student expression are reasonable in light of the forum in which the suspect oral communication is expressed.

FOCUS POINT: Expression Through Students' Written Communication

Student journalists have the same rights and responsibilities as any other journalists. Limits are placed on what adult journalists can write, and consequences are prescribed for, for example, copyright infringement and plagiarism, false advertising and the advertising of illegal products, inflammatory literature, obscenity, libel, invasion of privacy, fraud, and threats. Unlike regular newspapers and magazines, school newspapers are considered to be nonpublic forums and are thus subject to reasonableness-based censorship by school officials.

Just as the right of students to express themselves orally has undergone recent modification, their right to freedom of written expression has also been modified, most notably in the landmark case of *Hazelwood School District v. Kuhlmeier* (1988). The *Hazelwood* case involved a principal who deleted two full pages from the student newspaper produced in the journalism class. In his view, the deleted pages contained two "objectionable" articles that he characterized as "inappropriate, personal, sensitive and unsuitable." The court held that the First Amendment does not prevent educators from exercising editorial control over the style and content of school-sponsored student newspapers. The court reasoned that high school papers published by journalism classes do not qualify as "a public forum" open to indiscriminate use but one "reserved . . . for its intended purpose as a supervised learning experience for journalism students." School officials, therefore, retain the right to impose reasonable restrictions of student speech in those papers, and the principal, in this case, did not violate students' speech rights.

The "public forum doctrine" was designed to balance the right of an individual to speak in public places with the government's right to preserve those places for their intended purposes. Although there is considerable doctrinal conflict in recent public forum cases, the *Hazelwood* court placed school-sponsored activities in the middle ground of a "limited public forum." Although speech cannot be regulated in a public forum, it can be regulated in a nonpublic forum, and school-sponsored speech may be regulated if there is a compelling reason.

The court also drew a "two-tiered scheme of protection of student expression; one for personal speech, and the other for education-related speech." According to the *Hazelwood* decision, personal speech, of the type discussed in *Tinker,* is still protected by a strict scrutiny under the material and substantial disruption standard. However, speech that is curriculum related, whether in a class, an assembly, a newspaper, or a play, may be regulated. Such speech is protected only by a much less stringent standard of reasonableness.

Advertisements in Student Newspapers

Many schools permit students to solicit advertisements to be placed in school-sponsored publications. Problems can arise when school authorities determine that the content of an advertisement is inappropriate for a school paper. A federal court, in *Williams v. Spencer* (1980), found that protecting students from unhealthful activities was a valid reason to justify the deletion of a paid advertisement for drug paraphernalia in a student newspaper. The court affirmed the right of the school to prevent any conduct on school grounds that endangers the health and safety of students and upheld the prior restraint of material that encouraged actions that might endanger students' health or safety. Based on this decision, schools may restrict advertisements that promote unhealthy or dangerous products or activities. Schools have also been concerned about advertisements that promote controversial points of view. A court, in *San Diego Committee against Registration and the Draft v. Governing Board of Grossmont Union High School District* (1986), ruled that a school board cannot, without a compelling interest, exclude speech simply because the board disagrees with the content. Specifically, the school board cannot allow the presentation of one side of an issue but prohibit the presentation of another viewpoint. Because a school newspaper is clearly identified as part of the curriculum rather than a public forum, the school has greater latitude in regulating advertisements.

Non-School-Sponsored Publications

Courts that have supported schools' rights to regulate student newspapers have made a distinction between off-campus and on-campus publications. Courts, for example, in *Thomas v. Board of Education* (1979), have generally held that school authority is limited to school grounds, and school officials do not have the power to discipline students for distributing underground newspapers off campus.

However, some of the rules that apply to sponsored publications also apply to unofficial student publications. Unofficial publications must not interfere with the normal operation of the school and must not be obscene or libelous. Although students have the right to express themselves, schools retain the right to regulate the distribution of materials to protect the welfare of other students.

Prior Restraint

Prior restraint is generally defined as official government obstruction of speech prior to its utterance. As agents of the state, school districts or their agents may not exercise prior restraint unless the content of the publication

- Would result in substantial disruption of the education process
- Is judged to be obscene or pornographic
- Libels school officials or others
- Invades the privacy of others

Courts have ruled that a school board is not required to wait until the distribution of a publication takes place to determine whether any of these criteria have been met. Schools have the right to establish rules on prior review procedures as well as standards regulating the times, places, and manner of distribution of student publications. If a school chooses to establish rules that govern the distribution of student publications, these rules must be reasonable and relate directly to the prevention of disruption or disorder.

Examples of Management Cues

- A group of male journalism students wants to publish a satirical magazine parodying the school in the manner of a popular magazine. The journalism teacher does not support this effort and believes that articles that mock the school are apt to undermine school discipline. She wants the principal to ban the magazine.
- The high school athletic director tells the student editor of the school paper that she needs to review all sports-related articles and announcements prior to their publication, and he will quash any article that portrays an athlete or an athletic team or program in a negative way. The student editor claims this would be prior restraint and appeals to the principal for support.
- A principal is contacted by a parent who says, "Hey, I just read about this *Hazelwood* case that happened a number of years ago. We've got to get a PTA committee going to write our school's censorship policy." The principal is stunned that the parent is seeking a censorship policy rather than a policy dealing with censorship.
- The editor of the school newspaper receives a request to publish a paid advertisement announcing the formation of a support group for gay and

lesbian students. The editor accepts the ad, but the faculty advisor refuses to permit the ad to appear in the paper.

- Although an underground newspaper called *The Student Voice* is printed and distributed off school grounds, a number of copies are seized by teachers in the school. The main themes of the paper are that the food in the school cafeteria is overpriced and of poor quality and that a number of named teachers are incompetent. The faculty wants the principal to stop publication and distribution of the publication.

Suggested Risk Management Guidelines

- To develop a policy governing students' oral and written expressions,
  - Incorporate the substance and spirit of any districtwide policy promulgated by the board of education regarding the writing, editing, publication, and distribution of student-authored literature
  - Involve a committee composed of faculty, students, and parents to ensure that the interests of all are considered and incorporated into the final policy
  - Have the policy reviewed by the school district's legal counsel prior to implementation
  - Limit the scope of the policy regarding publication of unofficial student publications to writing, editing, or distribution that occurs on school grounds
  - Include reasonable and clearly stated rules concerning the distribution of student publications on school grounds and prohibiting material that is obscene, libelous, or inflammatory (a decision against the distribution of a publication is distinguished from a decision to deprive students of possession of a publication. The latter does not necessarily follow the former)
  - Include regulations that prescribe the procedures to be followed in the event that prior review is warranted. These rules should include
    o A definite period of time in which the review of materials will be completed
    o The specific person to whom the materials are to be submitted
    o The specific materials that are subject to prior review

  - Limit regulations regarding students' possession of literature that is allegedly obscene, libelous, or inflammatory to prohibit open display or distribution of such literature that causes or threatens to cause a substantial disruption of the education process
  - Clarify the purpose of each student publication—whether it is considered an open forum or curriculum based
  - Ensure that all policies and regulations regarding students' oral and written expression are written in clear, specific terms that describe

rational and fair provisions and are fully communicated to faculty, students, and parents

- In administering the policies and regulations concerning students' oral and written expressions, select a professional journalism teacher to supervise student publication classes and programs—one who will consistently select responsible student editors and provide them with clear guidance regarding their responsibility to see that the newspaper or other publications are free of libelous statements and inappropriate language.
- Consider the following general principles in developing policies and regulations regarding students' oral and written expression:
  - School officials must establish proof of substantial disruption before they can initiate disciplinary action against students. Disciplinary actions must be reasonable and fair. Actions by school officials are justified when there is evidence that a publication
    o Encourages disregard for school rules or disrespect for school personnel
    o Contains vulgar or obscene language, ridicules others
    o Violates policies on time, place, and conditions for distribution

  - School officials may not be held accountable for content in a non-school-sponsored newspaper.
  - Courts are in disagreement regarding the extent to which school officials may examine and make judgments on student publications prior to their distribution. Consider prior restraint only when there is a demonstrated and compelling justification for doing so.
  - Regarding distribution of a student publication, if limited review is legally justified, the following safeguards should be included:
    o A speedy review process
    o Identification of the persons authorized to approve or disapprove the material
    o The form in which the material is to be submitted
    o A clear and specific explanation of suspect items, with a rationale as to why they are suspect and should be prohibited
    o An opportunity for affected parties to appeal the decision

SECTION C: STUDENTS' RIGHTS TO FREEDOM OF ASSEMBLY

Students' freedom-of-assembly rights are protected by the First Amendment; however, the Tinker decision made it clear that students' First Amendment rights are protected only so long as they do not substantially disrupt the education process. Schools are well within the scope of their authority to adopt rules that restrict student gatherings to nondisruptive times, places, and behaviors.

❙ FOCUS POINT: Expression Through Freedom of Assembly

A school that allows students to gather, even peacefully, whenever they wish may not function efficiently or effectively. On the other hand, a school that does not allow adequate time for students to meet and discuss relevant issues, or that denies use of school facilities for such assemblies outside regular school hours, clearly discourages one of the most fundamental perquisites and options of good citizenship.

The key to distinguishing between the use and abuse of the students' right to assemble peacefully, then, lies in balancing the fundamental nature, necessity, and usefulness of the freedom itself with the duty to carry out the education process effectively. Although students' rights to freedom of assembly have not generated many court cases, school principals need to be sensitive to potential problems in this area.

Example of a Management Cue

- Nearly 80 percent of the school's 550 students participate in a peaceful sit-in that halts classes at the school for three hours. The students demand that the president of the school board meet with them to discuss the situation and answer their questions concerning the school board's vote to cut five teaching positions at the high school and to eliminate portions of the vocational education program.

Suggested Risk Management Guideline

- Have a written, board-approved plan for dealing with both peaceful and disruptive unauthorized assemblies of students that the entire staff is prepared to implement. Such a plan may prohibit

  - Disruptive demonstrations and protests that result in destruction of property, violation of school rules, or any other unlawful activities. Be advised that an activity involving students' right to freedom of expression cannot be banned because it conflicts with the personal views of school officials. Disruptive assemblies might, for example, include

    o Assembly of large groups of students called for the specific purpose of disrupting the school day
    o Demonstrations that deprive other students of their rights to pursue their education in an orderly environment or obstruct corridors or prevent free movement among students who are not participants

SECTION D: STUDENTS' RIGHTS TO HAVE WIRELESS COMMUNICATION DEVICES

Pagers, cellular phones, and other wireless communication devices have become increasingly popular with students. At this date, no case law is available to guide school administrators; however, the courts would probably support school officials' decisions to prohibit pagers and cell phones on school premises unless there is clear evidence that the policy violates a First Amendment right.

FOCUS POINT: The Prohibition of Wireless Communication Devices

It is well established that school authorities may prohibit student actions that create material or substantial disruption to the education process. When there is evidence that pagers and cellular phones create disruption or that they are being used for illegal purposes, school administrators can ban pagers and cell phones from the school, including school-related activities. A number of states have enacted regulations that prohibit the use of pagers and cell phones in public schools and outline expected consequences for policy violators and exceptions granted for *special* use. (See your state's Web site.)

Examples of Management Cues

- Teachers complain to the principal that the constant beeping of pagers and the muted ringing of cell phones are disrupting classes.
- The principal receives information from the police department that students in her school are using personal telephone equipment during school hours to make drug connections and deals.
- Students are complaining that their cell phones and pagers are being stolen.

Suggested Risk Management Guidelines

- Develop and implement a policy regarding use of pagers and cellular phones by students only if there is sufficient evidence of improper use. (Check state regulations.)
- If the use of pagers or cellular phones is permitted, develop specific guidelines governing the conditions under which they can be used.
- If the use of pagers or cellular phones is not permitted, consider allowing for exceptional cases when warranted.

EXAMPLES OF LEADING U.S. SUPREME COURT CASES ON EDUCATION

Admissions, Attendance, and Tuition

DeFunis v. Odegaard

Elgin v. Moreno

Martinez v. Bynum

Pierce v. Society of Sisters

Plyler v. Doe

Selective Service System v. Minnesota Public Interest Research Group

Toll v. Moreno

Vlandis v. Kline

Wisconsin v. Yoder

Due Process and Equal Protection

Cannon v. University of Chicago

Idaho Department of Employment v. Smith

Lau v. Nichols

Mississippi University for Women v. Hogan

O'Connor v. Board of Education of School District 23

Regents of the University of California v. Bakke

Freedom of Speech and Religion

Bender v. Williamsport Area School District

Bethel School No. 403 District v. Fraser

Board of Education v. Pico

Board of School Commissions v. Jacobs

Grayned v. City of Rockford

Hazelwood School District v. Kuhlmeier

Healy v. James

Minersville School District v. Gobitis

Papish v. University of Missouri

Police Department of Chicago v. Mosley

Tinker v. Des Moines Community School District

West Virginia Board of Education v. Barnette

ADDITIONAL CASES OF INTEREST TO EDUCATORS

Maintenance of Discipline in Schools

Blackwell v. Issaquena County Board of Education, 363 F.2d 749 (5th Cir. 1966). Maintenance of order in schools.

Brands v. Sheldon Community School, 71 F. Supp. 627 (N.D. Iowa 1987). Students do not have a substantive constitutional entitlement to participate in interscholastic athletics.

Clements v. Board of Trustees of Sheridan County School District No. 2, 585 P.2d 197 (Wyo. 1978). Discipline is reasonably necessary for the student's physical or emotional safety and the well-being of other students.

Clinton Municipal Separate School District v. Byrd, 477 So.2d 237 (Miss. 1985). Mandatory school discipline rules are not unconstitutional.

Fenton v. Stear, 423 F. Supp. 767 (W.D. Pa. 1976). Student conduct-in-school suspension.

McClain v. Lafayette County Board of Education, 673 F.2d 106 (5th Cir. 1982). Procedural due process is a flexible concept.

Nicholas B. v. School Committee, 412 Mass. 20, 587 N.E.2d 211 (1992). Imposing school discipline off school grounds is not arbitrary or capricious.

Wiemerslage v. Maine Township High School District 207, 29 F.3d 1149 (5th Cir. 1994). School district policy regarding "loitering" is not unconstitutionally "vague" or a violation of the First Amendment.

Student Rights

Alabama and Coushatta Tribes v. Big Sandy School District, 817 F. Supp. 1319 (Tex. 1993). School interest in dress code is not so compelling to overcome religious practice and belief.

Chandler v. McMinnville School District, 978 F.2d 524 (9th Cir. 1992). Speech in the form of buttons is evaluated in light of the *Tinker, Fraser (Bethel)*, and *Hazelwood* precedents.

Public Forum

Beussink v. Woodland R-IV School District, 30 F. Supp.2d 1175 (E.D. Mo. 1998). Home page created by student at home may be constitutionally protected speech.

Bystrom v. Fridley High School Ind. School District No. 14, 822 F.2d 747 (8th Cir. 1987). Underground newspapers can be controlled by the school.

Rivera v. East Otero School District R-1, 721 F. Supp 1189 (D. Colo. 1998). Students have a right to engage in political and religious speech.

CHAPTER RESOURCES

Bethel School District No. 403 v. Fraser, 755 F.2d 1356 (9th Cir. 1985), *rev'd*, 106 S.Ct. 3159 (1986).

Board of Education of School District 228, Cook County, Illinois. *Prohibiting gangs and gang activities*. Policy adopted April 24, 1984.

Burnside v. Byars, 363 F.2d 744 (5th Cir. 1966). See also *Tinker v. Des Moines Independent Community School District*, 393 U.S. 503 (1969); *Augustus v. School Board of Escambia City*, 361 F. Supp. 383 (N.D. Fla. 1973); *Banks v. Muncie Community Schools*, 433 F.2d 292 (7th Cir. 1970).

Crosby v. Holsinger, 852 F.2d 801 (4th Cir. 1988).

Gitlow v. New York, 268 U.S. 652 (1925).

Gusick v. Drebus, 431 F.2d 594 (6th Cir. 1971).

Hazelwood School District v. Kuhlmeier, 484 U.S. 260, 108 S.Ct. 562, 98 L.Ed.2d 592 (43 Ed. Law 515) (1988). See also *Kuhlmeier v. Hazelwood School District*, 607 F. Supp. 1450 (E.D. Mo. 1985).

Karr v. Schmidt, 460 F.2d 609 (5th Cir. 1972).

Olsen v. Board of Education of School District 228, Cook County, Illinois, 676 F. Supp. 829 (N.S. Ill. 1987). (See also Board of Education of School District 228.)

Richards v. Thurston, 424 F.2d. 1281 (1st Cir. 1970).

San Diego Committee against Registration and the Draft v. Governing Board of Grossmont Union High School District, 790 F.2d 1471 (9th Cir. 1986).

Smith v. Tammany Parish School Board, 448 F.2d 414 (5th Cir. 1971).

Stephenson v. Davenport Community School District, 110 F.3d 1303 (8th Cir. 1997).

Thomas v. Board of Education, 607 F.2d 1043 (2nd Cir. 1979).

Tinker v. Des Moines Independent Community School District, 393 U.S. 503 (1969).

West Virginia Board of Education v. Barnette, 319 U.S. 624 (1943).

Williams v. Spencer, 622 F.2d 1200 (4th Cir. 1980).

7

Student Discipline

One of the most difficult issues facing principals is the question of how to deal with unacceptable student conduct. Principals must be able to balance the school's interest in maintaining a safe and orderly environment against the rights of individual students to be free from *unreasonable* discipline. Although the doctrine of *in loco parentis* has been eroded by the courts, it still supports reasonable disciplinary control by school officials. The courts typically uphold school personnel in matters of student discipline *unless* a student's liberty or property rights are threatened or in cases in which the punishment is unreasonable or arbitrary.

School officials have a long-established right to make and enforce reasonable rules of student conduct. As long as the rules are necessary to carry out the school's education mission, the courts recognize the school's authority to adopt reasonable regulations for maintaining order. Rules and regulations for student conduct, the foundations of which should be adopted as official board policy, need to be specific enough so that both students and their parents know what actions will not be tolerated at school and school-related activities. These rules must not be vague and must be applied uniformly to all students. Punishments need to be appropriate to the offense and the circumstances. Current zero tolerance procedures bring the question of one-size-fits-all policies into the courts' scrutiny in the area of reasonableness and fairness.

School discipline of students is under continuous court review. In recent years, the courts have chosen to defer to school board decisions on the assumption that

AUTHORS' NOTE: Cases cited throughout this chapter have been selected on a precedent-setting or best-example basis regardless of jurisdiction or date of adjudication. (See Introduction for more information.)

school boards reflect the values of the community. Nevertheless, students and their parents continue to seek court action when they believe that their rights have been violated or that the school failed to follow proper procedures in taking disciplinary actions or that the punishment was unreasonable and arbitrary under the circumstances. When schools are careless, students tend to prevail.

Due Process

The right to due process of law is the cornerstone of civil liberty. It guarantees fairness for all citizens. The primary source of this guarantee is the Fifth Amendment, which protects individuals against double jeopardy and self-incrimination and guarantees that no person can be deprived of life, liberty, or property without due process of law. This protection is further defined in the equal protection clause of the Fourteenth Amendment. In addition, all 50 states have some form of due process language in their constitutions.

The states have total authority for education, and under state laws, schools are required to provide students and teachers with due process before they can be deprived of any right. Courts view due process in two ways:

1. *Substantive* due process requires that the rules or policies be fair in and of themselves.

2. *Procedural* due process requires that the policies, rules, and regulations be carried out in a fair manner.

Rather than defining an inflexible due process procedure universally applicable to every situation, the courts prefer to decide the required elements of due process on a case-by-case basis. The most commonly accepted elements of due process are

- Proper notice of the charges
- A fair and impartial hearing

However, courts generally follow precedent. This means that when a court rules a certain way, the same court or a lower court is obliged to rule the same way in similar cases. A court is not bound by precedent only if it can show that the case before it is significantly different from the precedent-setting case despite an apparent similarity.

SECTION A: EXCLUSION FROM SCHOOL

Schools are permitted by both statute and common law to regulate the conduct of students and have generally been given broad latitude in the areas of rules, control of misconduct, determination of guilt, and prescription of discipline and punishment. However, state statutes and the Constitution limit schools to rules that control behavior in ways that are reasonably related to legitimate education goals.

▌ FOCUS POINT: Short-Term Suspension

Much of the case law regarding short-term suspensions is derived from *Goss v. Lopez* (1975). In this case, students alleged that they had been suspended for up to 10 days without a hearing. They claimed that their suspensions were unconstitutional on the grounds that they were deprived, without a hearing, of their rights to an education—procedural due process under the Fourteenth Amendment. In ruling in favor of the students, the district court declared that minimum requirements of notice and hearing must take place before students can be suspended.

On appeal, the school district contended that the due process clause does not protect students from expulsion from a public school, because there is no constitutional right to an education at public expense. The Supreme Court disagreed and affirmed that the due process clause forbids deprivations of liberty. The *Goss* Court stated that "when a person's good name, reputation, honor, or integrity is at stake because of what the government is doing to him, the minimal requirements of the due process clause must be satisfied."

The *Goss* decision affirmed that education is one of the most important functions of state and local governments. It recognized that because of the complexity of public schools, discipline and order are essential for the education function to be performed. However, the Court required schools to set up hearing procedures that must be followed before students are suspended. These hearing procedures must include

- An oral or written notice of the charges against the student
- An explanation of the evidence the authorities have to support the charges
- The opportunity for the student to present his or her side of the problem

The court noted that if the continued presence of a student in a school poses a danger to persons or property, the student can be removed from school immediately. In this case, the notice and hearing must follow as soon as possible.

In *Wood v. Strickland* (1975), the Supreme Court held that, in the context of student discipline, school board members can be held liable for damages if they knew, or reasonably should have known, that the disciplinary action taken by the school would violate the constitutional rights of the affected student. Traditionally, educators and school board members enjoyed a good faith immunity from liability for damages, and educators who acted with no intent to commit a wrongful act were not held liable for their errors of judgment. The *Wood* decision demonstrates how far the pendulum has moved, from the earlier, hands-off policy that left education to the educators, to a policy that demands strict legal accountability on the part of educators.

Courts continue to be reluctant to become involved in the day-to-day operation of schools, and in the majority of short-term suspension cases, schools have been successful when they have followed procedures required by *Goss*. The intent of the *Goss* and *Wood* decisions was to respect both the discretionary powers of educators and the constitutional rights of students. These decisions formalized the requirement of fairness in the relationship between students and educators.

Example of a Management Cue

- A teacher reports that a student was involved in an incident that may fit the criteria for consideration for a 1- to 10-day suspension from school.

Suggested Risk Management Guidelines

- Ensure that all school officials involved in student discipline understand that students have clear constitutional rights.
- Ensure that all school officials involved in student discipline understand what constitutes due process procedures for short-term suspensions and what kinds of behaviors may merit consideration for short-term suspension.
- In the absence of explicit wording in state statutes, ensure that students (when students admit guilt, there is no requirement for a fact-finding hearing) are provided, at a minimum, with

  - An oral or written notification of the charges and the intended punishment
  - An opportunity to dispute the charges before an objective school administrator
  - An explanation of the evidence on which the charges are based

I FOCUS POINT: Long-Term Suspension and Expulsion

In general, the more severe the punishment, the more formal the due process requirements. Again, in *Goss*, the court prescribed a 10-day limit to separate short-term suspensions from long-term suspensions and expulsions. Because students who are suspended for more than 10 days or expelled from school altogether are deprived of certain constitutional rights, the courts require a more stringent due process to ensure the penalty is both deserved and fair. Under these more stringent due process requirements, students have, at a minimum, the following rights to

- Receive written notice of the charges and the school's intent to long-term suspend or expel, as noted in *Strickland v. Inlow* (1975)
- Receive prior notice of a hearing that specifies the time, place, and circumstances
- Be represented by legal counsel or other adult representative, as noted in *Black Coalition v. Portland School District No. 1* (1973)
- See adverse evidence prior to the hearing, as noted in *Graham v. Knutzen* (1973)
- Be heard before an impartial party (the hearing officer may be the school principal unless it can be shown that the principal cannot be fair and impartial), as noted in *Dixon v. Alabama State Board of Education* (1961)
- Compel supportive witnesses to attend the hearing

- Confront and cross-examine adverse witnesses, as noted in *Morrison v. City of Lawrence* (1904)
- Be protected from self-incrimination
- Testify on her or his own behalf and present witnesses
- Receive a transcript of the proceedings for use on appeal

Examples of Management Cues

- Three weeks prior to the end of the semester, two students are caught drinking beer at a track meet. Board policy requires expulsion.
- A student has been accused of a potentially expellable act. Cursory evidence supports both the student's and the school's claims.

Suggested Risk Management Guidelines

- Develop, publish, and disseminate written policies that spell out the due process procedures to which students are entitled.
- Provide students with the full protection of due process before suspending them for more than 10 days or expelling them.
- Document the due process carefully for future reference in the event of appeal.

SECTION B: CORPORAL PUNISHMENT, REASONABLE PUNISHMENT, EXCESSIVE PUNISHMENT, INTENTIONAL TORTS

Although the authors of this book believe that corporal punishment should not be allowed under any circumstances, it remains an acceptable action in some school districts across the country. As a result, we are compelled to include the focus point below.

▌FOCUS POINT: Corporal Punishment

Corporal or physical punishment continues to be a highly controversial issue in public education, and perhaps no other issue has drawn as much criticism. A majority of states now ban corporal punishment, and in other states in which it is allowed, a substantial number of school districts prohibit this kind of punishment. However, the courts still view corporal punishment as an acceptable form of discipline when administered in a reasonable manner.

The constitutionality of corporal punishment was confirmed in *Ingraham v. Wright* (1977), a landmark case in which the U.S. Supreme Court ruled that even severe corporal punishment may not violate the Eighth Amendment prohibition of cruel and unusual punishment. In its decision, the Court noted, however, that the use of corporal punishment deprives students of liberty interests protected by the Constitution, and as a result, *rudimentary* due process must precede its use. When corporal punishment is allowed, due process is satisfied with a brief explanation of the reason for the discipline coupled with an opportunity for the student to comment. However, reasonable school administrators take parents' wishes concerning this form of punishment into consideration and require an adult witness to be present when administering corporal punishment.

The common law rule on the subject of corporal punishment allows school administrators, standing *in loco parentis*, to use *reasonable* force as they reasonably believe necessary for a child's proper control, training, or education. The following factors, as identified in *Hogenson v. Williams* (1976), are generally considered in determining whether the amount of force used was reasonable:

- Age, gender, and condition of the child
- Nature of the offense or conduct and the child's motives
- The influence of the student's example on other students
- Whether the force was reasonably necessary to compel obedience to a proper command
- Whether the force was disproportionate to the offense, unnecessarily degrading, or likely to cause serious injury

Minimum Due Process

Before administering corporal punishment, school officials should develop, publish, and disseminate rules that provide students and their parents with *adequate notice* that specific violations may result in corporal punishment. The student to be punished should be informed of the rule violation in question and provided with an opportunity to respond. A brief but thorough informal hearing is a good way to allow the student the opportunity to present his or her side of the issue. Because the student's property rights are not involved, an extensive, full due process procedure is not necessary. However, the courts have identified as the minimal due process standards that

- Specific warning is given about what behavior may result in corporal punishment
- Evidence exists that other measures attempted failed to bring about the desired change in behavior
- Administration of corporal punishment takes place in the presence of a second school official
- On request, a written statement is provided to parents explaining the reasons for the punishment and the names of all witnesses

Reasonable Punishment, Excessive Punishment, Intentional Torts

Poor decisions regarding the use of corporal punishment may result in civil damage suits or even criminal prosecution of assault and battery. The court in *State v. Ingram* (1953), for example, identified two standards governing corporal punishment:

1. The reasonableness standard—punishment must be within the bounds of reason and humanity

2. The good faith standard—the person administering the punishment is not motivated by malice and does not inflict punishment wantonly or excessively

Excessive punishment occurs when the punishment is inflicted with such force or in such a manner that it is considered to be cruel and unusual. Excessiveness also occurs when no consideration is given to the student's age, size, gender, physical condition, or ability to bear the punishment. Assault and battery charges are normally associated with allegations of excessive punishment, and both are classified as intentional torts.

Privileged Force

Sometimes school employees need to use physical force to control a potentially dangerous situation. School personnel have an affirmative duty, for example, to break up a fight between or among students. When the use of physical force is necessary, the *Hogenson* court stated that school officials should use only the amount of force *reasonably* necessary to control a specific situation. The amount of force used should be proportionate to the prohibited activity.

Examples of Management Cues

- Two elementary students get into a fight on the playground and are warned that they will be paddled if they fight again. Several minutes later, they get into another fight. The teacher supervising the playground gives each student three swats on the buttocks with a paddle. One of the students develops severe bruises that required medical attention. The injured child's father files a complaint against the teacher.
- A middle school student is sent to the principal's office for showing a lewd photograph to a classmate. The principal informs the student that his punishment will be five swats with a paddle. After two swats, the student refuses to be hit again. The principal calls in a teacher to make the student bend over a chair to receive the additional three swats. In the ensuing struggle, the student hits his head on the corner of the desk and sustains an injury that requires medical treatment. The parents of the child are considering legal action.
- In what he considers an effort to "fire him up," a football coach yells at a player, strikes him on the helmet, and grabs his face mask. As a result of the coach's actions, the student is hospitalized and subsequently files charges of assault against the coach.
- While a teacher is reprimanding a student, the student turns and begins to walk away. The teacher grabs the student, slams him into the wall, then shakes him by the shoulders. The student breaks free, punches the teacher, then runs away. A few minutes later, the teacher pulls the boy out of another classroom and punches him several times.

- A student enters class a few minutes late and walks in front of another student who is giving a report. The teacher tells the tardy student to apologize and then be seated. The student mumbles something disrespectful. The teacher then twists the student's arm behind his back and shoves him down the hall to the principal's office.

Suggested Risk Management Guideline

- Jurisdictions that retain the right to discipline students with corporal punishment should have a written policy that, at a minimum,
  - Identifies the specific acts and kinds of misbehavior that may result in the use of corporal punishment
  - Identifies the school personnel authorized to administer the punishment
  - Identifies the minimal due process procedures that must be completed before corporal punishment is administered
  - Requires that corporal punishment be administered in private, without anger or malice, and in the presence of another adult witness
  - Prohibits punishment that could be considered cruel, unusual, or excessive
  - Requires written notification of the superintendent and the student's parents within a specified period of time after the punishment is administered

SECTION C: DISCIPLINING STUDENTS FOR ACTS OFF SCHOOL GROUNDS

School officials have broad authority to control the conduct of students, to take responsibility for conduct, and to punish misconduct that has a negative impact on the school where school-related activities are concerned (see also Chapter 15 on field trips). The authority to control student conduct is implied by state statutes and has developed over time through court cases. The courts generally uphold school officials' authority to discipline students for misconduct off the school grounds when the students are engaged in school-sponsored activities.

FOCUS POINT: Institutional Authority Off School Grounds

The common law basis for the school's authority to control student conduct or activities off school grounds is based on the assumption that the authority of school officials extends to any student acts that are detrimental to the good order and best interests of the school, whether the acts are committed during school hours, while students travel to and from school, or after the student has returned home. Schools can make rules and regulations governing students' extracurricular activities in athletic competitions, musical organizations, dramatic organizations and productions, social activities, class and school trips, cheerleading, school and class elective offices, literary and service clubs, scholastic activities, and honor groups. These rules and regulations are enforceable when student activities take place off school grounds as officially sanctioned school activities (see also Chapter 15 on field trips) or where it can be shown that the off-campus activities have a *detrimental effect* on the school.

Students are not deprived of constitutional rights of free speech and property interests when disciplined for behavior that is detrimental to the school, regardless of whether the incident took place on or off school property. A *reasonable* school regulation is one that is essential in maintaining order and discipline on school property and that measurably contributes to the maintenance of order and decorum within the educational system, as ruled in *Blackwell v. Issaquena County Board of Education* (1966).

A federal court in Pennsylvania, in *Fenton v. Stear* (1976), held that lewd comments made about a teacher on Sunday, off school premises, were sufficiently detrimental to the school to warrant disciplinary action. In this case, while a teacher was in a shopping center on a Sunday evening, a student shouted, "There's Stear." A second student loudly responded, "He's a prick." On Monday morning, when confronted about the incident by school authorities, the student admitted calling Stear a prick. The student was given an in-school suspension, was not allowed to participate in the senior trip, was not permitted to attend any extracurricular activities, and was placed on other restrictions at school. The student challenged the disciplinary action as a violation of his freedom of speech and denial of a property right to an education. The *Fenton* court stated that

> the First Amendment rights of the plaintiff were not violated. His conduct involved an invasion of the right of teacher Stear to be free from being loudly insulted in a public place by lewd, lascivious or indecent words or language. . . . It is our opinion that when a high school student refers to a high school teacher in a public place on a Sunday by a lewd and obscene name in such a loud voice that the teacher and others hear the insult, it may be deemed a matter for discipline in the discretion of the school authorities. To countenance such student conduct even in a public place without imposing sanctions could lead to devastating consequences in the school. Furthermore, because the student continued his education while serving the in-school suspension, he was not deprived of any property right.

In a case in which a student sold cocaine to an undercover police officer on three occasions, not on school property, the student was arrested at the high school and suspended by the principal and subsequently expelled. The student challenged the expulsion, claiming the school board lacked authority to expel him for a nonschool activity off school grounds. The court, in *Howard v. Colonial School District* (1992), upheld the school board, agreeing that the student was a threat to safety and welfare of other students even if he was an off-campus drug dealer.

In a case in which a student was expelled from school for committing battery on another student on a public street after school, the student challenged the school's authority to discipline him for off-school-grounds behavior. The court, in *Nicholas B. v. School Committee* (1992), upheld the school's action, observing that imposing discipline off school grounds was not arbitrary or capricious.

Where safety of students is compromised, school-based discipline clearly extends to activities beyond the school grounds. Two students, one in a jeep and the other in a pickup truck, blocked the progress of a school bus loaded with children traveling to school. The driver of the jeep positioned his vehicle in front of the bus while the pickup truck followed behind, and by alternately slowing and speeding up, they obstructed the operation of the bus. On arriving at the school, the students were cited by the highway patrol and suspended by the school. They challenged the disciplinary action by school authorities. The court, in *Clements v. Board of Trustees of Sheridan County School Dist. No. 2* (1978), stated,

> It matters little that the proscribed conduct occurred on a public highway. It is generally accepted that school authorities may discipline pupils for out-of-school conduct having a direct and immediate effect on the discipline or general welfare of the school. This is particularly true where the discipline is reasonably necessary for the student's physical or emotional safety and well-being of other students.

Examples of Management Cues

- One student intercepts another student several blocks from school. The first student knocks the second to the ground and steals his $100 basketball shoes. The victim's mother reports the robbery to the police, then calls the principal to inform him of the problem and request his assistance in recovering the shoes and prosecuting the guilty student.
- The football coach has a rule that forbids team members from drinking any alcoholic beverage. The starting quarterback is seen drinking a beer with his parents at a local restaurant. The coach suspends the student from the team. The student's father asks the court for a restraining order requiring his son be reinstated to the team.

Suggested Risk Management Guidelines

- Ensure that any and all students who frequently or infrequently are involved in school-sponsored field trips understand that the rules for away-from-school activities are the *same* as for in-school activities, including teacher and administrator authority.
- Develop clear guidelines for determining whether off-campus (out-of-school, off-school-grounds) conduct might be considered a punishable offense, that is, might have direct and immediate effect on the discipline or general welfare of the school.

SECTION D: LIABILITY FOR THE VIOLATION OF STUDENTS' RIGHTS

Section 1983 of Title 42 of the U.S. Code (the Civil Rights Act of 1871) authorizes a civil action for deprivation of federally protected civil rights against a person acting under state law, custom, or usage. Although this statute was enacted after the Civil War to protect the rights of freedmen, it has been extended to a variety of other situations, including school authorities' actions toward students. Under Section 1983, school districts cannot claim immunity for civil rights violations committed by an employee and can be held liable for damages if the injured party can demonstrate that there was an invasion of her or his federally protected constitutional rights, as noted in Owen v. City of Independence, Mo. *(1980).*

| FOCUS POINT: Liability for Violation of | Students' Rights—The Civil Rights Act of 1871

In 1975, the U.S. Supreme Court ruled that Section 1983 of the Civil Rights Act of 1871 applies to school officials who knowingly, willingly, or maliciously act to deprive a student of constitutional rights. Additional court rulings have expanded this coverage. In ruling that schools and school districts do not have immunity when civil rights violations are alleged, the courts have made it possible for individuals to file suit in federal court against schools and school officials to seek damages when their constitutional rights have been violated.

In establishing that school officials are covered under the law, the Supreme Court held that school officials may be liable to pay compensatory damages if they maliciously disregard a student's constitutional rights. This is true whether or not the school officials knew, or reasonably should have known, the results of their actions against the student. The Court subsequently clarified this ruling by limiting compensatory damages to those situations when an actual injury resulted from the violation of constitutional rights. This means that the student must prove an actual injury before any substantial compensatory monetary award will be allowed by federal courts. If it is determined that a civil rights violation has occurred, the plaintiff may also collect reasonable attorneys' fees under the Civil Rights Attorney's Fees Awards Act of 1976. An example of such a ruling can be found in *State of Maine v. Thiboutot* (1980).

Not only may school officials, as individuals, be sued under Section 1983, but the Supreme Court, in *Wood v. Strickland* (1975), also held that school boards as a whole can be sued for civil rights violations. And school boards can be held liable even when the constitutional violation was committed in good faith. In addition, the Court held that the liability of school boards is not limited to constitutional claims but also for claims under federal statutes. The Court ruled that local governments, including school boards, are not liable for punitive damages in civil rights suits.

Examples of Management Cues

- An elementary teacher, angry at a student, locks the child in a classroom closet for three hours as punishment.
- A wrestling coach determines that one of his wrestlers' hair is too long, according to the coaches' policy. As a punishment for appearing at a tournament with longer than acceptable hair, he takes the wrestler to the locker room and shaves his head.

Suggested Risk Management Guideline

- Inform all school employees on students' civil rights. Develop working guidelines in the areas of discipline, human rights, and so forth.

SECTION E: ZERO TOLERANCE

Many school districts have adopted zero tolerance policies in the wake of the Gun-Free Schools Act of 1994. The act mandates that all states receiving federal funds for education must require school districts to expel a student for at least a year for possessing a gun on school grounds. Many states have gone further and require students to be expelled for possession of any weapon—not just a gun. But even before this, school districts had other zero tolerance policies and regulations in place to ensure consistent handling of situations involving such issues as drugs and alcohol, threats and harassment, and so forth.

Before a school district attempts to develop or refine a zero tolerance policy, the primary question that should be asked is, How does the proposed or current zero tolerance policy define prohibited actions, substances, and possessions, and what, if any, room for interpretation of individual events does the policy permit? Secondary questions should include, What kinds of situations present a clear violation of policy? What constitutes a weapon, prohibited substance, threat or harassment under the policy? and Does the current or proposed policy offer any flexibility for interpretation?

FOCUS POINT: Zero Tolerance Policy Development and Implementation

Every school district needs tough policies that deal with weapons, drugs, threats, and so forth, but a zero tolerance policy can be difficult to enforce if (a) the policy is not well written and (b) those who administer the policy don't have some "interpretation" room. For example, any reasonable educator recognizes a gun or a knife as a weapon. A sharpened stick could be a weapon, but then so could a pencil. Zero tolerance policies need to be written in such a way that school district *credibility* is not going to be damaged by enforcement. Does the specific policy use the words *shall* or *will* (the policy dictates the decision, and individual cases cannot be evaluated by on-site administrators) or *may* (on-site school administrators have some decision-making power and can consider the merits of individual cases)?

School district attorneys have a tendency to advise school boards to develop zero tolerance policies that treat students as if one size fits all. Attorneys are sensitive to the demonstration of fairness in any policy. They are aware of the historical patterns of apparent inequitable disciplinary treatment of minority students, as reflected in suspension and expulsion rates. One of school districts' responses in recent years to address this apparent inequity in the meting out of discipline has been to create zero tolerance policies based on the assumption that all circumstances and all students are exactly equal. Yet on the other hand, schools commit to individualizing instruction and, in fact, in some cases, are legally mandated to do so. For example, the Individuals with Disabilities Education Act requires that school districts provide an individualized education program—an IEP. (Note: Recently the U.S. Commission on Civil Rights has announced plans to investigate whether enforcement of zero tolerance discipline policies in schools results in discrimination against minority and disabled students—because some recent data showed overrepresentation of minority students in student suspension rates [Robelen, 2000].)

Applying the letter of the zero tolerance law to cases like the following ones often makes school officials appear ridiculous. A school district in Pennsylvania suspended a kindergartner for bringing a plastic hatchet to school as part of his Halloween costume. A Chicago fourth grader who forgot to wear his belt was suspended for violating the school dress code. A 13-year-old Texas student was suspended for carrying a bottle of ibuprofen in her backpack instead of giving it to the school nurse. In Louisiana, an eight-year-old girl was suspended for bringing a family heirloom to show and tell: she brought a gold-plated pocket watch and fob with a one-inch knife attached to it. A New Jersey school district suspended four kindergartners who allegedly pointed their fingers like guns and shouted "Bang!" at other pupils during recess. A school district in Colorado expelled an honors student for accidentally packing a knife with her lunch. A school district in Virginia suspended a model student for writing in a note to her girlfriend that she was upset about the grade she was going to receive from a particular teacher, her parents would ground her "forever," and she "felt like killing herself and the teacher." In this case, the teacher discovered the note, and the school suspended the student for threatening a teacher, pending a hearing for expulsion (in accordance with a zero tolerance policy). Although the school board considered it a threatening note, they found it *not threatening enough to keep her out of school,* and ordered her reinstated—but at a *different* school in the same district. (Authors' note: Apparently, she was much less threatening at a different school?) The student and her parents appealed, community pressure heightened, the press had a heyday debating the issue, and then—quietly—the girl was allowed to return to her home school without any permanent record of the incident ever happening. Results? Do incidents like these demonstrate unfair treatment of students or examples of management decisions by school administrators *hamstrung* by zero tolerance policies that don't allow for leadership in decision making? All these examples caused substantial embarrassment to the school districts. The Virginia example, which was destined to be played out in the courts at the expense of the taxpayer, focused on the girl's alleged threat but ignored the girl's purported desire to kill herself. One threat was taken seriously to an illogical extreme—and the other was ignored. The conundrum that school districts find themselves in is to create zero tolerance policies that ensure consistent, fair, reasonable, and equitable treatment of all students in all circumstances.

In developing a zero tolerance policy, giving school administrators the opportunity to exercise their professional judgment and common sense in individual situations may provide the balance desired between the policy and individualization of discipline. The policy, like other aspects of instruction, should provide that the on-site administrator can be overridden, when necessary, through standard due process procedures—the classic checks-and-balances tenet of democracy. The following suggested policy statements include the provision that *on-site school administrators retain final authority* in determining what constitutes a weapon, threat, prohibited substance, harassment, and so forth—and whether the situation constitutes a potential danger. Consider the following examples.

- *In the area of weapons:* A policy statement such as the following balances the district's responsibility to act consistently and strongly with its responsibility to consider students as individuals:

  The school district strictly prohibits the possession, conveyance, use, or storage of weapons or weapon look-alikes on school property, at school-sponsored events, or in or around a school vehicle. This policy applies to students, employees, and visitors, including those who have a legal permit to carry a weapon. *On-site school administrators retain final authority in determining what constitutes a weapon and evaluating potential danger.*

  The problem of defining what constitutes a weapon surfaces. A policy statement might include the following definition:

  All the following are considered weapons: knife blades, razor blades, cutting instruments, martial arts hardware, lasers, BB guns, shockers, brass knuckles, metal pipes, sharpened sticks, stun guns, firearms, ammunition, Mace, pepper spray, acid, explosive devices, fireworks, pyrotechnics, slingshots, crossbows or noncrossbows or arrows, or any other instrument capable of inflicting serious injury. The brandishing of *any* instrument, piece of equipment, or supply item in the form of a threat of bodily harm to another will cause such instrument to be considered a weapon. Weapon look-alikes, such as toy guns, may also be considered weapons under this policy.

- *In the area of drugs:* A policy statement such as the following is suggested to again balance the need for a strong and consistent response with the importance of viewing students as individuals:

The school district strictly prohibits the possession, conveyance, use, or storage of drugs on school property, at school-sponsored events, or in or around a school vehicle. This policy applies to students, employees, and visitors. *On-site school administrators retain final authority in determining what constitutes a prohibited drug and in evaluating potential danger.*

Now, again, the problem arises in defining which drugs are prohibited and what the district considers to be a drug, so a policy statement should include examples (e.g., "All of the following are considered to be drugs and are strictly prohibited: . . .").

Using these areas as examples, zero tolerance policies could include threats to others, sexual harassment, child molestation or abuse, and a multitude of other areas that school districts believe need to be closely monitored. Whatever a school district decides, all zero tolerance policies should include, at a minimum, the following components:

- Exceptions to the policy (e.g., in a weapons policy, "Law enforcement officials may carry weapons on school property. . . . principals may issue exceptions for items such as cutting instruments used in a specific class or look-alikes for school drama productions"). Delineate exceptions in all other zero tolerance policies. Define the use of the words *shall* or *will* as opposed to *may*.
- Include a description of where and when such policies will be enforced. Any policy should specify the areas in which the policy will be enforced and the events—in addition to school hours—when students, employees, parents, or visitors are subject to the policy (e.g., field trips, school-sponsored events, school buses, and other school vehicles).
- Establish guidelines (local and state regulations) for notifying other authorities (e.g., police, social welfare).
- Provide disciplinary rules and procedures that include students, employees, and parents and other visitors. It is suggested that school districts include a statement such as, "The district will vigorously pursue prosecution through law enforcement agencies."
- Include an explanation of due process rights.

Any zero tolerance policy must comply with any existing state laws, should be reasonable—but tough—and be designed in such a way that both district credibility and exposure to liability are not compromised. To *preserve credibility,* any zero tolerance policy should state that the principal has the right to make the *final judgment* on what constitutes a weapon, a drug, abuse, harassment, and so forth. Exercising professional judgment is part of a principal's job as an effective leader.

Examples of Management Cues

- A sixth-grade student, attempting to play a practical joke, puts liquid hand soap in his teacher's coffee cup. The teacher feels that he could have been poisoned if he had drunk the tainted beverage.

- A high school student reports to the office that a student with a nearby locker has hidden a weapon in that locker.
- A fourth-grade student comes to the office complaining that another student continues to pinch her butt, despite the fact that she has repeatedly told him not to touch her.
- A teacher brings a backpack she found in the hall to the principal. When the backpack is opened to determine its ownership, the principal discovers a loaded gun and identification that shows the backpack belongs to a teacher in the school. On questioning, the teacher produces a permit to carry the gun.
- An eighth-grade boy is caught at the drinking fountain filling a translucent, fluorescent orange squirt gun.

Suggested Risk Management Guidelines

- *Ensure that you know the specific provisions of the district's zero tolerance policies.* For example, how weapons, prohibited substances, prohibited behaviors are identified and defined; what, if any, latitude do individual principals have in determining what constitutes a violation; and whether or not the violation created a potential danger.
- *Make sure that you have all the facts pertinent to the situation.* Your investigation should include any extenuating or mitigating circumstances. If the current policy does not permit introduction of mitigating or extenuating circumstances or individualization of cases, you, as principal, *must* follow the policy as written.

EXAMPLES OF LEADING U.S. SUPREME COURT CASES ON EDUCATION

Students' Rights—Discipline

Board of Curators v. Horowitz

Board of Education of Rogers v. McCluskey

Carey v. Piphus

Goss v. Lopez

Honig v. Doe

Ingraham v. Wright

New Jersey v. T.L.O.

Regents of the University of Michigan v. Ewing

Wood v. Strickland

CHAPTER RESOURCES

Black Coalition v. Portland School Dist. No. 1, 484 F.2d 1040, 1045 (9th Cir. 1973).

Blackwell v. Issaquena County Board of Education, 363 F.2d 749 (5th Cir. 1966).

Civil Rights Act of 1871, 42 U.S.C. § 1983.

Clements v. Board of Trustees of Sheridan County School Dist. No. 2, 585 P.2d 197 (Wyo. 1978). See also 53 A.L.R.3d 1124, 68 Am. Jur.2d, Schools §§ 256 and 266.

Dixon v. Alabama State Board of Education, 186 F. Supp. 945, *rev'd* 294 F.2d 15, *cert. denied*, 368 U.S. 930, 825 (Ct. 368 1961).

Fenton v. Stear, 423 F. Supp. 767 (W.D. Pa. 1976).

Goss v. Lopez, 419 U.S. 565, 955 S.Ct. 729, 42 L.Ed.2d 725 (1975).

Graham v. Knutzen, 362 F. Supp. 881 (D. Neb. 1973).

Hogenson v. Williams, 542 S.W.2d 456, 459 (Tex. Civ. App. Texarkana 1976).

Howard v. Colonial School District, 621 A.2d 362 (Del. Super. Ct. 1992).

Ingraham v. Wright, 430 U.S. 651, 97 S.Ct. 1401, 51 L.Ed.2d 711 (1977).

Morrison v. City of Lawrence, 186 Mass. 456, 460, 72 N.E. 91, 92 (1904).

Nicholas B. v. School Committee, 412 Mass. 20, 587 N.E.2d 211 (1992).

Owen v. City of Independence, Mo., 445 U.S. 622 (1980).

Robelen, E. W. (2000, March 1). Commission to investigate suspension rates. *Education Week*, p. 29.

State of Maine v. Thiboutot, 448 U.S. 1 (1980).

State v. Ingram, 237 N.C. 197, 74 S.E.2d 532 (1953).

Strickland v. Inlow, 519 F.2d 744 (8th Cir. 1975).

Wood v. Strickland, 420 U.S. 308; 95 S.Ct. 992; 43 L.Ed.2d 214 (1975).

8

The Principal's Responsibilities in Providing Special Education Services

A disability can impact a child's educational experience in a variety of ways. Sensory disabilities such as hearing impairments and visual impairments can limit the student's access to certain instructional formats such

---

AUTHORS' NOTE: This chapter was originally written by Janet M. Hamel while she was a doctoral candidate at George Mason University. Dr. Hamel is now an independent consultant and editor. For this second edition, the chapter was reviewed, revised, and expanded by Christina M. Diamond, a doctoral candidate and Learning Specialist in the Counseling Center at George Mason University.

Special education law, regulations, and procedures are very precise. School administrators should seek day-to-day guidance on such important (and potentially litigious) areas as disciplining students with disabilities, determining eligibility for services, changing educational placement, providing an appropriate education in the least restrictive environment, and so forth, from experts in their school district and, in problematic situations, from legal counsel.

Cases cited throughout this chapter have been selected on a precedent-setting or best-example basis regardless of jurisdiction or date of adjudication. (See Introduction for more information.)

as large group discussions and instructional materials such as textbooks. Other limitations resulting from a specific learning disability or traumatic brain injury can severely impact a child's ability to read, write, or do math at the same level as his or her nondisabled peers. However, children with disabilities did not always have the educational entitlements that are currently guaranteed under federal law. The purpose of this chapter is to introduce legislative history, key terminology, and principles in special education law and to describe scenarios along with procedures in accordance with special education law. According to the *Twenty-fourth Annual Report to Congress on the Implementation of the Individuals with Disabilities Education Act* (U.S. Department of Education, 2001), states reported serving 599,678 children ages 3 through 5 with disabilities and 5,775,722 students ages 6 through 21 during the 2000–2001 school year. When combined, these figures represent approximately 9 percent of the U.S. population in 2000–2001. It is quite remarkable to look at the current number of students receiving special education services today when you compare it to the estimated number of students who were excluded from public education 30 years ago due to their disabling conditions. Katsiyannis, Yell, and Bradley (2001) reported that "congressional findings in 1974 indicate that more than 1.75 million students with disabilities did not receive educational services," and "more than 3 million students with disabilities who were admitted to school did not receive an education that was appropriate to their needs" (pp. 324–325).

As this book goes to press, the U.S. Supreme Court in *Schaffer v. Weast* (US 546, November 14, 2005). On Writ Of Certiorari to The United States Court Of Appeals for The Fourth Circuit Court: (377 F. 3d 449) ruled that: The "Individuals [school and parents] must create an 'individualized education program' (IEP) for each disabled child. §1414(d). If parents believe their child's IEP is inappropriate, they may request an 'impartial due process hearing.' §1415(f). The Act is silent, however, as to which party bears the burden of persuasion at such a hearing. We hold that the burden lies, as it typically does, on the party seeking relief."

The figures above show the dismal state of special education 30 years after the passage of the Education of the Handicapped Act of 1970 (EHA). Although the EHA was the first federal law that addressed education for individuals with disabilities exclusively, the historical beginnings of the special education movement in the United States date back to the mid-1800s, when the federal government created grants to the states to fund "asylums for the deaf and the dumb" through an act to establish the Columbia Institution for the Instruction of the Deaf and Dumb and the Blind, which later became known as Gallaudet University (Martin, Martin, & Terman, 1996). Twenty-two years later, in 1879, Public Law No. 45-186 provided the American Printing House for the Blind funding to produce Braille materials for students who were blind or low-vision. Despite slow beginnings to federal involvement in special education, considerable progress has been made over the past 35 years and continues to be made as educators, families, students, and advocates dedicate their time and efforts toward improving educational services to individuals with disabilities.

Approximately 35 years have passed since students with disabilities were given the right to an education in the United States. Court cases that grew out of the racial desegregation movement of the 1950s and 1960s, such as *Brown v. Board of Education of Topeka (Brown I)* in 1954, affirmed that all children had a constitutional right to equal educational opportunities. Prior to this landmark case, educational decisions had been made at the state or local court level. The *Brown* case served as a foundational case for later litigation both at the federal level and in locales across the nation seeking to guarantee equal educational opportunities for all children. In the early 1970s, numerous parents of students with disabilities went to federal courts when their local school districts did not provide services to meet their children's educational needs. In *Pennsylvania Association for Retarded Citizens (PARC) v. Commonwealth of Pennsylvania* (1971, amended 1972), a Pennsylvania court ruled that all children, regardless of disability, have a basic right to an education under the Fourteenth Amendment. The court further stated that no law could postpone, terminate, or deny children access to a publicly supported education and described a basic order of preference for placement starting with the regular public school class, if possible:

> Placement in a regular public school class is preferable to placement in a special public school class. Further, placement in a special public school class is preferable to placement in any other type of program of education and training.

Soon afterwards, in *Mills v. Board of Education of the District of Columbia* (1972), a federal court ruled that District of Columbia schools could not exclude children with disabilities from the public schools, and that the lack of necessary funds claimed by the school district was not acceptable justification for not providing services. The Pennsylvania and District of Columbia cases were among a number of cases that focused public attention on the issue of educating children with disabilities, and social and political pressures resulted in landmark federal legislation that boldly addressed the educational rights of these children.

The two resultant laws—the Rehabilitation Act of 1973 and the Education for All Handicapped Children Act of 1975 (commonly referred to as EAHCA or Pub. L. No. 94-142)—provided federal funds and established regulations to protect equal access to a free, appropriate, public education (FAPE) for students with disabilities. EAHCA was actually an amendment to the EHA and "combined an educational bill of rights with the promise of federal financial incentives to states that chose to accept EAHCA funds" (Katsiyannis et al., 2001, pp. 325–326). These laws have been amended, reauthorized, and clarified by Congress and in the courts since their original passage. In addition, the Americans with Disabilities Act of 1990 (ADA) protects individuals with disabilities from discrimination and guarantees equal access and opportunities.

The major special education law in force as this book went to press was the Individuals with Disabilities Education Improvement Act, or IDEA, which reauthorized Public Law No. 105-17 in 2004. At press time, federal regulations and guidance detailing implementation of the reauthorized IDEA were not yet published; however, the proposed regulations had been drafted and were open for public comment. Once the public comment phase closes, the federal government is likely to complete regulations to implement IDEA 2004 in late 2005/early 2006. Then individual states will begin the process for writing their own regulations to conform to federal requirements.

Because the regulation process often takes time and portions of the new law differ significantly from Public Law No. 105-17, the Office of Special Education Programs (OSEP) in the U.S. Department of Education identified several issue areas and published fact sheets for guidance on issues where the new law is significantly different. These fact sheets are available online at http://www.cec .sped.org/cec_bn/briefs.html.

It is important to note that many states have additional laws and rules based on Public Law 105-17, and many of these state laws and rules exceed the minimum requirements of IDEA 2004. School-based administrators are encouraged to review the education laws and regulations in their states that affect students with disabilities. In addition, during the preparation phase of regulations implementing IDEA 2004, the regulations implementing Public Law No. 105-17 remain in effect, to the extent that they are consistent with the IDEA 2004 statute.

Every school-based administrator makes numerous decisions involving educating students with disabilities, and often, questions and challenges arise in individual cases about what is required and what is best for each student. The dynamic nature of special education law makes it difficult for administrators to stay well versed on the changing federal and state statutes and regulations. Special education law fills entire books (e.g., Huefner, 2000, and Turnbull & Turnbull, 2000). Therefore it is impossible to cover all scenarios in just one chapter. It is advisable to consult expert counsel whenever a difficult question or situation arises. This chapter summarizes the legislation that guarantees the rights of students with disabilities to receive a FAPE and also introduces suggested procedures to follow in a variety of situations. By necessity this chapter can provide only a general overview of this critical area of the law and does not purport to give detailed guidance for every dilemma involving special education. This chapter does not attempt to address every difficult situation and every procedural question that may arise in educating students with disabilities. Instead, the authors explain the key terminology and principles underlying federal special education law and describe, in a general manner, the related procedures mandated by such law. Due to space constraints, specific state laws and regulations, which in many cases go further than federal laws and regulations in requiring specific actions and procedures, are not presented in this book.

SECTION A: KEY TERMINOLOGY AND PRINCIPLES IN SPECIAL EDUCATION LAW

When considering the issues involved in educating students with disabilities, it is critical to understand specific terminology and key principles that have been defined both in legislation and through litigation. These terms and principles may sound straightforward, and their definitions may seem obvious. But frequently there are conflicting ways to interpret exactly what the law means by a certain term—and the courts often serve as the arbiters of such disagreements over definitions. Certain words have particular meanings in the special education arena. Knowing the special meanings of terms, as used in the context of special education, is a prerequisite for being able to meet the requirements of the law—and meet the educational needs of students with disabilities.

FOCUS POINT: Free, Appropriate, Public Education (FAPE)

All children with disabilities are guaranteed a FAPE under IDEA 2004. The law makes it clear that all state agencies must implement a zero reject policy; that is, they must provide special education and related services to meet the needs of all children with disabilities. This provision of the law is the premise on which special education is provided and all additional procedures and safeguards are based. Specifically, children with disabilities are entitled to an education "that emphasizes special education and related services designed to meeting their unique needs and prepare them for further education, employment, and independent living" (IDEA, 2004, 2651[d][1][A]). IDEA guarantees that students with disabilities have equal access to education provided at public expense, under public supervision and direction, and without charge. Such education must

- Meet the standards of the state educational agency
- Include an appropriate preschool, elementary school, or secondary school education in the state involved
- Conform with the individualized education program (IEP) required under Section 614(d) (Note: Developing IEPs will be discussed in the next section of this chapter)
- Include related services (defined later in this section) designed to enable a child with a disability to receive a FAPE as described in the IEP

Furthermore, the school and district or agency must make available all levels of schooling—preschool through secondary school education—to students with disabilities. Eligible students with disabilities are entitled to receive special education and related services from ages 3 through 21 or until they graduate from high school, whichever comes first. In addition, under Part C of IDEA, states that accept federal funding must provide federally assisted, early intervention services to infants and toddlers, from birth through age three, who would be at risk of experiencing a substantial developmental delay if early intervention services are not provided.

Examples of Management Cues

- A three-year-old girl enrolled in a community preschool has a limited vocabulary, is clumsy and prone to falling on the playground, and seems not to notice her classmates. Her teacher tells her parents that the girl's development is behind that of her same age peers and recommends that they take her for a comprehensive evaluation. The teacher refers the parents to their neighborhood elementary school.

- A 16-year-old former lacrosse star suffers oxygen deprivation and spinal injuries resulting from a diving accident. After completing a year-long rehabilitation program, he is ready to return to school (although as a differently abled student compared to before the accident). His doctors and rehabilitation therapists tell his parents he needs physical and occupational therapy, speech and language services, and special education in school. They assure the family that the school district is required to provide such services.

Suggested Risk Management Guidelines

- Know your school district's policies and procedures for special education referral, evaluation, eligibility, and placement decisions. In many large school districts, a centralized office, rather than individual schools, conducts evaluations of children not yet in kindergarten
- Find out who the special education experts are in your school district and in your school. Consult these experts whenever you have questions or doubts about particular situations.
- Never promise provision of services or tuition reimbursement strictly based on your own analysis of a child's individual case. Always follow your district's policies and procedures regarding serving students with disabilities.

▌FOCUS POINT: The IDEA Definition of Disability

According to IDEA, a child with a disability is a child with one or more of the following disabling conditions who, because of that disabling condition, needs special education and related services:

- Mental retardation
- A hearing impairment (including deafness)
- A speech or language impairment
- A visual impairment (including blindness)
- Emotional disturbance
- An orthopedic impairment
- Autism
- Traumatic brain injury
- Other health impairments
- A specific learning disability
- A developmental delay (ages three to nine or any subset of that age range)

Examples of Management Cues

- The parents of a high school junior demand that their son be tested for learning disabilities. They want the time limitations of the SATs and the state's standardized achievement tests to be waived for their son, because he experiences severe text anxiety and cannot do his best when tested under time pressure. The boy has never received special education services and is an average student taking standard curriculum courses (not honors courses). His mother, an attorney, feels her son is entitled to special testing accommodations because the "average" students had not received the benefits of the special and expensive extra services that students with disabilities and at-risk students received throughout their school years.

- A shy, first-grade student with no academic difficulties has a serious articulation problem. His classmates and teacher have a hard time understanding what he says, and his parents ask what the school can do for him.

Suggested Risk Management Guidelines

- Become familiar with the definitions and common characteristics of each disability area.
- Communicate honestly and empathetically with parents whose children experience difficulty learning. Recognize that the relationship you build from the start with such parents often determines how collaborative—or adversarial—future homeschool interactions will be.
- Get to know leaders of various disability advocacy groups in your community. Learn about the education-related issues that concern individuals and families affected with specific disabilities.

FOCUS POINT: Special Education, Related Services, and Supplementary Aids and Services

Special education is instruction that is specially designed to meet the unique needs of students with disabilities, including instruction conducted in the classroom, in the home, in hospitals and institutions, and in other settings, and instruction in physical education. Instruction that is specially designed is tailored to the child's needs and may differ in presentation, pacing, content, methodology, and mode of delivery, as appropriate. Such instruction must ensure that the child accesses the content included in the general education curriculum to meet the educational standards within the local school district and state that apply to all children.

IDEA defines related services to include transportation as well as any developmental, corrective, and other supportive services necessary to enable a student with disabilities to benefit from special education. In order for a student to receive related services, that child must first be found eligible for special education. (Note: Determining eligibility for services under IDEA is discussed later in this chapter.) Examples of related services that schools provide to students found eligible for such supports include

- Speech-language pathology and audiology services
- Interpreting services
- Psychological services
- Physical and occupational therapy
- Recreation, including therapeutic recreation
- Social work services
- School nurse services
- Counseling services, including rehabilitation counseling
- Orientation and mobility services
- Medical services for diagnostic and evaluation purposes only (does not include a medical device that is surgically implanted or the replacement of such device)
- Early identification and assessment services

Supplementary aids and services include aids, services, and other supports that are provided in regular education classes or other education-related settings to enable children with disabilities to be educated with their nondisabled peers to the maximum extent appropriate. These include devices, materials, modifications, adaptations, and accommodations to instruction that are required to meet the educational needs of the student with disabilities. Examples of such aids and services include the following:

- A device might be use of a computer on which to complete written assignments at school, or an augmentative communication device to use at school that can enable a student with a severe speech and language disability to communicate with teachers and students.
- Specialized materials might include books on tape or books with enlarged font or Braille.
- Modifications might address how to deliver instruction, how to modify class work and homework, or how to administer tests.

Adaptations to materials might include providing chapter outlines of textbook content or a different version of a classroom reading assignment (such as a novel) that is written at the student's reading level.

Accommodations that might be specified in a student's IEP include seating the student at the front of the classroom (to address visual impairments or poor attention), or providing a desk with a slant top to facilitate a student's completion of written work (to address certain fine motor difficulties).

Examples of Management Cues

- A student eligible for special education has learning disabilities that affect her organizational abilities. In addition to needing special education services to support her progression in the general education curriculum, she needs help organizing her homework assignments.

- Because an eight-year-old boy's visual impairment affects his ability to function in the regular third-grade classroom, his IEP team determines that he and his teacher need regular assistance from the itinerant vision specialist to ensure that materials are adapted to meet his needs.

Suggested Risk Management Guidelines

- Consider having at least one related service provider at IEP meetings when it is clear that a student will need related services (such as physical or occupational therapy, or speech and language therapy).
- Know the types of specialists that your school district has to provide related services and to assist a school in providing whatever supplementary aids and services a child may need.

❙ FOCUS POINT: Least Restrictive Environment (LRE)

IDEA mandates that students with disabilities be educated with their nondisabled peers to the maximum extent appropriate and that removal from the regular educational environment can only occur when the nature or severity of their disability is such that education in regular classes with the use of supplementary aids and services cannot be achieved satisfactorily. If it is determined that the general education classroom is the LRE for a child, it is equally important to ensure that the child is accessing the curriculum within that classroom rather than simply being *included*. "Access to the general education curriculum means more than simply being present in a general education classroom. Access requires that students with disabilities be provided with the supports necessary to allow them to benefit from instruction" (Nolet & McLaughlin, 2000, p. 9). Such an environment must be consistent with students' academic, social, and physical needs. While the general education classroom is most often the LRE, additional settings must be available along a continuum from least to more restrictive. Examples of additional settings include resource rooms, special classes, special schools, and hospitals or institutions.

IDEA 2004 includes an additional requirement related to LRE regarding states funding formulas for placement of students with disabilities. IDEA 2004 states,

[A] State shall not use a funding mechanism by which the State distributes funds on the basis of the type of setting in which a child is served that will result in the failure to provide a child with a disability a free appropriate public education according to the unique needs of the child as described in the child's IEP. (2678[i][A])

Therefore, it is now required that any state that does have a funding mechanism linked to student setting must revise its funding formulas to ensure that student placement is based on educational needs rather than streams of funding.

Examples of Management Cues

- Parents of a student with severe multiple disabilities want their child to attend her neighborhood school and be placed in a class with nondisabled children her own age. They argue that such a placement is the least restrictive environment for their daughter.
- A high school student with motor disabilities that necessitate her being in a wheelchair disagrees with her school district's efforts to change her placement from a high school 10 miles from her home to her neighborhood high school. She is attending the more distant school because it is a cluster school for many students with physical disabilities, and she likes having friends and classmates who deal with frustrations similar to hers. She also does not want to be the "only one" in a wheelchair at her neighborhood school. The district has a new policy initiative to place students in their neighborhood schools, in accordance with their commitment to fully include students with disabilities in regular classes.

Suggested Risk Management Guidelines

- Always consider placement in a regular classroom with same age/grade-level peers first when determining the most appropriate placement for a student with disabilities.
- The IEP team is responsible for making placement decisions for students receiving special education services. However, determining the place where a student receives services is secondary to educational programming. Therefore, the team must first make decisions about special instruction, related services, and supplementary aids and services before a placement decision is made.

| FOCUS POINT: Procedural Safeguards

IDEA delineates procedural safeguards that protect the due process rights of children with disabilities and their parents. These procedural safeguards are complex and were developed to hold the school and district accountable for complying with the law's provisions regarding the identification of a student as having a disability, the evaluations used to determine eligibility for services under IDEA, the placement of students with a disability to receive the special education services for which they are found eligible, and the provision of a FAPE.

Procedural safeguards must be provided and explained to the parents of a student with a disability in their native language at least annually. Typically, school districts have standard notices that are used districtwide to provide the required information to parents. Such notices describe specific rights guaranteed to parents (and to students of the age of majority) under IDEA, such as

- The parents' right to seek an independent educational evaluation
- The right to receive prior written notice of all meetings pertaining to their child (e.g., meetings where the district proposes to initiate or change or refuses to initiate or change the identification, evaluation, or educational placement)
- The right to have access to their child's educational records
- The right to present complaints and participate in the process for resolving such complaints
- The right to an impartial due process hearing conducted by an impartial hearing officer
- The policies related to their child's placement pending the outcome of due process proceedings
- Policies and procedures for alternative educational placements
- Policies pertaining to unilateral placement by parents of children in private schools at public expense
- Procedures for a due process hearing and the requirement for disclosure of evaluation results and recommendations
- State-level appeals (if applicable)
- Procedures for civil actions
- Policies regarding the payment of attorneys' fees
- Transfer of parental rights to the student on reaching the age of majority

Procedural safeguards provide for parent participation in all meetings where their child's identification, evaluation, program, or placement is discussed. Furthermore, parents must consent to initial educational evaluations, their child's initial placement, and any additional testing for the purposes of reevaluation (Katsiyannis et al., 2001). A due process hearing can be requested by the parents or the school for any disagreements related to a child's educational evaluation, placement or FAPE. A mediation hearing can be offered to parents willing to participate prior to going through a due process hearing. (Note: For more information on mediation, visit the Web site for the Consortium for Appropriate Dispute Resolution in Special Education at www.directionservice. org/cadre/index.cfm.)

In IDEA 2004, specific procedures were added to protect the rights of a child whenever the parents of the child are not known or the child is a ward of the state. Under these circumstances, an individual will be identified to act as a surrogate for the parents who is not an employee of the state educational agency, local school district, or any other agency that is involved in the education or care of the child.

Other areas addressed under IDEA's umbrella of procedural safeguards include disciplinary procedures, procedures for evaluation and determination of eligibility, considerations addressing least restrictive environment, and procedures regarding confidentiality of information. (Section B of this chapter discusses these special education procedures in more detail.)

Examples of Management Cues

- A parent who never responds to repeated phone messages and letters sent home, never comes to parent-teacher conferences, and, in fact, never has been seen by the child's teacher does not attend her son's IEP meeting. When the IEP form is mailed home for her approval and signature, via certified mail with return receipt, she calls the principal indignantly, stating that she would have attended the IEP meeting if she had been notified about it.
- A civil rights attorney calls the principal's office to notify her that the non-English-speaking parents of a student with disabilities were filing a claim against the school district for noncompliance with the parental notification requirements of IDEA. The attorney claims that the parents did not understand the IEP form that they had signed at the IEP meeting because a translator was not present.

Suggested Risk Management Guidelines

- Know your district's policies and procedures and timelines for providing required notifications to parents. The use of certain brochures, information sheets, or form letters may be required.
- Find out how to engage the services of a translator for providing required notices and procedural safeguards to parents in their native language.
- Find out your district's procedures for handling disputes and conflicts that may arise when working with students with disabilities and their parents. Know your district's policies and procedures for engaging the services of a mediator to help resolve issues before they escalate into a due process situation.

SECTION B: SPECIAL EDUCATION PROCEDURES

Special education law not only specifies eligibility criteria that must be met in order for a student to receive special education and related services, but it also mandates that certain procedures be followed in determining who is eligible for services, deciding on the appropriate placement for a student, and developing an individualized education program for each student with disabilities. In addition, the law contains provisions guaranteeing that parents be involved and informed in the process of making decisions regarding their child's education.

At times, administrators, teachers, and school support staff may disagree with parents about what type of placement, instructional approach, support services, and accommodations are appropriate for the students involved. School personnel must comply with procedural safeguards and notification requirements that are guaranteed to students with disabilities and their parents by law. Although students and parents have due process rights to appeal decisions with which they disagree, it is to everybody's advantage to prevent disagreements from escalating into adversarial relationships or, worse yet, litigation.

▌ FOCUS POINT: Conducting Prereferral Interventions

The prereferral intervention process is often confused with the referral process defined in IDEA. Historically, the referral process initiates the myriad decisions that identify, assess, refer, and place students in special education on the basis of their academic and behavioral needs. However, despite similar terminology, *prereferral intervention* does not imply special education. Rather, it represents a school-based intervention process that allows educational professionals and stakeholders to brainstorm ways to improve educational outcomes for students who are experiencing difficulty in the general education classroom. It is important to note that not all students who experience difficulty learning have disabilities. There are numerous other reasons why children are unsuccessful in school. Therefore, prereferral interventions typically occur prior to referral for special education services. Many schools and school districts have established formal prereferral intervention procedures, with the following purposes:

- To decrease the number of inappropriate referrals to special education and reduce the number of expensive evaluations for students who are eventually found ineligible for services under IDEA
- To provide multidisciplinary perspectives from a team of specialists to general education teachers in working with students who demonstrate a range of learning difficulties
- To provide specific strategies or accommodations that are implemented and evaluated by the referring teacher, or with outside assistance, to see if that support is sufficient to remedy the learning difficulties
- To ensure that students are served at the most cost-effective level that is appropriate to their individual learning needs
- To reduce the overidentification of students from culturally diverse backgrounds and decrease the likelihood that students will get erroneously labeled as "disabled"

A typical prereferral team might include the parent(s), other general education classroom teachers, administrators, a consulting special education teacher, and special services personnel, such as a school psychologist, a guidance counselor, a nurse, a social worker, a speech and language clinician, or other professionals, as needed. After reviewing the concern, an intervention plan is developed. According to Buck, Polloway, Smith-Thomas, and Cook (2003), the most commonly reported types of interventions include instructional modifications, behavior management strategies, curricular modifications, and counseling. Most often these interventions are conducted within the parameters of the general education class. An important component of prereferral intervention is communicating with the parents about the student's difficulties and how the school is trying to support the child. Teachers document the strategies they employ and how the student responds to the interventions. Even if the interventions are unsuccessful, the data collected during the intervention can prove valuable when others work with the same student in the future.

Prereferral interventions are not required under IDEA. However, results from the National Prereferral Intervention Survey, which included the 50 states and the District of Columbia, determined that 22 states and the District of Columbia require prereferral interventions, 15 states recommend them, 8 states do not mandate or recommend them, and in 6 states the decision to conduct prereferral interventions is at the discretion of the local school district (Buck et al., 2003). Even when not required, however, prereferral interventions are often part of school districts' service delivery model. Commonly used terms to describe these teams include *teacher assistance teams, support teams, child study teams,* and *instructional support teams.* Prereferral interventions may *not* be used by a school or district to postpone or delay evaluation for special education eligibility when there is a strong reason to suspect that a child has a disability that is impeding learning.

Examples of Management Cues

- A nine-year-old boy new to the teacher's class in January reads significantly below grade level. The first-year teacher has a master's degree in teaching mathematics, but she doesn't feel confident in assessing reading problems. The new boy has trouble sitting at his desk, and after trying unsuccessfully for a month to redirect his high energy level into his language arts work, the teacher refers him for testing because she feels he may have attention-deficit/hyperactivity disorder (ADHD) and possibly a specific learning disability in reading.
- One quiet child who sits in the back row and never causes any trouble also never turns in her homework. The teacher notices that she completes written assignments very slowly and with great effort. He worries that the girl may have some delays in fine motor development but isn't sure what steps to take to relieve some of the pressure of completing the written work. He wonders what he can do to ensure that the student is able to master the content and wants to consult with others to brainstorm strategies to encourage the child to complete her homework.

Suggested Risk Management Guidelines

- Establish a prereferral intervention process at your school (if one does not already exist) so a teacher with students experiencing difficulties learning will know
  - Whom to consult for specific types of assistance (e.g., behavior management, fine motor delays, attention and concentration problems)
  - When and how to involve parents in addressing their children's learning difficulties
  - Where to find appropriate strategies to try, to see if such strategies alleviate the problems
  - How to document the difficulties a student is experiencing and the different approaches used to try to alleviate the difficulties

- Provide time in teachers' schedules for them to meet regularly with colleagues to share successful instructional and behavior management techniques and strategies (include time for these discussions on team meeting agendas)

❚ FOCUS POINT: Early Intervening Services

The recent passage of IDEA 2004 introduced a new term to special education known as *early intervening services.* The purpose of early intervening services, similar to prereferral interventions, is to reduce the need to identify and label children as disabled; however, unlike prereferral interventions, IDEA allows school districts to use a portion of the federal money (not more than 15 percent) received each year out of Part B of IDEA to develop and implement interventions for students who have not been identified as needing special education or related services but who would benefit from additional academic and behavioral support to be successful in the general education classroom. Furthermore, early intervening funding will allow school districts who have a pattern of identifying a significant number of children from culturally diverse backgrounds as disabled to offer professional development to their teachers on the delivery of academic instruction and behavioral interventions, as well as the use of adaptive and instructional technology. Unlike prereferral interventions, data on early intervening services must be reported to the state annually and include information about the number of students who received services and the number of students who subsequently became eligible for special education and related services. These data are required under IDEA 2004.

For more information, see the Office of Special Education and Rehabilitation Services' (OSERS) IDEA-Reauthorized Statute fact sheet on Early Intervening Services available online at www.cec.sped.org/cec_bn/pdfs/EarlyIntervening Services.pdf.

Examples of Management Cues

- A first-grade general education teacher has two students in her reading group who are not progressing in the first-grade reading curriculum as defined by the school district. This teacher would like to spend extra time researching reading program alternatives that might help these two students succeed in reading, but doesn't have the time. She is aware that the special education program at her school has an alternative reading program that just might work for these two students. She does not want to refer these two students for a special education evaluation because she doesn't think they have a disability but thinks they might just need a jump-start on their reading skills. Therefore, she decides to talk to her principal about the possibilities for being trained in the use of the alternative reading program.

- A school district with predominantly white students and teachers has placed high numbers of their minority children in special education and in more restrictive settings. The state has warned the district that the percentage of minority students in special education should mirror the percentage of minority students in the general school population.

Suggested Risk Management Guidelines

- Know your state's and district's guidelines on early intervening services. State regulations may place more limitations on the use of funds than the federal law allows.
- Be aware of issues related to overidentification. If a district is found to have a disproportionate representation of students receiving special education based on race and ethnicity, the state will require the district to reserve the maximum amount of funds allowed under IDEA 2004 to provide comprehensive coordinated instructional supports.

FOCUS POINT: Determining Eligibility for Services Under IDEA

Children suspected of having a disability that affects their learning are referred for evaluation to determine whether they have a qualifying disability that makes them eligible for special education and related services. According to IDEA 2004, the evaluation process involves educators and related service providers using a variety of assessment tools and strategies to gather relevant functional, developmental, and academic information, including information provided by the parent, that may assist in determining (a) whether the child has a disability and (b) the content of the child's individualized education program, including information related to enabling the child to be involved in and progress in the general education curriculum or, for preschool children, to participate in appropriate activities. The evaluation committee should not use any single measure or assessment as the sole criterion for determining whether a child has a disability or determining an appropriate educational program for the child, and should use technically sound instruments that may assess the relative contribution of cognitive and behavioral factors, in addition to physical or developmental factors (IDEA, 2004, 2704 [2][A][i], 2705 [2][A][ii], 2705 [2][B], and 2705 [2][C]).

Assessments must be administered within a 60-day time frame (some states may have shorter time frames) from the receipt of parental consent and the student's native language, if using that language is most likely to yield accurate information about the child's academic, developmental, and functional status. Districts must also ensure that the assessments used are not discriminatory on a racial or cultural basis. In addition, assessment or measures must be valid and reliable and be administered by trained professionals.

IDEA directs schools to use sound evaluation procedures (and to eliminate unnecessary tests and assessments) to ensure that the performance of all students suspected of having disabilities is appropriately measured and analyzed to

- Determine whether the student is eligible to receive special education and related services, both initially and when reevaluated (Note: Reevaluation should occur at least once every three years)
- Determine the extent of the student's educational needs
- Rule out a lack of appropriate instruction in reading or math or limited exposure to English as a cause for the learning difficulties

Under IDEA 2004, there is no longer a requirement to conduct a full battery of assessments every three years to maintain ongoing eligibility. Now it is up to the IEP team (which includes the parents) to decide what types of assessments are necessary to determine continued eligibility. In conducting a reevaluation to determine whether a child's eligibility for special education services continues, the team reviews existing evaluation data (e.g., information provided by the parents, classroom-based assessments, and observations of teachers and related service providers). If the team agrees that determining the child's continuing eligibility and deciding whether existing services need to be changed or modified do not require collecting additional formal assessment information, then reevaluation activities need not involve formally reassessing the student. However, if the parents request that formal assessments be completed as part of the reevaluation, the assessments must be administered and evaluated (even if other team members do not consider the assessments necessary).

For more information, see the OSERS IDEA-Reauthorized Statute fact sheet on *Changes in Initial Evaluations and Reevaluations* available online at www.cec.sped.org/cec_bn/pdfs/EvaluationsandReevaluations.pdf.

Examples of Management Cues

- A Spanish-speaking second grader whose parents do not speak English is having difficulty learning language arts skills. The child also has a hard time sitting still in class and avoids her classmates on the playground. The classroom teacher is unsure about whether the student's problems are due strictly to the fact that English is her second language. She doesn't want to delay the possible provision of additional assistance to this child if underlying disabilities, in addition to the language barrier, are complicating her learning.
- Parents of a nonverbal five-year-old refuse to sign his IEP because they feel the intelligence test administered to their son and reported in the IEP is not appropriate for use with children who do not speak. They insist that he be reevaluated, at school district expense, using nonverbal, performance-based tests, and they identify the assessments they feel are appropriate.

Suggested Risk Management Guidelines

- Know the state and local school district requirements concerning assessment of children who may qualify for special education and related services under IDEA.
- Ensure that school psychologists, educators, and related service providers, when determining whether a child qualifies for services under IDEA, focus their evaluation activities on answering the following questions:
  - What is the nature and extent of the child's educational needs?
  - Does the child have a disability?
  - Does the disability affect the child's educational performance?
  - Because of the disability, does the child require special education and related services?
  - Because of the disability, does the child require special education, related services, assistive technology or services, particular accommodations, or supplemental aids to be involved in and progress in the general education curriculum?
  - For a preschool child with a disability, does the child require special education, related services, assistive technology or services, particular accommodations, or supplemental aids to be involved and progress in appropriate activities?

▌ FOCUS POINT: Developing a Student's IEP

Any student with a disability who is found eligible to receive special education and related services is entitled to receive an IEP. An IEP is a written plan describing the special education and related services specifically designed to meet the unique educational needs of a student with a disability. An IEP provides both a structure for identifying and addressing individual student needs and a written plan for ensuring that students with disabilities receive a free and appropriate public education. An IEP is developed after eligibility for services is determined, and it is reviewed and revised at least annually. A student's IEP document should contain

- A description of the student's present level of academic achievement and functional performance
- Measurable annual goals, including academic and functional goals, that enable the child to make progress in the general education curriculum (a description of benchmarks, or short-term objects, is necessary only for children who take alternate assessments aligned to alternate achievement standards)
- A description of how progress toward meeting annual goals will be measured and reported (such as quarterly or other periodic reports)

- A statement detailing the special education and related services and a description of the supplementary aids and services to be provided to the child (including any program modifications)
- An explanation of the extent, if any, to which the child will *not* participate with nondisabled children in the regular class and in other extracurricular or nonacademic activities
- A statement of any individual accommodations that are necessary for the child to participate in state and districtwide assessments or, if such assessments are not appropriate for the child, an explanation of why they are not appropriate and what alternate assessment they will take is required
- A projected date for the establishment of services and the frequency, location, and duration of each service
- Beginning not later than the first IEP to be in effect when the child is 16, a statement of the child's postsecondary goals and an assessment of the child's needs for transition services
- Beginning no later than one year prior to the student reaching the age of majority, a statement that the student has been informed of his or her rights that will transfer to him or her upon reaching the age of majority

A team consisting of multidisciplinary professionals and the student's parents develop the IEP in a collaborative process at a meeting that takes place at least once a year (or more often if needed). The IEP team consists of

- One or both parents (or legal guardian or surrogate parent)
- The student, whenever possible and appropriate
- At least one of the student's special education teachers (or service providers)
- At least one general education teacher, if the student is or may be participating in the general education environment
- A representative of the local education agency (LEA)—usually the school district—who is qualified to provide or supervise the provision of specially designed instruction to meet the unique needs of the student, is knowledgeable about the general education curriculum, and is knowledgeable about the availability of resources within the LEA
- An individual who can interpret the instructional implications of evaluation results (may be one of the team members already listed)
- Other individuals who have knowledge or special expertise regarding the student, including related service specialists, at the discretion of the parents or the LEA

The IEP team must meet at least annually—or more often as needed or as requested by any member of the IEP team—to review and revise the IEP. The law requires that the IEP must be completed and that the parents must agree with it before special education services can begin. IEP team members can be excused from participation in IEP meetings when that member's area of specialty is not being modified or discussed if both the parents and the district agree that the team member's attendance is not necessary.

In developing an IEP, the various IEP team members typically have certain responsibilities based on their areas of expertise. To maximize parent involvement in developing the IEP, some educators solicit parent input or send draft goals for parents to review prior to the IEP meeting. Doing so gives parents time to think about the draft IEP and about what contributions they want to make before the large group meeting—often conducted on a tight time schedule—is convened.

Students should understand the purpose and significance of the IEP meeting and understand their rights under IDEA as much as possible. Severe disabilities and chronological or developmental immaturity may prevent some students from participating as a contributing IEP team member. To prepare students to participate in IEP meetings, school personnel and parents can assist them in understanding their disability and helping them to be aware of their educational challenges.

IDEA 2004 mandates that the U.S. Department of Education publish model IEP forms and individualized family service plans (IFSPs) for children ages three to five no later than the date when the final regulations for implementing IDEA are released. To gain copies of these models, periodically check the OSERS Web site at www.ed.gov/about/offices/list/osers/index.html.

For more information on IEPs, see either the OSERS IDEA-Reauthorized Statute fact sheet on *Individualized Education Program* available online or their fact sheet on *Individualized Education Program (IEP) Team Meetings and Changes to the IEP*, available online at www.cec.sped.org/cec_bn/pdfs/IEPTeams.pdf.

Examples of Management Cues

- At her child's annual IEP meeting, a mother sits with her 12-year-old daughter at a long table. Also present are her daughter's special education teacher, the assistant principal, a psychologist, a social worker, the speech and language clinician, the physical therapist, and another teacher whom the mother has not met before: a total of seven educators, one parent, and one student. The mother hears everyone talk about her daughter's current level of functioning, academic and functional strengths, and areas to address, and tries to scan the pages and pages of draft goals and objectives the professionals have prepared and presented to her at the meeting. They all ask for her input and wait expectantly. One hour had been allotted for the meeting; the mother has to return to work, and the various educators also have pressing time commitments.
- The seventh-grade boy's IEP meeting is scheduled for one week after his parents receive a copy of the draft goals and objectives prepared by his teachers and therapists. The parents sit down with their son and explain what the staff proposes he work on in the coming school year. He expresses his frustration with difficulties in a particular subject, and with

his parents' help, he makes a list of things teachers did in the past that he knows helped him succeed in other classes. After considering their hopes and concerns for their son's education in relation to the draft IEP, the parents write some goals of their own to discuss with his school team. They send their ideas to the school so the staff can think about them ahead of the IEP meeting, at which time everyone will sit down together to develop the final IEP.

- Parents of a student with autism complain that their child's general education teacher is not modifying and adapting the curriculum for their son. His IEP lists several specific modifications that his teachers will make to adapt the curriculum to meet his needs.
- A student's IEP from her former school district specifies that she will have her own personal assistant accompany her throughout the entire school day. She has significant motor impairments and needs assistance with most aspects of daily living.

Suggested Risk Management Guidelines

- Familiarize yourself with every section of your district's IEP form.
- Attend training on developing IEPs that is provided by your school district for teachers and administrators.
- Ensure that all educators, specialists, and staff members involved with IEPs at your school have attended all district-level training and have a copy of the district's guidelines on proper IEP development.
- Encourage faculty and staff members to send draft IEPs home in advance of the scheduled IEP meeting so parents can read them thoroughly and prepare to provide their own input.
- Develop optional worksheets for parents and students to use when preparing for IEP meetings, to give them a structure for organizing the information that they want to discuss at the meeting (if your district does not have such worksheets available).
- Ensure that programming for students with disabilities includes a component that teaches students how to advocate for themselves.

▎ FOCUS POINT: Making Placement Decisions

After an IEP team has developed and reached consensus on a student's annual goals, they then consider the optimum setting in which the child will receive the special education and related services specified in the IEP. That is, first the IEP team determines what the child needs to make academic and functional progress, and then they decide how to meet that child's special needs. The IEP specifies what is needed—and how the needed services will be delivered. The guiding principle in determining a student's placement is the legal mandate for placement in the least restrictive environment. As mentioned in Section A, placement in the general education classroom is the first option the IEP team must consider. Removal of students with disabilities from the general education classroom should occur only when the nature or severity of the disability of a child is such that education in the general education classroom cannot occur satisfactorily with the use of supplementary aids and services. Schools must offer students with disabilities a continuum of services to ensure that students' education needs are met.

The proposed regulations for implementing IDEA state that unless the IEP requires other placements, the child should be educated in the school he or she would attend if not disabled. Furthermore, the child should be educated as close as possible to the child's home unless the parents agree otherwise (*Federal Register*, 2005). Each student with a disability has access to a continuum of placement options that include the following alternative settings, starting from the least restrictive setting and ending with the most restrictive placement:

- Regular class
- Special class
- Special school
- Home instruction
- Instruction in a hospital or institution

The student can receive different supplementary aids and services at different points on the above continuum during the same time period, to enable the student with disabilities to learn in that environment. For example, the student may spend part of the day in a general education classroom (regular class) with supportive, special education services and part of the day in a separate classroom (special class) receiving special education services.

Examples of Management Cues

- A family with a teenager who has severe emotional disturbance moves into a new school district. The child attends a private residential school. Her educational expenses were paid by the family's former school district. Her parents notify the new school district that they are having all tuition and other bills forwarded to that district and ask for the appropriate address.
- When a youngster with significant health impairments and developmental disabilities is ready to transition out of the district's preschool program, the principal and staff at her neighborhood elementary school are very nervous about being able to meet her physical care requirements along with her educational needs.

Suggested Risk Management Guidelines

- Know the continuum of services offered by the school district and how the district serves students with disabilities if the IEP team determines that the student's needs cannot be met within the district's continuum.

- Consider the following factors when deciding which placement will best meet the LRE criteria while also providing the specified services a student needs:
  - Does the placement under consideration provide the opportunity for the student, to the maximum extent appropriate, to participate with nondisabled, age-appropriate peers in academic, nonacademic, and extracurricular activities?
  - Where would the student be assigned if he or she did not have a disability? (Students with disabilities must be educated in the general education classroom of their neighborhood schools, with nondisabled peers, with appropriate supplementary aids and services, unless the IEP warrants the provision of services in a separate location.)
  - What time and distance would be involved in transporting the student from home to the school placement being considered?
  - Does the placement under consideration have the potential for harmful effects on the student or on the quality of services needed by the student (i.e., harmful effects that could prevent a student from reaching the IEP goals)?
  - What are the quality and appropriateness of the services provided at the placement, in relation to the services needed by the student?

FOCUS POINT: Implementing Required Procedural Safeguards

IDEA delineates certain protections and safeguards that exist to preserve students' and parents' rights. Parents and students of majority age have specific rights in the following areas:

- Notice—the right to receive written notice of
  - Provision of a FAPE for their child with a disability
  - Procedural safeguards delineated under IDEA
  - Scheduling of the student's IEP meeting (parents must be notified in advance)

- Consent—the right to provide informed consent for
  - Any evaluation to be conducted of a student with a disability
  - Initial placement of a child in a program providing special education and related services
  - Any change in the identification, evaluation, program, or placement of a child with a disability

- Transfer of parental rights at the age of majority (age determined by state law)
- Records—the right to inspect, review, and amend education records relating to the child
- Evaluation and eligibility procedures

- Discipline of students with disabilities
- IEP procedures
- Surrogate parent rights
- Appeals—the right to appeal any placement or education issue through requesting an administrative review, mediation, impartial due process hearing, and award of attorneys' fees

IDEA requires that schools notify parents of students with disabilities of the following specific events and provide them with the following information:

- Notice of evaluation: Parents of students with disabilities must be provided with prior written notice of evaluation and must provide their written consent for any proposed evaluation activities. If parents do not consent to proposed evaluations that school personnel believe are necessary to provide the student with a FAPE, then the LEA may choose to pursue consent for the evaluation via the mediation or due process hearing procedures.
- Notice of eligibility decision making: Parents of students with disabilities must be provided with prior written notice in advance of any meeting at which eligibility decisions will be made. As of the 1997 IDEA, parents can now vote in eligibility decision making.
- Notice of IEP-related meetings: Parents of students with disabilities must be provided with prior written notice of any IEP-related meetings, with sufficient time given to allow them to make arrangements to attend.
- Notice of procedural safeguards: Parents of students with disabilities must be provided with prior written notice of procedural safeguards (at least once annually) and of actions proposed or refused by the LEA:
  - On initial referral or parental request for evaluation
  - When filing a complaint about the services provided and requesting an impartial due process hearing
  - Whenever requesting a copy of such information

Any notice provided to parents must be written in clear language that is understandable to noneducators (i.e., free of jargon). If the native language of the parent is not English, or if the parents' mode of communication is not a written language, school districts must ensure that

- The notice is translated orally or by other means into the parents' native language or other mode of communication
- The parents understand the content of the notice
- There is documentation that these requirements have been met

Methods for contacting parents may include making telephone calls, mailing a letter, sending a letter home with the student, making a home visit, or contacting the parents through a friend or relative. It is important to document efforts made to notify parents of IEP meetings, in case the parents do not attend and the school determines that an education surrogate parent must be assigned to advocate for and represent the student's interests in the IEP process.

IDEA 2004 mandates that the U.S. Department of Education publish model forms of the notice of procedural safeguards and the prior written notice no later than the date when the final regulations for implementing IDEA are released. To gain copies of these models, periodically check the OSERS Web site at www.ed.gov/about/offices/list/osers/index.html.

For more information, see the series of three OSERS IDEA-Reauthorized Statute fact sheets on *Procedural Safeguards* available online at

- www.cec.sped.org/cec_bn/pdfs/ProceduralSafeguardsI.pdf
- www.cec.sped.org/cec_bn/pdfs/ProceduralSafeguardsII.pdf
- www.cec.sped.org/cec_bn/pdfs/ProceduralSafeguardsIII.pdf

Examples of Management Cues

- A six-year-old's parents do not speak English fluently, although they understand it better than they speak it. The district has translation services available for written communication as well as for translation at meetings and conferences. However, arranging for translators to be present at meetings and ensuring that documents get translated in a timely fashion means that school personnel need to prepare things far in advance. His teacher feels that his IEP goals are way off target, now that she has gotten to know him. She wants to rewrite the IEP.
- An 18-year-old student with learning disabilities is graduating from high school and wants to get all documentation of having ever received special education services removed from his permanent records. He said he wants to start his "adult life with a clean slate."

Suggested Risk Management Guidelines

- Ensure that faculty and staff know their responsibilities for implementing the procedural safeguards guaranteed to students and parents by IDEA and that they follow district procedures for notifying, and obtaining consent from, parents and students of majority age.
- Consult with the district's legal counsel whenever questions arise about mediation, due process rights, or procedural safeguards.
- Determine whether your school district has updated the content of the required notices to ensure that all documents are aligned with IDEA 2004.

FOCUS POINT: Participation of Students with Disabilities in State and Districtwide Assessments

According to the No Child Left Behind Act (NCLB) and IDEA, all children, including children with disabilities, are to be tested annually in Grades 3 to 8 and once between Grades 10 and 12. While the majority of students with disabilities will take the general state and districtwide assessments with necessary accommodations, as needed, a small group of students with more severe disabilities will be required to take alternate assessments as indicated in their IEP. Should the IEP team determine that a child will take an alternate assessment, a statement explaining why the child cannot participate in the regular assessment is required. In addition, the state must ensure that the alternate assessment is aligned with the state's challenging academic content.

On May 10, 2005, Secretary of Education Margaret Spellings issued a press release pertaining to students who participate in alternate assessments (U.S. Department of Education, 2005b). At press time, it appears that up to 3 percent of results for students who take alternate assessments can be reported as proficient for NCLB's adequate yearly progress (AYP) provisions. Decisions about the assessment of children with the most serious cognitive disabilities are a challenge for school districts across the country; however, until the final regulations are published, it is difficult to provide a comprehensive analysis of the proposed testing guidelines.

For more information, see the OSERS IDEA-Reauthorized Statute fact sheet on *Statewide and Districtwide Assessments* available online at www.cec.sped .org/cec_bn/pdfs/StatewideandDistrictwideAssessments.pdf.

Examples of Management Cues

- The IEP team of a nine-year-old student who is medically fragile and is receiving special education instruction on alternate performance standards determines that the child should not participate in the statewide annual assessment because this student's progress is well below his nondisabled peers.
- The parents of a seventh-grade student with a specific learning disability request that their child take a state's alternate assessment in place of the statewide assessment because their child is not good at taking tests. However, her IEP goals are aligned with the state's educational performance standards, and she is making progress in the general education curriculum.

Suggested Risk Management Guidelines

- School administrators concerned with meeting the requirements for AYP under NCLB should seek guidance from their school district or state on the procedures for calculating AYP, including requirements for students with disabilities who take alternate assessments.
- Become familiar with your state and district guidelines regarding the provision of appropriate accommodations for educational assessments.

| FOCUS POINT: Disciplining Students with Disabilities

Disciplining students with disabilities is as necessary as disciplining students who do not have disabilities. However, when a child requiring discipline for serious misconduct is a child with a disability who is eligible to receive a FAPE under IDEA, educators need to exercise great care to ensure that they comply with the law. While some people believe that students with disabilities cannot be held accountable for their conduct to the same degree as their nondisabled peers, the reality remains that certain behaviors and instances of misconduct are actual manifestations of the students' disabilities. Therefore, schools cannot stop providing services to students with disabilities, if it is determined that their behavior is a manifestation of their disability. However, appropriate consequences can be implemented for students with disabilities when their behavior is not related to their disability.

The overriding concerns of educators in any discipline situation are ensuring that all students, faculty, and staff are safe, and providing all children with the opportunity to learn. The civil rights of all individuals involved must be protected. In addition, however, mandated procedural safeguards that exist to protect the rights of students with disabilities must be implemented.

The area of discipline, as it relates to students with disabilities, is complex, and school districts generally provide their employees with specific guidance on these matters. *This chapter presents only a brief overview of this complicated issue. Readers are advised to learn the regulations for implementing the amended IDEA (once they are published) as well as the policies and procedures of their own states and local school districts in disciplining students with disabilities. Whenever questions arise, readers should consult with legal counsel.*

When a child with a disability commits a serious infraction of rules that requires disciplinary action, school administrators must consider the following questions:

- Does this student meet the IDEA definition of a "child with disabilities"?
  - If so, then all safeguards and provisions of IDEA must be afforded to that student. School districts must continue to provide special education and related services to the student through age 21 (or graduation), although it may be necessary to change the placement of the delivery of those services, depending on the type of infraction involved.
  - If not, then that student must be treated according to the school's or school district's standard disciplinary provisions.

- Was the problematic behavior or conduct a manifestation of the child's disability?
  - If so, then all safeguards and provisions of IDEA must be afforded to that student. In addition, the child's placement may not be changed as a disciplinary measure without the agreement of the IEP team, unless the misconduct involved weapons, violence, drugs, or other safety concerns. It must also be determined that the LEA has adequately implemented the IEP.
  - If not, then that student must be treated according to the same disciplinary provisions as would be applied for students without disabilities, except the student retains his or her IDEA rights and protections (e.g., FAPE, procedural safeguards).

- The review determining whether the misconduct was a manifestation of the student's disability must be conducted by the IEP team and completed immediately, if possible, or within 10 school days, if a child is removed from the previous placement through disciplinary actions.
- If the child carries to or possesses a weapon at school, knowingly possesses or uses illegal drugs, or inflicts serious bodily injury upon another person while at school, the school is permitted to remove the child to an alternate setting for not more than 45 school days without regard to whether the behavior is determined to be a manifestation of the child's disability.
- If the IEP team determines that the behavior was a manifestation of the child's disability, a *functional behavioral assessment* must be conducted and a behavioral intervention plan must be implemented. If the child's IEP already included a *behavioral intervention plan*, the plan must be reviewed and modified, as needed, to address the behavior.

Although it is true that schools cannot cease providing services to students with disabilities, regardless of the severity of the misconduct, principals and other administrators have the necessary authority—and the responsibility—to remove students with disabilities from immediate situations in which they pose a danger to themselves or others. Mandated services can be provided in alternative placements, and IDEA 2004 makes it easier for school personnel to move quickly when disciplining students with disabilities. In addition, although these students' rights to a free, appropriate, public education and to certain procedural safeguards are protected by IDEA, the law also protects the safety and learning of all students.

For more information, see the OSERS IDEA-Reauthorized Statute fact sheet on *Discipline* available online at www.cec.sped.org/cec_bn/pdfs/Discipline.pdf.

Examples of Management Cues

- An eighth grader is caught dealing drugs on the school soccer field during one lunch period and is sent home immediately with his parents. The principal acts swiftly in recommending the student for expulsion, in accordance with the district's zero tolerance policy for any incidents involving drug distribution on school premises. The boy has received special education and related services throughout his school years. According to evaluations in his student records, his primary disability is a significant hearing impairment; he also has been determined to have emotional disabilities.
- A fourth-grade girl constantly picks fights with other children in the cafeteria and on the playground. She targets younger, smaller children, whom she chases and then beats up, and she frequently hits and kicks staff members whenever they try to intervene. She brings a knife to school one day and brandishes it threateningly at her lunch table. The child functions academically several years below her grade level and is

classified as having mild mental retardation. The mother of one of her bullying targets threatens to sue the principal if she does not expel the child from that school.

Suggested Risk Management Guidelines

- Know and follow your district's policies and procedures for disciplining all students—students with disabilities and students who are not disabled. Keep in mind that protecting the safety of all students and adults in the school is of primary importance, followed by the responsibility of ensuring that all students are in a safe environment where learning can take place.
- Treat each student as an individual, and consider not just the punitive aspect of disciplinary actions but also the instructional opportunity.
- Find out where to find the specific expertise of particular value in disciplining students with disabilities—such as behavior management specialists, counselors, and speech and language clinicians.

FOCUS POINT: Determining Eligibility for Services Under Section 504 of the Rehabilitation Act of 1973

Some students with physical or mental disabilities who have difficulty learning are not found eligible for special education services under IDEA—they do not meet the eligibility criteria. For such students, Section 504 of the Rehabilitation Act of 1973 may apply. If a student has a physical or mental disability that substantially limits one or more major life activities and is not eligible for special education and related services under IDEA, that student may be eligible for services under Section 504 of the Rehabilitation Act of 1973. Life activities include the following: walking, seeing, hearing, breathing, speaking, learning, working, caring for oneself, and performing manual tasks.

Eligibility for services under Section 504 may also be considered for students who return to school after a serious illness or injury. Unlike IDEA, Section 504's implementing regulation does not limit coverage to specified and defined categories of disabilities.

In determining eligibility for services under Section 504, a team composed of persons knowledgeable about the student's needs, including the parents, should meet to determine eligibility and develop an educational plan. This team should base its eligibility decision on answers to the following questions:

- Does the student have a physical or mental impairment that affects and substantially limits at least one major life activity (i.e., walking, seeing, hearing, breathing, speaking, learning, working, caring for oneself, and performing manual tasks)?

- Would the student be qualified to participate in the academic, nonacademic, and extracurricular program under discussion if she or he did not need an accommodation or specialized services? (If the student is otherwise qualified to participate, then that student cannot be denied the opportunity to participate in the program.)

A 504 plan is a document describing the services and modifications the school district commits to provide to a student with a physical or mental impairment who does *not* qualify for services under IDEA but *does* require services, accommodations, or modifications to standard practice to experience educational benefit from the general curriculum and *does* qualify to receive services under Section 504. Students who receive IEPs (i.e., who qualify for special education and related services under IDEA) do not get 504 plans, as their IEP documents the needed supports and accommodations that the school will provide.

Examples of Management Cues

- A perpetually squirmy nine-year-old boy was recently evaluated by a psychiatrist and placed on medication for ADHD. Although this condition constitutes a disability, this student does not require special education services because he makes satisfactory progress in the general education curriculum. However, his parents request a meeting with his teachers to discuss accommodations that would help their son behave appropriately and complete his work more efficiently.
- A teenager has complicated orthopedic surgery that requires her to recover at home for several months. Although she does not qualify for special education services under IDEA, her physical condition qualifies her for services under Section 504. Her parents contact the school district to find out how to get their daughter the instruction she needs at home to keep up with her studies during her recuperation and rehabilitation from the surgery. They also request that the school district provide her with the use of a computer equipped with voice-activated word processing software.
- A student with ADHD has a 504 plan that documents her need for extended time periods for tests and certain modifications to the way assignments are presented in class.
- A student with a severe seizure disorder has a 504 plan that specifies steps to take and persons to contact in case a seizure occurs while the student is at school.

Suggested Risk Management Guidelines

- Know your district's policies and procedures for determining eligibility for assistance under Section 504 and for developing 504 plans. Ensure that your teachers, specialists, and staff are also fully knowledgeable.

- Consider holding meetings similar to IEP meetings to develop 504 plans for eligible students, if your district does not have specific procedural requirements. Although procedures for developing 504 plans are not spelled out in the federal legislation, a collaborative process involving parents and school personnel working together ensures that all concerns will be considered and addressed.
- Find out the district's policies and procedures for
  - Determining eligibility for services and accommodations under Section 504 of the Rehabilitation Act of 1973
  - Developing 504 plans for eligible students
  - Providing such services and accommodations

FOCUS POINT: Ensuring That School-Based Special Education Teachers Are Highly Qualified

Effective July 1, 2005, IDEA requires that all special education teachers meet highly qualified criteria. States will have the flexibility to allow educators to count a variety of formal and informal preparation experiences to achieve highly qualified status. The term *highly qualified* means that the teacher has

> obtained full state certification as a special education teacher (including certification obtained through alternative routes to certification), or passed the state special education teacher licensing examination, and holds a license to teach in the state as a special education teacher, except that when used with respect to any teacher teaching in a public charter school, the term means that the teacher meets the requirements set forth in the state's public charter school law. (IDEA, 2004, 2654 [10][B][i])

Once the regulations for implementing IDEA 2004 are released, more detailed information will be available regarding special education teacher requirements for teachers who are teaching to alternate achievement standards and those who teach multiple academic subject areas. Requirements for related service personnel and paraprofessionals (teaching assistants) will also be defined.

The Council for Exceptional Children (CEC) has created an easy-to-use reference guide to assist educators and school administrators in understanding the law, terminology, and requirements for being deemed highly qualified. This resource is available at www.cec.sped.org/pdfs/Highly_Qualified.pdf.

For more information, see the OSERS IDEA-Reauthorized Statute fact sheet on *Highly Qualified Teachers* available online at www.cec.sped.org/cec_bn/pdfs/HighlyQualifiedSpecialEducationTeachers.pdf.

Examples of Management Cues

- A newly hired special education teacher just completed his master's degree in special education teaching. He was hired to teach eighth-grade language arts and team-teach two sections of U.S. history. He is fully licensed in special education but has no experience teaching history.
- A teacher with 10 years of experience has just moved to your district from out of state because her husband was transferred to a local military base. In her previous state, she is certified to teach students with emotional disturbance and mental retardation; however, she has applied for a position to teach students with learning disabilities.

Suggested Risk Management Guidelines

- When considering assigning teaching duties to special educators that are outside their area of licensure, consult with your state or district licensure specialist.
- Know your state's policies for determining eligibility for licensure for teachers who transfer from out of state. Understand that licensure requirements and disability categories differ from state to state.

EXAMPLES OF LEADING U.S. SUPREME COURT CASES ON SPECIAL EDUCATION

Board of Education v. Rowley

Burlington School Committee v. Department of Education of Massachusetts

City of Cleburne, Texas v. Cleburne Living Center

Dellmuth v. Muth

Honig v. Doe

Honig v. Students of California School for the Blind

Irving Independent School District v. Tatro

Pennhurst State School and Hospital v. Halderman (Pennhurst I)

Pennhurst State School and Hospital v. Halderman (Pennhurst II)

School Board of Nassau County v. Arline

Smith v. Robinson

Southeastern Community College v. Davis

Traynor v. Turnage

University of Texas v. Camenish

Witters v. Washington Department of Services for the Blind

CHAPTER RESOURCES

Americans with Disabilities Act of 1990, 42 U.S.C. § 12101 et seq.

Brown v. Board of Education of Topeka (Brown I), 347 U.S. 453 (1954).

Buck, G. H., Polloway, E. A., Smith-Thomas, A., & Cook, K. W. (2003). Prereferral intervention processes: A survey of state practices. *Exceptional Children, 69*, 349–360.

Columbia Deaf, Dumb, and Blind Institution Incorporated, 1857, Pub. L. No. 34-5, 11 Stat. 161.

Education for All Handicapped Children Act of 1975, 20 U.S.C. § 1400 et seq.

Education of the Blind Acts of 1879, Pub. L. No. 45-186, 20 Stat. 467.

Education of the Handicapped Act of 1970, Pub. L. No. 91-230, 84 Stat. 175, Part B.

Education of the Handicapped Act Amendments of 1986, 20 U.S.C. § 1400 et seq.

Elementary and Secondary Education Act of 1965, Pub. L. No. 89-10, 79 Stat. 27.

Elementary and Secondary Education Act Amendments of 1966, Pub. L. No. 89-750, § 161, 80 Stat. 328.

Federal Register (2005, June 21). 34 C.F.R. Parts 300, 301, and 304. Assistance to States for the education of children with disabilities; Preschool grants for children with disabilities; and service obligations under special education—personnel development to improve services and results for children with disabilities; Proposed rule. U.S. Department of Education, 35782–35892.

Huefner, D. S. (2000). *Getting comfortable with special education law: A framework for working with children with disabilities.* Norwood, MA: Christopher-Gordon.

Individuals with Disabilities Education Act of 1990, 20 U.S.C. § 1400 et seq.

Individuals with Disabilities Education Act Amendments of 1997, Pub. L. No. 105-17. 20 U.S.C. § 1400 et seq.

Individuals with Disabilities Education Improvement Act of 2004, Pub. L. No. 108-446, 118 Stat. 2651.

Katsiyannis, A., Yell, M. L., & Bradley, R. (2001). Reflections on the 25th anniversary of the Individuals with Disabilities Education Act. *Remedial and Special Education, 22*, 324–334.

Martin, E. W., Martin, R., & Terman, D. L. (1996). The legislative and litigation history of special education. *The Future of Children, 6*, 25–39.

Mills v. Board of Education of the District of Columbia, 348 F. Supp. 866 (D.D.C. 1972).

Nolet, V., & McLaughlin, M. J. (2000). *Accessing the general curriculum: Including students with disabilities in standards-based reform.* Thousand Oaks, CA: Corwin.

Pennsylvania Association for Retarded Citizens (PARC) v. Commonwealth of Pennsylvania, 343 F. Supp. 279 (E.D. Pa. 1972).

Rehabilitation Act of 1973, § 504, 29 U.S.C. § 794.

Shaffer v. Weast (U.S. 546, November 14, 2005). On Write of Certiorari to The United States Court of Appeals for The Fourth Circuit Court: (377 F. 2d 449).

Silverstein, R. (2005). *A user's guide to the 2004 IDEA reauthorization (P.L. 108-446 and the conference report).* Washington, DC: Center for the Study and Advancement of Disability Policy. Retrieved June 16, 2005, from www.c-c-d.org/IdeaUserGuide.pdf

Turnbull, H. R., III, & Turnbull, A. P. (2000). *Free appropriate public education: The law and children with disabilities.* Denver, CO: Love.

U.S. Department of Education (2001). *Twenty-fourth annual report to Congress on the implementation of the Individuals with Disabilities Education Act.* Washington, DC: Author.

U.S. Department of Education (2005a). *New flexibility for states raising achievement for students with disabilities fact sheet.* Retrieved July 27, 2005, from www.ed.gov/policy/elsec/guid/raising/disab-factsheet.doc

U.S. Department of Education (2005b). Spellings announces new special education guidelines, details workable, "common-sense" policy to help states implement No Child Left Behind. Retrieved August 1, 2005, from www.ed.gov/news/press releases/2005/05/05102005.html

9

Academic Issues and Student Records

School districts employ a variety of criteria to determine whether students may be promoted or receive a diploma, including teacher-assigned grades, student performance on standardized tests or basic competency tests, and student attendance and conduct records. In recent years, school boards throughout the United States have adopted more stringent promotion standards for students, with the result that policies regarding grading, promotion, and retention are increasingly challenged in court. Policies that govern student participation in a variety of extracurricular activities are commonly subject to district rules and regulations, state high school activities associations, or other voluntary associations of member schools, and are also under close scrutiny by the courts.

SECTION A: GRADE ASSIGNMENT, GRADE REDUCTION, AND MINIMUM COMPETENCY TESTS

Courts have traditionally been reluctant to substitute their judgment for the expertise of educators. They recognize the classification of students as being rationally related to the permissible governmental end of furthering the education of students and, therefore,

---

AUTHORS' NOTE: Cases cited throughout this chapter have been selected on a precedent-setting or best-example basis regardless of jurisdiction or date of adjudication. (See Introduction for more information.)

support the authority of teachers to assign grades. Courts have also found policies authorizing retention of students who do not perform satisfactory work to be both acceptable and desirable. Teachers' grade assignments have been successfully challenged in court only when the teacher has

- *Discriminated against an identifiable or protected class of students*
- *Assigned grades in an arbitrary or punitive manner, or*
- *Assigned grades for other than actual academic achievement*

FOCUS POINT: Grade Assignment and Minimum Competency Testing

The majority of states have enacted some type of minimum competency testing. In a number of these states, students must pass a test as a prerequisite to receiving a high school diploma. Although these tests have been challenged as denying procedural due process or equal protection, courts have upheld both state-mandated and locally developed requirements for students to pass certain tests to qualify for a high school diploma.

Do the same standards apply to students who have learning disabilities? In *Brookhart v. Illinois State Board of Education* (1982), a federal court determined:

- The minimal competency test the school district used was a reasonable means to determine the effectiveness of the educational program.
- The test did not have to be modified to take into account a student's lack of mental ability or capacity.
- Regular high school diplomas could be denied to students with disabilities who failed to pass the competency test.

In general, students with disabilities who meet other requirements for graduation but fail to pass the minimum competency test may be given an alternative certificate of program completion instead of a diploma.

Examples of Management Cues

- A student who passes all his courses but fails to pass a district-administered competency test is prevented from graduating with his class.
- A student who is identified as being moderately mentally disabled, but attends classes with nondisabled students, is not required to do the same level of academic work as his classmates. At graduation he is given a "special education" diploma.

Suggested Risk Management Guideline

- Adhere to state and district requirements for graduation as they relate to competency tests. Standards for graduation that include competency testing should comply with legal requirements that students be

- Given adequate notice of the requirements
- Provided with remedial classes if they need them
- Tested with tests that are reliable, valid, and nondiscriminatory
- Tested on what they were actually taught

FOCUS POINT: Grade Reduction and Student Attendance

Some schools and school districts have policies that authorize the reduction of a student's grade or the denial of credit in a course as punishment for truancy. Although the courts are generally reluctant to interfere with the academic decisions of local school officials, they have intervened in cases in which the penalty

- Was out of proportion to the conduct being punished
- Violated the state's attendance statute
- Did not bear a reasonable relationship to some legitimate educational purpose

Such policies must be administered fairly and objectively, and courts have held that students are entitled to proper notification of the process available to contest any penalty before a grade can be reduced. Courts are more willing to require a student to receive a hearing in cases in which no school board policy authorizes the use of grade reduction for truancy.

Example of a Management Cue

- A high school teacher has a class rule that students must earn a 70 percent average to pass the course. This average includes scores for attendance and class participation. A student who earns above-average grades on his tests, often comes to class late, and seldom hands in his assignments on time has his grade reduced to below 70 percent because of his behavior and attendance.

Suggested Risk Management Guidelines

- Any school or school district policy that intends to penalize unauthorized absenteeism and truancy by reducing a student's grades should clearly state:
  - Absenteeism will result in reduction of the student's grades in the classes missed.
  - When a student misses a stated number of classes, the student will be dropped from individual classes with a no-credit or failing grade.

- Any school or school district policy that intends to penalize unauthorized absenteeism and truancy by reducing a student's grades should establish a *clear relationship* between the absenteeism and the grade reduction.

FOCUS POINT: Grade Reduction, Withholding a Diploma, and Student Misconduct

Courts in general have been unsympathetic toward rules that penalize students academically for disciplinary offenses and have clearly stated that academic grades should not be enhanced or reduced based on activities *unrelated* to academic performance.

Withholding a Diploma

Once a student has successfully completed all the district's required courses, the awarding of a diploma is a ministerial act that the school district must comply with. Refusal of a student, for example, to attend graduation or to perform some act that is not part of the school district's curriculum or not part of school regulations cannot be used to justify withholding a diploma. A school district, as noted in *Swany v. San Ramon Valley Unified School District* (1989), may bar a student from attending graduation as a disciplinary measure but cannot withhold a diploma unless a student is academically deficient.

Examples of Management Cues

- A student drinks a glass of wine in a restaurant while on a field trip with her class. In addition to being expelled from the cheerleading squad and National Honor Society, she is suspended from school for five days, and each of her individual class grades is reduced two percentage points for each day of absence.
- A student refuses to wear a cap and gown to graduation ceremonies.

Suggested Risk Management Guidelines

- Review current policies to ensure that the policies that address disciplinary issues are separate from those that address academic performance.
- Revise as appropriate any policies that permit grade reductions for student misconduct that is not directly related to academic performance.
- Ensure that any policy developed can be judged to deter targeted misconduct.

SECTION B: PARTICIPATION IN EXTRACURRICULAR ACTIVITIES

The majority of states have adopted uniform guidelines governing academic eligibility standards for athletic and nonathletic extracurricular activities.

FOCUS POINT: Academic and State Standards for Athletics and Other Extracurricular Activities

Texas was the first state to enact a no pass/no play statute. This legislation grew out of a concern that participation in extracurricular activities necessarily meant time away from studies and that the school day should be preserved for academic pursuits. When this statute was challenged on the grounds that it classified students by achievement levels, the Texas Supreme Court, in *Spring Branch v. Stamos* (1984), upheld its constitutionality. In its ruling, the court held that there is *no "fundamental right" to participate* in extracurricular activities. The court further indicated that even though there may be a "disproportionate impact on minority and learning disabled students, that alone will not support a finding that the statute [violated the constitution]."

A West Virginia State Board of Education policy recognizes and addresses the differences between students and protects the interests of disabled students. This policy provides for statewide grade standards for all nonacademic activities in Grades 7–12 that are not closely related to the program of study, such as interscholastic athletics, cheerleading, student government, class offices, and clubs. To protect the interests of students with disabilities, the policy allows students with disabilities to include grades received from placements in both regular classrooms and special education classrooms when computing their GPAs. Students placed in ungraded programs are eligible for participation in extracurricular activities if their records indicate that they are making satisfactory progress in meeting the objectives of their individualized education program (IEP) (West Virginia Code 18-2-5, 1984).

In an important case, the Montana Supreme Court, in *State ex rel. Bartness v. Board of Trustees of School District No. 1* (1986), ruled in favor of a school district that set *higher* standards for extracurricular participation than were required by the state for either extracurricular participation or graduation. In its ruling this court held that the district's policy was substantially related to an important governmental objective.

A number of states delegate authority to state high school activities associations or other voluntary associations of member schools to enact extracurricular activity participation standards. Students who participate in extracurricular activities are then subject to the rules and regulations of these associations governing eligibility, transfer, and discipline. Legal questions often emerge when school authorities deny student participation in certain extracurricular activities under rules promulgated by state associations.

Generally, the courts will intervene with state associations only when the rules or procedures demonstrate

- Fraud
- Denial of a student's substantive rights or procedural due process
- Lack of jurisdiction
- Evidence that the organization has exceeded its general powers

Rules regarding participation in extracurricular activities must be based on legal and rational reasons and must be applied uniformly. Schools may not arbitrarily allow a privilege to some students and not to others. If a school or association can show a rational basis for excluding some students, then such decisions will withstand court scrutiny unless the basis for exclusion is illegal (for example, racial or gender classifications).

The courts have held that participation in extracurricular activities is a privilege and not a property right. A school or a voluntary association may withdraw a privilege if a student fails to qualify for it. Because participation in such activities is not a property right, due process is not required to withdraw that privilege. However, a federal court, in *Pegram v. Nelson* (1979), suggested that total exclusion from extracurricular activities for a lengthy period of time, depending on the circumstances, could be sufficient deprivation to require due process.

Historically, residency requirements and transfer rules that require a definite period of residence in a school district before a student may participate in athletics, or that prohibit for a fixed time the right of transfer students to play, have been upheld by the courts as a reasonable exercise of state power. In addition, such transfer rules have been found not to violate the U.S. Constitution.

However, courts may reduce some of the authority of state high school athletic associations. In one case, *Crocker v. Tennessee Secondary School Athletic Association* (1988), a student transferred from a private school to a public school and, under the state athletic association's rules, was barred from interscholastic athletic participation for a year after transfer. The student's parents and the high school appealed to the state athletic association for an exception to the transfer rule. The association found no hardship and denied each appeal. It was then determined that the student had a learning disability and was certified as handicapped under the federal Education of the Handicapped Act (EHA). The parents sued the state association, claiming that its refusal to allow their son to participate in interscholastic sports deprived him of his rights under the EHA. The U.S. District Court ruled that although the EHA does not require local and state education agencies to provide extracurricular activities for students with disabilities, it does prohibit discrimination against those students. Therefore, the student was allowed to participate in athletics.

| FOCUS POINT: Disabled Student Athletes

Generally, athletic eligibility is governed by the rules and regulations of state athletic/activities associations. Although these state rules are superimposed on all rules and regulations of the individual school districts, they are governed by three federal statutes: the Rehabilitation Act of 1973, Section 504 of the Individuals with Disabilities Education Act, and the Americans with Disabilities Act of 1990. The question of disabled athletes participating in high school sports depends on an understanding of what constitutes "disabled" and what constitutes "otherwise qualified." When these questions have come before courts, the courts had to balance the rights of the individual athlete to participate against the concerns about possible detrimental consequences that participating could cause the athlete or other participants. Generally, trial courts have allowed the disabled athlete to participate. According to Heckman (2000), if the disability involves a clearly apparent physical disability, the case law demonstrates an inclination by the trial courts to grant the student participation, especially where a hold harmless waiver shields the school from liability. However, athletes have not been as successful in cases brought against state athletic/ activities associations' participation rules.

Examples of Management Cues

- The grade average of a three-year letterman on the football team falls below the standards adopted by the school district, and he is dropped from the football team. The student's parents argue that this action denies their son an opportunity to receive a college football scholarship and is, therefore, an unconstitutional denial of his liberty interest.
- The state high school activities association approves a rule that prevents students from participating in any extracurricular activity in the semester following their 19th birthday. A student who turns 19 on October 29 is allowed to play on the basketball team during the second semester.

Suggested Risk Management Guideline

- Make sure that any rules developed by the school, school district, or applicable state association
  - Demonstrate a recognized, legitimate educational purpose
  - Can be reasonably judged to deter the targeted misconduct
  - Are definite and provide sufficient notice of their requirements

FOCUS POINT: Participation Fee Plans

As school districts encounter economic hard times, an increasing number of school districts have begun to shift the burden of financial support of athletics and extracurricular activities to the students and their parents. School systems from Arizona to Connecticut now employ participation fee plans. In Colorado, for example, about 60 percent of the schools have pay-to-play plans (Gillis, 1995). Some of these plans are designed to provide supplemental financial support for athletics and activities through a nominal fee structure. Others are intended to offset the entire cost of the athletic or activity program by passing on those costs directly to the participants under either a flat rate or a variable rate plan. Although there are ethical questions relating to equity and decreased participation, there seem to be no legal barriers to implementing such programs. *San Antonio Independent School District v. Rodriguez* (1973) clearly put decisions concerning educational programs into the hands of the state court systems. Consequently, various state courts have been called upon to answer the legal questions concerning student participation fees, and it is not surprising that the courts have differed in their interpretations of this pay-for-play issue. For example, in the case of *Hartzell v. Connell* (1984), the California Supreme Court reversed a lower court decision that permitted the collection of participation fees for athletics and activities. The court held that "the imposition of fees for educational activities offered by public high school districts violates the free school guarantee. The constitutional defect in such fees can neither be corrected by providing waivers to indigent students, nor justified by pleading financial hardship."

A case in Michigan illustrates the opposing point of view. In *Attorney General v. East Jackson Public Schools* (1985), the state attorney general filed a suit to prevent two school districts from continuing to collect participation fees. On appeal, the Michigan Court of Appeals ruled for the districts, citing that "the fee in question only funds an extra curricular activity which is not required and for which no credit is given to a participant." The court noted that "[t]here is a confidential process under which students who do not have means to pay will have the fees waived," and "we cannot say that the school board had acted in an arbitrary and unreasonable manner." The issue of pay-to-play fees remains unsettled, and school districts considering implementation of such programs should be sure that they are in compliance with the court decisions in their particular states.

SECTION C: STUDENT RECORDS

As a result of growing concern about the potential invasion of privacy associated with the amount and type of personally identifiable data that were being collected by various agencies, the Family Education Rights and Privacy Act (FERPA) was passed in 1974. This act, also known as the Buckley Amendment, guarantees parental access to the education records of their children as well as limiting the disclosure of those records.

FOCUS POINT: Family Rights and Privacy Act (FERPA), aka The Buckley Amendment

In 1974, the U.S. Congress enacted legislation in the form of the Buckley Amendment, which became known as the Family Education Rights and Privacy Act (FERPA). (See also FERPA in Chapter 2.) This act set forth several guidelines related to the protection and sharing of student records. Prior to the passage of FERPA, educators maintained student records and shared the contents of those records at their own discretion, including the posting of student grades. As a result, it was possible for incorrect, misleading, embarrassing, or damaging information to be maintained and disclosed without the knowledge or consent of the parent or student. Furthermore, parents had no access to the records or any right to correct inaccurate information.

FERPA was enacted to correct some of the real or potential abuses in the access to and disclosure of education records. FERPA established students' right to privacy in their education records. For purposes of this legislation, the term *education records* means those records, files, documents, and other materials that

- Contain information directly related to a student
- Are maintained by an education agency or institution or by a person acting for such agency or institution

Education records do not include notes, memory aids, and other similar information that is maintained in the personal files kept by school officials and is not accessible or revealed to authorized school personnel or any third party. Such information can be shared with the student or parent, but if it is released to authorized school personnel or any third party, it becomes part of the student record subject to all the provisions of FERPA.

FERPA requires that schools formulate a policy and procedures related to parental access to the education records of their children. This policy should provide parents with the right to

- Inspect and review the education records
- Amend the education records
- Limit the disclosures of personally identifiable information from education records

Education records may not be destroyed when there is a current request by a parent or student to see them.

In 1978, FERPA was amended to restrict the purpose for which psychiatric examinations, testing, or treatment may be used. The new section specifies that no student shall be required to submit to any psychiatric examination, testing, or treatment for which the primary purpose is to reveal information concerning

- Political affiliations
- Mental and psychological problems potentially embarrassing to the student or family
- Sex behavior and attitudes
- Illegal, antisocial, self-incriminating, and demeaning behavior
- Critical appraisals of other individuals with whom respondents have close family relationships
- Legally recognized privileged and analogous relationships, such as those of lawyers, physicians, and ministers

FERPA gives parents the right to

- Review the education records of their children
- Have access to the education records of their children within 45 days of the initial request

- Have a hearing to challenge the content of the student's education records
- Correct or delete any inaccurate, misleading, or inappropriate data contained in the education records and insert into the records their written explanation regarding the content of such records
- Give or withhold consent for the records to be released (the right of consent shifts to the student at age 18, or when the student enters an institution of postsecondary education)

Courts have ruled that both parents have the right to inspect their child's records unless the noncustodial parent waives such a right in a separation agreement. FERPA provides that a school can release a student's education records without the written consent of the parents to

- Other school officials determined by the school to have a legitimate education interest in the information
- Officials of other schools or school systems in which the student seeks or intends to enroll (provided that the student's parents are notified of the transfer, receive a copy of the records if desired, and have an opportunity for a hearing to challenge the content of the records)
- Certain authorized representatives of the federal government and state education authorities, in connection with the audit and evaluation of federally sponsored education programs or with the enforcement of the related federal legal requirements
- Local and state officials to whom information is specifically required to be reported or disclosed pursuant to state statutes in connection with a student's application for or receipt of financial aid
- Organizations conducting studies, with certain specific limitations
- Accrediting organizations when performing their responsibilities
- Parents of a dependent student
- Authorized persons, as specified, in connection with an emergency

Any and all personally identifiable information must remain confidential and must be destroyed when no longer needed.

Directory Information

Directory information refers to information that is generally available through various sources and is often reported by the schools in student directories, athletic programs, and news releases. The law requires that public notice must be given by any school regarding the categories of directory information that it intends to make public. A reasonable period of time must be given after the notice so that a parent can inform the school of any material that cannot be released without the parent's prior consent. Directory information includes

- Name, address, and telephone number
- Date and place of birth

- Major field of study
- Participation in officially recognized activities and sports
- Weight and height of members of athletic teams
- Dates of attendance
- Degrees and awards received
- Most recent previous school attended
- Other similar information

Enforcement

If the U.S. Department of Education finds that FERPA has been violated, the parties must be notified, and the secretary of education must attempt to effect compliance through voluntary actions. If the school system fails or refuses to comply, the school district may have its federal education funds terminated. The act does not create any independent cause of action. If it is found that the school district's actions deny students' civil rights, damages and attorneys' fees may be awarded.

▌ FOCUS POINT: FERPA and IDEA

When the Elementary and Secondary Education Act (ESEA) and the Individuals with Disabilities Act (IDEA) were reauthorized in 1997, IDEA incorporated FERPA language. However, specific details of IDEA provide additional protections related to age of consent procedures for students who receive special and related services. For example, IDEA allows the disclosure of a student's special education records without parental consent

- When it affects law enforcement officials' ability to serve the student
- When necessary to protect the health or safety of the student or other persons
- To school-employed campus police solely for law enforcement purposes
- Under court order or subpoena

However, even in these cases, the school administrator must make a reasonable effort to notify the student or the student's parents.

▌ FOCUS POINT: FERPA and Privacy in the Classroom

Although FERPA was enacted in 1974, it is only recently that federal courts have become involved in interpreting its implementation. In 2002, the U.S.

Supreme Court, on an appeal of an earlier decision in the Tenth Circuit, *Falvo v. Owasso* (2000), rendered a decision interpreting the constitutional right of privacy as a result of a grading practice used by many teachers. *Owasso Independent School District I-001 v. Falvo* (2002) concerned the practice of students exchanging papers and grading each other's work as the teacher went over the answers. In this case, the teacher permitted students to announce aloud the grades on papers that they had graded. The Court ruled that student grading of assignments does not violate the provisions of FERPA. The Court offered five reasons for its decision: (1) the teacher does not maintain a grade until it is recorded, (2) by grading assignments, students do not constitute persons acting for an educational institution within FERPA, (3) peer-graded items do not constitute education records protected by FERPA until a teacher collects the students' papers or other items and records the grades in the teacher's grade book (in reaching its conclusion, the Court noted that peer-graded items were not maintained within the meaning of FERPA, as the student graders only handled the items for a few moments), (4) permitting parents to contest each student's graded work would bury the school in hearings, and (5) Congress did not mean to intervene in this drastic fashion with traditional state functions. This case is particularly important because it reinforces the long-standing tradition of the courts' reluctance to substitute their opinion for those of professional educators when it comes to issues of instruction. According to Mawdsley and Russo (2003), "the Court refused to be drawn into classroom management of public schools. The Court made it clear that peer grading is a matter of pedagogy and not a proper matter within the expertise of courts."

Examples of Management Cues

- A high school journalism teacher is preparing to leave on summer vacation when she receives a phone call from the president of a community service organization. The president tells the teacher that one of the teacher's former students is being considered for a college scholarship and asks about the student's grades in her class.
- A third-grade teacher posts the test papers of his better students on the class bulletin board. He feels that this practice recognizes the effort of his better students and serves as a motivator for his weaker students.
- A special education teacher is frustrated that the school does not have enough money to allow her to take her students on two field trips. She decides to raise the money by asking local business owners to make contributions. Before speaking with the businesspeople, she intends to bring her camera to school and take candid photographs of all her students. She will then label a photo album with the caption, "Don't you want these special children to have the best education possible?" She plans to use the album for publicity purposes.
- A student lives with his grandmother. Although she is not his legal guardian, she attends all parent-teacher conferences and wants to be

kept informed about her grandson's attitude and grades and to receive his formal grade reports. She is also an active member of the school's PTA.

- A principal is notified that several students are in possession of handguns. The police are called to the school. When they arrive, the principal informs the police that one of the students is receiving special education services and will require additional hearings. The principal informs the police that he will not release the student's records.

Suggested Risk Management Guidelines

- Publish and distribute an annual notice to parents and students explaining their rights under FERPA. (See Annual Notice in Chapter Resources for more information.)
- Develop and implement legally defensible policies and procedures consistent with the requirements of FERPA. Principals should implement to the letter and *monitor* all procedures required by the board of education or the act itself. Inform students, parents, and legal guardians about their rights under this act.
- Require each time (and for each item) the consent of the student and one parent or guardian whenever the student's record is requested to be divulged to persons other than certified professional personnel.
- Maintain accurate records describing any and all examinations of student files. Include information about why the file was examined.
- Make sure that any corrections or adjustments to student records are dated and initialed by the person responsible.
- Allow students and parents or guardians to submit any materials to the record, for example, results of outside testing and evaluation, medical or psychological reports, and explanations of unfavorable evaluations.
- If it is necessary to place disciplinary information in student records, any information should be detailed and include, as a minimum, the infraction committed, time, place, and witnesses as appropriate.
- Refrain from discussion with third parties regarding confidential information found in student records.
- Store student records in a safe and secure place. Student records should not be removed from school premises by anyone unless proper authorization is secured.
- Unless prohibited by court order, a noncustodial parent should be given the same right to examine student records as the custodial parent.
- Provide assistance, when necessary, to enable students and their parents or guardians to understand the material in their records.
- Be advised that in the event a decision of a principal or other official regarding any of the provisions of FERPA is not satisfactory to students or parents, they have the right to appeal to the superintendent of schools.

CHAPTER RESOURCES

Annual Notice

The following is a suggested format for an annual notice to parents and students regarding FERPA rights, which should contain, at a minimum, the following information:

- *Parental Rights:* The Family Educational Rights and Privacy Act (FERPA), 20 U.S.C. § 1232g, C.F.R. Part 99, Protection of Pupil Rights Amendment, 20 U.S.C. § 1232h, 34 C.F.R. Part 98, Elementary and Secondary Education Act, 20 U.S.C. §§ 7165, 7908, and 10 U.S.C. § 503 provide certain notice, inspection, and participation rights to parents, students who are over age 18, and emancipated minors. This booklet provides you with information about those rights.

- This booklet includes opt-out forms that you should submit to your child's school principal if you do not want your student to participate in a given activity. If you have no objection to the activities described in this booklet, do not sign or submit any of the forms.

- *Consent to Surveys:* You have the right to consent before your student participates in any federally funded survey asking about any of the following: political affiliation or belief of the student or parent; mental or psychological problems of the student or family; sexual behavior or attitudes; illegal, antisocial, self-incriminating, or demeaning behavior; critical appraisals of others with whom the student has close family relationships; legally privileged or analogous relationships such as those with lawyers, physicians, and ministers; religious practices, affiliations, or beliefs of student or parent; and income (other than required to determine program eligibility).

- *Survey Inspection and Opt-Out Rights:* You have the right to inspect any survey dealing with the above topics, regardless of funding source, and to opt your student out of participation. You may also inspect instructional materials used in connection with such surveys.

- *Inspection of Educational Materials:* You have the right to inspect any instructional materials used as part of the educational curriculum. School district policies and regulations provide more detail about curriculum materials.

- *Physical Examinations:* Federal law requires that parents be permitted to opt the student out of certain physical examinations if the examinations are not authorized by state law.

- *Inspection of Student Records:* You have the right to inspect and copy all records relating to your student within 45 days of the school's receipt of your request. You should submit a written request, identifying the records you want to inspect, to your student's principal. The principal will notify you of the time at which and the place where records may be inspected. You may be charged a fee if you request copies.

- *Amendment of Student Records:* You have the right to request an amendment of any education record that you believe is inaccurate or misleading. You should write the school principal, clearly identify the part of the record you want to have changed, and specify why it is inaccurate or misleading. The school district will notify you, if applicable, of your right to a hearing regarding the amendment request, and provide additional information regarding the hearing procedures.

- *Education Records Consent:* You have the right to consent before the school district discloses personally identifiable information from your student's education records, unless federal law specifically authorizes release without consent. Consent is not required for disclosures to school officials with legitimate educational interests, however. A school official is (a) a person employed by the school district as an administrator, a supervisor, an instructor, or a support staff member (including school nurses, clinic room aides, and law enforcement personnel), (b) a person serving on the school board, (c) a person or company with whom the school district has contracted to perform a special task (such as an attorney, an auditor, a medical consultant, or a therapist), or (d) a parent or another volunteer serving on a special committee, such as a disciplinary or grievance committee, or helping another school official perform his or her tasks. "Legitimate educational interest" means the need to review the record in order to fulfill a professional responsibility. Consent is also not required to release education records to officials of another school or school district if your student seeks or intends to enroll there. The school district forwards such records on the request of the other school or school district.

- *Opt-Out Options:* As a general policy, the school district does not release student addresses, phone numbers, parent information, or demographic information (such as primary language or gender) to the press or the general public, even though it is directory information. The school district does provide limited directory information to school-related organizations, such as PTAs, and to state and county agencies to help provide services. If you do not want directory information released to these entities, you may select one of the options below. (Include opt-out forms as described below in your notice.)
  - *Choice A:* Omit your child from school directories. The school district will not provide student addresses and phone numbers to the press or the general public. Unless you opt out, however, it does provide that information to PTAs and other school-related organizations, which may use that information to publish student directories and may contact your family about school-related activities. Check Choice A if you want your child to be included in all school publications except student addresses and telephone directories.

- *Choice B:* The school district also provides directory information, such as student address and phone number, parent or guardian name, address, and phone number, and demographic information to state and county agencies if the district determines that such information will help provide services to students or the school community. Check Choice B if you do not want state and county agencies to receive this type of information about your child, but you do want your child included in school publications.
- *Choice C:* Omit your child from photographic productions and other types of district-sponsored publicity and media coverage. The district produces, and participates in, television, videotape, motion picture, audio recordings, and still photograph productions that may use your child's name, likeness, or voice. Such productions may be sold or used for educational purposes and may be copyrighted, edited, and distributed by the district. News media often cover the public school system and sometimes photograph, videotape, or broadcast likenesses of students during school hours. Check Choice C if you do not want your child's image, name, or voice featured in such productions.
- *Commercial Use of Student Information:* You have the right to opt your child out of any collection of personal information if that information will be marketed or sold by the school district or if the district collects it for others to sell. The school district provides names and addresses of seniors to commercial photographers, who photograph each senior during the graduation ceremonies and then contact the graduates by mail to sell the photographs. If you do not want to receive a solicitation from a commercial photographer to purchase photos of your student graduating, complete the opt-out form provided.
- *Military Recruiters:* Federal law requires secondary schools to release the names, addresses, and telephone numbers of secondary students to military recruiters who request this information. You or the student (even if the student is not 18 or emancipated) may prohibit the release of this information to military recruiters by completing the opt-out form provided.

- *Guidance and Counseling:* You have the right to withdraw your student from academic or career guidance provided by the school or personal-social counseling provided by the school, or both. The guidance program is part of the comprehensive education provided to all students and focuses on teaching positive approaches toward school and learning and the knowledge and skills for life and employment. It includes
  - Academic guidance, which helps students and their parents learn about required curriculum and testing and choose appropriate courses leading to graduation and a transition to college, career and other educational opportunities

– Career guidance, which helps students acquire information and skills in order to plan for work, jobs, apprenticeships, and postsecondary education and career opportunities

– You may excuse your child from academic or career guidance or from personal-social counseling at any time by completing the appropriate opt-out form. Parents who elect to have their child excused from academic or career guidance shall have sole responsibility to ensure that all academic and graduation requirements are fulfilled.

- *Complaints:* If you have a complaint regarding any of the above rights, you may contact your school principal. In addition, if you believe that your rights in regard to surveys, educational materials, commercial use of information, physical examinations, military recruiters, inspection or amendment of student records, directory information, or privacy of student records have been violated, you may file a complaint with the Family Policy Compliance Office, U.S. Department of Education, 400 Maryland Avenue, S.W., Washington, DC 20202-4605.

Attorney General v. East Jackson Public Schools, 372 N.W. 2d 638.

Brookhart v. Illinois State Board of Education, 534 F. Supp. 725 (C.D. Ill. 1982).

Crocker v. Tennessee Secondary School Athletic Association, 735 F. Supp. 753 (1988).

Falvo v. Owasso Independent School District, Filed U.S. Ct. App. (10th Cir., July 2000).

Family Education Rights and Privacy Act, 20 U.S.C.S. § 1232g (2002).

Gillis, J. (1995). 15-member Colorado association staff serves 285 schools across state. *National Federation News, 12*(5), 23–25.

Hartzell v. Connell, 35 Cal.3rd 899 (1984).

Heckman, D. (2000). *Athletic associations and disabled student-athletes in the 1990's.* 143 Ed. Law Rep., 1.

Individuals with Disabilities Act (IDEA), 20 U.S.C.S. § 1415 (2002).

Mawdsley, R. D., & Russo, C. J. (2003). *FERPA, Student privacy and the classroom: What can be learned from Owasso School District v. Falvo?* 171 Ed. Law Rep., 397.

Owasso Independent School District I-001 v. Falvo, 534 U.S. 426 (February 19, 2002).

Pegram v. Nelson, 469 F. Supp. 1134, 1140 (M.D. N.C. 1979).

San Antonio Independent School District v. Rodriguez, 411 U.S. 907 (1973).

Spring Branch v. Stamos, 695 S.W.2d 556 (Tex. 1984).

State ex rel. Bartness v. Board of Trustees of School District No. 1, 726 2d 801 (Mont. 1986).

Swany v. San Ramon Valley Unified School District, 720 F. Supp. 764 (N.D. Cal. 1989). See also *Valentine v. Independent School Dist. of Casey,* 191 Iowa 1100, 183 N.W. 434 (1921).

West Virginia Code 18-2-5 (1984).

10

Copyright Law

C opyright is a form of protection provided by the laws of the United States (Title 17, U.S. Code) to the authors of "original works of authorship," including literary, dramatic, musical, artistic, and certain other intellectual works. This protection is available to both published and unpublished works. Section 106 of the 1976 Copyright Act generally gives the owner of a copyright the exclusive right (a) to reproduce the work and to authorize others to do so, (b) to prepare derivative works based on the work, (c) to distribute copies of the work, (d) to perform the work, or (e) to display the work.

It is illegal for anyone to violate any of the rights provided by the copyright law to the owner of a copyright. These rights, however, are not unlimited in scope. Sections 107 through 121 of the 1976 Copyright Act establish limitations on these rights. In some cases, these limitations are specified exemptions from copyright liability. One major limitation is the doctrine of "fair use," which is given a statutory basis in Section 107 of the act. In other instances, the limitation takes the form of a "compulsory license," which permits certain limited uses of copyrighted works upon payment of specified royalties and compliance with statutory conditions.

Only the author or those deriving their rights through the author can rightfully claim a copyright. In the case of works made for hire, the employer and not the employee is considered to be the author. Section 101 of the copyright

---

AUTHORS' NOTE: Cases cited throughout this chapter have been selected on a precedent-setting or best-example basis regardless of jurisdiction or date of adjudication. (See Introduction for more information.)

law defines a "work made for hire" as (a) a work prepared by an employee within the scope of his or her employment or (b) a work specially ordered or commissioned for a specific use.

The U.S. Copyright Office makes it clear that mere ownership of a book, manuscript, painting, or photograph, film or DVD, or sound recording (i.e., record, tape recording, CD, etc.) does not give the possessor the copyright. This is the critical point. It does not matter that you bought the greeting card; you do not have the right to make 20 copies of the cartoon image to decorate your classroom. It does not matter that your school purchased a word processing program; teachers may not copy it and install it on their laptops. Intellectual property is just like any other property; it is owned by someone. Using someone's intellectual property is analogous to stealing another's possession.

▌ FOCUS POINT: What Copyright Protects

Copyright protects "original works of authorship" that are fixed in a tangible form of expression. The Copyright Act of 1976 protects such items of expression as literary, dramatic, and musical works; pantomimes and choreography; pictorial, graphic, and sculptural works; audiovisual works; sound recordings; and architectural works. As soon as an original expression is fixed in some tangible form, it is eligible for copyright protection. Consequently, even without applying for a copyright, almost any original expression is protected as soon as it is created. For example, a Web page would be protected as soon as the file is saved as an .html file. Therefore, it is important for educators and students to understand that most of the items they access on the Internet are most likely protected by a copyright.

Copyright protection generally covers such literary works as books, periodicals, manuscripts, sound recordings, computer programs, film, tapes, and disks. Copyright protection generally covers such musical and dramatic works as musical compositions, stage plays, screenplays, television plays, pantomimes and choreography, still or motion pictures, and other audiovisual media. The copyright law also protects such pictorial, graphic, and sculptural works as fine art, graphic art, applied art, photographs, prints and art reproductions, maps and globes, charts, technical drawings, diagrams, models, sculptures, statues, figures, and forms. Copyright protection also extends to sound recordings of music, the spoken word, and sound effects.

Copyright protection applies to trademarks and logos but does not extend to names, short phrases, and slogans; familiar symbols or designs; mere variations of typographic ornamentation, lettering, or coloring; the mere listings of ingredients or contents; or works consisting entirely of information that is common property and containing no original authorship (e.g., standard calendars, height and weight charts). Ideas, procedures, methods, systems, processes, concepts, principles, discoveries, or devices are protected by patent.

▌ FOCUS POINT: The Source of Copyright Law

The source of copyright law is the copyright clause of the U.S. Constitution, which states, "To promote the Progress of Science and useful Arts, by securing for limited Times to Authors and Inventors the exclusive Right to their respective Writings and Discoveries." (See U.S. Constitution.) Title 17 of the U.S. Code extends this protection to any original works of authorship in any tangible medium of expression.

Over the past several decades, copyright law has been significantly modified. Publication is no longer the key to obtaining a federal copyright, as it was under the Copyright Act of 1909. Since January 1, 1978, registration is also no longer necessary, although it is recommended by the Copyright Office. Consequently, a copyright is secured automatically when it is fixed in a copy for the first time. "Copies" are material objects from which a work can be read or visually perceived either directly or with the aid of a machine or device, such as books, manuscripts, sheet music, film, videotape, microfilm, cassette tapes, LPs, or computer disks (CDs, DVDs, etc.). By registering the work with the Copyright Office, the author has more legal remedies under the law against unlawful use than with an unregistered work. Substantial statutory damages for willful infringement of registered copyright may total up to $100,000 per work infringed. The copyright owner may also recover any actual damages, including any profits the infringer gained as a result of the infringement, an award of attorneys' fees, injunctive relief against future infringement, and impoundment and destruction of infringing material. In addition, registration is a deterrent to violators, because most copy centers are reluctant to copy works when each item has the copyright mark (*Basic Books, Inc. v. Kinko's Graphics Corp.*, 1991).

With the passage of the Sonny Bono Copyright Term Extension Act (CTEA) in 1998, the copyright for works created after January 1, 1978, endures for the life of the author plus an additional 70 years. The extension may be even longer under other circumstances. Any work no longer protected by copyright is in the public domain and may be used by anyone without prior permission.

A copyright notice contains the following three elements:

1. The symbol © or the word *Copyright*

2. The year of first publication of the work

   In the case of compilations or derivative works incorporating previously published material, the year date of first publication of the compilation or derivative work is sufficient. The year date may be omitted when a pictorial, graphic, or sculptural work and any accompanying textual matter is reproduced in or on greeting cards, postcards, stationery, jewelry, dolls, toys, or any useful article.

3. The name of the individual owner of the copyright or an abbreviation by which the name can be recognized or a generally known alternative designation of the owner

The three elements of the notice should appear together on the copies or on the label and should be affixed to copies in such a way as to "give reasonable notice of the claim of copyright." Section 106 of the Copyright Act gives copyright owners the "exclusive rights of reproduction, adaptation, publication, performance and display" without obtaining permission.

▌ FOCUS POINT: Public Domain

The public domain is that repository of all works that for whatever reason are not protected by copyright. As such, they are free for all to use without permission. Works in the public domain include the following classifications: originally noncopyrightable, lost copyright, expired copyright, and government documents. Facts, names, short phrases, ideas, and titles are noncopyrightable. Although it is difficult to lose copyright protection today, works published prior to January 1, 1978 that were not copyrighted may be considered in the public domain. If, for any reason, a copyright owner failed to renew his or her copyright, the material generally reverts to the public domain. Federal documents and publications are not copyrighted and therefore are considered to be in the public domain. Consequently, laws, statutes, agency circulars, federal reports, and any other documents published or generated by the federal government are not protected. However, if the document was contracted by an individual for use by the federal government, the work is copyrighted.

▌ FOCUS POINT: Fair Use Doctrine

For educators, one of the most important limitations on the exclusive rights of copyright owners is the fair use doctrine. This doctrine is broadly expressed in 17 U.S.C. Sections 107, "Limitations on exclusive rights: Fair use"; 108, "Limitations on exclusive rights: Reproduction by libraries and archives"; 110, "Limitations on exclusive rights: Exemption of certain performances and displays"; and 117, "Limitations on exclusive rights: Computer programs."

Fair use is the legal principle that defines the limitations on the exclusive right of the copyright holder. Electronic publication and communication technologies, including computers and computer networks and Internet Web sites and e-mail, have combined to significantly modify how information is published and disseminated. The courts, legislatures, and consumers are in a constant state of flux as they attempt to respond to this rapidly changing technology. The January 2000 lawsuit between the Recording Industry of America and the MP3.com Web site illustrates how technology developments can place copyright owners at odds with entrepreneurs. (See Snider, 2001.) This case challenged the legality of a company, MP3.com, enabling computer owners to copy and save copyrighted musical tracks in a password-protected area of the Web site for later listening via any Internet access device. The recording industry argued that this practice creates an illegal database "with no permission and no license." Two other suits have been brought by the motion picture and music industries against Scour.com, a site that lets users locate and copy music and movies directly from other users' computers, and the Napster music trading site.

Over the years, a substantial number of court decisions have sought to balance the rights of copyright owners to profit from their creativity and the legitimate interests of educators to use and disseminate copyrighted works. The primary impact of the fair use doctrine is the elimination of the need to obtain permission or pay royalties for purposes such as criticism, comment, news reporting, teaching (including multiple copies for classroom use), scholarship, and research. Unfortunately, the statute does not specifically delineate what a teacher may and may not do. Consequently, every decision must be made on a case-by-case basis according to the guidelines set forth in the statute.

The following four factors must be considered in determining whether the proposed use of copyrighted work constitutes fair use:

1. The purpose and character of the use, including whether the use is of a commercial nature or is for nonprofit educational purposes

   Nonprofit, educational purposes seem to be less strictly controlled than commercial purposes.

2. The nature of the copyrighted work

   Newspaper articles and other material that are very timely or out of print are more likely to be considered fair use than books or video programs. However, more and more newspaper stories are carrying a copyright notice.

3. The amount and substantiality of the portion used in relation to the copyrighted work as a whole

   This aspect may be the most difficult to understand. Even the Copyright Office holds that there is no specific number of words, lines, or notes that may be safely taken without permission. Excerpts are more likely to be permissible than are entire works. If large portions of the work, or that part of the work that is considered to be the core of the work, are copied, there is a higher likelihood of copyright infringement.

4. The effect of the use on the potential market for or value of the copyrighted work

   Courts give this factor greater weight than the other three. If a reasonable person would conclude that the work was copied to avoid purchasing the copyrighted work, or it is proven that the market for the work was damaged as a result of the copying, a court is likely to consider this to be a copyright infringement.

Each of these four factors must be considered when determining if the copying falls under fair use.

Fair use has been generally defined as the privilege of people other than the owner to use copyrighted material in a reasonable manner without consent (Henn, 1988, quoting *Rosemont Enters. v. Random House, Inc.*, 1966). School leaders face the challenge of encouraging teachers and students to discover and use the most current research while still complying with copyright law.

In school settings, timely access to tools and resources that enhance the teaching and learning process is of paramount importance. Although the vast majority of teachers would not think of stealing something, many educators routinely use copyrighted material *without* permission. Most teachers violate copyright law because they are uninformed or confused about what they may and may not legally copy.

Congress has developed guidelines to clarify the fair use doctrine. These guidelines establish minimum standards and have won acceptance by some courts. (See, for example, *Marcus v. Rowley*, 1983.) They allow teachers to make single copies of a chapter from a book, an article from a periodical or newspaper, a short story, short essay, or short poem, or a chart, graph, diagram, or cartoon for research or teaching purposes. Teachers may make multiple copies for classroom use if the copying meets the test of brevity, spontaneity, and cumulative effect.

- Brevity is defined to mean 250 words of a poem or not more than two pages of poetry; a complete article, story, or essay of fewer than 2,500 words; an excerpt of 10 percent of a work or 1,000 words; or one graph or one cartoon.
- Copying is spontaneous when done at the inspiration of an individual teacher and when it occurs so close in time to the use of the work that it would be unreasonable to expect the teacher to obtain permission to copy.
- The cumulative-effect limitation is violated if the copying is for more than one course in the school; more than one poem, story, or article or two excerpts are copied from the same author; more than three items are taken from a collective work or periodical volume during one class term; or a teacher uses multiple copies more than nine times in one course during one class term.

| FOCUS POINT: School-Sponsored Internet

The vast majority of the items accessed from the Internet are protected by copyright law. However, though not yet tested in the courts, it is unlikely that school districts will be held liable for student or employee Internet copyright infringements. Title II of the Digital Millennium Copyright Act (DMCA) indicates that direct or vicarious liability will occur only if the district received direct financial benefit from the violation and had the ability and right to control the acts of the primary infringer. Conn and Zirkel (2000) suggest, however, that districts should "consider requiring users of the school Internet to sign 'acceptable use policies,' that include simple explanations of what constitutes copyright infringement" (p. 22). They also warn districts to be aware that in some circumstances, "caching" is another potential copyright infringement. *Caching* is the term used to describe the material that is often stored on the computer's RAM or at the district's server. The infringement is generally related to copyright infringement when a site supported by advertising is cached for lengthy periods of time (Conn & Zirkel, 2000). An infringement might occur if the advertiser was disadvantaged by having inaccurate information accessed from the district's site. Liability, in this case, would be reduced if there was a clear policy requiring regular review and deletion of cached information. It is also prudent for districts to educate all Internet users of the liabilities and dangers associated with clipping and pasting links from one site to another.

Conn and Zirkel (2000) also warn school districts about two other liability issues relating to the use of school-sponsored e-mail: (1) interception and privacy of e-mail messages and (2) e-mail used as a tool for sexual harassment. School district Internet use policies should clearly state that the district retains unlimited access to all e-mails on the system, and that the use of user names and passwords does not entitle users to an expectation of privacy. Although Title I of the Electronics Communications Privacy Act (ECPA) of 1986 protects e-mail from being intercepted, this act is not generally applicable to a system retrieving mail from electronic storage.

While a detailed discussion of sexual harassment is presented later in this book, in this chapter it is important to note that the Internet and e-mail provide additional opportunities for harassment to occur. Pervasive interaction through electronic communication in all sections of our society, including our schools, has given rise to issues regarding inappropriate behavior and harassment. As early as 1994, NBC ran a segment in its *Dateline* series titled "Predators On-Line," which discussed seduction, preying on naïve victims, intimidation, harassment, stalking, and even rape as issues relevant to electronic communication. Electronic harassment is no less harmful than harassment in a face-to-face situation. Every school district should have a policy that clearly describes the kinds of communication that are inappropriate and harassing and offers avenues of recourse to users who have been harassed.

School administrators should also be aware of liability issues related to the development and use of school Web sites. Increasingly, school districts use district and school-based Web sites to facilitate school identification, enhance learning, and promote student achievement. These sites may contain copyrighted material, student work assignments, and artistic, musical, or dramatic productions. These sites also may link to other sites or import other material into the district's site. Lipinski (1999) warns that the same fair use guidelines that govern printed musical, photographic, and audiovisual works also pertain to material placed on an educational Web site.

▌ FOCUS POINT: Educational Media Projects

In 1996 the Subcommittee on Courts and Intellectual Property of the U.S. House Judiciary Committee created a set of guidelines to clarify the application of the fair use doctrine to copyrighted works as teaching methods are adapted to new learning environments. These guidelines reaffirm that all use of copyrighted material in multimedia projects is subject to copyright law, and the resulting projects should include proper attribution and citations. Students may incorporate portions of lawfully acquired copyrighted works when producing their own educational multimedia programs for a specific course. They may also perform or display their own educational multimedia projects and may use them in portfolios for their own use. Similarly, educators may incorporate portions of lawfully acquired copyrighted work when producing educational multimedia programs to use as teaching tools in support of curriculum-based activities at educational institutions. They may use this material for their own face-to-face instruction, remote instruction in real time, and for review if safeguarded by a password and protection that prevents copies being made of the copyrighted material.

Examples of Management Cues

- Your counselor uses overheads of copyrighted material in making a presentation to community members at a public meeting.
- A teacher hands out copyrighted material at a local, regional, or national workshop.
- Your industrial arts teacher is hired as a consultant and distributes material copyrighted by the school district to his clients.
- Your librarian uses copyrighted materials in overheads in a televised distance-learning class.
- One of your teachers locates an article from a recent journal that is relevant to his lesson plan of that day. He not only makes enough copies for his current class but also makes several hundred extra copies to be used in future classes.
- Students create individual and class Web pages on which they post scanned pictures from magazines and posters.
- Some of your teachers make copies of software programs for installation on their home computers.
- Teachers make copies of pictures from greeting cards and cartoons to decorate their classrooms.
- Teachers make packets of readings by copying recent articles and sections from new textbooks.
- A teacher scans several journal articles onto the district network and instructs the students on how to access them so that they can complete the class assignments.
- A teacher has lawfully obtained a piece of music, a picture, and a piece of videotape, which she uses in face-to-face instruction. She now plans to

reproduce these short items onto one compact disc to prevent their loss or deterioration, keep them organized, and show them in the class by using a single piece of equipment.

- Students are asked to create an "electronic term paper" using lawfully acquired resources from the institution's library and media center. While doing research, one student photocopies the bibliography and several pages of images and text and then uses the school computer lab to scan the material into his electronic term paper.
- A teacher has lawful access to research on the Internet. The teacher downloads the document to a computer disk and prints the document.
- A teacher photographs and makes slides of a number of reproductions of artworks from a book on the National Gallery. She plans to show the slides to the students enrolled in her course.
- A special education teacher makes closed-captioned versions of several videotapes to serve the needs of special education students. This teacher also makes large print copies of some materials. Some of these materials are electronically delivered to disabled students in their homes.
- A national education association sponsors a teleconference on school discipline. Your school is 1 of over 40 sites across the country that participates. At each site, the satellite broadcast is down-transmitted to receiving dishes, and the signal is translated into video and audio images and viewed on television monitors. The director of your media center makes a video copy of this broadcast and makes it available to teachers who were not able to attend the presentation.
- Two years ago, when the middle school's 11-station computer room was set up, the software was purchased under a "one package to one workstation" license agreement. Many of the software programs have had several updates. Because there is not enough money to buy 11 updates of each software package, your computer teacher buys one copy of each program and makes 11 "backup" copies.
- As a "treat" for being especially well behaved, a fifth-grade teacher rents a popular movie to show to her class. To make the afternoon especially enjoyable, she allows them to invite their preschool brothers or sisters to come.
- A pay television channel shows a series of children's classic films. One of your teachers videotapes several of these movies for future use in her classroom.
- Because of a budget cut, no new textbooks are purchased for several years. As principal, you tell teachers to use some creativity and generate some "teacher-made" material. The advanced placement history teacher responds by spending his summer reviewing and compiling journal articles. Just before school starts, he gives a packet of 30 articles to the copy room staff and tells them to make 100 copies.
- Your band director buys the sheet music for several marches, duplicates them, and hands them out for his students to practice during summer vacation.

Suggested Risk Management Guidelines

Note: The suggested guidelines presented here should assist educators in making educationally and legally sound decisions regarding the permissibility of quoting, photocopying, downloading, or making other uses of copyrighted materials. However, the increased use of electronic methods is likely to increase the need for obtaining permission. Although copyright owners are under no obligation to respond, most are cooperative. The person desiring permission must contact the author or publisher directly. Permission may be denied, granted with no fee, or granted on the condition of paying a fee. Oral permission granted over the telephone may be valid. However, it is a better practice to have written documentation of all permissions.

- Inservice faculty and staff may believe that because they have purchased a book, CD, DVD, software program, or Internet subscription, they have permission to make copies of these items. Ensure that all understand that these works are protected by copyright law, and that violation of the copyright law could result in a civil action.

Educational Uses of Music

- It *is* permissible to

  - Copy sheet music in an emergency situation (providing replacement copies are purchased) and excerpts of no more than 10 percent of the whole work, and to edit (as long as the fundamental character of the work is not distorted or lyrics altered or added)
  - Make a single copy of a sound recording of a student performance for evaluation or rehearsal purposes, as long as it is only used for exercises or examinations

- It *is not* permissible to

  - Create anthologies or compilations
  - Copy from "consumables" like workbooks
  - Copy to substitute for purchase of sheet music or recordings (emergency copying is the only allowable use of copying for performances, and all copies made must include the copyright notice and a citation)

Off-Air Recording of Broadcast Programming for Educational Purposes

- It *is* permissible to

  - Make copies of "Cable in the Classroom" types of programs (These programs offer commercial-free educational programming with liberal copyright clearances. A pamphlet distributed by Cable in the Classroom, *All About Copyright: Fair Use in the Multimedia Age,* discusses a wide range of fair use topics.)

- Make off-air tapes to be held for a 45-calendar-day retention period (During the first 10 consecutive school days, the tapes may be used once in teaching activities and repeated once for reinforcement. After the first 10 days, the tapes may only be used for teacher evaluation purposes. At the end of the 45-day retention period, the tapes must be erased.)

- It *is not* permissible to

  - Make copies of off-air programming at the request of individual teachers
  - Conduct advance taping in anticipation of possible teacher requests
  - Alter recorded programs or include them in anthologies or compilations
  - Omit copyright notice and a citation from any copy

Face-to-Face Teaching Activities

- It *is* permissible to perform copyrighted material, such as a videotape, without having to obtain a public performance license if certain conditions are met.

  - A performance or display of a copyrighted work must take place in a classroom or similar place of instruction (such as a school library).
  - The performance or display must be directly related to the curriculum and not connected with recreation or a reward. For example, treating a class to a movie (unrelated to course content) would require obtaining permission.

Transmission of a Performance

- It *is* permissible to

  - Transmit certain copyrighted works, including singing a song, reciting a poem, reading a short story aloud, or displaying paintings—providing the performance is a "regular part of systematic instructional activities" and "directly related and of material assistance to the teaching content" (Also, such transmissions must be received in a classroom or similar place of instruction.)
  - Perform a copyrighted nondramatic literary or musical work (a) if the transmission is part of the activities of a governmental body or a non-profit educational institution, (b) the performance or display is directly related and of material assistance to the teaching content of the transmission, (c) the transmission is made primarily for (i) reception in classrooms or similar places normally devoted to instruction or (ii) reception by persons to whom the transmission is directed because their disabilities or other special circumstances prevent their attendance in classrooms or similar places normally devoted to instruction or (iii) reception by officers or employees of government bodies as a part of their official duties or employment

- It *is not* permissible to transmit copyrighted plays, movies, and most audiovisual works.

Transmission of Live Performance

- It *is* permissible to
  - Transmit a nondramatic literary or musical work without having to obtain a public performance license if the performance is without commercial advantage and nondramatic (a concert, choral work, or poetry reading, for example)
  - Transmit a performance of a nondramatic literary or musical work otherwise than in a transmission to the public, without any purpose of direct or indirect commercial advantage and without payment of any fee or other compensation for the performance to any of its performers, promoters, or organizers, if (a) there is no direct or indirect admission charge or (b) the proceeds, after deducting the reasonable costs of producing the performance, are used exclusively for educational purposes, where the copyright owner has served notice of objection to the performance

Transmission for Distance Learning

Note: The Conference on Fair Use (CONFU) was unable to agree on Educational Fair Use Guidelines for Distance Learning. *Until more specific guidelines are published, it is prudent to obtain permission before using any copyrighted material in distance learning.* Some legal experts consider interactive television (compressed video) to be covered, or at least defensible, under the classroom exemption. However, other experts believe that very little copyrighted material may be transmitted or broadcast over a distance education network without proper written permission or licensing agreements.

Multimedia

Note: As more teachers are creating new learning environments in their classrooms and helping students develop educational multimedia projects, it is important to keep the fair use doctrine in mind. The following guidelines are adapted from material developed by Groton Public Schools Media Technology Services (Groton Public Schools, 2005):

- It *is* permissible for
  - Students to perform and display their own educational multimedia projects for the course for which they were created and may use them in their own portfolios as examples of academic work
  - Educators to perform and display their own education multimedia projects for face-to-face instruction, assigning to students for directed self-study, peer conferences, and evaluation
- Educators must seek individual permissions for all copyrighted works incorporated in their educational multimedia projects for noneducational

or commercial purposes, duplication beyond guidelines limitations, and for distribution over an electronic network other than the remote instruction uses described above.

Material Downloaded from the Internet and Internet Use by Students

- Unfortunately, much of the material on Internet Web sites has been posted without permission from the copyright holder. Because the Internet is so readily accessible, it is easy to forget that digital material is often copyrighted. Because the copyright law and related guidelines have not specifically addressed this new technology, the best strategy is to apply existing law to the Internet.

  - Alterations of copyrighted works must support specific instructional objectives.
  - Fair use guidelines do not preempt or supersede license agreements and contractual obligations.
  - Access to works on the Internet does not automatically mean that these works can be reproduced and reused without permission or royalty.

- It *is not* permissible to

  - Download copyrighted software of any kind via the Internet
  - Download material from an Internet Web site and store it in an offline browser without obtaining permission from the site's Webmaster
  - Paste materials from the Internet onto a school Web page or incorporate such material into a multimedia project without obtaining permission

- Although many educators learned to use computers and "surf the Web" only after we reached adulthood, the current generation of schoolchildren has grown up using computers for everything from education to entertainment. Children's comfort level with the Internet may leave them vulnerable to abuse by unscrupulous adults. To protect the children entrusted to our care and reduce our school districts' potential liability, prudent educators should act affirmatively to teach children to use the Internet wisely and safely by providing clear guidelines. The following "Six Online Safety Tips for Kids," developed by America Online Childhelp (n.d.) and the National School Boards Foundation, provide a useful model for all educators. We recommend that the following, or similar, guidelines be posted in each classroom and computer lab in which students have access to the Internet:

1. Never give out your name, home address, age, phone number, or school name—or any personal information—to strangers online.

2. Don't give out your password to anyone, either online or offline.

3. Never agree to meet an online friend in person without one of your parents also being present.

4. Don't e-mail pictures of yourself to strangers online.

5. Never accept things from strangers online, such as e-mails, files, pictures, or Web links.

6. If someone says or does something online that makes you feel unsafe or uncomfortable, tell an adult right away.

Computer Software and Courseware

- It *is* permissible for

  - The owner of a computer program to make another copy or adaptation of the program for archival (backup) purposes
  - Nonprofit libraries to lend computer programs, providing a warning of copyright is affixed to the program

- You should always read the terms and conditions of license agreements, especially clauses relating to permitted uses, prohibited uses, restrictions, and copying limitations before you use a computer program.

School Library Copying

Note: The DMCA amends Section 108, subsection (a)(3), by adding requirements to the notice of copyright that must appear on a copy. The reproduction or distribution of the work includes a notice of copyright that appears on the copy or sound recording that is reproduced under the provisions of this section, or includes a legend stating that the work may be protected by copyright if no such notice can be found on the copy or sound recording that is reproduced under the provisions of this section. The DMCA also amends Section 108, subsections (b) and (c), by allowing libraries to make three copies (now including digital ones) from their collections for archival or replacement purposes. These exceptions to the single-copy limit, still in force under subsection (a), apply only if certain conditions are met:

- The library must prominently display a warning of copyright in accordance with regulations from the Register of Copyrights. This notice should be at the place where the copying requests are accepted and be included on its request form.
- It *is* permissible for a library to

  - Duplicate an unpublished work for purposes of preservation and security or for research use
  - Duplicate a published work for purposes of replacement if the work is damaged, deteriorating, lost, stolen, or in an obsolete format
  - Scan an article from a periodical issue, a chapter, or portions of other copyrighted works and provide an electronic copy to the user

Figure 10.1

WARNING CONCERNING COPYRIGHT RESTRICTIONS

The copyright law of the United States (Title 17, U.S. Code) governs the making of photocopies or other reproductions of copyrighted material. Under certain conditions specified in the law, libraries and archives are authorized to furnish a photocopy or other reproduction. One of these specified conditions is that the photocopy or reproduction is not to be "used for any purpose other than private study, scholarship, or research." If a user makes a request for, or later uses, a photocopy or reproduction for purposes in excess of "fair use," that user may be liable for copyright infringement.

NOTICE

The copyright law of the United States (Title 17, U.S. Code) governs the making of photocopies or other reproductions of copyrighted material. The person using this equipment is liable for any infringement.

- – Fax or otherwise transmit a copy to the user (however, the library must not retain the incidental copy made to facilitate transmission)
- – Print a copy of an article, a chapter, or portions of other copyrighted works at the request of a user if the library interprets the purpose to be *fair use*
- – Download a copy of an article, a chapter, or portions of other copyrighted works to satisfy the request of a user and forward it electronically to the user
- – Make a single copy of a single article or a copy of a small part of a copyrighted work in the library's collections

- It *is not* permissible for a library to

  - – Systematically reproduce or distribute single or multiple copies to substitute for a subscription or purchase of a work
  - – Distribute digital copies in digital format
  - – Make copies available to the public in digital format outside the premises of the library

Coin-Operated Copying Machines

- Libraries (media centers) must refuse to accept a copying order if the fulfillment of the order would violate copyright law.
- Libraries (media centers) must post a warning concerning copyright restrictions. The warning must be printed on heavy paper or other durable material, in type at least 18 points in size, and displayed prominently so as to be clearly visible, legible, and comprehensible to a casual observer within the immediate vicinity of the place where orders are accepted.

- The warning should be placed on all coin-operated copying machines in the school building. The warning should notify the user of potential liability for any copyright violation. The content of the proposed warning is shown in Figure 10.1.

CHAPTER RESOURCES

America Online Childhelp. (n.d.). Retrieved May 4, 2005, from www.safetychecks.com/hasflash.html

Basic Books, Inc. v. Kinko's Graphics Corp., 758 F. Supp. at 1532–1533 (1991).

Cable in the Classroom. (n.d.). Retrieved from www.ciconline.com

Conn, K., & Zirkel, P. (2000). *Legal aspects of Internet accessibility and use in K–12 public schools: What do school districts need to know?* 146 Ed. Law Rep., 1.

Educational Multimedia Fair Use Guidelines Development Committee. (1996, September 27). *Fair use guidelines for educational multimedia.* Adopted by the Subcommittee on Courts and Intellectual Property, Committee on the Judiciary, U.S. House of Representatives.

Groton Public Schools. (2005). *Copyright implementation manual.* Mystic, CT: Author.

Henn, H. G. (1988). *Copyright law: A practitioner's guide* (2nd ed.). New York: Practicing Law Institute.

Lipinski, T. A. (1999). *Designing and using Web-based materials in education: A Web page legal audit.* 137 Ed. Law Rep., 9.

Marcus v. Rowley, 695 F.2d 1171 (9th Cir. 1983).

Rosemont Enters. v. Random House, Inc., 366 F.2d 303, 306 (2d Cir. 1966).

Snider, M. (2001). "Fair use" is the cry at MP3.com. *USA Today.* Retrieved February 13, 2001, from www.usatoday.com/life/cyber/tech/review/crg965.htm

Title I of the Electronic Communications Privacy Act (ECPA), 18 U.S § 2511 (1) (a).

Title II of the Digital Millennium Copyright Act (DMCA), Pub. L. No. 105-304.

U.S. Constitution, Article I, Section 8, Clause 8 (copyright clause).

11

Search and Seizure

The courts have balanced the school's legitimate need to obtain information and the students' right to privacy using several variables:

- The purpose of the search
- The person doing the searching
- The place being searched
- The background of the person being searched
- The severity of the penalties resulting from the search
- The degree to which the person's privacy was invaded by the search

The *in loco parentis* theory—namely, that school officials act in place of the parents and not as agents of the state—is used as the basis for some court rulings regarding search and seizure. However, in some more recent cases, courts have rejected the *in loco parentis* argument as being out of touch with contemporary reality, affirming that schools act as representatives of the state and not as surrogate parents.

Principals acting with malice toward a student or in ignorance or disregard of the law may be held liable for violating a student's constitutional rights. Absent these conditions, the principal has general immunity.

AUTHORS' NOTE: Cases cited throughout this chapter have been selected on a precedent-setting or best-example basis regardless of jurisdiction or date of adjudication. (See Introduction for more information.)

FOCUS POINT: Proper or Improper Search and Seizure

Searches for drugs and weapons have ranged from routine inspections of lockers, cars, pockets, and purses to very intimate strip searches.

The Fourth Amendment to the Constitution guarantees the right of people to be secure in their persons, houses, papers, and effects against unreasonable searches and seizures without probable cause. In *Mapp v. Ohio* (1961), the U.S. Supreme Court ruled that the Fourth Amendment protects citizens from the actions of state as well as federal governments.

Although police officers generally must convince a magistrate that probable cause exists before a warrant is issued for a search, courts have been mixed in their opinions on how the Fourth Amendment applies in cases of school personnel searching students on school grounds. Some have argued that because school personnel are private persons and not agents of the state, the Fourth Amendment does not apply to them. Court decisions that reinforce this argument are based on the *in loco parentis* theory that the school is acting in place of the parent and not as an agent of the state. When students have pled that warrantless searches conducted by school officials infringe on their constitutional rights guaranteed by the Fourth Amendment, school officials have claimed that such searches are compelled by their affirmative duty to protect people and places.

The U.S. Supreme Court ruled, in the case of *New Jersey v. T.L.O.* (1985), that the Fourth Amendment applies to school searches and seizures. Although this decision left some questions unanswered, it did give educators some guidance. Asking the following five questions prior to conducting a search helps school officials in particular situations determine whether a search is justified at its inception and reasonable in its scope:

1. Is there reasonable suspicion that a student has violated a law or school policy?

   • Before conducting a search of a student's person or property, including school lockers, a school official must have a reasonable suspicion that a student has violated a law or school policy, and in conducting the search, the school official must use methods that are reasonable in scope. The search must be reasonably related to the objectives of the search and not excessively intrusive in light of the age and sex of the student and the nature of the infraction. Considerations of student age, sex, and emotional condition are directly applicable as inhibitions to searches that must be justified by reasonableness.

2. Was the source of information suggesting the need for a search *reliable* and *credible?*

   • A school official's good judgment applies to the determination of whether the information recommending the need for a search came from a reliable source. The courts have generally agreed that school officials may reasonably rely on information by school personnel or by a number of students, but information from a single student or from an anonymous source should be weighed more carefully before any action is taken.

3. Does the school official's past experience or knowledge of the student's prior history provide reasonable suspicion to justify a search?

   - Reasonable suspicion would be based on the details of the information and whether those details are credible in the current overall situation. Reasonable suspicion may be based on the school official's knowledge of the student's prior history or on the official's past experience.

4. Is the intended search method reasonable in relation to the objectives of the search and the nature of the suspected infraction?

   - Once the school official has met the standards of reasonable suspicion, reasonable scope is considered. The place or person identified through reasonable suspicion has a direct bearing on the scope of the search.

5. Is the intended search method not excessively intrusive, given the nature of the suspected infraction?

   - The closer the searcher comes to the person, the higher the intrusiveness and, as a result, the stronger that reasonable suspicion must be to justify a search. The highest degree of intrusiveness would be the strip search of a person. The lowest degree of intrusiveness would be the search of an inanimate object such as a locker.

A school official's reasonable suspicion that a search will reveal evidence that a student has violated or is violating a law or school policy is a less rigorous test than the probable cause required for a police officer to obtain a search warrant. In an education setting, a school official may rely on his or her good judgment and common sense to determine whether there is sufficient probability of an infraction to justify a search. Furthermore, the level of suspicion may vary depending on the circumstances of the particular situation. In emergency situations that are potentially dangerous or where the element of time is critical, less suspicion is necessary to justify a search (e.g., the suspected presence of a weapon or explosive device or of drugs that might be quickly disposed of).

Locker Searches

There is some question about whether a search of a student's locker falls within the protection of the Fourth Amendment. The Fourth Amendment protects only a person's reasonable expectation of privacy. Therefore, some courts have ruled that because students know when they are issued a locker that the school administrator keeps a duplicate key or a copy of the combination, their expectation of privacy in the locker is so diminished that it is virtually nonexistent. Courts have noted that students have use of the lockers, but the lockers remain the exclusive property of the school. School authorities, therefore, have both the right and duty to inspect a locker when they believe that something of an illegal nature may be stored in it or simply to remove school property at the end of the school year. Therefore, locker searches may be conducted with a fairly low degree of suspicion.

Before police or other law enforcement officials may search students' lockers, they must have a search warrant. They must demonstrate "probable cause" as the basis to justify the issuance of a search warrant. This also holds true when a law enforcement official requests that school personnel do the actual searching. By acting with the police, the school official becomes an arm of the state and subject to due process requirements and illegal search and seizures sections of the U.S. Constitution; therefore, a search warrant is necessary. Evidence seized without a warrant will not be admissible in court.

Whether uniformed or plainclothed, school security personnel are generally considered by the courts to be law enforcement officers. As such, they must apply the higher standard of "probable cause" (as opposed to "reasonable suspicion") in conducting searches.

Cars

The search of a student's car, even when the car is on school grounds, is highly controversial. Because a car is privately owned, the search of a car is a greater invasion of privacy than the search of a locker. However, because the car is parked on school property, in public view, the expectation of privacy is reduced. However, courts have identified degrees of privacy. For example, objects in open view are less protected than objects in the trunk or glove compartment. Generally, principals will want to avoid searching a student's car unless there is clear reason to believe that there is imminent danger either to the student or to others, should the student come into possession of the items.

Tote Bags and Purses

A search of a student's personal effects requires a higher standard of protection than a car search, because such a search involves personal belongings in which the student has a higher expectation of privacy. Although lockers are the property of the school, personal effects are the property of the individual. School personnel are not forbidden to search student possessions, but they must exercise greater care in doing so. The court in *New Jersey v. T.L.O.* affirmed that students do not waive all rights to privacy in such items by bringing them onto school grounds.

Metal Detectors

In an effort to reduce the number of guns, knives, and metal weapons carried into schools, some school districts use metal detectors. School districts that use these devices argue that they are one of the less intrusive techniques for searching for dangerous items. Opponents of this method argue that such searches are violations of students' privacy rights.

Pocket, Pat Down, and Strip Searches

When a school employee actually touches a student's clothing while engaged in a search, the search becomes more invasive. The risks of this type of search increase if it is conducted by a person of the opposite gender. Courts have warned that because this type of search may inflict indignity and create strong resentment, it should not be undertaken lightly. The most controversial search of students is the strip search. There have been situations in which school officials have ordered students to remove their clothes down to the undergarments in a search for stolen money or illegal drugs. Even though in most cases the boys and girls were placed in separate rooms and searched by school personnel of the same sex, the courts have generally condemned strip searches in the public schools as impermissible and, in some cases, have awarded money damages to the students who were illegally searched in such a manner. A body cavity search is the most intrusive type of search and should *not* be conducted by school employees.

Surreptitious Observation

This is not recommended.

Dog Sniff Searches

The courts are split on the legality of using dogs in a dragnet search of students. In the case of *Horton v. Goose Creek* (1982), the court held that because the canine actually touched the students while sniffing, the students' Fourth Amendment right to be free from unreasonable searches was violated. The court also found that the school district failed to establish an individualized suspicion of the students searched.

In the case of *Doe v. Renfrow* (1979), the court held that the use of dogs to sniff out drugs was not a search within the meaning of the Fourth Amendment and, therefore, not a violation of the Fourth Amendment. This court's opinion seems to suggest that if a school district clearly establishes an individualized suspicion of certain students, then the use of dogs might be appropriate.

When school authorities find the use of dog sniffs necessary to combat a drug problem, it is suggested that they coordinate the proposed search with law enforcement officials who have search warrants. In addition, the use of dogs should be subject specific rather than a dragnet of all students and should be done in private.

Informed Consent, Emergency, and Administrative Searches

Students may willingly waive their rights of privacy under the Fourth Amendment. However, this waiver must be given free of even the slightest coercion. Principals are not protected from liability because students give permission for any kind of search. Courts have determined that students cannot freely give consent to a search because they are expected to cooperate in a school setting.

In an emergency situation, when school authorities are faced with a situation that demands immediate action to prevent injury or substantial property damage, the requirements of the Fourth Amendment are relaxed.

Reasonable Suspicion Versus Probable Cause

Even though school administrators can follow the lesser standards of "reasonable suspicion" rather than "probable cause," courts will still scrutinize the conditions surrounding any search. To determine whether a search is reasonable, the courts consider the magnitude of the suspected offense and the extent of the intrusiveness to the student's privacy. To establish reasonable suspicion, a school administrator must have some evidence regarding a specific suspicion that would lead a reasonable person (experienced school administrator) to believe that something is hidden in violation of school policy. In addition, the Fourth Amendment clearly states that the issuance of a warrant must "describe the place to be searched and the persons or things to be seized." Even though school administrators may conduct a warrantless search, they must be guided by a degree of specificity, for example, What is the suspected offense? Do I have definitive knowledge of where the suspected contraband is located? Do I know who the subjects in question are?

Examples of Management Cues

- Incidents of school violence reported in the media (e.g., shootings, bombs)
- Smell of marijuana coming from a certain area or certain student
- Student report of other student engaging in illegal activities (e.g., selling drugs, using drugs, carrying a weapon, stealing)
- Dog search for drugs, leading to a specific student's locker
- Smoke from cigarettes coming from restroom
- Reports of missing student, faculty, or school property

Suggested Risk Management Guidelines

- All boards of education should maintain clear rules and regulations regarding search and seizure activities by school administrators, as official policy.
- School administrators should always be knowledgeable about legal requirements and district policy regarding search and seizure and should always follow the most restrictive standards.
- All in-school searches should be authorized by the principal, based on reasonable suspicion, conducted using a method that is reasonable in scope, and initiated from information from *credible* sources. Credible sources are identified as and range from most to least in the following order: (1) school personnel, (2) more than one student, (3) a single, highly reliable student, (4) an outside or anonymous informant.

- Locker searches should be conducted in the presence of another staff member, and the student should be present if applicable.
- Any search of students' clothing or personal effects must be subject specific and not conducted randomly.

Note: Drug testing through urinalysis is covered by the Fourth Amendment, is considered a highly invasive search, and requires strong reasonable and individualized suspicion that the student is a drug user.

ADDITIONAL CASES OF INTEREST TO EDUCATORS

Cornfield v. Consolidated High School District No. 230, 991 F.2d 1316 (7th Cir. 1993). No violation of the Fourth Amendment—strip search of student was reasonable.

DesRoches v. Caprio and School Board of Norfolk, 156 F.3d 571, 129 Educ. L. Rep. 628 (4th Cir. 1998). The school had reasonable suspicion to search student's backpack for stolen tennis shoes.

Isiah B. v. State of Wisconsin, 176 Wis.2d 639, 500 N.W.2d 637 (1993). A student does not have a reasonable expectation of privacy when storing personal items in a school locker.

Vernonia School District 47J v. Acton, 515 U.S. 646, 115 S.Ct. 2386 (1995). School district's drug policy of random urinalysis for interscholastic athletics was constitutionally legitimate.

CHAPTER RESOURCES

Doe v. Renfrow, 475 F. Supp. 1012 (N.D. Ind. 1979).
Horton v. Goose Creek, 690 F.2d. 470 (5th Cir. 1982).
Mapp v. Ohio, 367 U.S. 643 (1961).
New Jersey v. T.L.O., 105 S.Ct. 733 (1985).

12

The Principal's Responsibilities in Program Management

A school administrator's affirmative responsibilities in program management are as diverse as they are difficult. The areas examined in this chapter are ever changing, often challenged, and frequently driven by politics. School administrators need to continuously update their personal knowledge and skills in program management issues to be able to effectively reduce the risk of litigation.

SECTION A: SCHOOL ATTENDANCE

Since the end of the 18th century, most states have enacted compulsory attendance laws, and the courts generally have defended compulsory attendance as a duty for the public good. The U.S. Supreme Court held, in Pierce v. Society of Sisters (1925), *that the state's right to require school attendance did not give it the right to limit attendance only to public schools.*

The court found that such a law violated parents' rights to control the education and upbringing of their children and was an unreasonable exercise of

---

AUTHORS' NOTE: Cases cited throughout this chapter have been selected on a precedent-setting or best-example basis regardless of jurisdiction or date of adjudication. (See Introduction for more information.)

state power. Thus compulsory attendance can be satisfied in both public and private schools.

In 1944, the U.S. Supreme Court, in *Prince v. Massachusetts,* reaffirmed the right of the state to regulate school attendance. The Court declared that "the family itself is not beyond regulation in the public interest. . . . [N]either rights of religion nor rights of parenthood are beyond limitations."

Each state has enacted its own compulsory attendance laws. Most state statutes include (a) the beginning and ending ages for required attendance, (b) the various ways that compulsory education can be accomplished (i.e., public schools, private schools, homeschooling), (c) the length of the school day and school year and the minimum attendance that is required, (d) any basis for granting exemptions to compulsory attendance, (e) provisions for enforcing compulsory attendance, and (f) any penalties for violation of compulsory attendance laws. The two general exceptions to the compulsory attendance laws are (1) conflicts with religion, as noted in *Wisconsin v. Yoder* (1972), and (2) statutory exemptions (i.e., excusing students who live more than a specified distance from the nearest school).

In addition to affirming the state's right to require compulsory school attendance, courts have also affirmed the right of a school district to require residence requirements for school attendance, as demonstrated in *Martinez v. Bynum* (1983). States have their own specific residency statutes, ranging from open admission to requiring permission from the sending and receiving districts before students are allowed to attend a school outside their home district.

▌ FOCUS POINT: Constitutional Right to an Education

In *Plyler v. Doe* (1982), the U.S. Supreme Court was asked if the equal protection clause of the U.S. Constitution entitled illegal alien children residing in Texas to attend the public schools of Texas free of charge. The Court found, "For purposes of the Fourteenth Amendment's equal protection clause which prohibits states from denying equal protection to any person 'within its jurisdiction,' undocumented aliens, despite their immigration status, are persons within the jurisdiction of a state entitled to the equal protection of its law. Use of the phrase, 'within its jurisdiction,' confirming that the protection of the Fourteenth Amendment extends to anyone, citizen or stranger, who is subject to the laws of a state, and reaches into every corner of a state's territory, and that until he [sic] leaves the jurisdiction, either voluntarily or involuntarily in accordance with the Constitution and laws of the United States, a person is entitled to the equal protection of the laws that a state may choose to establish."

Therefore, states may not withhold funds from local school districts for the education of children not legally admitted into the United States, and authorizing districts to deny enrollment to such children is a violation of the equal protection clause. Although public education is not a "right" under the equal protection clause, neither is it merely some government "benefit." Consequently, to deny education to alien children would impose a lifetime of hardship on a discrete class of children, and such discrimination of the funding statute is not rational.

I FOCUS POINT: Home Instruction

Although many parents prefer to enroll their children in public, private, or parochial schools, others have sought the right to educate their own children through home instruction. According to the National Center for Education Statistics (2003), 1.1 million students were homeschooled in 2003.

Although homeschooling is permitted in all 50 states, there is considerable variation in how each state regulates this type of instruction. Regardless of the specifics of the various statutes, responsibility for ensuring that the quality of home instruction meets at least the minimum requirements prescribed by state law rests with local school superintendents. The majority of states require that parents notify the state department of education or the local school district that they plan to homeschool their child. However, other specific regulations vary widely from state to state. When issues relating to home instruction find their way into the courts, they generally focus on either (a) interpretations of the statute or (b) the rights of homeschooled students to receive some of the benefits, that is, participation in course work, available through the public school system.

In *Yoder*, the U.S. Supreme Court modified the state's power to impose regulations on parents. The Court held that Wisconsin could not require members of the Old Order Amish religious sect to send their children to formal schools beyond the eighth grade. The Court said that even though the state had the power to impose reasonable regulations governing school attendance, the exercise of the power must not inhibit the deeply held religious beliefs of parents. In this case, the parents' right to the free exercise of religion was sufficient to override the state's power to compel formal school attendance to age 16. The general application of the Court's ruling is limited because the Amish objected only to post-eighth-grade compulsory attendance of 14- and 15-year-olds. The fact that the Amish beliefs were of long-standing tradition and an important part of their total religious culture were the key considerations in this case.

Efforts to extend the *Yoder* decision have been unsuccessful. The West Virginia Supreme Court refused to extend the ruling of *Yoder* to Biblical Christian parents who chose to educate their children at home. In *State v. Riddle* (1981), when the Riddle family refused to comply with the state's compulsory attendance laws, they were arrested by a local truancy officer. The court found that even though the family was apparently doing a good job of educating their children and were sincere in their beliefs, the state had the right to require compliance with its attendance laws. (See also *Department of Education Religious Expression Guidelines*, 2001.)

Homeschooled Students' Participation in Public School Programs

Frequently, parents of homeschooled students wish to have their children participate in some public school courses or extracurricular activities. Although a school district may adopt a policy that allows homeschooled students to enroll on a part-time basis, the district may not receive state aid for such students. Generally, parents have no legal rights to insist that their children be permitted to participate in programs in public schools in which they are not enrolled. For example, a New York Court, in *Bradstreet v. Soboal* (1996), rejected the argument that denying a homeschooled child the right to participate in interscholastic activities was a violation of the student's right to equal protection under the Fourteenth Amendment. In the case of *Swanson v. Guthrie* (1998), the U.S. Court of Appeals for the Tenth Circuit ruled that not allowing a homeschooled student to attend public school on a part-time basis did not violate the student's rights under the free exercise clause of the U.S. Constitution. However, it should be noted that several states have enacted specific legislation that permits homeschooled students to use school facilities and participate in extracurricular activities.

Examples of Management Cues

- Your football coach informs you that his starting middle linebacker is going to be homeschooled next year, and the student would like permission to continue to play on the school's football team.
- A parent requests that she be allowed to borrow a school-owned VCR to show educational programs to her homeschooled child.
- A group of parents request that their homeschooled children be allowed to take part in chemistry class, because the parents are not able to afford the specialized equipment.
- A parent of a homeschooled child asks that the school allow her child to play on the playground during the school's recess periods in order for her child to have interaction with other children.

Suggested Risk Management Guidelines

- Ensure that all your teachers and support staff understand that any parent has the legal right to educate a child at home.
- Ensure that all parents and teachers understand your state statute and district policy regarding the rights of homeschooled pupils to enroll in courses or take part in extracurricular activities.

I FOCUS POINT: Homeless Children and Youth

Because homeless families move frequently, and the length of stay in shelters is often restricted, it is often difficult for homeless children to attend school regularly. (See Homeless in Chapter Resources.) In addition, guardianship requirements, delays in transfer of school records, and lack of a permanent address and immunization records often prevent homeless children from enrolling in school. Furthermore, homeless children who are able to enroll in school face another obstacle—the inability to get to school because of a lack of transportation.

The McKinney-Vento Education for Homeless Children and Youth (McKinney-Vento) program, authorized under Title VII-B of the McKinney-Vento Homeless Assistance Act (McKinney-Vento Act), was originally established by Congress in 1987 in response to reports that over 50 percent of homeless children were not attending school regularly. The McKinney-Vento program provides formula grants to state education agencies (SEAs) to ensure that all homeless children have equal access to the same free, appropriate education, including preschool education, provided to other children. State and local educational agencies receive McKinney-Vento funds to review and revise laws, regulations, practices, or policies that may act as a barrier to the enrollment, attendance, and success in school of homeless children.

In 1990, the McKinney-Vento program was amended, and its authorized funding level was increased to enable states to provide grants to local education agencies (LEAs) or direct services to carry out the purposes of the program. This legislation requires that each state review school attendance residency requirements to ensure that homeless children have access to a free, appropriate, public education that is comparable to the services provided to other students. Homeless children may either continue to be enrolled in the school district of origin for the remainder of the year or enroll in the school district in which they are living, whichever is in the children's best interests. Education records for each child must be maintained so that the records are available in a timely fashion.

The McKinney-Vento Act defines "homeless children and youth" as individuals who lack a fixed, regular, and adequate nighttime residence. The term includes children who

- Share the housing of other persons due to loss of housing, economic hardship, or a similar reason (sometimes referred to as *doubled-up*)
- Live in motels, hotels, trailer parks, or camping grounds due to lack of alternative adequate accommodations
- Live in emergency or transitional shelters
- Are abandoned in hospitals
- Are awaiting foster care placement
- Have a primary nighttime residence that is a public or private place not designed for, or ordinarily used as, a regular sleeping accommodation for human beings
- Live in cars, parks, public spaces, abandoned buildings, substandard housing, bus or train stations, or similar settings
- Are migrant children who qualify as homeless because they are living in circumstances described above

Homeless children and their parents have been successful in challenging their exclusion from public education. For example, when four children living with their parents in a tent in a Massachusetts state park were denied enrollment in the local school, they appealed to the state commissioner of education. The commissioner ruled that Massachusetts state law requires local communities to be responsible for educating the children within their boundaries, "irrespective of their living situation" (First & Cooper, 1989). In 1994, the Circuit Court of the District of Columbia ruled, in *Lampkin v. District of Columbia* (1994), that the McKinney-Vento Act permits homeless children to sue government officials to obtain the educational rights guaranteed by the act.

Examples of Management Cues

- You read an article in your local paper that informs you that your local homeless shelter houses a number of children who are not attending school.
- You become aware that several large farms in your area employ migrant workers at several seasons during the school year.
- You attend a service club meeting in which the director of the women's crisis center reports that they need children's clothing and toys for the children of residents of the shelter. She also reports that they also need textbooks so that the shelter can provide transient education services.

Suggested Risk Management Guidelines

- Train all school enrollment staff, secretaries, guidance counselors, school social workers, and administrators on the legal requirements regarding immediate enrollment.
- Review all regulations and policies to ensure that they comply with the McKinney-Vento requirements.
- Develop affidavits of residence or other forms to replace typical proof of residency. Such forms should be carefully crafted so that they do not create further barriers or delay enrollment.
- Develop caregiver affidavits, enrollment forms for unaccompanied youth, and other forms to replace typical proof of guardianship. Again, such forms should be carefully crafted so they do not create further barriers or delay enrollment.
- Establish school-based immunization clinics or other opportunities for on-site immunizations.
- Collaborate with community-based or public agencies to provide school uniforms within a district and among neighboring districts.
- Accept school records directly from families and youth.
- Contact the previous school for records and assistance with placement decisions.
- Develop short educational assessments to place students immediately while awaiting complete academic records.

- Inform families and youth in a language they can understand or in an accessible format, as appropriate, of their right to attend either their school of origin or local school.
- Inform families and youth in a language they can understand or in an accessible format, as appropriate, of their right to transportation and immediate enrollment.
- Develop clear, understandable, and accessible forms for written explanations of decisions and the right to appeal.
- Expeditiously follow up on any special education and language assistance referrals or services.
- Be sure that your school has reviewed its attendance residency requirements to ensure that any homeless child has access to a free, appropriate, public education that is comparable to the services provided to other students.
- Remove any barriers to enrollment.
- Maintain records of each homeless child and make them available in a timely fashion.
- Develop strategies aimed at recruiting, enrolling, and retaining homeless children in school.
- Develop strategies to involve homeless parents in the life of the school.
- Provide all homeless shelters, crisis centers, and churches with information regarding school enrollment.

SECTION B: BILINGUAL AND SPECIAL LANGUAGE PROGRAMS

With each passing year, our nation's student population becomes more diverse. The most recent figures available indicate that language minority students, including culturally and linguistically diverse (CLD) students (sometimes referred to as limited-English-proficient students [LEP]), are the fastest growing group of students in the United States today. The number of families whose children could be considered CLD continues to grow in school districts across the country. Many of these students need special language programs to overcome the language barriers to an equal education and to equal participation in the life of society.

FOCUS POINT: Court Rulings That Have Affected The Education of Language Minority Students

Note: Includes newcomer centers. (See History in Chapter Resources for a brief overview of policymaking foundations.)

A number of federal court cases have defined the parameters of bilingual or special language programs in local school districts and established a legal basis for challenges to school districts that fail to provide bilingual or special language programs or provide inadequate programs. An early test case was *Lau v. Nichols* (1974), a case brought by a group of Chinese CLD students who alleged that they were not receiving any special assistance to learn English. The federal court supported the school district's contention that it had no obligation to specifically respond to the communication difficulties of the non-English-speaking students because the Chinese-speaking students were being taught in the same facilities, by the same teachers, at the same time as everyone else. Because they had equal opportunities, there was no discrimination.

In reviewing the court's decision in *Lau*, the U.S. Supreme Court strongly supported the right to a quality education for language minority students and ruled that the school district had violated the rights of Chinese-speaking students by failing to provide them with an education commensurate with their special language needs. The Court wrote that "merely by providing students with the same facilities, textbooks, teachers, and curriculum; for students who do not understand English [they] are effectively foreclosed from any meaningful education." Consequently, schools have an obligation to take action to rectify language barriers that result in the exclusion of linguistic minority children from meaningful participation in educational programs. In addition, the Court noted:

> Basic skills are at the very core of what these public schools teach. Imposition of a requirement that before a child can effectively partici-pate in the educational program he must already have acquired these basic skills is to make a mockery of public education. We know that those who do not understand English are certain to find their classroom experiences wholly incomprehensible and in no ways meaningful.

The *Lau* court further required that action be taken to address the special language needs of the non-English-speaking children. The Court's rationale was based on Section 504 of the Civil Rights Act of 1964, which states: "No person in the United States, on the ground of race, color, or national origin, shall be excluded from participation in, be denied the benefits of, or be subjected to dis-crimination under any program or activity receiving federal financial assistance." Because the school district in this case was receiving federal funds, it could not discriminate against non-English-speaking students by refusing to provide them with the benefits of public education through meaningful programs.

On remand to the federal district court, a consent decree was entered into by the school district providing for bilingual-bicultural programs for Chinese, Filipino, and Spanish-language groups within the district, and implementation of English as a second language (ESL) and other special programs, including bilingual education where feasible, for students from other language groups. Although a consent decree is not precedent setting, it is enforced by the court that accepted it (Teitelbaum & Hiller, 1977).

The Equal Educational Opportunities Act (EEOA) was passed in 1974. Under this act, an education agency's failure to take appropriate action to over-come language barriers that impede equal participation by students in instruc-tional programs is an unlawful practice that gives individuals the right to sue.

Another important result of the *Lau* decision was an intensive evaluation of school districts by the Department of Health, Education, and Welfare (HEW) and the Office of Civil Rights (OCR) to determine the extent of violations identified by the Court's decision in *Lau*. This investigation resulted in administrative guidelines known as the *Lau* Remedies or *Lau* Guidelines issued jointly by HEW and OCR in 1975. Although never enacted by Congress nor officially adopted as federal policy, the *Lau* Remedies have become recognized, even by many courts, as the minimal standards for designing or evaluating an educationally effective program to overcome discriminatory practices against limited-English-speaking students (Teitelbaum & Hiller, 1977). The *Lau* Guidelines require school districts to identify all students who might be limited-English speakers and develop programs to assist them. Students involved in special language programs must remain in them until they can compete on an equal basis with their English-proficient peers.

In 1980, Title VI Language Discrimination Guidelines were distributed. These rules contain the basic components of the *Lau* Remedies, including identification, assessment, program assignment, and exit criteria, although they differ in the specific requirements in each area. In addition, the regulations specify that no minimum number of students is required before the mandated programs must be implemented.

Other contemporary court cases followed the same logic as the *Lau* court. In *Serna v. Portales* (1974), a federal court ruled that a city school district must implement a bilingual and bicultural curriculum, revise procedures for assessing achievement, and hire bilingual personnel to provide equal education opportunities for students whose home language and culture was Hispanic. In *Cintron v. Brentwood* (1978), a federal court ordered a school district to retain its bilingual program rather than substitute a program that would segregate Spanish-speaking children from their English-speaking peers in certain classes. In *Ríos v. Reed* (1978), a federal court ruled that a school district's transitional bilingual program was really an English immersion program that denied Spanish-speaking students equal education opportunity by not providing academic instruction in Spanish. The court further ruled that "a denial of educational opportunities to a child in the first years of schooling is not justified by demonstrating that the educational program employed will teach the child English sooner than a program comprised of more extensive Spanish instruction."

Castañeda v. Pickard (1981) is generally regarded as the most significant court decision affecting language minority students after *Lau*. In responding to the plaintiffs' claim that their school district's language remediation programs violated the EEOA of 1974, a federal appeals court formulated a set of basic standards to determine school district compliance with EEOA. The tripartite *Castañeda* test includes the following criteria:

- *Theory:* The school must pursue a program based on an education theory recognized as sound or, at least, as a legitimate experimental strategy.
- *Practice:* The school must actually implement the program with instructional practices, resources, and personnel necessary to transfer theory to reality.

- *Results:* The school must not persist in a program that fails to produce results.

By applying this test, the court is able to determine the degree to which actions taken by a school district are appropriate. However, the *Castañeda* decision imposed the additional dual obligation to (1) teach students English while taking appropriate action to ensure that English-language deficiencies do not constitute a barrier to the acquisition of substitutive knowledge and (2) overcome all barriers to an equal education. (Note: Under the Fourteenth Amendment of the U.S. Constitution, as ruled in *Plyler v. Doe*, 1982, the state does not have the right to deny a free public education to undocumented immigrant children.)

The *Castañeda* test was applied in *Keyes v. School District No. 1* (1983), in which the school district argued that it had asserted a good faith effort to provide services to students in need. The court ruled that "good faith" alone is not an adequate defense and stated, "What is required is an effort which will be reasonably effective in producing the intended result of removing language barriers to participation in instruction programs offered by the district." The *Keyes* court also required programs to

- Include the proper identification and classification of students in need of services, at the outset of a student's educational program
- Evaluate services at regular intervals throughout to ensure that progress is being made (Note: The Seventh Circuit Court of Appeals ruled, in *Gums v. Illinois State Board of Education*, 1987, that state education agencies are *also* required under EEOA to ensure that language minority students' educational needs are met.)

Newcomer Centers

Many school districts have established centers to serve CLD students when they first enter the school district. The purpose of these centers is to help these students make a successful transition to a new environment and culture. Such centers may be housed in separate buildings or within the regular school. Sometimes CLD students attend the centers for part of the day and spend the rest of the day with regular students. Generally, these centers separate CLD students from the general student population while they are given intensive instruction in English and content area instruction in their native language.

Because of the danger of segregating students and consequently discriminating against them, in 1990, the OCR issued a memorandum that provides guidance to schools in implementing a newcomer center. Some of the key points included in this memorandum are as follows:

- The district must not be operating under an order to desegregate its schools.
- Enrollment in the newcomer center is voluntary.
- The newcomer center should be multiethnic, multiracial, and multilinguistic.
- Attendance at the center is limited to no more than one year.

- Students attend the center based on their need for both language services and assistance in adjusting to American culture.
- The facilities and range of courses and extracurricular activities are comparable to those at the district's other schools. (Friendlander, 1991)

In 1998, California voters adopted a referendum that amended the California Education Code to require that all children in California public schools be taught English by being taught in English—and requiring that "all children be placed in English language classrooms" (Cal. Edu. Code 305). In a related case, a federal district court, in *Martin Luther King Jr. Elementary School Children v. Michigan Board of Education* (1978), extended the reasoning of *Lau* to require schools to take special steps to address the needs of speakers of the dialect known as Black English. (See National Clearinghouse for Bilingual Education in the Chapter Resources.)

Examples of Management Cues

- The elementary school curriculum encourages and supports bilingualism and biliteracy. However, the majority of the high school teachers have no training in bilingual education, and the curriculum stresses an English-only approach.
- In the halls and on the playgrounds, Latino students regularly make fun of their Latino peers who speak English in class. They accuse them of "acting white."
- A high percentage of students from South America are placed in remedial or basic classes. They are rarely placed in advanced classes such as algebra and geometry.
- Students in a fifth-grade language arts class are asked to keep a journal recording their observations about their reading. At the end of the unit, when the teacher collects the journals for evaluation, she notices that the journal of the one nonnative speaker is mostly blank and the few messages are unreadable.
- A teacher states that he wants to treat all students fairly and alike. Consequently, he does not wish to know which students are CLD.
- The state department of education requires that all students take a standardized test in English to measure student and school district achievement.

Suggested Risk Management Guidelines

- Ensure that all school employees understand that being a nonnative English speaker is not a disability or a handicapping condition.
- Develop policies and procedures to ensure that everyone in the school understands that the school district is committed to facilitate students' use of their native language to facilitate academic and social growth.

- Ensure that limited-English-speaking students are not disproportionately represented in special education classes.
- Ensure that all employees understand that academic success cannot be attributed to language or cultural background.
- Ensure that non-native-English-speaking students are offered an appropriate education that takes into consideration their developing language.
- Ensure that all students are given the opportunity to learn subject matter content while they are becoming fluent in English, and ensure that program assessment is an ongoing and integral part of all programs.
- Be aware that CLD students are at a significant disadvantage when evaluated using norm-referenced standardized tests.

I FOCUS POINT: Education of Migrant Children

The Migrant Education Program (MEP) is authorized by Part C of Title I of the Elementary and Secondary Education Act (ESEA). The MEP provides formula grants to SEAs to establish or improve education programs for migrant children. These grants assist states in improving educational opportunities for migrant children to help them succeed in the regular school program, meet the challenging state academic content and student academic achievement standards that all children are expected to meet, and graduate from high school.

The general purpose of the MEP is to ensure that migrant children fully benefit from the same free public education provided to other children. To achieve this purpose, the MEP helps SEAs and local operating agencies address the special educational needs of migrant children to better enable migrant children to succeed academically. More specifically, the purposes of the MEP are to

- Support high-quality and comprehensive educational programs for migrant children in order to reduce the educational disruption and other problems that result from repeated moves
- Ensure that migrant children who move between states are not penalized in any manner by disparities among the states in curriculum, graduation requirements, and state academic content and student academic achievement standards
- Ensure that migrant children are provided with appropriate educational services (including supportive services) that address their special needs in a coordinated and efficient manner
- Ensure that migrant children receive full and appropriate opportunities to meet the same challenging state academic content and student academic achievement standards that all children are expected to meet
- Design programs to help migrant children overcome educational disruption, cultural and language barriers, social isolation, various health-related problems, and other factors that inhibit their ability to do well in school

and to prepare them to make a successful transition to postsecondary education or employment

- Ensure that migrant children benefit from state and local systemic reforms

SECTION C: RELIGION IN PUBLIC SCHOOLS

Note: Because all the Focus Points in this section are built on the same foundation, Examples of Management Cues and Suggested Risk Management Guidelines are included at the end of the *section* rather than at the end of each Focus Point.

"Congress shall make no law respecting an establishment of religion, or prohibiting the free exercise thereof" (First Amendment to the U.S. Constitution; see establishment of religion clause of the First Amendment). At first reading, these 16 words appear to be relatively straightforward. However, the appropriate relationship of religion and public schools is a sensitive and controversial issue that has divided Americans and resulted in more contention between community groups than any other issue in school law.

The first major governmental debate regarding religious freedom occurred in 1789, when the First Amendment to the U.S. Constitution was written. The first part of the First Amendment is commonly known as the establishment clause, and the second part is known as the free exercise clause. Although one might assume that the framers of the U.S. Constitution had a clear understanding of what this phrase meant, it has been the focus of much debate. The origin of the debate is found in the 1946 U.S. Supreme Court decision, *Everson v. Board of Education,* that barred a state from levying a tax to support any religious activities or institutions. Much of the contemporary confusion can be traced to the 1962 U.S. Supreme Court decision, *Engel v. Vitale,* that banned state-sponsored school prayer. Some people have interpreted this to mean that all religious expression is prohibited. In fact, this decision did not preclude individual students, in their personal capacity, from expressing their religious faith. Because of the *Engel* decision, a national debate continues between those groups that favor organized classroom prayer as part of the regular school experience and those who oppose any form of religious speech in the public schools. Much of this debate has taken place in the courts as they have struggled to balance the requirements of the establishment clause with the free speech clause.

In 1971, the U.S. Supreme Court, in *Lemon v. Kurtzman,* gave schools some direction when it articulated a three-part test, known as the *Lemon* test, to be used to evaluate state statutes and local school board policies under the establishment clause. In order for a statute or policy to be constitutional, it must have (1) "a secular legislative purpose," (2) "a primary effect that neither advances nor inhibits religion," and (3) "it must not foster excessive entanglement between government and religion." To satisfy the establishment clause, governmental action must pass all three prongs of this test.

Since 1971, subsequent U.S. Supreme Court rulings arguably have modified the *Lemon* test, and courts are now more likely to apply the "endorsement test" or the "coercion test."

Pauken (2005) notes:

The *Lemon* test has not been overturned. However, after 30 years, several courts and commentators have modified it and argued in favor of two newer standards that may reflect a changing balance. The "endorsement test" articulated in Justice O'Connor's concurring opinion in *Lynch v. Donnelly* (1984) rewrites the first two questions of *Lemon* to address the intention of the government's activity or policy and the actual message that the activity or policy conveys. The questions become: (1) Is the intent of the government action or policy to endorse religion? (2) Regardless of the intent, does the action or policy actually convey a message of endorsement?

In *Lynch,* Justice O'Connor argued that "[e]ndorsement sends a message to nonadherents that they are outsiders, not full members of the political community, and an accompanying message to adherents that they are insiders, favored members of the political community. Disapproval sends the opposite message." Operative in the application of the endorsement test is whether a "reasonable observer" would perceive the government action or policy to endorse religion.

The "coercion test," adopted by the Supreme Court in the landmark graduation prayer decision in *Lee v. Weisman* (1992), holds that a government action is unconstitutional if it has a coercive effect with respect to religious practices. In *Lee,* a student graduating from a public middle school complained that the school's policy of inviting local religious leaders to deliver the commencement ceremony's invocation and benediction violated the establishment clause. The Supreme Court agreed and struck down the policy. In the majority opinion, Justice Kennedy articulated a "coercion" test, under which governmental entities may not coerce anyone to support or participate in a religious exercise. In furtherance of this directive and in application to a public school's use of a religious leader to deliver a graduation prayer, Justice Kennedy stated the following:

Of course, in our culture standing or remaining silent can signify adherence to a view or simple respect for the views of others. And no doubt some persons who have no desire to join in a prayer have little objection to standing as a sign of respect for those who do. But for the dissenter of high school age, who has a reasonable perception that she is being forced by the State to pray in a manner the conscience will not allow, the injury is no less real.

Each of the three establishment clause tests has been applied regularly in cases involving legal challenges and defenses to the inclusion of religion in public schools. And along with the litigation-heavy establishment clause also come claims of free speech and free exercise infringement.

Courts attempt to balance the right of free exercise of religion against the right not to have a religion established. Problems arise when these two rights are perceived as being in conflict. In 1995, the U.S. Department of Education published guidelines regarding religious expression in public schools (Riley, 1985). These guidelines reflect two basic and equally important obligations of public school officials: (1) schools may not forbid students acting on their own from expressing their personal religious views or beliefs solely because they are of a religious nature and (2) schools may not discriminate against private religious expression by students but must, instead, give students the same right to engage in religious activity and discussion as they have to engage in other comparable activity. Generally, this means that students may pray in a nondisruptive manner during the school day when they are not engaged in school activities and instruction, subject to the same rules of order that apply to other student speech. At the same time, schools may not endorse religious activity or doctrine and may not coerce participation in religious activity. Among other things, of course, school administrators and teachers may not organize or encourage prayer exercises in the classroom. Students do not have the right to make repeated invitations to other students to participate in religious activity in the face of a request to stop.

FOCUS POINT: Official Neutrality Regarding Religious Activity

Teachers and school administrators, when acting in those capacities, are representatives of the state and are prohibited by the establishment clause from soliciting or encouraging religious activity and from participating in such activity with students. Teachers and administrators also are prohibited from discouraging activity because of its religious content and from soliciting or encouraging antireligious activity.

In *Mitchell v. Helms* (2000), the U.S. Supreme Court removed virtually all constitutional barriers that previously prevented the flow of taxpayer dollars to Catholic schools. The court redefined "neutrality" as meaning that if the tax funds were not used for one religious group over another and the funds used did not discriminate between religious factions, then the statute distributing the funds is constitutional.

FOCUS POINT: School Prayer and Bible Reading

Note: Includes prayer at school board meetings, prayer at athletic events, student prayer and religious discussion, school employees' personal prayer, graduation prayer and baccalaureates, and period of silence.

Prayer at School Board Meetings

In 1999, in *Coles v. Cleveland Board of Education*, the court was asked to consider the issue of prayer at a school board meeting. A student appearing at a school board meeting to accept an award indicated that she was shocked and surprised when the board began the meeting by having a Baptist minister offer a prayer that she believed showed favor to Christians and was offensive to anyone of another religion attending the meeting. A teacher who was similarly offended by this practice joined in filing a suit alleging that the board's practice violated the establishment clause. The district court concluded that the board meeting was fundamentally an adult gathering to conduct the business of schools. The judge felt that prayer at a school board meeting should be treated in a similar manner to prayers that open legislative sessions.

The Sixth Circuit rejected the board's contention that a school board meeting fell within the legislative exception found in *Marsh v. Chambers* (1983). The *Marsh* decision held that "paying a chaplain with public funds to offer an opening prayer for a Nebraska legislative session was not unconstitutional." The court followed the Supreme Court's lead in striking down any instance of government-sponsored religious expression or involvement in public education. In striking down the school board prayer as unconstitutional, the court asserted that the practice had the primary effect of endorsing religion and further reasoned that prayer at a board meeting was arguably more coercive than at a graduation.

Prayer at Athletic Events

In 2000, the U.S. Supreme Court handed down its decision in *Santa Fe Independent School District v. Doe.* Prior to 1995, a student who was elected as Santa Fe High School's student council chaplain delivered a prayer over the public address system before each home varsity football game. A number of Mormon and Catholic students and their families filed a suit challenging this practice under the establishment clause. While the suit was pending, the school district adopted a different policy that authorized two student referenda, the first to determine whether "invocations" should be delivered at games and the second to select the spokesperson to deliver them. After the students voted to authorize such prayers and select a spokesperson, the district court entered an order modifying the policy to permit only nonsectarian, nonproselytizing prayer. The federal Fifth Circuit Court held that, even as modified by the district court, the football prayer policy was invalid.

The U.S. Supreme Court affirmed the decision of the circuit court and ruled that the district's policy permitting student-led, student-initiated prayer at football games violates the establishment clause. In its decision, the Court was guided by the principles endorsed in *Lee v. Weisman* (1992). In *Lee*, the court had ruled that a prayer delivered by a rabbi at a graduation ceremony violated the establishment clause. The Court held that, at a minimum, the Constitution guarantees that government may not coerce anyone to support or participate in religion or its exercise or otherwise act in a way that establishes a state religion or religious faith, or tends to do so. Furthermore, the Court ruled that the delivery of a message such as the invocation—on school property, at school-sponsored events, over the school's public address system, by a speaker representing the student body, under the supervision of school faculty, and pursuant to a school policy that explicitly and implicitly encourages public prayer—is not properly characterized as "private" speech. The *Santa Fe* Court ruled that the policy involved both perceived and actual endorsement of religion. For some students, such as cheerleaders, members of the band, and the team members themselves, attendance at football games was mandated, sometimes for class credit.

Student Prayer and Religious Discussion

The establishment clause does not prohibit purely private religious speech by students. Students, therefore, have the same right to engage in individual or group prayer and religious discussion during the school day as they do to engage in other comparable activity. For example, students may read their Bible or other scriptures, say grace before meals, and pray before tests. Local school authorities possess substantial discretion to impose rules of order or other restrictions on student activities, but they may not structure or administer such rules to discriminate against religious activity or speech.

Generally, students may pray in a nondisruptive manner when not engaged in school activities or instruction—subject to the rules that normally pertain in the applicable setting. Specifically, students in informal settings, such as cafeterias and hallways, may pray and discuss their religious views with each other. Students may also speak to and attempt to persuade their peers about religious topics, just as they do with regard to political topics. School officials, however, should intercede to stop student speech that constitutes harassment aimed at a student or a group of students. Students may also participate in beforeschool or afterschool events with religious content, such as "see you at the flag pole" gatherings, on the same terms as they may participate in other noncurricular activities on school premises. School officials may neither discourage nor encourage participation in such an event.

The right to engage in voluntary prayer or religious discussion free from discrimination does not include the right to have a captive audience listen, or to compel other students to participate. Teachers and school administrators should ensure that no student is in any way coerced to participate in religious activity.

School Employees' Personal Prayer

It is important for teachers and others in the school setting to remember that they are employees of the government and subject to the establishment clause and thus required to be neutral concerning religion while carrying out their duties. Consequently, school employees may not pray with or in the presence of students during the school day. This, of course, does not mean that an employee is prohibited from praying silently or outside the presence of students. Employees are permitted to wear nonobtrusive religious jewelry, such as a cross or Star of David. But employees should not wear clothing with a proselytizing message (i.e., a "Jesus Saves" T-shirt).

Although many teachers prefer not to answer questions about their personal religious beliefs, others choose to answer the question in the interest of an open and honest classroom environment. Before answering the question, however, the teacher should consider the age of the student. The critical issue is, Would the student be likely to interpret the teacher's personal view as the official position of the school?

Graduation Prayer and Baccalaureates

The U.S. Supreme Court has consistently held that invocations and prayers at high school graduation ceremonies violate the establishment clause. School officials may not mandate or organize prayer at graduation or organize religious baccalaureate ceremonies. If a school generally opens its facilities to private groups, it must make its facilities available on the same terms to organizers of privately sponsored religious baccalaureate services. However, a school may not extend preferential treatment to baccalaureate ceremonies and may, in some instances, be obliged to disclaim official endorsement of these ceremonies. In *Lee v. Weisman* (1992), the U.S. Supreme Court ruled that even though the graduation ceremony may be voluntary, it is not appropriate for the state to place a student in the position of choosing whether to miss the graduation ceremony or attend and listen to a prayer that the student might find objectionable. The court reasoned that even though the graduation ceremony is not mandatory, it is still one of life's most significant occasions.

Period of Silence

In an effort to circumvent U.S. Supreme Court decisions that prohibit schools from conducting prayer, some school districts and state legislatures have enacted policies and statutes that authorize a moment of silence for meditation or silent prayer. The Supreme Court ruled, in *Wallace v. Jaffree* (1985), that such a statute in Alabama violated the first prong of the *Lemon* test that required the statute to have a secular legislative purpose. The court ruled that Alabama's statute was not motivated by a secular purpose and had the purpose of endorsing religion.

FOCUS POINT: Distribution of Religious Literature by Students

Students have a right to distribute religious literature to other students on the same terms as they are permitted to distribute other literature that is unrelated to school curriculum or activities. Schools may impose the same reasonable time, place, and manner or other restrictions on distribution of religious literature as they do on nonschool literature generally, but they may not single out religious literature for special regulation.

FOCUS POINT: Accommodation of Students With Special Religious Needs

Various religions have practices that may require a student to perform a specific task or refrain from performing a specific task. For example, Muslim students need a quiet place at lunch or during breaks to fulfill their prayer obligation during the school day. At schools attended by Jehovah's Witness students, principals are frequently given a brochure that describes the beliefs of Jehovah's Witnesses and requests that these children be excused from singing anthems and school songs; from being involved in elected offices, cheerleading, and homecoming king or queen; and from celebrating birthdays or holidays. As long as honoring these requests are feasible, school officials may do so under the First Amendment. However, schools must not permit school employees to monitor or enforce a child's compliance with a particular religious requirement.

I FOCUS POINT: Teaching About Religion

Note: Includes guest speakers on religion, student assignments, and teaching about creationism.

Public schools may not provide religious instruction, but they may teach about religion, including the history of religion, comparative religion, the Bible (or other scripture) as literature, and the role of religion in the history of the United States and other countries. Similarly, it is permissible to consider religious influences on art, music, literature, and history. Although public schools may teach about religious holidays, including their religious aspects, and may celebrate the secular aspects of holidays, schools may not observe holidays as religious events or promote such observance by students. In *School District of Abington Township v. Schempp* (1963), the U.S. Supreme Court found required reading of verses from the Bible to be a violation of the establishment clause. The Court stated:

> [I]t might well be said that one's education is not complete without a study of comparative religion or the history of religion and its relationship to the advancement of civilization. It certainly may be said that the Bible is worthy of study for its literary and historic qualities. Nothing we have said here indicates that such study of the Bible or of religion, when presented objectively as part of a secular program of education, may not be effected consistently with the First Amendment.

As a result of this and other court decisions, the question is not, May teachers teach about religion? but rather, How should religion be taught? The answer is simply that instruction concerning religions may not include religious education or indoctrination.

Guest Speakers on Religion

Frequently, teachers invite outside speakers to their classes to supplement their teaching. Many districts have board-approved policies regulating this practice. These policies should be consulted prior to inviting an outside speaker. However, when community members are invited to speak on a religious topic, it is very important that they have appropriate academic credentials and understand that they are to speak about religion and cannot proselytize.

Student Assignments

Students may express their beliefs about religion in the form of homework, artwork, and other written and oral assignments free of discrimination based on the religious content of their submissions. Home and classroom work should be judged by ordinary academic standards of substance and relevance and against other legitimate pedagogical concerns identified by the school (i.e., a student writing about her activities at a church camp or a student singing a religious song at a talent show would be permitted).

Teaching about Creationism

Efforts to clarify the interpretation of the establishment clause and the free exercise clause have resulted in five major evolution-creationism cases. The first is the well-known 1927 case of *Scopes v. State of Tennessee* (often referred to as the Scopes Monkey Trial). In this case, John Scopes volunteered to be the defendant in a test case challenging Tennessee's antievolution statute. He was charged with teaching the theory of evolution in violation of Tennessee's antievolution statute, was found guilty, and was fined $100. A year later, the decision of the district court was reversed by the Tennessee Supreme Court on a technicality.

The U.S. Supreme Court decided a second case in 1968. In *Epperson v. Arkansas*, the Court invalidated an Arkansas statute that prohibited the teaching of evolution. The Court held the statute unconstitutional on grounds that the First Amendment does not permit a state to require that teaching and learning must be tailored to the principles or prohibitions of any particular religious sect or doctrine.

In 1987, the U.S. Court of Appeals ruled, in *Mozert v. Hawkins County Board of Education*, that a group of fundamentalist Christian students in Tennessee had to participate in the classroom use of a basic reading series that exposed students to competing ideas and philosophies, some of which were contrary to the students' religious beliefs. This ruling reversed a lower court's decision to allow those students to opt out of a reading curriculum because of their objection to the textbooks used. The Court held that "the students were merely being exposed to the materials and were not compelled to either do an act that violated their religious convictions or communicate an acceptance of a particular idea or affirm a belief."

In *Edwards v. Aguillar* (1987), the U.S. Supreme Court held unconstitutional Louisiana's Creationism Act. This statute prohibited the teaching of evolution in public schools, except when it was accompanied by instruction in "creation science." The Court found that, by advancing the religious belief that a supernatural being created humankind, which is embraced by the term *creation science*, the act impermissibly endorses religion. In addition, the Court found that the provision of a comprehensive science education is undermined when it is barred from teaching evolution except when creation science is also taught.

In 1997, the U.S. District Court for the Eastern District of Louisiana rejected a policy requiring teachers to read aloud a disclaimer whenever they taught about evolution, ostensibly to promote "critical thinking." The court wrote, in

Freiler v. Tangipahoa Parish Board of Education, that "in mandating this disclaimer, the School Board is endorsing religion by disclaiming the teaching of evolution in such a manner as to convey the message that evolution is a religious viewpoint that runs counter to . . . other religious views." In 1999, the Fifth Circuit Court of Appeals upheld the lower court ruling, noting that the actual effect of the disclaimer was to establish religion by encouraging them to read about religious "alternatives" to evolution. In June 2000, the U.S. Supreme Court denied the petition for *a writ of certiorari,* allowing the decision of the appeals court to stand.

Under the Tenth Amendment to the U.S. Constitution, federal control over education is secondary to the power exercised by the states. Consequently, public school curriculum decisions are delegated to state boards of education. In the late 1990s, the creationism-evolution controversy moved from the federal courts to various state boards of education. For example, a 1999 decision by the Kansas Board of Education to delete any mention of evolution from the state's science curriculum became one of the most far-reaching efforts by creationists in recent years to challenge the teaching of evolution in schools (Kansas Board of Education, 2001).

▐ FOCUS POINT: Religious Holidays

There is a difference between teaching about and celebrating religious holidays. Teaching is permissible, celebrating is not. Teachers may not use the study of religious holidays as an opportunity to proselytize or otherwise inject personal religious beliefs into the discussion.

If any religious symbols are incorporated into the teaching unit, they may be displayed only on a temporary basis as part of the academic lesson. When students have the opportunity to work on projects, they may choose to create artwork with religious symbols. However, teachers must not assign or suggest such creations.

▐ FOCUS POINT: Religious Excusals

Subject to applicable state laws, individual school districts have substantial discretion to excuse individual students from lessons that are objectionable to the student or the students' parents on religious or other conscientious grounds. However, students generally do not have a federal right to be excused from lessons that may be inconsistent with their religious beliefs or practices. School officials may neither encourage nor discourage students from opting out of certain activities.

▐ FOCUS POINT: Released Time

Subject to applicable state laws, schools have the discretion to dismiss students to off-premises religious instruction, provided that schools do not encourage or discourage participation or penalize those who do not attend. Schools may not allow religious instruction by outsiders on school premises during the school day.

I FOCUS POINT: Character Education

Although schools must be neutral with respect to religion, they may play an active role with respect to teaching civic values and ethics. The fact that some of these values are held by various religions does not make it unlawful to teach them in school.

It is generally agreed that teachers may, and in fact should, teach the personal and civic virtues widely held in our society, such as integrity, honesty, fairness, and caring. However, this must be done without invoking religious authority or denigrating the religious or philosophical beliefs of students and parents. It is in the best interest of teachers and students if there is a district-approved, comprehensive plan for character education, developed as a cooperative effort with parents and other community members that represent a very broad range of points of view.

I FOCUS POINT: Student Attire

Schools enjoy substantial discretion in adopting policies relating to student dress and school uniforms. Students generally have no federal right to be exempted from school dress rules based on their religious beliefs or practices. Schools may not single out religious attire in general, or attire of a particular religion, for prohibition or regulation. Students may display religious messages on items of clothing to the same extent that they are permitted to display other comparable messages.

I FOCUS POINT: The Equal Access Act

Note: Includes lunchtime and recess—limited open forum, religious clubs, use of school facilities.

In response to community demands, many school districts have expanded their programs of community and adult education. These programs have resulted in schools offering a wide range of enrichment, academic, recreational, and social courses and activities. Consistent with the First Amendment, the Equal Access Act (1984) was enacted to ensure that student religious activities are accorded the same access to public school facilities as are student secular activities. Based on decisions of the federal courts, as well as their interpretations of the act, the Department of Justice has advised that the act should be interpreted as providing, among other things, that student religious groups at public secondary schools have the same right of access to school facilities as is enjoyed by other comparable student groups. Under the act, a school receiving federal funds that allows one or more student non-curriculum-related clubs to meet on its premises during noninstructional time may not refuse access to student religious groups.

The Equal Access Act made it unlawful for any public secondary school to deny equal access to school facilities to students wishing to conduct religious, political, or philosophical meetings. It specifically gave students the right to conduct these meetings if the school received federal financial aid and had a limited open forum. The act defines an open forum as a school district's action that "grants an offering to, or an opportunity for, one or more non-curriculum-related student groups to meet on school premises during noninstructional time." Noninstructional time is defined as that time set aside by the school before actual classroom instruction begins or after instruction ends.

The law specifically states that school districts have the option of not being subject to the provisions of the act. To exercise that option, they must avoid creation of a limited open forum by keeping their facilities closed to all non-curriculum-related student meetings and activities, including religious meetings. Historically, school administrators who sought guidelines for deciding whether or not to allow students to participate in religious-oriented activities on school property could look to the three-pronged *Lemon* test established by the Supreme Court. Strictly following those guidelines, public schools could ban students from conducting religious activities on school property.

In 1989, the Supreme Court ruled for the first time on the constitutionality of the Equal Access Act in *Mergens v. Board of Education of West Side Community Schools*. This case began in 1985 when several students at a high school were denied permission to form a Christian group devoted to fellowship and Bible study. The students filed a suit arguing that their rights under the Equal Access Act had been violated. They contended that their school had sanctioned several extracurricular clubs on topics ranging from chess to scuba diving. School officials countered that all their clubs were related in some way to the broad goals of the school curriculum. They also argued that the Equal Access Act violated the First Amendment. The Court ruled that the act does not violate the First Amendment's prohibition against government establishment of religion. In its decision, the Court said that if a school sanctions even one student group that is not directly tied to course work, the act comes into play and the school cannot discriminate against other student organizations based on the religious, philosophical, or political views of their members. The decision further stated that "there is a crucial difference between government speech endorsing religion, and private speech endorsing religion, which the Free Speech and Free Exercise Clause protects." According to the *Mergens* Court: "A student group directly relates to a school's curriculum if: the subject matter of the group is actually taught, or will soon be taught, in a regularly offered course, if the subject matter of the group concerns the body of courses as a whole, if participation in the group is required for a particular course, or if participation in the group results in academic credit." The Court gave the example of a French club, which would be considered curriculum related if the school offered a French course. However, chess or stamp collecting, for example, would most likely be considered non-curriculum-related, and thus their existence would create a limited open forum at the school, requiring the accommodation of religious groups. School districts have three options: (1) drop all extracurricular programs to ensure a closed forum, (2) only permit those groups that directly relate to the curriculum, or (3) open their doors to all student groups.

Lunchtime and Noninstructional Time—Limited Open Forum

A school creates a limited open forum under the Equal Access Act, triggering equal access rights for religious groups, when it allows students to meet during their lunch periods or other noninstructional time during the school day, as well as when it allows students to meet before and after the school day.

Religious Clubs

The critical issue relating to student clubs is, Does the school allow other student clubs? Student religious groups at public secondary schools have the same right of access to school facilities as is enjoyed by other comparable student groups. The Equal Access Act is intended to protect student-initiated and student-led meetings in secondary schools. According to the act, outsiders may not "direct, conduct, control, or regularly attend" student religious clubs, and teachers acting as monitors may be present at religious meetings in a nonparticipatory capacity only. A meeting, as defined and protected by the Equal Access Act, may include a prayer service, Bible reading, or other worship exercise.

In addition, a school receiving federal funds must allow student groups meeting under the act to use school media—including the public address system, the school newspaper, and the school bulletin board—to announce their meetings on the same terms as other non-curriculum-related student groups. Any policy concerning the use of school media must be applied to all non-curriculum-related student groups in a nondiscriminatory manner. Schools, however, may inform students that certain groups are not school sponsored.

According to Fields (2005), one organization, the Child Evangelism Fellowship (CEF), which sponsors Good News Clubs for children, has successfully challenged the limited public forum rulings by arguing that religious speech is "private speech," not "governmental speech," in a number of jurisdictions. Although CEF's initiatives have not always been successful, their approach presents another challenge in the area of separation of church and state. (For more information, see Child Evangelism Fellowship and the Good News Clubs in Chapter Resources.)

Use of School Facilities by Religious Groups

Under the Equal Access Act, a school district may not deny access to school facilities to religious groups if a school district has made itself a "limited open forum" by permitting other nonreligious groups, for example, recreational organizations, to use its facilities (*Lamb's Chapel v. Center Moriches Union Free School District*, 1992).

FOCUS POINT: Using Federal Funds for Remedial Education Services

In *Agostini v. Felton* (1997), the U.S. Supreme Court reversed its 1985 decision in the case of *Aguilar v. Felton*, ruling that New York City could spend Title I funds to provide remedial educational services inside private religious schools.

FOCUS POINT: Pledge of Allegiance

The issues surrounding the flag salute could be discussed as a religious freedom issue or as a First Amendment freedom of expression issue. The first flag salute statute was passed in 1898, shortly after the United States declared war on Spain. Certain religious groups, most notably Jehovah's Witnesses, immediately expressed their opposition to any mandatory pledge of allegiance based on their religious teaching that forbade reverence to a national symbol. Various state courts upheld the expulsion of students who refused to salute the flag. In the midst of the nationalistic sentiments just prior to the Second World War, the Supreme Court ruled that national unity and national security takes precedence over individual religious liberties (*Minersville School District v. Gobitis*, 1940). However in 1943, the U.S. Supreme Court again addressed this issue when a West Virginia state law required all students to recite the pledge under threat of expulsion from school and criminal prosecution. The Jehovah's Witnesses argued, in *West Virginia State Board of Education v. Barnette* (1943), that being required to recite the Pledge of Allegiance forced them to worship something other than Jehovah. They argued that their refusal was not an indication of disrespect or antigovernment sentiments, bolstering their argument by quoting from the *Encyclopedia Americana*: "The flag, like the cross, is sacred."

The U.S. Supreme Court, in a reversal of a lower court decision, affirmed the state's right to adopt a curriculum designed to "inspire patriotism and love of country." The Court concluded that although the state's purpose in requiring a flag salute was valid, its methods overstepped constitutional bounds. It stated that "the actions of the local authorities in compelling the flag salute and pledge transcends constitutional limitations on their power." This decision does not prohibit schools from including a flag salute in a school's daily program. Several courts, for example *Steirer v. Bethlehem Area School District* (1993), have stated that the pledge's reference to God does not violate the First Amendment.

During the 2003–2004 term, the Supreme Court had an opportunity to settle the question of the constitutionality of the words *under God* in the pledge. The Court sidestepped this opportunity. In *Elk Grove School District v. Newdow* (2004), a noncustodial California father argued that his daughter was injured by being compelled to watch and listen as her teacher led her classmates in what he described as a ritual proclaiming that there is a God. Because of the unusual set of facts in this case, the Court's decision focused on procedural issues rather than the substantive issue of the words *under God*. The noncustodial father did not inform the custodial mother that he was acting, in spite of the fact that the mother reported that neither she nor her daughter were troubled by her reciting the pledge. The federal trial court dismissed the case. On review, the Ninth Circuit reversed in favor of Newdow and struck down the 1954 statute that added the words *under God* to the pledge. The Supreme Court chose to ignore the constitutional issue and decided that since the state courts had yet to clarify issues surrounding Newdow's standing and custodial status, it would have been improper for the Supreme Court to have resolved the merits of his claim. Consequently, although a student cannot be required to recite the pledge, the pledge remains intact.

▮ FOCUS POINT: The Ten Commandments

It is unlikely that school leaders will be confronted with any issue more emotionally and politically charged than those involving the display of the Ten Commandments. In 1980, in *Stone v. Graham,* the U.S. Supreme Court overturned a Kentucky law calling for the Ten Commandments to be posted in public schools. Since then there have been a number of lower court decisions pertaining to the display of the Ten Commandments. In 2004, the Supreme Court agreed to review two such cases (Kentucky and Texas), in which the Fifth and Sixth Circuits reached opposite conclusions. In the 1950s and 1960s, the Fraternal Order of Eagles donated monuments of the Ten Commandments to a number of communities. The Texas case involves a red six-foot-tall granite monument of the Ten Commandments that is displayed 75 feet from the state capitol building (*Van Orden v. Perry,* 2003). The Fifth Circuit found no constitutional violation in this display. In the Kentucky case, the Sixth Circuit ruled that the display of framed copies of the Ten Commandments in two county courthouses and a school district violated the establishment clause (*ACLU v. McCreary County, Kentucky,* 2003).

▌ FOCUS POINT: Distribution of Bibles in Public Schools

Historically, some schools have allowed outside groups, such as the Gideons, to come into schools and distribute Bibles to students. The Fifth Circuit Court, in *Meltzer v. Board of Public Instruction of Orange County* (1977), prohibited this practice, stating that the practice favored the Gideons and consequently was not a neutral act. However, in *Peck v. Upshur County Board of Education* (1996), a federal court in West Virginia ruled that as long as the distribution was conducted in an area that is open to other outside organizations and the students are free to refuse the Bibles, the distribution is permitted.

The issue of Bible distribution in schools continues to find its way into the courts. For example, in 1997, a case in Alabama concerned a teacher who argued that the distribution of Bibles to public school students during homeroom by an outside group did not violate the First Amendment because no instruction took place during homeroom. The court ruled against permitting the distribution, stating that because the homeroom was surrounded by other school activities, such a practice gave the impression that the school endorsed the religious activity (*Chandler v. James*).

▌ FOCUS POINT: Public Aid to Private Schools

In 2000, the U.S. Supreme Court decided the case of *Mitchell v. Helms*, a case that involved Chapter 2 of the Education Consolidation and Improvement Act of 1981. This act channels federal funds via SEAs to LEAs, which in turn lend educational materials and equipment, such as library and media materials and computer software and hardware, to public and private elementary and secondary schools to implement "secular, neutral, and non-ideological" programs.

The enrollment of each participating school determines the amount of Chapter 2 aid that it receives. The district court agreed with the *Mitchell* plaintiffs' allegations that Chapter 2, as applied in this school district, violated the First Amendment's establishment clause and had the primary effect of advancing religion because the materials and equipment loaned to the Catholic schools were direct aid and the schools were pervasively sectarian. While the appeal was pending, the U.S. Supreme Court, in *Agostini v. Felton* (1997), approved a program under Title I of the Elementary and Secondary Education Act of 1965 that allowed public employees to teach remedial classes at religious and other private schools. The Fifth Circuit invalidated Chapter 2. However, the Supreme Court reversed the decision of the Fifth Circuit. The Court concluded that Chapter 2, as applied in this case, is not a law respecting an establishment of religion simply because many of the private schools receiving Chapter 2 aid in the parish are religiously affiliated. The Court modified the traditional *Lemon* test and set out three primary criteria for determining a statute's effect:

"Government aid has the effect of advancing religion if it (1) results in governmental indoctrination, (2) defines its recipients by reference to religion, or (3) creates an excessive entanglement."

FOCUS POINT: The Religious Freedom Restoration Act

In 1993, Congress passed the Religious Freedom Restoration Act (RFRA) prohibiting government at any level from enforcing generally applicable laws that burden the free exercise of religion, unless the burden is the least restrictive means of furthering a compelling government interest. This act would have prohibited states from enforcing any limit on student absence for religious observance as long as any possible method of allowing the absent student to make up for lost work could be conceived. In 1997, the U.S. Supreme Court, in *City of Boerne v. Flores*, struck down the act, affirming the district court's conclusion that by enacting RFRA, Congress exceeded the scope of its enforcement power under Section 5 of the Fourteenth Amendment.

Examples of Management Cues

- A parent registers a complaint that the art teacher discusses religious themes in art class and the music teacher has students perform some music that has religious overtones.
- A group of parents complain that their children's teacher decorates her room with religious symbols at various times during the year.
- A teacher passes out advertising for a summer Bible class that she is instructing at her church and welcomes her students to attend.
- A high school teacher reads magazine articles in class and mocks those articles that focus on religion.
- A local pastor has been elected to the public school board and wears his clerical regalia to board meetings.
- A local radio station informs its listeners that five minutes before the kickoff of all home football games, the station will broadcast the Lord's Prayer. The station suggests that all listeners take portable radios to the game and turn the volume up during this broadcast.
- An elementary school student screams Bible passages at recess.
- A teacher keeps a very large Bible on her desk and reads it during free reading time.
- A Jehovah's Witness parent requests that her child not participate in any classroom parties. The child, however, wants to go to the parties. The parent learns of her child's attendance and informs the school that they must remove the child from the room during such events.

- A teacher and coach sponsor the Fellowship of Christian Athletes and require that all athletes attend the meetings.
- A teacher announces that her church is having its annual revival meeting, and she invites students to attend.
- A child remains seated during the morning Pledge of Allegiance. He is ridiculed and threatened during recess.

Suggested Risk Management Guidelines

- Every school district should have a clear policy that informs all staff members about the appropriate relationship of religion and public education.
  - These policies should emphasize that religion is included for educational reasons, not for proselytizing, and any policies developed must conform to state statutes and state board of education policies. The keywords for policy development should be *academic* as opposed to *practice*, *exposure* as opposed to *imposure*, *educational* as opposed to *promotional* or *denigrating*.
  - All teachers who deal with religiously contested matters should discuss the content of their syllabi and various course activities with their principal.
  - If there are courses that deal with comparative religion or world religions, the principal should ensure that there are teachers competent to teach them.
  - All textbooks and other curriculum materials should be reviewed by a school committee to ensure that the material is appropriate.

- It *is* permissible
  - To use art, drama, music, or literature with religious themes if it serves a sound educational goal in the curriculum
  - To include religious themes on the basis of their academic or aesthetic value, not as a vehicle for promoting religious belief
  - To sing or play sacred music as part of the academic study of music
  - For school concerts to include a variety of selections that include religious music (see *not* permissible below)
  - For school officials to accommodate the requests of parents and students to be excused from classroom discussions or activities for religious reasons
  - For school officials to routinely grant requests for excuses from specific discussions, assignments, or activities
  - To excuse students from particular lessons if the school cannot prove a compelling interest in requiring attendance
  - To provide speech, hearing, and psychological services at a parochial site or a neutral site

- It *is not* permissible
  - For concerts or music programs to be dominated by religious music, especially when they coincide with a particular religious holiday

- To loan materials and equipment other than textbooks to parochial schools
- To assist a parochial school to pay for transportation on field trips
- To assist a parochial school to pay for facility maintenance
- To assist a parochial school to pay for remedial or enrichment courses during the school day
- To assist a parochial school to pay for community education programs on parochial school grounds during nonschool hours
- To allow student religious speech to turn into religious harassment aimed at a student or a group of students

SECTION D: THE MARKETPLACE OF IDEAS

A long line of U.S. Supreme Court opinions recognize that schools foster moral, cultural, and intellectual qualities in children in a uniquely important way and identify the classroom as a marketplace of ideas. Text and library book selection and the use of technology can exert a powerful influence on curriculum. (See, for example, Ambach v. Norwick, *1979;* Keyishian v. Board of Regents, *1967.) This section focuses on topics of critical significance to public education: (a) What are the rights of teachers to teach and students to learn? (b) Who is ultimately in charge of a school's curriculum? (c) What is academic freedom?*

In *Meyer v. State of Nebraska* (1923), the U.S. Supreme Court recognized that there is a substantive constitutional interest in teaching and learning. The Court ruled that a Nebraska law forbidding, "under penalty, the teaching, in any private, denominational, parochial or public school, of any modern language, other than English, to any child who has not attained and successfully passed the eighth grade, invades the liberty guaranteed by the Fourteenth Amendment and exceeds the power of the State." Although this case was decided in 1923, it is still highly relevant because it established the foundational tenet that the freedom to teach may not be interfered with under the guise of protecting the public interest.

I FOCUS POINT: Community Service

In the 1990s, Rye Neck School District's public high school, located in Mamaroneck, New York, instituted a mandatory community service program as part of the high school curriculum. Under the program, in order to graduate, all students were required to complete 40 hours of community service sometime during their four high school years. They were also required to participate in a corresponding classroom discussion about their service. The program had no opt-out provision for students who objected to performing community service. There were rules regarding the organizations to which the students could donate their services and the nature of the work they could perform. For their efforts to count toward the 40-hour requirement, students could not receive pay for their services, nor could their services displace activities performed by paid employees of the organization being served. Furthermore, while up to 20 hours of service could be provided to the school itself or to younger students at the school, at least 20 hours had to be provided to an organization outside the school (*Immediato v. Rye Neck School District*, 1996).

Daniel Immediato, a student at the district's high school, objected to the program on the grounds that charitable activities and community service, while admirable, must be left to an individual's conscience and should not be mandated by the school. He also desired to keep private any information about what community service he did or did not perform. In addition, Daniel's parents expressed a fear that the school's mandatory community service program would teach Daniel that guidance on moral issues should come from the government, rather than from within. In their suit, his parents contended that the mandatory community service program conditioned the right to public education on the surrender of their constitutional rights. Specifically, they asserted that the program (a) imposed involuntary servitude upon Daniel, in violation of the Thirteenth Amendment, (b) infringed on Daniel's parents' Fourteenth Amendment right to direct his upbringing and education, (c) infringed on Daniel's personal liberty, in violation of the Fourteenth Amendment, and (d) violated Daniel's right to privacy, in violation of the Fourteenth Amendment. The plaintiffs asked the district court to declare the program unconstitutional and to permanently enjoin the defendants from imposing the program. The school district denied that the program violated any of the plaintiffs' constitutional rights.

The U.S. District Court for the Southern District of New York granted summary judgment for the school district, and the student and his parents appealed. The Court of Appeals held that the high school's mandatory community service program did not rise to the level of "involuntary servitude" prohibited by the Thirteenth Amendment. The court further held that because the school district's mandatory community service program for high school students was reasonably related to the state's legitimate function of educating its students, it did not violate parents' substantive due process rights in the upbringing of their children. The court also held that the state has a compelling interest in educating its youth to prepare them both to participate effectively and intelligently in an open political system and to be self-reliant and self-sufficient participants in society (*Immediato v. Rye Neck School District*, 1996).

I FOCUS POINT: Censorship of Print Material

One of the major issues in the selection of textbooks, library books, and other instructional material, including technology, is censorship. Censors may be state appointed or self-appointed. They may be school employees, members of citizens' groups, or talk show hosts. They are found on both the right and the left ends of the political spectrum.

The National Council of Teachers of English (NCTE) suggests that teachers are uniquely qualified to judge their own instructional materials' strengths and weaknesses and that the textbook selection process should always include teachers' evaluations of the books (NCTE, 1989). The process should be shared with parents and other interested members of the community.

The American Library Association (ALA) asserts that intellectual freedom is the right of every individual to both seek and receive information from all points of view without restriction. It provides for free access to all expressions of ideas through which any and all sides of a question, cause, or movement may be explored (ALA, 2005). In 1986, in response to inquiries from librarians facing book or material challenges for the first time, the Intellectual Freedom Committee developed the following list of definitions to clarify terminology associated with challenges:

- *Expression of concern:* An inquiry that has judgmental overtones
- *Oral complaint:* An oral challenge to the presence and/or appropriateness of the material in question
- *Written complaint:* A formal, written complaint filed with the institution (library, school, etc.), challenging the presence and/or appropriateness of specific material
- *Public attack:* A publicly disseminated statement challenging the value of the material presented to the media and/or others outside the institutional organization in order to gain public support for further action
- *Censorship:* A change in the access status of material based on the content of the work and made by a governing authority or its representatives. Such changes include exclusion, restriction, removal, or age/grade level changes. (ALA, 2005)

The ALA collects information regarding efforts to restrict, remove, or ban books, and of the 6,364 challenges between 1990 and 2000, the ALA reported that

- 1,607 were challenges to "sexually explicit" material
- 1,427 were to material considered to use "offensive language"
- 1,256 were to material considered "unsuited to age group"
- 842 were to material with an "occult theme or promoting the occult or satanism"
- 737 were to material considered to be "violent"
- 515 were to material with a homosexual theme or "promoting homosexuality"
- 419 were to material "promoting a religious viewpoint"

Other reasons for challenges included "nudity," "racism," "sex education," and "anti-family" (ALA, 2005). (See also Challenges in Chapter Resources.)

Some people claim they are engaged in a battle to determine who will use the schools to indoctrinate young people. Others claim they have a right to remove educational material that fosters sexual stereotypes. Other advocates say they have a right to remove books that are racist, profane, or obscene and replace them with books that present positive role models for racial and ethnic minorities. Whatever the challenge, principals need to follow school district policy and procedures to the letter before removing materials from the classroom, library, or school.

About half of the states delegate the responsibility for textbook selection to local boards of education, while the other half exercises this authority directly. In adoption states, a single text is selected for each subject, and publishers supply them statewide. Typically, local school districts, in adoption states, may not use state funds to buy books that are not on the state list.

Although the courts have ruled that citizens of the community cannot use court action to require a board of education to use a certain textbook, school boards are very responsive to vocal pressure. In some cases, textbooks have been removed from schools as the result of pressure from less than a dozen citizens. In *Mozert v. Hawkins County Board of Education* (1987), a parent challenged the requirement that all students participate in a particular reading program that contained stories and poems with ideas contrary to the parent's religious beliefs. A federal court of appeals held in favor of the school board and recognized the broad discretion of school boards to establish curriculum even in the face of parental disagreements.

In addition to attacking textbook adoptions, school patrons and individual board members sometimes demand that certain materials they consider objectionable be removed from classrooms or libraries. School boards, faced with such complaints, have often been willing to order school administrators to remove the materials from the schools. In some cases, school officials have ordered not only that materials be removed from schools, but also that their content not be discussed in classrooms. School boards have justified their actions by asserting that they have absolute discretion in all curriculum matters in the school and that they must be permitted to establish and apply the curriculum in such a way as to transmit community values. Those who oppose the removal of school curriculum materials or library books from schools argue that the practice is a violation of the First Amendment's guarantee of free speech.

A number of federal courts have heard cases involving efforts to censor various reading materials in the schools. In *Presidents Council District 25 v. Community School Board No. 25* (1972), a federal appeals court upheld the right of a school board to remove Piri Thomas's *Down These Mean Streets* from junior high school libraries because some patrons believed that some of the language and scenes in the book were "ugly and violent." The court found no violation of any basic constitutional right and concluded that any intrusion on any First Amendment right was only "minuscule."

On the other hand, in *Minarcini v. Strongville City School District* (1976), another federal appeals court overruled a lower court and denied a school board's right to remove Joseph Heller's *Catch-22* and Kurt Vonnegut Jr.'s *Cat's*

Cradle from a high school library. The court ruled that if a school board sets up a library, that library becomes a forum of silent speech protected by the First Amendment. Therefore, it is unconstitutional to place conditions on its use based solely on the social or political tastes of school board members.

In 1982, in *Island Trees Union School District v. Pico*, the U.S. Supreme Court heard its first school library book-banning case. This case of censorship involved the removal of nine books from a school library within the Island Trees District. The board defended its decision by claiming the books contained "material which is offensive to Christians, Jews, Blacks, and Americans in general," as well as "obscenities, blasphemies, brutality and perversion beyond description." The board's action prompted Steven Pico and four other high school students to sue the school district. They charged that the board ignored the advice of literary experts, libraries, teachers, and publications that rate books for secondary students, and based its decision solely on a list of objectionable books put out by a conservative parents' group. In hearing the *Pico* case, the Court affirmed the appellate court's decision that school officials can be taken to federal court if they are challenged about removing books from school libraries. The Court noted that the "right to receive ideas is a necessary predicate to the exercise of speech, press and political freedom."

The *Pico* decision sent the message that board members have discretion in curriculum matters by reliance on the duty to support community values in the schools, but that duty is misplaced when boards extend their discretion beyond the compulsory environment of the classroom into the library, in which voluntary inquiry is paramount. In addition, although school boards have significant discretion to determine the library's content, such discretion cannot be exercised in a narrowly partisan or political manner. The *Pico* Court ruled that "[o]ur Constitution does not permit the official suppression of ideas."

The courts have ruled that books cannot be removed simply because school officials disagree with the ideas. Removal decisions should be based on a book's or other curriculum material's educational suitability, considering such "politically neutral" factors as relevance, quality, pervasive vulgarity, and appropriateness to age and grade level. (See also *Hazelwood v. Kuhlmeier*, 1988; *Virgil v. School Board of Columbia County*, 1989.)

I FOCUS POINT: The Harry Potter Argument

Courts have uniformly ruled that, although there is a legitimate community interest in allowing the values of a community to be transmitted through the school curriculum, these interests must not be determined in a narrowly partisan and political manner. The debate about J. K. Rowling's Harry Potter series is the most recent, and perhaps the most intense, example of the role of parental offense in curricular decisions. The Harry Potter series follows the exploits of an orphaned boy wizard at the Hogwarts School of Witchcraft and Wizardry.

The two sides of the debate can be seen in *Counts v. Cedarville School District* (2003). Parents of a child attending the Cedarville School District became concerned when they learned that the Harry Potter books were in circulation in the district's school libraries. They contacted their child's school librarian and were told that, under the district's policy, they would have to complete a Reconsideration Request Form. The parents completed the form and requested that *Harry Potter and the Sorcerer's Stone* be withdrawn from circulation. The school's library committee considered the request and recommended, without reservations, that the board of education keep the book in circulation. The school board voted to restrict the circulation of all of the books in the Harry Potter series to only those students who provide a signed permission statement from their parent or guardian. The parents of Dakota Counts brought a suit alleging that her rights under the First and Fourteenth Amendment were being abridged. In ruling that Counts had sufficient injury to give her standing to pursue her claims, the Court stated, "The right to read a book is an aspect of the right to receive information and ideas, an inherent corollary of the rights of freedom of speech and the press." The Court found that the school district's policy of restricting access to the Harry Potter books infringed on Counts's First Amendment rights.

Examples of Management Cues

- A parent complains that the band director has selected the song "White Rabbit" for an upcoming concert. The parent states that the song was recorded in the 1960s and alludes to drug use, and he calls the music "almost an anthem for the drug culture."
- A primary teacher selects the book *Nappy Hair* by Carolivia Herron to read with the children in her third-grade class. She thinks that reading the book will be a celebration of the mostly Hispanic and African American class's diversity. The book is a semiautobiographical account of the author's uncle's teasing praise for her hair as a girl. The teacher notes that her students are enamored with the tale, but a parent, who claims that the book is a racist attack on the black community, is organizing a protest against the school and the teacher unless the book is banned from the school.
- A teacher sends a permission slip home with all the students in her advanced-level government course, giving parents the opportunity to have their children excused from any discussion of the Clinton-Lewinsky scandal. Although the students' families give their approval, the school counselor strongly objects, believing that the material is not appropriate.
- While passing through the high school library during open house, a father, who is also a school board member, is concerned when he sees the cover of a *Rolling Stone* magazine featuring the cast of *Saturday Night Live*. In the photo, one cast member is touching the fully covered breast of another cast member, and a female cast member dressed as a cheerleader is touching her own buttocks. He believes that the magazine is inappropriate material for high school students, calling some of the content "pornographic." He insists that the magazine be removed and the subscription be cancelled.

- A community patron comes into the high school library and asks the librarian to compile a list of books depicting "alternative lifestyles." When asked to clarify what she means, she responds, "Gays." The librarian is able to come up with a list of 14 titles, and the patron asks that they be removed immediately.
- A middle school librarian finds the photos in the swimsuit issue of a popular sports magazine to be "in bad taste." She sends the magazine back to the publisher and posts the following note on the shelf where the magazine is usually displayed: "This issue of this magazine is banned from this library because of obscene photographs."
- A parent asks the teacher of his fourth grader to stop using *The Gnats of Knotty Pine* by Bill Peet. The parent believes the story wrongly depicts hunters as "macho types" who harm little animals.
- One of your elementary teachers removes all copies of the *American Heritage Dictionary* from her classroom on the grounds that it defines vulgar and scatological phrases.

Note: Many of the above examples are drawn from events that took place in 1999 and are adapted from "Attacks on the Freedom to Learn" (1999).

Suggested Risk Management Guidelines

- Assume personal responsibility for ensuring that all curriculum and library materials are educationally sound and appropriate to the age and maturity of students. Encourage teachers to consider the age and maturity of the student when making assignments. Provide inservice instruction for all academic staff.
- Develop procedures that ensure that the selection of educational material is based on an evaluation of how the material will assist the student to reach previously agreed-upon goals.
- Make provision for alternative materials for those students whose parents object to specific material.
- Follow school district policy and procedures for handling complaints. Such a policy should include
  - A *specific* procedure to follow in the cases of material being challenged
  - A standardized form for filing complaints; all office staff members, librarians, and teachers should receive inservice instruction on the implementation of this policy and the use of the standardized form
  - A districtwide committee to review any requests for review of materials

❙ FOCUS POINT: Issues Related to the Use of the Internet

Note: Includes Internet privacy for staff files, filtering software, and district liability.

With increased access to Internet services by students comes the legitimate concern about appropriate use of this technology. In April 1998, the Associated Press reported that the Utah Education Network (UEN) documented that public school students tried to access prohibited material 275,000 times in just one month. In another month, students tried more than 250,000 times to access Internet sites that were sexual in nature or dealt with sexuality. The filters used by UEN were successful in blocking most of the inappropriate sites, although it is impossible to block all unwanted material because new sites are added daily (*Filtering Facts,* 2001).

The key point here is not what access is bad, but what access is inappropriate in a PreK–12 school environment. It is appropriate for districts to exert control over the use of the district's Internet access system and to establish that the system is for a limited educational purpose. Both employees and students have a duty to use the district system only for professional and educational purposes. Schools must be aware that some risks are associated with providing students with access to technology resources. Generally, these risks are (a) viewing or reading inappropriate material, (b) inviting physical molestation or harassment, and (c) personal or commercial exploitation. (See Technology in the School in Chapter Resources.)

Internet Privacy for Staff Files

In *O'Connor v. Ortega* (1987), the U.S. Supreme Court relied on the *T.L.O.* standards (see Chapter 11, *New Jersey v. T.L.O.*). The Court held that employees had constitutionally protected privacy interests in the work environment, but that the reasonableness of employees' expectation of privacy must be determined on a case-by-case analysis. The Court then applied the *T.L.O.* standards of reasonableness to employer intrusions of employee privacy for noninvestigatory, work-related purposes as well as for investigations of work-related misconduct. Employees should have no expectation of privacy when material reviewed or downloaded was created on school time using school-owned equipment, including school cable or phone lines.

Filtering Software

Filtering software may be somewhat effective in restricting access to inappropriate material and dealing with online predators if the software is used to block access to chat rooms, which are a primary location for predators. However, filtering software has limitations and will not alleviate all possible areas of concern. Computers in classrooms, libraries, or labs should be monitored by school personnel at all times. Equipment should be placed so that adult supervisors have clear visibility of computer monitors. (See *Downloading* in Chapter Resources.) Because all transactions conducted using a district's technology resources may be perceived as being authorized by the school district, it is important that the district have clear policies and practices.

District Liability

Some sections of the Communications Decency Act of 1996 were ruled unconstitutional; however, Section 230 of the act, which provides federal immunity from liability to service providers for the speech of third-party content providers, remains in force. In *Kathleen R. v. City of Livermore* (1998), a mother of a teenage boy sued the city library because her son had accessed sexually explicit pictures through the library's Internet service. The city argued that Section 230 applied. The action was dismissed.

Other liability concerns include defamation, harassment, invasion of privacy, copyright infringement, and computer security violations. It is possible that a school district could be held liable for harm caused by material transmitted through the system by students due to a lack of adequate supervision. Although the immunity provided by Section 230 would likely apply in such a situation, it is possible that an action based on negligence would succeed if the school could reasonably have foreseen the risk and did not take reasonable steps to protect students. (See Chapter 15 on negligence. See also Chapter 13 on sexual harassment and Chapter 10 on copyright infringement.)

Examples of Management Cues

- A student or someone else, using a terminal in the school library, sends a threatening e-mail to the principal's office. The sender uses a teacher's password.
- A student using a lab computer to do research for a term paper on safe ground-covering material to place under swings and other playground equipment inadvertently accesses a pornographic Web site and prints several pictures from the site. His parents find the pictures and are now complaining about poor supervision at the school.
- A teacher complains that another teacher is harassing her through the school e-mail because she refuses to see him socially. When she asked him to stop, he continued. As a result, school security asks permission to monitor the sending teacher's school e-mail account.

Suggested Risk Management Guidelines

- Develop and widely publicize a technology acceptable-use policy.
- Describe what is considered to be an *educational purpose* and outline what activities are considered acceptable and unacceptable. For example, *acceptable activities* might include class assignments and career development activities for students, and professional development and communication. *Unacceptable activities* might include materials that contain racist, profane, or obscene language; using the network for financial gain or political or commercial activity, including attempting to send anonymous or threatening messages of any kind; and using the network to provide addresses or other personal information that others may use inappropriately.
- Place computers with access to the Internet in a location in which a supervising adult can view the screen. Ensure that instructional staff members carefully monitor students using the Internet.
- Install filtering software; however, do not consider this a stand-alone protection.

- Develop an education program that assists students and staff members in understanding district or school-based restrictions on computer use.
- Assign individual access passwords to all users of the system, including teachers, staff, and students.
- If possible, require all users to record and state the purpose of activities.
- Prohibit participation in online group discussions that are not related to education.
- Allow only limited incidental personal communication.
- Inform all users that the technical system administrators and technical services personnel have the ability to access personal files and monitor online use.
- Investigate any unusual activity on the system.

I FOCUS POINT: Internet Privacy for Student Files

In 1998, the U.S. Congress enacted the Children's Online Privacy Act, which authorizes the Federal Trade Commission (FTC) to develop rules that place restrictions on companies that solicit personal information from children under the age of 13. The FTC has developed regulations to implement this act.

Educators need to balance the interest in protecting privacy with the need for effective monitoring and supervision. The manner in which the district addresses these issues may depend on a variety of factors, including the age of the students and the community environment. Whatever the district decides, students should be given clear notice of the standards and expectations. All users should be informed that

- They have only limited privacy in the contents of their personal files or records of Web research activities, and routine maintenance and monitoring of the system can lead to discovery of policy violations.
- The district has the right to conduct a search if there is reasonable suspicion that a student, teacher, or staff member has violated policy.
- Parents have the right to request to see the content of student e-mail files.

There also may be educational or disciplinary reasons for a student's e-mail not to be considered private.

There are four basic areas of concerns regarding privacy: (1) student information that is placed on the district Web site or otherwise distributed through the Internet by school staff members or other students, (2) disclosure of confidential student information by staff members via electronic communications, (3) information that students disclose about themselves in e-mail messages or on various Web sites, and (4) school-corporate partnerships that provide the opportunity for companies to gather or solicit personal information from students. (See National Center for Missing and Exploited Children, n.d., which has excellent materials on child safety on the Internet.)

Examples of Management Cues

- A teacher insists that students who are absent from school for more than one day obtain their homework assignments and submit their work via the school's Internet Web site. The teacher contends that "by now," all students should have computers in their homes.
- A student doing research for a term paper requests information to be e-mailed or mailed to her concerning sexually transmitted diseases.
- A student is accused of using school equipment to send harassing e-mail to a student in another school in the district.
- A counselor sends information about students' grades, attendance, and scholastic aptitudes to college admissions officers to assist students in gaining admission.

Suggested Risk Management Guidelines

- Do not post students' names, class work, or pictures on a district Web site without parental consent. This action falls under the provisions of the Family Rights and Privacy Act. (See section on student records in Chapter 9.)
- Obtain written permission before posting any personal information about staff members.
- Develop a policy that prohibits students from disclosing personal information.
- Ensure that school-site policies and procedures cover the items listed below and provide comprehensive inservice to ensure that all personnel understand and implement adopted policies and procedures.
- Ensure district cooperation with local, state, or federal officials in any investigation concerning or relating to any illegal activities conducted through district system technology.
- Monitor to ensure that any attempts by employees or students to gain unauthorized access to the district system, or to any other computer system through the district system, or go beyond their authorized access is blocked. (This includes attempting to log in through another person's account or access another person's files.)
- Monitor to ensure that any deliberate attempts by employees or students to disrupt the computer system performance or destroy data by spreading computer viruses or other means is blocked. (Employees and students must follow district virus protection procedures if they download software.)
- Monitor to ensure that any deliberate attempts by employees or students are blocked if they attempt any of the following activities:
  - Engaging in any illegal act, such as arranging for a drug sale or the purchase of alcohol, engaging in criminal gang activity, threatening the safety of persons, and so forth
  - The use of obscene, profane, lewd, vulgar, rude, inflammatory, threatening, or disrespectful language
  - The posting of information that, if acted on, could cause damage or a danger of disruption

– Engaging in personal attacks, including prejudicial or discriminatory attacks, or harassing another person

– Knowingly or recklessly posting false or defamatory information about a person or organization

– Using the district system to access material that is profane or obscene (pornography), that advocates illegal or dangerous acts, or that advocates violence or discrimination toward other people (hate literature)

• It is appropriate, and strongly recommended, that principals designate a school Web manager to be responsible for the Web site and to monitor class, teacher, student, and extracurricular Web pages. It is also appropriate to permit teachers to establish Web pages and students to create a Web site as part of a class activity. Copyrighted or trademarked material belonging to others should not be included in any Web page without written permission.

▌ FOCUS POINT: Technology and Student Misconduct

With the advent of cellular telephones, e-mail, Blackberries, iPods, instant messaging, blogging, pod casting and the Internet, school leaders are being confronted with significant challenges relating to student misconduct. In discussing the need to balance the likelihood of disruption against students' free speech rights, Fossey and Horner (2003) identified several cases that focus on technology misuse by students. In *J.S. v. Bethlehem Area School District* (2002), a student-authored Web site titled "Teachers Sux" included audio and visual statements casting teachers and the principal in an unflattering light. The site also included a portion captioned "Why Should She Die? (referring to an algebra teacher). The FBI and the police declined to file charges against the student. At the end of the school year, the student was informed that he would be expelled for the next school year. Although the court found that no serious threat to the teacher existed, it upheld the school's punishment based on the substantial disruption the Web site caused. However, in another student Web site case, the court ruled that a student's Web site did not cause a material and substantial interference with school discipline. The federal district court in Missouri overturned the suspension of the site's author (*Beussink v. Woodlend R-IV*, 1998).

Another type of student misuse of technology can be seen in *Boucher v. School Board of School District of Greenfield* (1998). In this case, a student wrote an article in an "underground" newspaper explaining how to "hack" into the school's computer system. According to Fossey and Horner, the appeals court vacated the trial court's injunction prohibiting the school from expelling the author of the article. According to the appellate court, the action of the student was "palpably transgressive."

And now there is e-bullying. As this book goes to press, Harvard-Westlake High School, a private school in Los Angeles, is facing a $100 million lawsuit filed by the parents of a 15-year-old student who got anonymous death threats on his personal Web site. The suit alleges that Harvard-Westlake failed to protect the student and to discipline those who confessed to using school computers to post menacing messages.

Bullies have added the Internet to their harassment methods, and schools faced with threats of litigation should take protective measures (i.e., tightening restrictions on Internet access at school and/or barring students from accessing personal e-mail accounts from school servers) to prevent e-bullying and avoid possible litigation.

Suggested Risk Management Guidelines

Note: The following Management Guidelines are adopted from Fossey and Horner's (2003) recommendations for practice by school districts

- Have a board-approved acceptable use policy and consent form for student use of the school's computers.
- Use filtering software.
- Clearly state that the school owns the hardware and the server and there is no expectation of privacy.
- Prohibit all personal use of the school's technology.
- Protect the confidentiality of educational records stored on computers.
- Create and disseminate a specific listing of unacceptable use of the district's network.

SECTION E: HEALTH AND SAFETY ISSUES

School administrators are responsible for the success of all students by ensuring management of the organization, operations, and resources of the school for a safe, efficient, and effective learning environment. An important step in creating such schools is to implement a districtwide or school-site safe-school plan.

The National School Safety Center (n.d.) recommends the following steps to create a safe school: (a) establish clear behavior standards, (b) provide adequate adult presence and supervision, (c) enforce the rules fairly and consistently, (d) supervise closely and sanction offenders consistently, (e) cultivate parental support, (f) control campus access, (g) create partnerships with outside agencies. This section focuses on the legal context surrounding the following health and safety issues: (a) school violence, (b) drug testing of students and teachers, (c) child abuse, (d) child abduction, (e) students with AIDS, and (f) immunization.

FOCUS POINT: School Violence and Liability for Failing to Protect Students

Concerns for school safety have become even stronger as a result of the events that took place at Columbine High School in Littleton, Colorado, during the 1998–1999 school year. This tragedy will be remembered not only because two students bearing a variety of sophisticated armaments opened fire, shot, and killed 13 people at their school. It will also be remembered for the extensive and intensive media coverage of the issue of school violence that it generated. As the media described the "crisis of school violence," there were calls for zero tolerance to school crime, particularly those forms that expose other children to danger. (See the section on zero tolerance in Chapter 7.) Some states have adopted safe-school acts that require all school boards to report certain specified categories of criminal activity to law enforcement officials.

In a 1997 national survey conducted by Columbia University (see Studies in Chapter Resources), 86 percent of respondents supported a zero tolerance drug and alcohol policy in schools (possession of any illegal drugs or alcohol would result in automatic suspension), and 93 percent supported a zero tolerance weapons policy in schools (automatic suspension for any student found carrying a weapon of any kind). A national poll of 1,350 elementary school principals was also included in the survey. Ninety percent of respondents said that tough discipline policies were absolutely essential for keeping schools safe, despite an increase in student suspensions; 83 percent reported that they spent too much time dealing with disruptive, dangerous students; and 78 percent criticized federal law for unreasonably limiting their ability to manage disruptive or dangerous special education children.

In light of the survey, it is interesting to note that most researchers agree that schools are safe places for children. According to the U.S. Departments of Education and Justice, of the more than 2,500 children who were murdered or committed suicide in the first half of the 1997–1998 school year, less than 1 percent were at school or at a school-sponsored event. It is also important to remember that the problem is not school violence, it is youth violence. Most juvenile crime occurs off school grounds and peaks between 3 p.m. and 4 p.m. on school days. (See Fairchild & Bell, 1999.)

The National School Safety Center has compiled a list of characteristics designed to help educators identify potentially violent students. This checklist includes such items as gang involvement, weapons possession, a history of disciplinary or drug abuse problems, and social marginality. Stephens (2001) noted that many public schools have zero tolerance policies covering serious offenses, and many states have policies that require lengthy suspensions, expulsions, or both for students who possess a weapon on school property.

School administrators must have knowledge and understanding of the principles and issues relating to school safety and security and to human resources management and development. They must facilitate processes and engage in activities that recognize emerging trends and apply strategies aimed at maintaining a safe and orderly learning environment. However, strategies for reducing school violence must be weighed against their consequences. Obviously, everyone wants school violence to be reduced and all students to feel safe in school. However, some consequences, such as the stigmatizing of "profiled" students and increased anxiety about the potential for violence, might lead to counterproductive measures and to resistance on the parts of students and their parents. Educators must attempt to balance the rights of the students to a safe school against the constitutional protections granted to all students.

School's Liability for Failing to Protect Students

Historically, the common-law doctrine of official immunity protected public officials from liability for torts committed during the performance of their official duties. However, the enactment of 42 U.S.C. 1983 abrogated this common-law doctrine and allowed victims of school violence to sue public school officials. (See Section 1983 in Chapter 2.) Consequently, school board members, teachers, and administrators can be sued in their individual capacities if they deprive a person of a federal right.

In *Ingraham v. Wright* (1977), the U.S. Supreme Court held that students' rights to their bodily integrity is a liberty interest that is protected by the Constitution. Therefore, students who are victims of school violence can argue that they were deprived of an existing federal right. In addition, victims of school violence may sue school officials in state court under theories of negligence, gross negligence, strict liability, and failure to supervise.

Examples of Management Cues

- School administrators, teachers, and support staff should be alerted to the potential of violence *when a student exhibits the following characteristics* (see National School Safety Center, n.d., and Stephens, 2001):
  - Has a history of tantrums and uncontrollable angry outbursts
  - Characteristically resorts to name calling, cursing, or abusive language
  - Habitually makes violent threats when angry
  - Has previously brought a weapon to school
  - Has a background of serious disciplinary problems at school and in the community
  - Has a background of drug, alcohol, or other substance abuse or dependency
  - Is on the fringe of a peer group with few or no close friends
  - Is preoccupied with weapons, explosives, or other incendiary devices
  - Has previously been truant, suspended, or expelled from school
  - Displays cruelty to animals
  - Has little or no supervision or support from parents or a caring adult
  - Has witnessed or been a victim of abuse or neglect in the home
  - Has been bullied or bullies or intimidates peers or younger children
  - Tends to blame others for difficulties and problems she or he causes herself or himself
  - Consistently prefers TV shows, movies, or music expressing violent themes and acts
  - Prefers reading materials dealing with violent themes, rituals, and abuse
  - Reflects anger, frustration, and the dark side of life in school essays or writing projects
  - Is involved with a gang or an antisocial group on the fringe of peer acceptance
  - Is often depressed or has significant mood swings
  - Has threatened or attempted suicide

While the FBI discourages profiling, it recommends considering four areas in assessing whether a student is likely to carry out a specific threat:

1. *Personality traits and behavior:* Student collects injustices and nurses resentments; dehumanizes others; shows exaggerated sense of entitlement, signs of depression, and a pathological need for attention; has trouble managing anger; shows a dramatic behavior change; has unusual interest in sensational violence.

2. *Family dynamics:* Student's relationship with own parents is particularly difficult or turbulent; parents accept or minimize pathological behavior, setting few limits and possibly seeming intimidated by student; student has access to weapons; and there is little monitoring of what student watches on TV and sees on the Internet.

3. *School dynamics:* Student is detached from other students, teachers, and school activities; school does little to prevent or punish disrespectful behavior or bullying; a pecking order exists among students, who also have a code of silence about telling staff members of their concerns about other students; access to computers and Internet is unsupervised.

4. *Social dynamics:* Student is intensely and exclusively involved with a group that shares a fascination with violence or extremist beliefs; student's use of drugs and alcohol, and any outside interests, should be examined. The period after a violent incident that receives widespread media attention is a particularly dangerous time because of possible copycat behavior.

Suggested Risk Management Guidelines

Note: See also Chapter 1, "Preventive Law: Developing Risk and Crisis Management Programs."

- Ensure that a comprehensive school safety plan, which gives specific instructions for handling any emergency, is posted in every classroom.
- Provide regular inservice training for all school employees regarding the safety plan.
- Regularly evaluate the safety plan.
- Ensure that staff members recognize that children today often don't have a single problem but many.
- Develop a process of links between school personnel and other community health providers.
- Develop partnerships in the community and establish good relationships with law enforcement, clergy, mental health services, youth services, and others.
- Provide regular inservice for staff regarding how to identify risk factors such as drug and alcohol abuse, family instability, school failure, negative peer influences, and bullying.
- Develop and implement a comprehensive conflict resolution program for all students. Consider a program of peer mediation.

- Provide for the observations and insights of students at all levels of education in the development of the safety plan.
- Provide for the observations and insights of parents and other community members in the development of the safety plan.
- Consider afterschool programs for all students.
- Develop mentoring programs for all students and not only for the disadvantaged.
- Develop partnerships with social service organizations, such as the Boy Scouts, Girl Scouts, Boys and Girls Clubs, Big Brothers and Big Sisters, and faith-based organizations.
- Develop an Internet home page that keeps everyone informed about what is happening in the school and community.

I FOCUS POINT: Drug Testing of Students

Note: Includes drug testing of all students, drug testing of students involved in extracurricular activities, and drug testing of athletes.

Concerns about the use of drugs by students and employees have led some school districts to develop drug testing programs in an ongoing effort to eliminate drug use from schools. (See Studies in Chapter Resources.) These testing programs raise numerous constitutional, employment law, and statutory questions. Because school officials are actually government officials or employees, school districts that wish to drug test their employees or students must do so within the protection of the Fourth Amendment. (See Chapter 2.) If a district chooses to have a drug testing policy, it must demonstrate a sufficient interest in public health and welfare to outweigh the employees' and students' privacy interests. School districts should establish clear, concise, and reasonable policies that have wide input and expert counsel.

The U.S. Supreme Court, in *Skinner v. Railway Labor Executives' Association* (1989), held that drug testing constitutes a search for purposes of Fourth Amendment analysis. Generally, the use of drug tests has been upheld, provided that the tests are nondiscriminatory and involve a minimal infringement of a person's privacy.

Several types of drug testing polices regarding students exist in school districts across the country. Schools have initiated policies that (a) require mandatory random testing of student athletes, (b) provide for voluntary testing of students, and (c) call for testing of a student if there is a reasonable suspicion that the student is under the influence of drugs.

Various state statutes have detailed provisions regarding sample collection, storage, and transportation requirements, and labs that may perform the tests. The process of drug testing typically includes the following: (a) if the test result indicates the presence of illegal or banned substances, the positive result is verified; (b) once verification of the positive result is complete, the outside company notifies the school principal; (c) the principal contacts the student's parents and may set up a meeting; (d) the student receives some type of discipline; (e) the student may be required to participate in a drug treatment program. Some schools automatically suspend a student who tests positive; others do not. Some schools automatically send results to juvenile or criminal authorities. Others only send results if they receive a subpoena or other legal request. In the case of athletes, most policies require students to be retested before they are allowed to participate in athletics again.

Proponents of drug testing cite dramatic evidence that drug testing has been effective in reducing drug abuse. They argue that drug testing results in a safe and orderly environment. Arguments against drug screening center on both technological and constitutional considerations. Some opponents cite charges of inaccuracy and outright fraud and of medical unreliability of detection technology. Opponents argue that drug testing causes greater harm than benefit, given documented, widespread, false-positive errors caused by common substances, including herbal teas, poppy seeds, medication, and passive inhalation. Urinalysis, the most common detection method, is only 95 percent accurate. Opponents also charge that any detection method, especially urinalysis, necessarily invades privacy by requiring a witness to specimen collection. Mandatory drug screening is seen as a humiliating and intrusive governmental action not outweighed by either security concerns or overriding social benefit.

Drug Testing of All Students

The Carlstadt-East Rutherford, New Jersey, School District was the first in the United States to adopt a policy under which all the students at a high school would be required to submit to a chemical test for the identification of illicit drugs. The test was part of a more comprehensive physical examination required of all students. A state superior court judge ruled the proposed program unconstitutional. In *Odenheim v. Carlstadt-East Rutherford School District* (1985), the court ruled that drug testing was an unreasonable search, and the school's interest in discovering student drug use did not justify the interference with student privacy that the testing program involved. The court also held that the school district's program violated the students' right to due process because of the possibility that the results of the test could lead to suspension or expulsion from school without following the usual rules for such actions.

Drug Testing of Students Involved in Extracurricular Activities

In the fall of 1998, the U.S. Supreme Court refused to hear *Todd v. Rush County Schools*, a case in which a lower court had held that it was constitutional for the district to test all students involved in extracurricular activities for drugs. Consequently, some school districts have adopted policies that require all students who wish to participate in extracurricular activities to agree to submit to a drug test. In 1999, the U.S. Supreme Court refused to hear the *Anderson Community School v. Willis by Willis* case in which a high school's policy required all students who were suspended for fighting to be tested for drugs.

A 2002 U.S. Supreme Court decision illustrates the continuing trend of the Court to place school safety over the Fourth Amendment protection of students. In *Board of Education of Independent School District No. 92 of Pottawatomie County v. Earls,* a group of Oklahoma high school students and their parents challenged a district's policy that required all middle and high school students to consent to urinalysis testing for drugs in order to participate in any extracurricular activity. They argued that this policy resulted in an unconstitutional suspicion-less search in violation of the Fourth Amendment. The Court held that the policy was a reasonable means of furthering the school district's important interest in preventing and deterring drug use among its students, and therefore did not violate the Fourth Amendment.

Drug Testing of Athletes

Schools that test student athletes for drugs argue that the tests are preventative, not punitive. Most drug testing procedures are similar in that they make participation in athletic programs conditional on consent to drug testing at the beginning of each season. Typically, a district randomly selects athletes for testing each week throughout the athletic season. Selection is made from the entire athletic team regardless of whether the student has already been tested that season. Once selected, students who refuse to be tested are treated as if they had tested positive for drugs.

In 1995, the U.S. Supreme Court considered the constitutionality of a school's program of mandatory drug testing for athletes. In *Vernonia School District 47J v. Acton*, the Court held that the Fourth Amendment permits school districts to randomly search high school athletes without cause through drug testing.

Examples of Management Cues

- Signs that a student or employee may be abusing drugs or alcohol include
  - The smell of alcohol on the breath, or sudden, frequent use of breath mints
  - Abrupt changes in mood or attitude
  - Sudden decline in attendance or performance at school
  - Losing interest in school, sports, or other activities that used to be important
  - Sudden resistance to discipline or school
  - Uncharacteristic withdrawal from family, friends, or interests
  - Heightened secrecy about actions or possessions
  - Associating with a new group of friends whom the student refuses to discuss

Suggested Risk Management Guidelines

- Drug testing policies should
  - Leave no room for misinterpretation and should be widely disseminated and explained

- Be clear in intent, and the consequences for violating them should be specific, to prevent claims of failure to notify under due process considerations
- Be more concerned with prevention than detection
- Where sanctions result, require that the district provide notice and due process hearing in conformity with constitutional, statute, and local due process requirements

I FOCUS POINT: Drug Testing of School Employees

A drug-free school environment includes more than just students and must include teachers, administrators, bus drivers, coaches, custodial workers, secretaries, and food service workers. Some schools have attempted to test all people who enter a school building (DeMitchell, 1997). There is a distinction between drug testing for students and for employees. The testing of school employees is concerned with determining an individual's fitness for employment, and the effect of causeless search may result in loss of employment, contractual rights, and possible criminal charges. The primary object of student search is to preserve safety in schools (*People v. Scott D.*, 1974).

Regarding school employees, school districts have initiated policies that require (a) drug testing of all prospective employees, (b) drug testing of employees who exhibit some signs of drug use (reasonable-suspicion testing), (c) random drug testing of current employees, (d) random drug testing of current employees in safety-sensitive positions, (e) drug testing of employees who are involved in accidents, and (f) drug testing as part of an annual physical examination.

In 1987, the New York Court of Appeals dealt with the issue of drug testing of teachers in *Patchogue-Medford Congress of Teachers v. Board of Education.* The school district required that all teachers eligible for tenure submit to random drug testing. The court of appeals held that the policy was unconstitutional under the constitutions of both the United States and New York State. It then held that the particular testing involved was not reasonable. However, the court did indicate that "under certain special circumstances it may be reasonable to permit the government to search without a warrant on grounds not amounting to probable cause."

Some state and federal courts have used the U.S. Supreme Court's "special needs" doctrine to justify the testing of employees in safety-sensitive positions. For example, the Sixth Circuit's decision in *Knox County Education Association v. Knox County Board of Education* (1998) was at odds with the New York Court of Appeals' decision in *Patchogue,* holding that teachers applying for promotion could be tested. In *Knox,* teachers were considered to be in safety-sensitive positions. The policy developed by the school board permitted suspicionless testing for people applying for safety-sensitive positions, including "principals, assistant principals, teachers, traveling teachers, teacher aides, substitute teachers, school secretaries and school bus drivers." Potential candidates for employment or employees seeking a transfer or promotion were drug tested before the hiring or promotion. The policy did not, however, provide for random drug testing. The Court said,

> [W]e can imagine few governmental interests more important to a community than that of insuring the safety and security of its children while they are entrusted to the care of teachers and administrators. . . . [W]hile serving in their *in loco parentis* capacity, teachers are on the "front line" of school security, including drug interdiction.

The Court concluded,

> On balance, the public interest in attempting to ensure that school teachers perform their jobs unimpaired is evident, considering their unique in loco parentis obligations and their immense influence over students. These public interests clearly outweigh the privacy interests of the teacher not to be tested because the drug-testing regime adopted by Knox County is circumscribed, narrowly tailored, and not overly intrusive, either in its monitoring procedures or in its disclosure requirements. This is particularly so because it is a one-time test, with advance notice and with no random testing component, and because the school system in which the employees work is heavily regulated, particularly as to drug usage.

Courts have consistently permitted drug testing based on reasonable individualized suspicion. Reasonable-suspicion drug testing means drug or alcohol testing based on a belief that an employee is using or has used drugs or alcohol, in violation of the covered employer's policy, drawn from specific objective facts and reasonable inferences drawn from those facts, in light of experience.

It has been indicated that drug testing as part of a physical examination is less intrusive than other forms of drug testing. In *Allen v. Passaic County* (1986), the court said that "the requirement of physicals at the commencement of employment or regular annual physical checkups are common and normal employment practices and should not be deemed as rendered impermissible by this decision."

Examples of Management Cues

- A school employee shows physical symptoms of being under the influence of a drug or alcohol.
- A school employee demonstrates erratic behavior while at school or a significant deterioration in work performance.
- A parent informs the principal that at a parent-teacher conference, she smelled a strong odor of alcohol on a teacher's breath.
- A teacher is arrested for drug possession or driving while under the influence.

Suggested Risk Management Guidelines

- Drug testing utilizing urinalysis is a "search" under the Fourth Amendment.
- Generally, drug testing policies for employees holding safety-sensitive positions where even a momentary lapse of attention can have disastrous consequences are considered reasonable.
- Schools may require preemployment testing, postaccident testing, reasonable-suspicion testing, random drug testing of employees in safety-sensitive positions, and testing during a regularly scheduled physical examination.

I FOCUS POINT: Child Abuse

Note: Includes what child abuse and maltreatment are, and mandatory reporting laws.

For more than 5 million American children, punishment at home has meant being shot, stabbed, kicked, beaten, poisoned, burned, or bitten by their parents. In addition to suffering abusive punishment, many children are raped, starved, and psychologically damaged by parents or relatives in their homes. In 1997, an estimated 984,000 children were victims of maltreatment nationwide; 440,994 children were victims of neglect; 197,557 were victims of physical abuse; 98,994 were victims of sexual abuse; and 49,338 were victims of psychological abuse or neglect. (See *Reports from the States to the National Child Abuse and Neglect Data System,* 1997.) A survey of high school adolescents showed that 17 percent of girls were physically abused and 12 percent were sexually abused, whereas 12 percent of boys were physically abused and 5 percent were sexually abused. (See Commonwealth Fund, 1999.)

The key federal law addressing child abuse and neglect is the Child Abuse Prevention and Treatment Act (CAPTA), originally enacted in 1974. This act has been amended several times and was most recently amended by the Child Abuse Prevention and Treatment Act Amendments of 1996. CAPTA provides federal funding to states to support prevention, assessment, investigation, prosecution, and treatment activities and also provides grants to public agencies and nonprofit organizations for demonstration programs and projects.

What Is Child Abuse and Maltreatment?

Child abuse and neglect are defined in both federal and state legislation. The federal legislation provides a foundation for states by identifying a minimum set of acts or behaviors that characterize maltreatment. This legislation also defines what acts are considered physical abuse, neglect, and sexual abuse. CAPTA, as amended and reauthorized in October 1996 (see Public Law 104-235 in Chapter Resources), provides the following definitions. (Note: "Child" is defined as a person who has not attained the lesser of the age of 18, except in cases of sexual abuse, and the age specified by the child protection law of the state in which the child resides.) There are four major types of abuse and maltreatment: physical abuse, neglect, sexual abuse, and emotional abuse. Although state definitions may vary, operational definitions generally include the following:

- Physical abuse includes any physical injury that results from punching, beating, kicking, biting, burning, shaking, or otherwise harming a child.
- Child neglect is characterized by failure to provide for the child's basic needs. Neglect can be physical, educational, or emotional. Physical neglect includes refusal of or delay in seeking health care, abandonment, expulsion from the home or refusal to allow a runaway to return home, and inadequate supervision. Educational neglect includes the allowance of chronic truancy, failure to enroll a child of mandatory school age in school, and failure to attend to a special educational need.
- Sexual abuse includes fondling a child's genitals, intercourse, incest, rape, sodomy, exhibitionism, and commercial exploitation through prostitution or the production of pornographic materials.
- Emotional abuse (psychological and verbal abuse and mental injury) includes acts or omissions by the parents or other caregivers that have caused, or could cause, serious behavioral, cognitive, emotional, or mental disorders. In some cases of emotional abuse, the acts of parents or other caregivers alone, without any harm evident in the child's behavior or condition, are sufficient to warrant child protective services intervention. Emotional neglect includes such actions as marked inattention to the child's needs for affection, refusal of or failure to provide needed psychological care, spouse abuse in the child's presence, and permission of drug or alcohol use by the child.

Although any of the forms of child maltreatment may be found separately (see U.S. Department of Health and Human Services, Children's Bureau, 1999), they often occur in combination. Emotional abuse is almost always present when other forms are identified. Although injuries can occur by accident, child abuse should be suspected if the explanations do not fit the injury or if there is a pattern of repeated injury. Also, the existence of several injuries in different stages of healing may demonstrate that they did not happen as a result of one accident. A child who is consistently withdrawn or overly aggressive, who complains of soreness or wears inappropriate clothing for the weather, or who is a chronic runaway may be a victim of abuse.

Mandatory Reporting Laws

Because attendance in school is compulsory, few youngsters do not come into contact with teachers and principals. In fact, educators may be the only professionals to whom the child is exposed on a regular basis. Because of this, educators have an affirmative obligation to be aware of child abuse warning signs and to report suspected cases to proper authorities.

Every state has enacted reporting laws requiring certain professionals, including teachers and administrators, to report suspected cases of child abuse. Each of these state laws has a clause providing a degree of immunity from prosecution for those reporting, without malice, cases of suspected abuse. Each state statute also specifies the penalties for mandatory reporters who fail to report cases of suspected child abuse.

School personnel are expected to report suspected cases of child abuse "immediately." Typically, "immediately" is interpreted to mean as soon as there is sufficient evidence from which it is "reasonable" to conclude that a child has been or is being abused. The question then arises, How much information is necessary to establish sufficient evidence from which it is reasonable to conclude that abuse has occurred? It is not the intent of mandatory reporting statutes to require educators to investigate child abuse cases. These statutes require educators to report if they "have reason to suspect." This language is important because the original standard in most states was some variation of "reason to believe." Recently, several states have changed the standard required of mandatory reporters to that of "reason to suspect," explaining that less evidence is required to establish a suspicion than to establish a belief. Reasonableness invariably is defined with reference to the hypothetical reasonable person similarly situated. In this case, the standard of reasonableness would be the actions of a competent school administrator or teacher. School personnel should use common sense in trying to figure out if a child is being abused. For example, normal, active children get some bruises and bumps from everyday playing. These bruises are mostly over bony areas such as knees, elbows, and shins. However, a child with injuries on other parts of the body, such as the stomach, cheeks, ears, buttocks, mouth, or thighs, or showing black eyes, human bite marks, or round burns the size of a cigarette, should clearly be considered a possible abused child. (See American Academy of Pediatrics, 1995.)

Examples of Management Cues

- The following observable signs may identify abused or neglected children. *These are only indicators and should not be considered absolute.* The child
  - Has had many unusual injuries or injuries that can't be explained
  - Seems sad and cries a lot
  - Fights with classmates, acts out in the classroom, or destroys things; throws objects across a room or is violent toward another student
  - Seems very tired; talks about trouble sleeping and often has nightmares
  - Seems afraid of a parent or other adults, such as teachers or babysitters
  - Spends a lot of time at the playground and doesn't want to go home after school, as if afraid of something there
  - Finds it hard to make friends
  - Tends to be pushy and hostile
  - Has difficulty learning, is overly active, or has reported problems such as bed wetting or soiling

  – Acts falsely grown up, has to care for adults or others far beyond what should be expected for the child's age (see American Academy of Pediatrics, 1995)

- Other signs that might mean a child is being abused are that the child's parents
  – Stay away from other mothers and fathers in the neighborhood
  – Do not take part in school activities
  – Have a drinking or drug abuse problem
  – Don't want to talk about their child's injuries or seem nervous when they do

Suggested Risk Management Guidelines

- Strictly follow state, local, and school district policy including reporting procedures.
- Provide inservice training concerning family violence, child abuse, and teachers' legal requirements in reporting suspected child abuse.
- Consider forming parenting classes after school to help new parents understand the issue of child abuse.
- Develop formal communication and support between the school and local and state agencies responsible for investigating suspected child abuse.
- Ensure that the school receives feedback about action taken after reports of suspected child abuse. Such information is important to maintain the involvement of teachers as mandated reporters.

▌ FOCUS POINT: Teacher Abuse of Students

Note: See Chapter 13 for an in-depth examination of sexual abuse.

No national statistics document how many teachers and other school employees are sexually abusing students. However, the results of a nationwide search conducted by *Education Week* make it clear that teacher-to-student sexual abuse is a serious problem that demands serious attention (see Hendrie & Drummond, 1998). This study covered the six-month period from March through August of 1998 and identified 244 cases that involved inappropriate sexual behavior. This behavior ranged from "unwanted touching" to "years-long sexual relationships and serial rape." "Seven out of ten suspects were teachers. However, principals, janitors, bus drivers, and librarians were also among the accused. Although most were men, 20% were women." Authorities ultimately concluded that students had fabricated claims in only two cases. Signs of possible teacher-to-student sexual abuse include overly affectionate behaviors; inappropriate, noneducation-related contact; and inappropriate, nonprofessional behavior. (For a discussion of false complaints, see Chapter 13.)

Examples of Management Cues

- A parent reports that she saw one of your teachers in the shopping mall last evening with a friend's daughter, a student at your school. She noted that the teacher had his arm around the girl.
- A number of sophomore girls voice anger over a teacher's propensity to tell sexually explicit jokes in class.
- A parent calls to ask whether there is a school policy about where play rehearsals are held. Her son, who has the lead role in the spring musical, has been spending three or more evenings a week rehearsing at the female drama coach's house.
- A first-grade teacher reports that a male colleague, a new teacher on staff, insists on personally taking his first-grade students to the restroom. She's concerned about the children left alone in the classroom and wonders whether it's necessary for him to stay in the restroom waiting for each child to finish.

Suggested Risk Management Guidelines

- Acknowledge that teacher-to-student sexual abuse is a serious problem.
- Strictly administer and enforce district policies that specifically describe inappropriate behaviors and make it clear that sexual harassment and sexual abuse will not be tolerated.
- Continuously scan the environment for information. This includes making daily observations in the school and asking questions.
- Don't make judgment errors because of bias in favor of the student or teacher.
- Conduct appropriate training for all staff members and students.
- Ask the right questions in the preemployment process.

I FOCUS POINT: Child Abduction

Because schools can be held legally responsible, school administrators should be concerned about releasing a child to an adult. Administrators must be alert not only to the possibility of a stranger taking a child without permission but also to the possibility of a child being taken by a parent, contrary to a custody decree. When deciding whether or not to release a child from school, the first issue to be resolved is the question of who has parental rights. The legal parent is the person the legal system recognizes as having the legal rights of parenthood. Usually, both parents' rights are recognized. Therefore, either parent, acting alone, has the legal right to make decisions on behalf of the child. Because the law has traditionally respected the privacy of the family, the law presumes that when a man and woman present themselves to be married and live together as husband and wife, they are married (Stenger, 1986). In states that have not adopted Uniform Parentage Acts, if a child is born to biological parents who are not married, the mother alone enjoys parental rights. (See Uniform Parentage Act in Chapter Resources.) The biological father can gain parental rights only by marriage or by a court finding of paternity. The U.S. Supreme Court ruled, in *Lalli v. Lalli* (1978), that states must recognize the parental rights of a father who has married the mother or been adjudicated as the legal father. In the case of divorce, the issue of child custody is determined in the dissolution proceedings. The court may grant custody to one parent or it may grant joint custody to both parents. In the case of sole custody, the custodial parent alone has the power to make parental decisions.

Modern adoption laws have created a new and exclusive parent-child relationship and have established parental rights and duties where they would not otherwise exist. When a court issues a decree of adoption, the natural parents no longer have a legal relationship to the child.

School personnel should be very cautious about the physical custody of children. If the school has no information to the contrary, it can assume that both parents have parental rights. However, if the school is informed that there has been some modification of parental rights, then the noncustodial parent does not have the right to remove the child from school without permission of the custodial parent. Although it may cause some embarrassment or inconvenience, it is better to err on the side of protecting the child. (See National Center for Missing and Exploited Children, 1999; Viadero, 1990; Parental Kidnapping Prevention Act; International Child Abduction Remedies Act.)

Examples of Management Cues

- A person the teacher or other school employee does not recognize attempts to pick up the child from school.
- A police officer attempts to remove a student from school without a court order.
- A parent informs the teacher that she or he is having difficulty with a noncustodial parent.
- A school employee observes heated or violent arguments, on school grounds, between the parents of a student.

Suggested Risk Management Guidelines

- Ensure that every door to the school has a notice informing all visitors to report to the office. Include outside doors to individual classrooms if applicable.
- Ensure that all school employees understand that they must inform the office of any strangers they see in the building.
- Note the status of guardianship in each student's school record. Ensure that the record is checked before a child is released from school.
- When a person other than a legal parent seeks possession of a child, school personnel should ask for some authorization and should notify the parent before the child is released into the other person's custody.

- In the case of a person who cares for a child on a regular basis, such as a neighbor, child caregiver, or grandparent, the school should request that the parent give written permission prior to the release of the child.
- Request to see a court order before releasing a child to a public employee such as a police officer or social worker.

I FOCUS POINT: Students With AIDS

Note: Includes confidentiality rights.

By the end of 2003, there were 8,549 reported AIDS cases among children under 13 years of age in the United States. Of those cases reported between 1996 and 2003, 20 percent acquired AIDS by injection drug use and 42 percent acquired AIDS from heterosexual contact (Centers for Disease Control and Prevention, 2005).

Young people in the United States are at persistent risk for HIV infection. Continual prevention outreach and education efforts are required as new generations replace the generations that benefited from earlier prevention strategies. An estimated 38,490 young people in the United States received a diagnosis of AIDS. An estimated 10,041 young people with AIDS died. The proportion of young people with a diagnosis of AIDS increased. In 1999, 3.9 percent of all persons with a diagnosis of AIDS were aged 13–24. In 2003, 4.7 percent were aged 13–24. Research has shown that a large proportion of young people are not concerned about becoming infected with HIV (Kaiser Family Foundation, 2000).

The Centers for Disease Control and Prevention (CDC) and most other medical groups tell us that AIDS cannot be transmitted through casual contact or the airborne route and that AIDS victims normally need not be excluded from school. The type of contact that occurs in a school setting does not result in a very significant degree of risk for infection.

Prior to the introduction of treatments known as antiretroviral therapy, many children infected with the virus were very ill and were not able to function normally in school. Successful drug treatments have enabled more HIV-infected children to attend school, causing the American Academy of Pediatrics (AAP) to ask teachers and school administrators to provide students infected with HIV with the same education and services that they provide for those with other chronic illnesses. The AAP indicates that there is no reason to isolate a child with HIV (see American Academy of Pediatrics, n.d.).

Although the AAP strongly encourages parents who have school-age children and teens with HIV infection to tell their children the truth about their illness, they also emphasize the need for schools to maintain confidentiality about HIV infection. Teachers must obtain parental consent before disclosing a student's infection with the virus.

The CDC recommends that school districts develop an administrative process for responding to the needs of both the afflicted person and the other students. They suggest that a panel of experts be established to review the individual facts and make a recommendation. This panel should include (a) the student's parent or guardian, (b) public health personnel, (c) school officials, and (d) the child's physician. In resolving the student's placement, a panel should weigh the risks and benefits to both the infected child and the child's classmates.

State laws guarantee that a public education is the legal right of every child in this country. The courts have recognized that children benefit from the socialization process in a class of their peers and that education has a great impact on their social and psychological well-being. As a result, children with HIV or AIDS have the legal right to a free public education with their peers. Problems arise because all states also have communicable disease laws that compel school officials to provide a safe, healthy learning environment. Some argue that, in the face of an incurable, inevitably fatal, infectious disease, the schools are legally and morally obligated to exclude a child with HIV or AIDS from school to protect the health of other students. Proponents of this argument believe that children with HIV or AIDS should be provided with an alternative means of education, usually through tutoring or private home instruction.

Because the HIV virus destroys lymphocytes, a child with HIV or AIDS clearly has a "physical impairment" and thus is considered handicapped within the meaning of the Rehabilitation Act. The U.S. Department of Justice believes that the disabling consequences of AIDS infection qualify as handicaps, but the mere presence of the HIV virus in the body does not. In other words, individuals experiencing the opportunistic infections of full-blown AIDS are protected as handicapped under the act, but those who are asymptomatic are not handicapped by the virtue of their communicability.

In determining whether or not to exclude a child from school, some courts have ruled that the district must evaluate each case individually. This appraisal must consider such factors as the characteristics of the disease, the behavior of the child, and the particular options available to the school in reducing the likelihood of transmission. If the risk is low, the school is obligated to enroll the student in a regular classroom. The question then centers on whether the unconfirmed possibility of transmitting the disease is sufficient to bar such pupils from the classrooms.

Medical research indicates that AIDS cannot be transmitted through casual physical contact. The school-aged child infected with the disease presents a negligible risk for transmission to his or her classmates or to adult school personnel and thus does not affect their health and safety. Therefore, children with AIDS, in most instances, should continue to attend school and fully participate in programs and activities offered by the school district. Although removal of a student infected with AIDS from the school setting normally is not justified, guidelines need to be established for a case-by-case review process. (See Shoop, 1989.)

Educational Placement of a Child with AIDS

Martinez v. School Board of Hillsborough County (1988) involved the appropriate educational placement of a mentally retarded child infected with AIDS. At the time the action was filed, the child was seven years old and had an IQ of 41. The child was not toilet trained and suffered from thrush, a disease that can produce blood in the saliva. She sucked her thumb, resulting in saliva on her fingers. Section 504 of the Rehabilitation Act provides that no otherwise qualified handicapped individual shall, solely by reason of his or her handicap, be excluded from participation in the benefits of school. The court was asked to balance the risks to the child versus the benefits from attendance at school. The court held that the remote theoretical possibility of transmission from saliva, tears, and urine did not support segregating the child from a regular trainable mentally handicapped classroom.

Confidentiality Rights of Students with AIDS

The Family Educational Rights and Privacy Act (FERPA) requires that student records be kept confidential (see FERPA in Chapter 9). Therefore, if a parent voluntarily discloses to school officials a student's medical condition, this information is entitled to all the protections of FERPA. School districts need compelling reasons to justify any disclosure.

Many of the major health care organizations and professional education associations have published policy recommendations concerning AIDS. Among the recommendations is one that school districts clearly state their position on confidentiality. The need to preserve the privacy of students with AIDS remains paramount.

Examples of Management Cues

- A teacher who is informed that a student has AIDS refuses to teach the child.
- A child with AIDS wishes to participate in interscholastic sports.
- A parent enrolls a child in school and informs the principal that the child has AIDS and the teachers are not to be informed.
- Rumors begin to circulate about the illness of one of your teachers.

Suggested Risk Management Guidelines

- School districts should adopt board policies and building procedures for dealing with *all* contagious diseases. When school officials are notified that a student is infected, they should have a procedure in place to ensure safety of persons in the school setting and provide support for the person with the illness.
  - The policy should include the designation of the individual person responsible for ensuring compliance with the policy.
  - The policy should specifically state that the identity of an infected individual will only be known by the staff members designated for

decision making: the coordinator of nursing services, the personal physician of the infected person, and a public health official or medical person, unless the infected person or guardian chooses to inform other people.

- A team should be appointed to assist the school district in implementing its policy. This team should consist of a school staff person, the coordinator of nursing services, the infected person's physician, the infected person, the student's parents or guardians, and a public health official or medical personnel. In determining whether a person who is infected constitutes a recognized risk in the school setting, the team should consider (a) the behavior, neurological development, and physical condition of the student, (b) the expected type of interaction with others in the school setting, and (c) the impact on both the infected student and others in that setting. The team should also consider ways in which the school district may anticipate and meet the needs of the infected student. If there is a secondary infection that constitutes a medically recognized risk of transmission in the school setting, it may be necessary to develop an individually tailored plan for the student.
- Schools may not initiate mandatory screening for communicable diseases that are not spread by casual everyday contact, such as HIV infection. Screening should not be a condition for school entry or attendance. Disclosure of HIV status may not be required for entry to schools or child care programs.
- Because disclosure of a child's HIV status to schools is not required, educators should treat all children as potentially HIV-infected.
- If an infected student with a secondary infection is not able to attend classes or participate in the school activities, the district should offer the student an appropriate alternative education. The special education department should be consulted regarding possible homebound instruction or assignment to an alternative placement.
- A contingency plan should be developed for reentering students with AIDS when public attention has become an issue.
- A case manager should be appointed to coordinate monitoring and consultation with representatives of the medical community.
- There should be a comprehensive AIDS education program for all students and staff.
- Persons who may have contact with blood, or body fluids containing blood, should be educated about CDC's standard precautions to prevent transmission of HIV and other blood-borne pathogens.
- Children who are known to be HIV-infected should be encouraged to participate in all school activities as long as they are able to do so.
- Athletes and the staff of athletic programs should take special steps to protect themselves from human HIV, hepatitis B virus (HBV), or hepatitis C virus (HCV). Any athlete who has active bleeding should be removed from practice or competition as soon as possible, until the bleeding has stopped and the wound has been cleaned and covered. Athletes

should be told not to share personal items, such as razors, toothbrushes, and nail clippers, that might be contaminated.

FOCUS POINT: Medication Administration

Note: See Chapter 15, Section C, under Postinjury Treatment, for text and guidelines in this important area of legal liability.

FOCUS POINT: Immunization

Although there continues to be some public resistance and legal challenges to mandatory vaccination, all states require some immunization for most children prior to the admission to public school to protect them from infectious diseases. Medical exemptions are permitted if a physician states that a specific child would be endangered by immunization. Twenty-two states provide exemptions for philosophical reasons, and religious exemptions are permitted in every state except two. All states have statutes requiring vaccination for diphtheria, measles, rubella, and polio. There are state-by-state variations in the requirements for vaccines for tetanus, whooping cough (pertussis), and mumps. Parents who refuse permission for their child to be vaccinated and who do not qualify for some exemption may be fined or even imprisoned.

Most challenges arise where parents' religious beliefs do not allow them to have their children vaccinated. When groups have challenged legislation requiring all schoolchildren to be immunized, the courts have held that a person's religious freedom ceases when it overlaps and transgresses the rights of others. The courts have reasoned that other schoolchildren have a right to be free from mandatory association with persons not immunized against deadly diseases. This right is so compelling that it overrides religious freedom rights. *Maack v. School District of Lincoln* (1992) is one example of the many cases that affirm that the protection of public health permits the state to require the vaccination of all persons for the common good. In this case, the question was whether a school could exclude children from school who had not been immunized against a dangerous disease. In this case, the Supreme Court of Nebraska held that (a) the board of education was legally authorized to exclude the children under the circumstances and (b) classification between unimmunized and insufficiently immunized students did not violate unimmunized students' equal protection rights.

Examples of Management Cues

- A parent refuses to provide a record of immunization for her child.
- A parent learns from a newspaper article that some of the children at school have not been immunized for measles. He wants to know if any of

those children are in his child's classroom, and if so, he wants his child placed in a classroom in which all the children have been immunized.

Suggested Risk Management Guideline

- Strictly enforce state laws and school district policies that require students to present proof of appropriate immunization prior to enrollment.

EXAMPLES OF LEADING U.S. SUPREME COURT CASES ON EDUCATION

Defining the Establishment Clause—The *Lemon* Test

Aguilar v. Felton

Committee for Public Education and Religious Liberty v. Nyquist

Committee for Public Education v. Regan

County of Allegheny v. American Civil Liberties Union

Early v. DiCenso

Grand Rapids School District v. Ball

Hunt v. McNair

Lemon v. Kurtzman (Lemon I)

Lemon v. Kurtzman (Lemon II)

Levitt v. Committee for Public Education and Religious Liberty

Lynch v. Donnelly

Meek v. Pittinger

New York v. Cathedral Academy

Pre-School Owners Association v. Illinois Department of Children and Family Services

Roemer v. Board of Public Works

Sloan v. Lemon

Tilton v. Richardson

Wolman v. Walter

Establishment of Religion in Public Schools

Abington School District v. Schempp

Doremus v. Board of Education

Edwards v. Aguillar

Engel v. Vitale

Karcher v. May

Stone v. Graham

Wallace v. Jaffree

Widmar v. Vincent

ADDITIONAL CASES OF INTEREST TO EDUCATORS

Gun-Free School Zones

United States v. Lopez, 131 L. Ed.2d 626, 115 S.Ct. 1624 (1995). The Gun-Free School Zones Act created by Congress violates the commerce clause.

Child Abuse

C.B. v. Bobo, 659 So.2d 98, Ala. (1995). Duty to report child abuse.

Korunka v. Dept. of Children and Family Services, 259 Ill. App.3d 527, 197 Ill. Dec. 537, 631 N.E.2d 759 (4th Dist. 1994). Teacher grabbed a student and left a "mark." The court found no abuse by teacher.

McDonald v. State, by and for CSD, 71 Or. App. 751, 694 P.2d 569 (1985). Statutory reporting of child abuse-immunity.

CHAPTER RESOURCES

ACLU v. McCreary County, Kentucky, 354 F.3d 438 (6th Cir. 2003).

Agostini v. Felton, 521 U.S. 203 (1997).

Aguilar v. Felton, 473 U.S. 4902 (1985).

Allen v. Passaic County, 530 A.2d 371 (N.J. Super. Ct. Law Div. 1986).

Ambach v. Norwick, 441 U.S. 68, 76–79 (1979).

American Academy of Pediatrics (AAP). (n.d.). Retrieved February 13, 2001, from www.aap.org/advocacy/archives/janhiv.htm

American Academy of Pediatrics (AAP). (1995). Some more things you should know about physical and emotional child abuse. (Adapted from American Academy of Pediatrics, 1995, *Caring for your school-age child: Ages 5 to 12.* New York: Bantam). Retrieved February 13, 2001, from www.aap.org/advocacy/childhealthmonth/ABUSE2.HTM

American Library Association (ALA). (n.d.). *Censorship and challenges.* Retrieved May 30, 2005, from http://www.ala.org/Template.cfm?Section=Intellectual_Freedom_Issues&Template=/ContentManagement/ContentDisplay.cfm&ContentID=24501

American Library Association (ALA). (n.d.). *Support for dealing with or reporting challenges to library materials.* Retrieved May 30, 2005, from http://www.ala.org/ala/oif/challengesupport/challengesupport.htm

American Library Association (ALA). (2005). *Challenged and banned books.* Retrieved May 30, 2005, from http://www.ala.org/ala/oif/bannedbooksweek/challenged banned/challengedbanned.htm

Anderson Community School v. Willis by Willis, 158 F.3d 415 (7th Cir. 1998), *cert. denied,* 119 S.Ct. 1254 (1999).

Attacks on the freedom to learn. (1999). E-mail newsletter, 3(1). Retrieved February 13, 2001, from www.pfaw.org/issues/education/aflo/aflo.3–1.html#ofallon

Beussink v. Woodlend R-IV, 30 F. Supp.2d 1175, 131 Ed. Law Rep. 1000 (E.D. Mo. 1998).

Board of Education of Independent School District No. 92 of Pottawatomie County v. Earls, 536 U.S. 822 (2002).

Boucher v. School Board of School District of Greenfield, 134 F.3d 821, 828 (7th Cir. 1998).

Bradstreet v. Sobol, 630 N.Y.S.2d (Sup. Ct. 1996).

Castañeda v. Pickard, 648 F.2d 989 (5th Cir. 1981).

Centers for Disease Control and Prevention. (2005). *Fact Sheet: HIV/AIDS among youth.* Atlanta, GA: CDC-NCHSTP-Divisions of HIV/AIDS Prevention. Retrieved June 1, 2005, from http://www.cdc.gov/hiv/pubs/facts/youth.htm

Challenges. The ALA Office for Intellectual Freedom received a total of 547 challenges in 2004. A challenge is defined as a formal, written complaint, filed with a library or school, requesting that materials be removed because of content or appropriateness. According to Judith F. Krug, director of the Office for Intellectual Freedom, "Three of the 10 books on the 'Ten Most Challenged Books of 2004' were cited for homosexual themes—which is the highest number in a decade. Sexual content and offensive language remain the most frequent reasons for seeking removal of books from schools and public libraries. The books, in order of most frequently challenged, are: 1) 'The Chocolate War' for sexual content, offensive language, religious viewpoint, being unsuited to age group and violence, 2) 'Fallen Angels' by Walter Dean Myers, for racism, offensive language and violence, 3) 'Arming America: The Origins of a National Gun Culture' by Michael A. Bellesiles, for inaccuracy and political viewpoint, 4) Captain Underpants series by Dav Pilkey, for offensive language and modeling bad behavior, 5) 'The Perks of Being a Wallflower' by Stephen Chbosky, for homosexuality, sexual content and offensive language, 6) 'What My Mother Doesn't Know' by Sonya Sones, for sexual content and offensive language, 7) 'In the Night Kitchen' by Maurice Sendak, for nudity and offensive language, 8) 'King & King' by Linda de Haan and Stern Nijland, for homosexuality, 9) 'I Know Why the Caged Bird Sings' by Maya Angelou, for racism, homosexuality, sexual content, offensive language and unsuited to age group, and 10) 'Of Mice and Men' by John Steinbeck, for racism, offensive language and violence." Off the 2004 list, but on the list for several years past, are the Alice series of books by Phyllis Reynolds Naylor, *Go Ask Alice* by Anonymous, *It's Perfectly Normal* by Robie Harris, and *The Adventures of Huckleberry Finn* by Mark Twain.

Chandler v. James, 985 F. Supp. 1094 (M.D. Ala. 1997).

Charter Schools Program, Non-Regulatory Guidance, Title V, Part B. The Charter Schools Program (CSP) was authorized in October 1994 under Title X, Part C, of the Elementary and Secondary Education Act of 1965 (ESEA), as amended, 20 U.S.C. 8061–8067. The program was amended in October 1998 by the Charter School Expansion Act of 1998 and in January 2001 by the No Child Left Behind Act of 2001.

Child Abuse Prevention and Treatment Act of 1974 (CAPTA), Pub. L. No. 93-247.

Child Abuse Prevention and Treatment Act Amendments of 1996, Pub. L. No. 104-235.

Child Evangelism Fellowship and the Good News Clubs. Cathie L. Fields, Esq., a California attorney, presented an unpublished paper titled *Good News? Advancing*

Religion Through Litigation Against the Public Schools at the Oxford University Round Table on School Law and Policy in July 2005. Some of the issues she presented should be of interest to readers. She notes, for example, that among the many nonschool groups vying for the attention of "nearly 50 million American school children," one religious group, the Child Evangelism Fellowship (CEF), has taken a different and fairly successful tack. CEF has established 2,000 Good News Clubs in public schools and has won more than 50 lawsuits against public schools. "In asserting the Good News Clubs' right of access to public school facilities, CEF typically argues the clubs teach character-building and 'moral values,' and are distinguishable from organizations such as the Boy Scouts and Girl Scouts only in that the Good News Clubs address these subjects from a religious perspective." The distinction between these inherently religious activities and the morality- and character-building activities of secular organizations may be obvious, but has not altered the courts' analyses in Good News Club cases. The Supreme Court, in *Good News Club v. Milford Central School* (99–2036) 533 U.S. 98 (2001) 202 F.3d 502, reversed and remanded, held that "quintessentially religious" activities could be "characterized properly as the teaching of morals and character development from a particular viewpoint." The high court majority has not taken the opportunity to distinguish "worship services" from other "religious activities." In *Good News Club*, the dissenting justices—Stevens, Souter, and Ginsburg—perceived the club's religious speech to be sufficiently different from that in *Lamb's Chapel* (a film on family life from a religious viewpoint) to require the opposite result. The dissenting justices identified three types of religious speech: (1) "religious speech that is simply speech about a particular topic from a religious point of view," such as the film in *Lamb's Chapel*, (2) "religious speech that amounts to worship, or its equivalent," and (3) an "intermediate category that is aimed principally at proselytizing or inculcating belief in a particular religious faith." The Good News Clubs' meetings, in their estimation, fell into the third or proselytizing category. The majority agreed with the dissenters' description of the club's activities, but concluded those activities "do not constitute mere religious worship, divorced from any teaching of moral values." The majority saw "no reason to treat the Clubs' use of religion as something other than a viewpoint merely because of any evangelical message it conveys." The Court determined that "what matters is the substance of the Club's activities, which we conclude are materially indistinguishable from the activities in *Lamb's Chapel v. Center Moriches Union Free School District*, 508 U.S. 384, 113 S. Ct. 2141 (1993) or in *Rosenberger v. University of Virginia* (94–329), 515 U.S. 819 (1995)." Under *Good News Club*, then, the standard is not whether access to public school facilities is sought for inherently religious activities or worship services but whether the activities constitute *"only* religious worship" or include some (unquantifiable) element of "teaching of moral values." Because virtually any religious service may be characterized as teaching moral values, under the current case law, schools risk legal challenges if they deny access to organizations that engage in exclusively religious activities. Fields concludes her paper with the following admonition: "Case law is clear on a few points: (1) if schools allow outside groups to use their facilities, they may not deny access based on the 'viewpoint' of a particular group; (2) an organization's inherently and exclusively religious activity will be considered 'teaching of morals from a religious perspective,' regardless of the proportion of such teaching to activities such as prayer, Bible study, worship, and proselytizing; (3) a school creates a limited public forum when it agrees to distribute outside literature of any kind, and must therefore distribute religious materials to the same extent and in the same manner as secular materials; and (4) parental permission may (possibly must) be required for school children to participate in privately sponsored after school activities. It also appears, under decisions such as *Hills v. Scottsdale Unified School District,* 329 F.3d 1044 (9th Cir. 2003) that schools may require a disclaimer of sponsorship on the religious materials they agree to distribute. Only one appellate court, *Wigg v. Sioux Falls School District 49–5,* 382 F.3d 807 (8th Cir. 2004), has held thus far that a schoolteacher must be permitted to participate in the Good News Club at the campus where she teaches. That decision is directly at odds with the Equal Access Act's express prohibition on school employee participation in *student* clubs. Indeed, questions of employee rights and restrictions as to participation in these religious activities may create the next legal battleground for school districts."

Children's Online Privacy Act of 1998, 15 U.S.C. 6501–6506 (1999).

Cintron v. Brentwood, 455 F. Supp. 57 (1978).

City of Boerne v. Flores, 521 U.S. 507 (1997).

Cohen, R. (1986, August 20). Drug use testing: Costly and corruptible. *New York Times,* p. A23.

Coles v. Cleveland Board of Education, 171 F.3d 369 (1999).

Commonwealth Fund. (1999). *Improving the health of adolescent girls: Policy report of Commonwealth Fund Commission on Women's Health.* New York: Author.

Communications Decency Act of 1996, 47 U.S.C. 230(c) (1999).

Counts v. Cedarville School District, 295 F. Supp.2d 996 (2003).

DeMitchell, T. A. (1997). Security within the schoolhouse gate: An emerging fundamental value in educational policy making. *Education Law Report, 49*(120), 379–386.

Department of Education religious expression guidelines, retrieved February 13, 2001, from www.ed.gov/inits/religionandschools. See also *A teacher's guide to religion in the public schools,* published by the Freedom Forum, retrieved February 13, 2001, from www.freedomforum.Org/newsstand/reports/teachersguide/teachersguide.word format.doc; and *A parent's guide to religion in the public schools,* published by the National Congress of Parents and Teachers, retrieved February 13, 2001, from www .fac.org/publicat/parents/parents.htm

Downloading. Retrieved February 13, 2001, from www.protectkids.com/index.html

Edwards v. Aguillar, 482 U.S. 578 (1987).

Elk Grove School District v. Newdow, 124 S. Ct. 2301 (2004).

Engel v. Vitale, 370 U.S. 421 (1962).

Epperson v. Arkansas, 393 U.S. 97 (1968).

Establishment of Religion Clause of the First Amendment, 736 F. Supp. 1247, 1253 (1990).

Everson v. Board of Education, 330 U.S. 1 (1946).

Fairchild, M., & Bell, J. D. (1999). School violence: Lessons learned. *State Legislatures,* February.

Fields, C. L. (2005, July 14). *Good news? Advancing religion through litigation against the public schools.* Paper presented at the Oxford Roundtable: Education Law and Public Policy. Oxford University, Oxford, England.

Filtering facts. Retrieved February 13, 2001, from www.filteringfacts.org

First, P., & Cooper, G. (1989). Access to education by homeless children. *Education Law Reporter, 53*(757), 759.

Fossey, R., & Horner, J. (2003). Student misconduct involving the misuse of technology. *Western Education Law Reporter, 179*(1), 1.

Freiler v. Tangipahoa Parish Board of Education, 975 F. Supp. 819 (1997). See also *Freiler v. Tangipahoa Parish Board of Education,* 201 F.3d 602 (2000); *Tangipahoa Parish Board of Education v. Herb Freiler,* 120 S.Ct. 2706 (2000).

Friendlander, M. (1991). *The Newcomer Program: Helping immigrant students succeed in U.S. schools.* Program Information Guide 8. Washington, DC: National Clearing House for Bilingual Education.

Gums v. Illinois State Board of Education, 811 F.2d 1030 (7th Cir. 1987).

Hazelwood v. Kuhlmeier, 484 U.S. 260 (1988).

Hendrie, C., & Drummond, S. (1998). A trust betrayed: Special report. *Education Week.* December 2, December 9, and December 16. Retrieved March 5, 2001, from www.edweek.org/sreports/abuse98.htm

History. (1) In the 1920s–1960s, English immersion or "sink-or-swim" policies were the dominant method of instruction for language-minority students. Few or no remedial services were available, and students were generally held at the same grade level until enough English was mastered to advance in subject areas. (2) In 1963, several successful, two-way bilingual programs for Cuban refugee children were conducted in Dade County, Florida, which inspired the implementation of similar programs elsewhere. (3) With the passage of the Civil Rights Act in 1964, Title VI prohibited discrimination on the basis of race, color, or national origin in the operation of all federally assisted programs. The Bilingual Education Act, Title VII of the Elementary and Secondary Education Act of 1968, established federal policy for bilingual education for economically disadvantaged language-minority students; allocated funds for innovative programs; and recognized the unique educational disadvantages faced by non-English-speaking students. In 1970, the OCR issued a memorandum interpreting Title VI's prohibition against discrimination on the basis of "national origin" to require school districts to take affirmative steps to rectify the language deficiency, to open its instructional program to students who had limited ability to speak and understand the English language. The May 25th memorandum included a number of provisions designed to give direction to school districts when confronted with children with special language needs. Local school districts were required to implement programs to help overcome the language deficiencies of national origin minority students, but the regulations did not specify the types of programs or methods to be used in the effort (Office for Civil Rights, Identification of Discrimination of Denial of Services on the Basis of National Origin, 35 Fed. Reg. 1, 595; May 25, 1970). Although the term *language deficiencies* was peculiar to the May 25th memorandum and to the time period, it is important to understand that for many people, such language in legislation and in subsequent, administrative guidelines has been a contributor to a deficit orientation toward culturally and linguistically diverse (CLD) students. More contemporary guidelines and approaches are more careful to minimize this perspective on CLD student backgrounds and potential.

Homeless. Most studies indicate that homeless children and youth are the fastest growing segments of the homeless population. About 40 percent of families who become homeless have children (M. Shinn & B. Weitzman, 1996, Homeless Families Are Different, in *Homelessness in America,* National Coalition for the Homeless, Washington, DC, 202/737–6444; retrieved March 7, 2001, from octhands5.html). A survey of 30 U.S. cities found that in 1998, children accounted for 25 percent of the urban homeless population, and unaccompanied minors accounted for 3 percent of the urban homeless population (U.S. Conference of Mayors, *A status report on hunger and homelessness in america's cities: 1998.* U.S. Conference of Mayors, Washington, DC). Research indicates that families, single mothers, and children make up the largest group of people who are homeless in rural areas (Y. Vissing, 1996, *Out of sight, out of mind: Homeless children and families in small town America.* Lexington: University Press of Kentucky).

Immediato v. Rye Neck School District, 73 F.3d 454, 519 U.S. 813 (1996).

Ingraham v. Wright, 430 U.S. 651 (1977).

International Child Abduction Remedies Act (ICARA), 42 U.S.C. 11601(a)(1995).

Island Trees Union School District v. Pico, 102 U.S. 2799 (1982).

J.S. v. Bethlehem Area School District, 807 A.2d 847 (Pa. 2002). *Education Law Report, 302.*

Kaiser Family Foundation. (2000). *National survey of teens on HIV/AIDS.* Retrieved June 1, 2005, from www.kff.org/youthhivstds/loader.cfm?url=/commonspot/security/getfile.cfm&pageid=13570

Kansas Board of Education. Retrieved March 6, 2001, from www.nytimes.com/library/national/081299kan-evolution-edu.html

Kathleen R. v. City of Livermore, V-015266–4 Cal. Sup. Ct. (Oct. 21, 1998).

Keyes v. School District No. 1 of Denver, Colorado, 576 F. Supp. 1503, 1510 (N.D. Col. 1983).

Keyishian v. Board of Regents, 385 U.S. 589, 603 (1967). See also *Virgil v. School Board of Columbia County,* 862 F.2d 1517 (1989).

Knox County Education Association v. Knox County Board of Education, 158 F.3d 361 (6th Cir. 1998).

Lalli v. Lalli, 439 U.S. 259 (1978).

Lamb's Chapel v. Center Moriches Union Free School District et al., 508 U.S. 384, 506 U.S. 813 (1992).

Lampkin v. District of Columbia, 27 F.3d 605 (D.C. Cir. 1994).

Lau v. Nichols, 414 U.S. 563 (1974); *Lau v. Nichols,* 483 F.2d 791 (1974). In addition, see *Serna v. Portales,* 499 F.2d 1147 (10th Cir. 1974); *Aspira v. New York,* 58 F.R.D. 64 (S.D. N.D. 1975); *Clinton v. Brentwood Union Free School District,* 455 F. Supp. 547 (E.D. N.Y. 1978); *Keys v. School District No. 1, Denver,* 413 U.S. 189 (1973); *Morgan v. Kerrigan,* 401 F. Supp. 4341 (E.D. Tex. 1981). See also J. Lyons (1988, revised 1992), *Legal responsibilities of education agencies serving national origin language minority students,* Washington, DC: Mid-Atlantic Equity Center; and A. S. Sosa (1994). *20 Years After Lau: In pursuit of equity not just a language response program,* San Antonio, TX: Intercultural Development Research Association.

Lee v. Weisman, 505 U.S. 577 (1992).

Lemon v. Kurtzman, 403 U.S. 602 (1971).

Lynch v. Donnelly, 465 U.S. 668 (1984).

Maack v. School District of Lincoln, 241 Neb. 847 (1992).

Marsh v. Chambers, 463 U.S. 783 (1983).

Martin Luther King Jr. Elementary School Children v. Michigan Board of Education, 451 F. Supp. 1324 (E.D. Mich. 1978).

Martinez v. Bynum, 461 U.S. 321, 103 S. Ct. 1838 (1983).

Martinez v. School Board of Hillsborough County, 861 F.2d 1502 (1988).

McKinney-Vento Homeless Assistance Act, 42 U.S.C. 11421 et seq.

Meltzer v. Board of Public Instruction of Orange County, 548 F.2d 559 (5th Cir. 1977).

Mergens v. Board of Education of West Side Community Schools, 867 F.2d 1076 (8th Cir. 1989).

Meyer v. State of Nebraska, 262 U.S. 390 (1923).

Migrant Education Program (MEP), §§ 1301–1306(a) of Title I, Part C; § 9302 of Title IX; § 421(b) of GEPA.

Minarcini v. Strongville City School District, 541 F.2d 577 (6th Cir. 1976).

Minersville School District v. Gobitis, 310 U.S. 586 (1940).

Mitchell v. Helms (98–1648), 530 U.S. 793 (2000), 151 F.3d 347.

Mozert v. Hawkins County Board of Education, 827 F.2d 1058 (6th Cir. 1987).

National Center for Education Statistics. (2003). *1.1 million homeschooled students in the United States in 2003.* Retrieved June 1, 2005, from http://nces.ed.gov/ nhes/home school/

National Center for Missing and Exploited Children. (n.d.). Retrieved February 13, 2001, from www.ncmec.org

National Center for Missing and Exploited Children. (1999). *1998 missing children statistics fact sheet.* Alexandria, VA: Author.

National Clearinghouse for Bilingual Education (NCBE). (n.d.). Retrieved March 1, 2001, from www.ncbe.gwu.edu

National Council of Teachers of English (NCTE). (1989). Retrieved February 13, 2001, from www.ncte.org/resolutions/textbook891989.html

National School Safety Center. (n.d.). Retrieved February 13, 2001, from www.nssc1 .org/

O'Connor v. Ortega, 480 U.S. 709 (1987).

Odenheim v. Carlstadt-East Rutherford School District, N.J. Super. Ct., 510 A.2d 709 (1985).

Parental Kidnapping Prevention Act (PKPA), 28 U.S.C.A. 1738(a) (1994).

Patchogue-Medford Congress of Teachers v. Board of Education, 510 N.E.2d 325 (N.Y. 1987).

Pauken, P. D. (2005, July 12). *Religion in public school curricula in the United States and Ireland: The legal balance between educational authority and individual rights.* Paper presented at Oxford Round Table: Education Law and Public Policy, Oxford University, Oxford, England.

Peck v. Upshur County Board of Education, 941 F. Supp. 1465 (N.D. W.Va. 1996).

People v. Scott D., 34 N.Y.2d 483 (1974).

Pierce v. Society of Sisters, 268 U.S. 510 (1925).

Plyler v. Doe, 457 U.S. 202 (1982).

Presidents Council District 25 v. Community School Board No. 25, 457 F.2d 289 (2d Cir. 1972), *cert. denied,* 409 U.S. 998 (1972).

Prince v. Massachusetts, 321 U.S. 158 (1944).

Public Law 104-235, § 111; 42 U.S.C. 5106g.

Religious Freedom Restoration Act (RFRA), Pub. L. No. 103-141, Nov. 16, 1993.

Riley, R. W. (1995). *Religious expression in public schools.* Retrieved February 13, 2001, from www.ed.gov/Speeches/08-1995/religion.html

Ríos v. Reed, 480 F. Supp. 14 (E.D. N.Y. 1978).

Rowling, J. K. (1999). *Harry Potter and the prisoner of Azkaban.* New York: Scholastic.

Santa Fe Independent School District v. Doe, 120 S.Ct. 2266 (2000).

School District of Abington Township v. Schempp, 374 U.S. 203 (1963).

Scopes v. State of Tennessee, 154 Tenn. 105, 289, S.W. 363 (1927).

Serna v. Portales, F.2d 1147 (10th Cir. May 1974).

Shoop, R. J. (2004). *Sexual exploitation of students: How to spot it and stop it.* Thousand Oaks, CA: Corwin.

Skinner v. Railway Labor Executives' Association, 489 U.S. 602, 633–34 (1989).

State v. Riddle, 285 S.E.2d 359 (1981).

Steirer v. Bethlehem Area School District, 987 F.2d 989 (3rd Cir. 1993).

Stenger, R. (1986). The school counselor and the law. *Journal of Law & Education, 1*(15), 12–17.

Stephens, R. D. (2001). *The art of safe school planning.* National School Safety Center. Retrieved February 13, 2001, from www.nssc1.org

Stone v. Graham, 449 U.S. 39 (1980).

Studies. *School Safety Study 1998:* National Center on Addiction and Substance Abuse at Columbia University; *Back to School 1998.* See also *National Survey of American Attitudes on Substance Abuse IV: Teens, Teachers and Principals,* CASA, retrieved February 13, 2001, from www.casacolumbia.org. See also *School Safety Study 1997: Gallup Organization and Phi Delta Kappan 29th Annual Phi Delta Kappa/Gallup Poll of the Public's Attitudes Toward the Public Schools,* Gallup Organization. Telephone: 609/924–9600; *Phi Delta Kappan* telephone: 800/ 766–1156.

Swanson v. Guthrie Independent School District, 135 F.3d 694 (1998).

Technology in the School. For a comprehensive discussion, see R. Bagby, G. Bailey, D. Bodensteiner, and D. Lumley (2000), *Plans and policies for technology in education: A compendium* (2nd ed.). Alexandria, VA: National School Boards Association.

Teitelbaum, H., & Hiller, R. J. (1977). *The legal perspective in bilingual education: Current perspectives* (Vol. 3). Arlington, VA: Center for Applied Linguistics.

Title VI Language Discrimination Guidelines, 45 Fed. Reg. 152, 52056 (1980).

Title VII-B of the McKinney-Vento Homeless Assistance Act (42 USC 11431 et seq.) (McKinney-Vento Act). The program was originally authorized in 1987 and, most recently, reauthorized by the No Child Left Behind Act of 2001.

Todd v. Rush County Schools, 139 F.3d 571 (7th Cir. 1998), *cert. denied,* 525 U.S. 824 (1998).

Uniform Parentage Act, 9A U.L.A. 579 (1983).

U.S. Department of Health and Human Services, Children's Bureau. (1999). *Child maltreatment 1997: Reports from the states to the national child abuse and neglect data system.* Washington DC: Author.

Van Orden v. Perry, 351 F.3d 173 (5th Cir. 2003).

Vernonia School District 47J v. Acton, 515 U.S. 646, 652 (1995).

Viadero, D. (1990, May 16). 350,000 abductions by family members documented. *Education Week,* pp. 21–22.

Virgil v. School Board of Columbia County, 862 F.2d 1517 (1989).

Wallace v. Jaffree, 472 U.S. 38 (1985).

West Virginia State Board of Education v. Barnette, 319 U.S. 624 (1943).

Wisconsin v. Yoder, 406 U.S. 205 (1972).

13

Sexual Harassment

Sexual harassment is a serious offense. It is not about flirting, humor, raging hormones, or horseplay. It is about power and the harasser's need to exert it over a victim. Many targets of sexual harassment would rather try to deal with incidents informally, but many do not have the necessary skills. In the workplace, victims of sexual harassment are just as likely to change jobs as a result of sexual harassment as they are to take formal action. Students usually do not have the option of leaving school. Consequently, they often suffer in silence. (See Shoop, 2004.) The concepts of sexual harassment as described and discussed in this chapter are equally applicable to adults as employees and children as students under expected duty and standards of care.

Sexual harassment is a violation of Title VII of the Civil Rights Act of 1964 and Title IX of the Education Amendments of 1972. Title VII prohibits employers of more than 15 people from discriminating on the basis of race, color, religion, gender, or national origin in all aspects of employment. Later amendments permit employees and applicants to file suit in federal court if they are not satisfied with the employer's disposition of their complaints. This act covers all aspects of employment, including pay, promotion, hiring, dismissal, and working conditions.

In 1980, the Equal Employment Opportunity Commission (EEOC) issued guidelines that declared sexual harassment a violation of Title VII, establishing criteria for determining when unwelcome conduct of a sexual nature constitutes sexual harassment, defining the circumstances under which an employer

---

AUTHORS' NOTE: Management cues are embedded within and evident throughout this chapter. Therefore, no examples of management cues are included. All suggested risk management guidelines, in comprehensive form, are at the end of the chapter.

may be liable, and suggesting affirmative steps an employer should take to prevent sexual harassment. The Equal Opportunity Employment Commission (EOEC) guidelines were reinforced in 1986 by the U.S. Supreme Court in *Meritor Savings Bank v. Vinson,* the Court's first decision regarding sexual harassment in the workplace. So effectively did the Supreme Court clarify the nature of sexual harassment and the responsibility employers have for preventing or remedying harassment, that in 1988, the EEOC published definitive guidance for employers, victims, EEOC officials, and attorneys. These guidelines have shaped all subsequent interpretations of both Title VII and Title IX in the area of sexual harassment. According to these guidelines, unwelcome sexual advances, requests for sexual favors, and other verbal or physical conduct of a sexual nature is harassment if

- Submission to such conduct is made either explicitly or implicitly a term or condition of an individual's employment
- Submission to or rejection of such conduct by an individual is used as the basis for employment decisions affecting that individual
- The conduct has the purpose or effect of unreasonably interfering with an individual's work performance or creating an intimidating, hostile, or offensive working environment

Title VII was amended in 1991 to allow sexual harassment plaintiffs to sue for monetary damages. This amendment limits recovery of compensatory damages to cases of intentional discrimination and punitive damages to nonpublic employers who act with malice or reckless indifference. In general, Title VII is enforced by the EEOC. In 1993, the U.S. Supreme Court ruled, in *Harris v. Forklift Systems,* that employees alleging sexual harassment on the job do not have to prove psychological injury to collect damages under Title VII. In 1997, the U.S. Supreme Court, in *Oncale v. Sundowner Offshore Services, Inc.,* ruled that same-sex sexual harassment in the workplace is actionable as sex discrimination under Title VII.

Title IX prohibits discrimination on the basis of sex in education programs or activities that receive federal financial assistance. Title IX covers both employees and students and virtually all activities of a school district. The prohibition covers discrimination in employment of teachers and other school personnel as well as discrimination in admissions, financial aid, and access to educational programs and activities of students. Title IX states:

> No person in the United States shall on the basis of sex be excluded from participating in, be denied the benefits of or be subjected to discrimination under any education program or activity receiving federal financial assistance.

Under Title IX, school employees and students may sue to collect monetary damages from the school, or the school may lose federal funds. In general, the EEOC enforces Title IX for the Office of Civil Rights (OCR) of the

U.S. Department of Education. OCR defines the education program of a school as *all* of the school's operations: (a) academic, (b) educational, (c) extracurricular, (d) athletic, and (e) other programs of the school. The school is responsible for ensuring a safe place to learn, whether the education activity takes place (a) in the facilities of the school, (b) on a school bus, (c) at a class, on a field trip, athletic event, or training program sponsored by the school at another location, or (d) anywhere else if the activity is school related.

As on-site representatives of a school district's central administration, principals are responsible for preventing and remedying sexual harassment in their schools. Principals must clearly understand what constitutes sexual harassment and what they must do to protect their teachers, students, and other staff members from this kind of discrimination.

FOCUS POINT: Sexual Harassment Defined and Categorized

Sexual harassment is unwelcome contact of a sexual nature that interferes with school employees' ability to do their jobs or with students' ability to enjoy the benefits of an education. EEOC guidelines describe sexual harassment as unwelcome sexual conduct that is a term or condition of employment. In *Meritor*, the Supreme Court clarified this definition by identifying two kinds of sexual harassment: *quid pro quo* (this for that) and environmental. Several other courts have expanded the definition of environmental sexual harassment to include nonsexual conduct (physical or verbal aggression or intimidation) that creates a hostile environment that would not exist but for the sex of the employee. The EEOC guidelines also identify a third type of sexual harassment, "sexual favoritism," that is a possible result of *quid pro quo* harassment. Incidents of *quid pro quo* and hostile education environment are daily occurrences in schools. (See American Association of University Women, 1992.) Although it is sometimes difficult to distinguish between the two categories, it is important to do so because school districts are held to different standards for each.

- *Quid pro quo sexual harassment* exists whenever a supervisor makes unwelcome sexual advances toward an employee and implicitly or explicitly threatens that the victim's continued employment and advancement are contingent on submission. Once the fact of the sexual (or sex-based) conduct of the supervisor is confirmed, the next question to be determined is whether the conduct was unwelcome. In this inquiry, the question of whether the victim voluntarily submitted to the supervisor's advances is irrelevant. The court will not fault a victim who has made a clear protest for submitting to an offending supervisor rather than face real or perceived job-related consequences. When an employment opportunity or benefit is granted because of an individual's submission to sexual advances, other employees have grounds to sue on the basis of sexual discrimination under Title VII (sexual favoritism).

Quid pro quo sexual harassment is the easiest type of harassment to recognize in schools. It occurs when sexual demands are made on a student or a school employee in exchange for education participation, advancement, or other benefits, or under the threat of punishment. OCR defines an employee as any agent of a school district. In addition to certified and classified staff, anyone with whom the school contracts to provide services for the school is considered an employee. Student teachers who are given authority to assign grades may be considered employees. An incident of sexual bribery or sexual intimidation is considered *quid pro quo* sexual harassment even if it happens only once. Because of the age and vulnerability of students, in the case of a student who "consents" to the sexual attention, both the school and the adult employee are liable for sexual harassment.

• *Environmental sexual harassment* exists when a pattern of unwelcome and offensive conduct, which would be considered abusive by any reasonable person under the same circumstances, creates a hostile work environment that inhibits the work performance of an employee. The court views similarly offensive conduct that is sexual in nature and aggressive nonsexual conduct that is focused on an employee because of her or his sex.

In the workplace, this type of harassment is called *hostile work-environment sexual harassment.* In a school setting, it is referred to as a *hostile education environment.* A hostile education environment is the most frequent type of sexual harassment in schools. This form of harassment is less tangible and less discrete, and it often occurs over a period of time. Although one inappropriate touch, comment, or joke may be offensive, to cross the threshold into sexual harassment, the behavior must either be very severe (e.g., touching the breast, crotch, or buttocks) or be persistent and pervasive (e.g., a teacher making sexual comments to or about a student on a regular basis). Hostile-environment harassment may be the conduct of an employee or another student, may include unwelcome sexual advances, requests for sexual favors, and other verbal or physical conduct of a sexual nature. If this behavior is sufficiently severe, persistent, or pervasive and limits a student's ability to participate in or benefit from an education program or activity, a hostile or abusive education environment exists.

• *Sexual favoritism* occurs when a less qualified applicant receives employment opportunities or benefits as a result of the individual's submission to the employer's sexual advances or requests for sexual favors. Sexual favoritism is often a form of harassment claimed by employees or students when another employee or student has benefited from *quid pro quo* harassment.

In addition to these legal categories of sexual harassment, educators need to keep in mind three manifestations of harassment: employee to employee, employee to student, and student to student.

Sexual activity between two consenting adults as coworkers is not illegal. Sexual activity is not sexual harassment unless it is unwanted. However, sexual activity between an adult and a minor student is always illegal. Because of the special relationship between the school and the student, schools have a duty to protect students from sexual abuse by school employees. Sexual activity between an adult employee and a student, or propositions for such activity, is grounds for dismissal and for criminal action against the adult. Sexual assault, sexual battery and rape, and sexual activity with a minor, in addition to qualifying as sexual harassment, are forms of child abuse and violations of criminal law and must be reported.

Sexual Harassment Statutes

Every state has some form of gender discrimination law. In some state statutes, sexual harassment is specifically prohibited; in others, sexual harassment is included under the prohibition against sex discrimination. Individual state statutes reinforce federal law and often define harassment more specifically. It is clear, however, that school districts and individual schools are required to take all steps necessary to prevent sexual harassment. Specifically, school districts must *formulate and disseminate* a strong, clearly stated policy and *implement an effective procedure* for resolving complaints that does not require the victim to complain first to the offending supervisor or, in the case of a student, the adult offender. School districts and individual schools are required to investigate thoroughly every complaint of sexual harassment, deal appropriately with offenders, and resolve the problem.

| FOCUS POINT: School Liability for Sexual Harassment

School districts and individual schools are always liable for *quid pro quo* harassment because the action (promotion, demotion, transfer, termination) taken by an employee is an exercise of authority delegated by the district. School districts and individual schools are liable for environmental harassment if the district has no strong, widely disseminated, and consistently enforced policy against sexual harassment and has no effective complaint procedure in place. Without these clear protections in place, employees and students can reasonably assume that a superior has "apparent authority" (tacit approval) to practice sexual harassment. School districts and individual schools are also liable for environmental harassment if senior management does not take immediate and appropriate steps to terminate harassing conduct and discipline the offending party. (Note: When immediate and appropriate action has not been taken in response to a complaint, school districts have been found liable for sexual harassment by independent contractors—for example, by roofing, electrical, and plumbing contractors and those who provide contracted services such as custodial, food preparation, etc.)

School Liability for Adult Sexual Harassment

Sexual harassment in the employment relationship is definitively described in the Supreme Court's ruling in *Meritor*. The employer's responsibility for preventing and dealing with sexual harassment is clearly outlined in the EEOC guidelines discussed at the beginning of this chapter.

School Liability for Teacher-to-Student Sexual Harassment

In 1992, the U.S. Supreme Court confirmed that damages might be awarded in sex discrimination action under Title IX. In the case of *Franklin v. Gwinnett County School Board*, the Court ruled that schools owe their students protection from sexual harassment, a form of discrimination, by school employees and by other students. A student in a high school in Georgia filed a complaint in a federal district court against the school district under Title IX. In her complaint, the student alleged that (a) she was subjected to continual sexual harassment and abuse, including coercive intercourse, by a male teacher at the school, (b) teachers and administrators were aware of the teacher's conduct but took no action to halt it, and (c) the school closed its investigation of the teacher's conduct after the teacher resigned on the condition that all matters pending against him be dropped. The district court dismissed the complaint on the grounds that Title IX did not authorize an award of damages. Although an appeals court upheld the district court, the U.S. Supreme Court reversed the decision and ruled that money damages can be awarded for an action brought to enforce Title IX.

In 1998, the U.S. Supreme Court ruled, in *Gebser v. Lago Vista Independent School District*, that school districts may be held liable under Title IX of the Education Amendments of 1972 (20 U.S. §§ 1681–1688) for sexual harassment of a student by an employee in which (a) an official representative of the educational institution who had authority to take constructive steps to stop the harassment actually knew of the harassment and (b) the educational institution responded with deliberate indifference. The case involved an eighth-grade student who, after joining a book discussion group led by a teacher, began to have sexual intercourse with the teacher. This relationship continued until her sophomore year, when a police officer discovered them having sexual intercourse in a car and arrested the teacher. The school district terminated his employment, and the state revoked his teaching credentials.

The student brought suit against the school district, claiming that the school should be liable under Title IX. She also argued that the court should follow Title VII's imposition of liability for "constructive knowledge": "If one by exercise of reasonable care would have known a fact, he is deemed to have had constructive knowledge of such fact" (*Black's Law Dictionary*, 1979, p. 477). A district and an appeals court ruled in favor of the school district. The U.S. Supreme Court also rejected the constructive knowledge argument and ruled that the district could only be found liable in the case of actual knowledge.

A school district would be held liable for sexual harassment if a teacher abuses delegated authority over a student to create a hostile environment, for example, if a teacher explicitly or implicitly threatens to fail a student unless the student responds to her or his sexual advances, even though the teacher fails to carry out the threat. Often the line between *quid pro quo* and hostile-environment discrimination is blurred, and the employee's conduct may constitute both types of harassment.

Janitors or cafeteria workers may be considered to be in positions of authority—or appear to have authority if authority is actually given to the employee (e.g., in some schools, a cafeteria worker or paraprofessional may have authority to impose discipline or report infractions). The age of the student is an important factor. Generally, the younger the student, the more likely it is that he or she will consider any adult employee to be in a position of authority.

School Liability for Student-to-Student Sexual Harassment

In 1999, the U.S. Supreme Court, in *Davis v. Monroe County Board of Education*, ruled that school boards could be held liable under Title IX for "deliberate indifference" to known student-to-student sexual harassment that is "severe, pervasive, and objectively offensive." In this case, a fifth-grade student alleged ongoing verbal and physical sexual harassment at the hands of a male classmate. The male classmate was charged and pled guilty to sexual battery. The girl's mother had reported each incident of harassment to a teacher. One teacher had reported the matter to the school's principal. When the student had attempted to report the event directly to the principal, a teacher had told her that if the principal "wants you, he'll call you." When the girl's mother spoke to the principal, he said, "I guess I'll have to threaten him a little bit harder." The principal then asked the mother why her daughter was the only one who was complaining. The family sued the school district under Title IX. The district court rejected their claim. On appeal, the circuit court reversed the district court's holding. The U.S. Supreme Court ruled that schools may be held liable for student-to-student sexual harassment if (a) the school exercises substantial control of both the harasser and the context in which the known harassment occurs, (b) the school is deliberately indifferent to peer harassment or their response or lack of response is clearly unreasonable under the circumstances, and (c) the harassment is so severe, pervasive, and objectively offensive that it deprives the victims of a school's educational benefits.

Although in the majority of sexual harassment cases the victim is a female, a significant number of males report being targets as well. It is important to note, too, that same-sex sexual harassment is also a serious problem. In fact, other boys perpetrate much of the sexual harassment of boys. Boys calling other boys "queer," "faggot," or "homo" is a form of sexual harassment.

FOCUS POINT: Appropriate Physical Contact Versus Unwelcome Conduct or Hostile Environment

Title IX's prohibition against sexual harassment does not extend to nonsexual touching or other nonsexual conduct. There are legitimate reasons for an employee to touch a student or another employee or for one student to touch another student. For example, a vocal music teacher showing a student the correct way to breathe, an instrumental music teacher demonstrating the proper way to hold a musical instrument, a basketball coach demonstrating the proper way to block out another player, or an elementary schoolteacher comforting a child with a skinned knee by putting an arm on the child's shoulder to console the child are appropriate forms of physical contact.

Some school districts are so worried about having an employee charged with sexual harassment that they have adopted policies prohibiting school employees from having any physical contact other than a handshake. This may be an overreaction to the problem. There is a clear difference between appropriate and inappropriate touching.

Conduct is unwelcome when an adult or a student being harassed did not solicit or incite it and regarded the conduct as undesirable or offensive. The fact that the victim does not complain or report the harassment does not mean that the conduct is welcome.

In attempting to determine if harassment occurred or if the behavior was welcome or unwelcome, the totality of the circumstances must be taken into consideration. For example, in attempting to resolve the dispute, the following should be considered:

- Statements by any witnesses to the alleged incident
- Evidence about the relative credibility of the allegedly harassed victim and the alleged harasser
- The level of detail and consistency of each person's account and of corroborative evidence

Severe, Persistent, or Pervasive Harassment

Although a single instance of *quid pro quo* harassment is a violation of Title IX, hostile-environment sexual harassment must be sufficiently severe, persistent, or pervasive to limit an employee's ability to work or a student's ability to participate in or benefit from the education program, or it must create a hostile or abusive educational environment. Everything sexual is not sexual harassment. If a student drives by another student and shouts a sexual comment out the window or makes an obscene gesture, this is certainly inappropriate. However, usually one isolated incident does not cross the threshold into sexual harassment.

Hostile-environment sexual harassment may result from either one incident of intense, aberrant behavior or a number of lesser behaviors that take place over a period of time. For example, a single incident of a severe behavior, such as grabbing a female's breast, crotch, or buttocks or threats of rape or assault, would constitute a hostile environment as well as be a criminal action. On the other hand, a situation that may not appear to be too serious may be sexual harassment when it is pervasive and persistent. For example, when one person (student or employee) is the target of name calling, taunting, propositions, rumors, and graffiti, and the offensive behavior occurs almost every day and is initiated by several people, there is a serious cumulative impact.

The context of the behavior is also an important factor. For example, it is not sexual harassment to ask someone for a date. However, it can become sexual harassment if the request is continually rejected to the point that a reasonable person would understand that the behavior is unwanted.

FOCUS POINT: Harassment of Males

The EEOC has seen the number of sexual harassment complaints by men more than double in the past years. Sexual harassment is not just something that happens to women. According to Uggen (2004), "All women are at some risk of sexual harassment, but males are also likely to be targeted if they seem vulnerable and appear to reject the male stereotype." Uggen found that if a man refuses to go along with sexual joking, wears an earring, or engages in activity typically attributed to women, he is more likely to be harassed. The harassers tend to be men who are flaunting their heterosexual masculinity over all forms of femininity. Victims were not just women but also men who had challenged the stereotypical male ideals.

The sexual harassment of men appears to be underreported. In Uggen's research, young adults and adolescents were asked if they'd ever experienced sexual harassment. Uggen found that one of every three women and one of every seven men who took part in the study reported they had been sexually harassed by the time they reached their mid-20s. Yet, many of those men and women had never told anyone about their experience prior to their participation in the study. School districts should encourage males to report all incidents of sexual harassment and learn how to identify it early. "When these adolescents remain quiet, they risk experiencing greater levels of harassment as they enter adulthood" (Uggen, 2004).

FOCUS POINT: Duty to Prevent Antigay Student Harassment

Some of the material in this section touches upon issues that are covered in other sections of the book. However, because all of these topics are associated with antigay harassment, this Focus Point addresses a variety of topics as they relate to lesbian, gay, bisexual, and transgender (LGBT) students.

LGBT students face tremendous challenges as they grow up, including rejection, isolation, verbal harassment, and physical violence in schools. And in many schools, they also face teacher homophobia and discrimination.

In its passive form, this harassment results in a lack of protection for students. In its more active form, it exists as discrimination, open ridicule, and violence. According to the Office for Civil Rights (OCR, 2000), "[H]arassing conduct of a sexual nature directed toward gay or lesbian students (e.g., if a male student or group of male students target a gay student for physical and sexual advances) may create a sexually hostile environment and, therefore, be prohibited by Title IX." In addition, various reports and studies make it clear that harassment of LGBT students is an everyday occurrence in many of our public schools. The National School Boards Association (NSBA, 2004) reports, "Over the past decade, controversies surrounding students' sexual orientation and gender identity have become increasingly common in K–12 schools." Other studies reported the following:

- Forty-five percent of gay males and 20 percent of lesbians suffer harassment in high school, resulting from perceptions about their sexual orientation (AAUW, 1992).
- Thirty-one percent of gay youth had been threatened or injured at school in the last year alone (Chase, 2001).
- More than 90 percent of participants reported hearing homophobic remarks in their schools, including the use of the word *gay* to mean something that is considered bad or valueless, as in "that's so gay," just as one might use the words *dumb* or *stupid*. Almost all participants reported hearing homophobic remarks from other students—81.8 percent reported hearing such remarks often or frequently from other students. Over a third (40.5 percent) reported hearing these remarks from most of the students at their schools. Less than a quarter of the youth reported that faculty or staff intervened most or all of the time when present at the time such remarks were made (Kosciw, 2004, p. 8).
- Ninety-seven percent of public high school students report regularly hearing homophobic remarks from their peers (Massachusetts Governor's Commission, 1993).
- Seventy-eight percent heard remarks such as "faggot" or "dyke" frequently at school, and 39.1 percent had been physically assaulted at school because of their sexual orientation. Of those same students, 64.3 percent felt unsafe in their school because of their sexual orientation (*Gay, Lesbian, Straight Education Network,* 2003).

LGBT students are guaranteed equal protection under the Fourteenth Amendment and freedom of speech and association under the First Amendment. Like other student clubs, LGBT-related student groups are guaranteed equal treatment and access under the Equal Access Act (EAA) of 1984. Some courts have held that Title IX offers protections to LGBT students in certain circumstances, and some states and communities have enacted specific prohibitions against discrimination on the basis of sexual orientation and gender identity.

Questions about the legal rights of LGBT students generally focus on (a) student organizations and clubs, (b) student dress codes, (c) curriculum and LGBT issues, (d) student involvement in school events, and (e) harassment of LGBT students.

Student Organizations and Clubs

In *Westside Community Schools v. Mergens* (1990), the courts found that the EAA requires schools to treat student clubs that address LGBT issues the same as other student groups. When students establish a club in a public school that both receives federal money and provides an "open forum," the EAA requires the school to allow LGBT-oriented clubs the same access to school facilities that other student groups enjoy. (See the Chapter 12 Focus Point regarding the EAA.) It is important to note that courts have not looked favorably on school districts that have changed the rules regarding "noncurriculum" clubs in attempting to exclude LGBT clubs (*Boyd County High School Gay Straight Alliance v. Board of Education of Boyd County,* 2003).

Student Dress Codes

Since the *Tinker* case in 1969, courts have recognized that school districts must balance their interest in maintaining a safe and orderly learning environment against the rights of students to freedom of speech and expression. *Bethel School District No. 403 v. Fraser* (1986) and other cases have allowed schools to prohibit spoken, written, or symbolic speech that is deemed to be lewd, vulgar, indecent, or clearly offensive, and speech contrary to the school's educational mission. Some courts have held that messages or images that are at odds with values such as civility were contrary to a school's educational mission (*Boroff v. Van Wert City Board of Education,* 2000). Speech that does not fall into one of the above-mentioned categories may be regulated only if it substantially disrupts or interferes with the work of the school (*Sypniewski v. Warren Hills Regional Board of Education,* 2002). Courts have made it clear that mere disagreement or dislike of a message does not meet the disruption test. In order to prohibit expression, the school does not need to wait for a disruption, but must have *well-founded* concerns. (See the Chapter 6 Focus Point regarding Expression Through Students' Written Communication.) Consequently, prohibiting clothing that conveys a message that might be construed as pro- or antigay, but is not likely to disrupt the learning environment or interfere with other students' rights, risks legal challenge.

Although some courts have supported the actions of schools that restricted clothing on the basis of a student's gender and on the basis that such clothing distracted from learning, such actions are open to challenges on the basis of sexual discrimination. For example, prohibiting a boy from wearing a dress to school might be viewed as a disruption in one community and be seen as permissible in another. The National School Boards Association (NSBA, 2004) recommends: "Schools with sex specific dress codes might consider making a narrow exception for transgender students—students who are biologically of one gender, but psychologically identify with the opposite gender."

Curriculum and LGBT Issues

Courts have consistently ruled that parents do not have the right to control the content of a curriculum. As long as the curriculum is based on sound education rationale such as age appropriateness, relevancy, and currency of the information, districts have great leeway. However, the NSBA (2004) recommends: "Districts may want to consider adopting a complaint-and-review procedure for resolving challenges to school curriculum. Including teachers, parents, and community members on the review panel will foster a sense of fairness in any decision made. All parents should be advised of their right to use this process." Some states require written parental consent before students can participate in classes where such topics as sex, sexuality, and AIDS are discussed. The federal Protection of Pupil Rights Amendment (PPRA, 2004) gives parents the right to limit their child's participation in surveys or questionnaires that may contain controversial and/or sexual subject matter.

Student Involvement in School Events

Increasingly, student groups are asking permission to take part in such events as "Diversity Days" or a "Day of Silence." Unless the activity will substantially disrupt the work of the school, such activities as remaining silent for all or part of a day to raise awareness for LGBT students must be accorded the same rights that would be given to any other school group.

Harassment of LGBT Students

Antigay bias has been referred to as the last "acceptable" form of discrimination in the United States" (Walker, 2002). There have been two significant federal cases that have affirmatively held that school districts have a legal obligation under the equal protection clause of the Fourteenth Amendment to protect students from discrimination, harassment, and abuse based upon their sexual orientation.

In a 1996 case, *Nabozny v. Podlesny*, Jamie Nabozny, a gay man, was awarded $900,000 in the first federal trial against a school for not protecting gay students. In this case against the Ashland School District in northern Wisconsin, Nabozny alleged that he had been harassed from the time he entered middle school in 1988 until he dropped out of high school as a junior in 1993. Nabozny said that abuse by other students ranged from name calling to being shoved, beaten, spat upon, and even having his head pushed in a urinal. He said he was kicked in the stomach so many times that he later required surgery.

The award in the *Nabozny* case was groundbreaking in that it affirmed that a school district's failure to protect a gay student from peer harassment violated the federal equal protection clause. The case also affirmed that the student was protected by Title IX's prohibition on sex discrimination, because he alleged that the harassment was based on his failure to conform to male stereotypes.

The OCR (2000) states that "sexual harassment directed at gay or lesbian students that is sufficiently serious to limit or deny a student's ability to participate in or benefit from the school's program constitutes sexual harassment prohibited by Title IX." An important point to keep in mind is that school boards may be held liable for harassment of students by their peers if the harassment—verbal or physical—has been severe and persistent and the school took no action after learning of the misconduct. As in any other case of alleged sexual harassment, a trained investigator should investigate complaints of harassments based on sexual orientation thoroughly and promptly.

In *Flores v. Morgan Hill Unified School District* (2003), the U.S. Court of Appeals for the Ninth Circuit held that local school officials who did not take formal action when consistent discrimination and abuse were evident could be held liable. The plaintiffs sued the school district, administrators, and school board members under Section 1983, claiming that the defendants' response or lack of response to complaints of student-to-student antihomosexual harassment denied them equal protection. The plaintiffs alleged that, during their time as students in the Morgan Hill Unified School District, they suffered antigay harassment by their classmates. The case settled in early 2004 after a five-year court battle, with the district agreeing to make extensive policy changes, provide training for all district staff on how to appropriately respond to harassment, and pay a total of over $1.1 million.

▌ FOCUS POINT: Affirmative Response to a Complaint

To avoid liability for sexual harassment of students or employees, a school must take immediate and appropriate corrective action when it is notified of or has suspicion of an incident of alleged harassment. In the case of an allegation of sexual harassment, the accused person should be separated from any contact with the victim until an investigation has been completed and a finding reached. A school is considered to be on notice as soon as an agent or responsible employee of the school receives notice. Notice occurs when

- A student or employee files a grievance
- A student or employee complains to an administrator or other school employee
- A parent or other responsible individual contacts a school employee
- A responsible employee of the school witnesses the harassment or finds some other evidence of harassment

All reports of sexual harassment (superior to employee, employee to employee, employee to student, student to employee, student to student) should be taken seriously and promptly investigated. Even unsubstantiated reports of possible sexual harassment should receive scrutiny by a principal.

▌ FOCUS POINT: Defense Against Allegations

Note: This Focus Point is included *only* to demonstrate how points of law enter into issues of alleged sexual harassment.

Defenses That Have Been Successful against Allegations of Sexual Harassment

Examples of defenses that may be allowed in sexual harassment cases include the following:

- *No harassment occurred.* Although it is possible that the complaint is a complete fabrication invented by a disgruntled employee or malicious student, it is critical that all complaints be investigated. If the school district or OCR completes an investigation and no evidence of sexual harassment is found, the school district is not liable. The burden of proof is on the person bringing the complaint.

- *The event occurred, but it was not unwelcome.* If the actions were solicited, incited, or encouraged, it will be difficult for the person bringing the complaint to prevail. However, this defense must be used with extreme care, because the consent may have been given out of fear and, therefore, would not have been voluntary. Students are not legally capable of entering into a consensual relationship. Consequently, even if the student agreed to a sexual relationship with the teacher or other student, it is a violation of state laws.
- *Harassment was not based on sex.* Overtures were made to both sexes, or conduct was equally offensive to both sexes. It must be remembered that just because there was a sexual content, it is not necessarily sexual harassment. A boy hanging out the window of a bus and making obscene gestures may be a violation of the school's discipline policy, but unless this action was part of a persistent pattern and was directed at a specific student or faculty member, it is unlikely that a court will find it to be sexual harassment.
- *Harassment was not severe.* To be sexual harassment, the behavior must be sufficiently severe or pervasive to alter the conditions of the employee's employment or the student's ability to learn, and the behavior must create an abusive environment.
- *Employer had no knowledge of the harassment.* If it can be demonstrated that the school did not know of the sexual harassment, and if there was a clearly defined and well-publicized grievance procedure for claims, it is unlikely a court would find it to be sexual harassment.
- *It happened, but the school took prompt and appropriate actions.* If, upon notice of the complaint, the school conducted a prompt and thorough investigation, and if it was determined that sexual harassment took place and prompt punishment was commensurate with the severity of the harassment, it is unlikely that a court would find the school district to be liable. This would especially be true if the school district's actions were aimed at preventing future incidents of sexual harassment.

Defenses That Have Been Unsuccessful Against Allegations of Sexual Harassment

In recent court cases, some school districts have offered defenses that were *not accepted* by the courts.

- *She or he is crying wolf.* Some people do not believe that sexual harassment is real. They see it as a way of getting back at a teacher or student who rejected them. Although there may be false complaints, it is the responsibility of the school to take all complaints seriously and to investigate all complaints. If no grounds for the complaint are found, there may be discipline for the person bringing the false complaint. Recent studies indicate that most victims of sexual harassment do not report the harassment, and on investigation, most complaints prove to be valid.

- *He or she failed to promptly report the sexual harassment.* Clear evidence indicates that many victims of sexual harassment do not report the harassment because they are afraid they will not be believed, will be blamed for the harassment and don't know how to complain, or fear retaliation for reporting the sexual harassment. Although there are statutes of limitations for reporting sexual harassment, courts frequently allow cases to be brought forward that exceed this time frame.

- *No real harm resulted from the harassment.* Often a school district will attempt to dismiss a complaint of sexual harassment by saying that no significant harm resulted from the harassment.

- *The complainant behaved in a "sexually provocative" manner.* Although the behavior, speech, dress, and demeanor may be admissible in a sexual harassment proceeding, it is not a defense for inappropriate behavior by the harasser.

▌ FOCUS POINT: Protecting Teachers' Reputations

The fear of false accusations of sexual harassment and abuse has a negative impact on educators. It is important to recognize that a false allegation of harassment may significantly damage an educator's reputation and destroy his or her career. This is another reason that every allegation of sexual harassment should be quickly and thoroughly investigated and disposed of. If an accusation is proved to be true, then definitive action to punish must be demonstrated. If the accusation is proved false, then definitive action should be taken to punish the false accuser. Include *prohibition against false complaints* in any sexual harassment prevention policy. Including such a prohibition is an important component in protecting the reputation of innocent victims. Students and employees must understand the damage that can be done by a false complaint and that serious punishment will be given to any person who makes a false complaint.

Suggested Risk Management Guideline
(Prohibited Conduct regarding Sexual Orientation)

- School district agents and employees must not
  - Fail to respond promptly and appropriately to any complaints or allegations of harassment or discrimination on the basis of actual or perceived sexual orientation or gender identity
  - Knowingly engage in, sanction, or allow harassing conduct on the basis of actual or perceived sexual orientation or gender identity
  - Retaliate against, or take any actions that have the impact of adversely affecting, any student or employee because that student or employee

has made allegations, filed, or participated in a complaint with the district or any federal, state, local, or nongovernmental entity concerning harassment or discrimination on the basis of actual or perceived sexual orientation or gender identity
- Coerce a student to enroll in alternative education or independent study programs because he or she has complained of harassment or discrimination on the basis of actual or perceived sexual orientation or gender identity

Suggested Risk Management Guideline (Advice for Parents)

- Education about sexual harassment and abuse prevention should extend to the parents of school-aged children. A notice like the following might be incorporated into a parent newsletter under the title "What to do if your child reports sexual abuse to you."
  - Be patient: This is a difficult thing for your child to share with you.
  - Let your child tell you about the abuse in his or her own words. Don't interrogate.
  - Listen to what your child is telling you, and believe your child.
  - Acknowledge what your child is feeling and how difficult it is for him or her to tell you.
  - Let your child know how proud you are of him or her for having the courage to tell about the abuse.
  - Let your child know you will do everything you can to keep your child safe from now on.
  - Don't make any promises you may not be able to keep.
  - Let your child see your distress, but be careful how you express your anguish; you don't want to worry your child.
  - When you have a free moment alone, write down everything that your child has told you; use your child's words whenever possible and avoid interpreting what your child has said.

Suggested Risk Management Guidelines (Policy Development)

- The clearest way that a school district can demonstrate that it takes sexual harassment prevention seriously is to have a comprehensive board-adopted policy regarding sexual harassment prevention. *However, individual building principals must affirmatively enforce such a policy.* A formal policy provides a structure under which everyone in the school district can understand his or her individual rights and responsibilities. Furthermore, having such a policy will help prevent sexual harassment, provide guidance in how to respond to incidents of sexual harassment, and provide some protection from liability in the event of a lawsuit. *The policy should be written in nonlawyer language that is user friendly and should include a separate section for staff and a separate section for*

students. In developing, implementing, or enforcing a policy, remember that a school will be held to be liable for hostile-environment sexual harassment by its employee if the employee
- Acted with apparent authority (i.e., because of the school's conduct, the employee reasonably appears to be acting on behalf of the school, whether or not the employee acted with authority)
- Was aided in carrying out the sexual harassment by her or his position of authority within the institution

- A comprehensive sexual harassment prevention policy should include
  - A statement prohibiting sexual harassment, indicating that sexual harassment is illegal
  - A definition of sexual harassment, with examples
  - A description of who is covered by the policy
  - A description of the complaint procedures
  - A time frame for filing and responding to formal complaints
  - A description of the appeals process
  - A list of consequences
  - A statement prohibiting retaliation
  - A statement about confidentiality
  - A statement about coverage of off-campus violations
  - Identification of the school employee who should be notified if there is a complaint
  - A statement about false charges
  - A statement about other legal remedies available to complainants
  - An indication of how the school community will be notified about the policy
  - A statement regarding the ongoing training of school staff and students
  - A requirement for ongoing review, evaluation, and improvement

Suggested Risk Management Guidelines
(Policy Implementation and Enforcement)

- Ensure that administrators are thoroughly familiar with the policy.
- Include a copy of the policy in faculty and staff handbooks.
- Train all certified and classified staff members in how to recognize and prevent sexual harassment.
- Train investigators in investigation protocols.
- Include a comprehensive presentation of sexual harassment prevention in student handbooks.
- Inform off-campus sites about the school district's sexual harassment prevention policy.
- Integrate information about sexual harassment prevention across the curriculum.
- Display posters in prominent places in district buildings that explain what people should do if they believe they are being sexually harassed.

- Include questions regarding sexual harassment in any surveys conducted to assess school climate.

Suggested Risk Management Guidelines (Codes of Conduct and Training to Support Policy)

- There should be a code of conduct for teachers, other school staff members, and volunteers. This document should explicitly state that all romantic and sexual relationships between students and teachers, regardless of the student's age, are prohibited and what the consequences will be if the code is violated.
  - If the allegations involve improper language or a nonphysical form of sexual harassment, it may be possible to allow the teacher to remain in the classroom. However, if the complaint involves sexual intimidation, inappropriate contact, stalking, sexual propositions, or sexual intercourse, the school has a duty to remove the teacher to ensure student safety. A range of options, including suspension or reassignment to nonclassroom duties, may be considered.
  - If the complaint was false, there must be serious consequences for the accuser. The punishment must be strong enough to make it clear to employees and all others that a false complaint is a very serious matter.
  - In the event of a false complaint, the employee should be reinstated, and efforts must be made to rehabilitate the employee's reputation.

- There should be a code of conduct for students. This document should explicitly state what types of conduct are not permitted and what the consequences will be if the code is violated (e.g., suspension, expulsion, transfer, criminal charges).
  - If a false complaint is filed, there must be serious consequences for the accuser. The punishment must be strong enough to make it clear to students and all others that a false complaint is a very serious matter.

- Provide training in prevention strategies. Specific training is necessary to reduce the confusion between appropriate and inappropriate physical or verbal contact.

Suggested Risk Management Guideline (For Teachers and Other Employees)

- The best way that teachers can protect themselves from false accusations is to avoid behaviors that can be misconstrued. Teachers and other school employees should not
  - Be alone with a student in a schoolroom, outside of the regular school day, without informing the principal
  - Be alone with a student behind a closed door; if a room door does not have a window, request that one be installed
  - Make a habit of meeting students outside of school

- Counsel students in nonacademic matters
- Regularly transport students in your own vehicle or allow students to have access to it
- Give students hall passes to come to your room on non-school-related business
- Allow students to engage you in conversations regarding their romantic or sexual activities. Don't discuss your personal problems with students
- Entertain students in your home unless it is a school-sponsored activity
- Make sexual comments, comments about their bodies, tell sexual jokes, or share sexually oriented material with students
- Put your hands on a student in a manner that a reasonable person could interpret as inappropriate

Suggested Risk Management Guidelines (Cautions)

- Don't assume that otherwise "good teachers" will not harm children.
- Don't assume that only certain types of students engage in sexual harassment.
- Don't assume that only certain types of students can be victims of sexual harassment.
- Don't confuse sexual harassment with flirting or giving someone a compliment.
- Don't assume that sexual harassment did not take place if there are no witnesses.
- Don't assume that sexual harassment is an isolated incident.
- You have an affirmative duty to
  - Protect students and employees from potential harm
  - Ensure that no retaliation is taken against a person who reports abuse
  - Promptly investigate all complaints
  - Report the suspected abuse to the appropriate state agency if required
  - Report the suspected abuse or complaint of abuse to the appropriate school district person (e.g., Title IX compliance officer)
  - Document the investigation process
  - Evaluate the circumstances in the case of an unsubstantiated complaint to determine if any actions could be misconstrued, and eliminate these actions
  - Provide ongoing education about sexual harassment by (a) reminding all staff members of the importance of appropriate behavior, (b) reminding all staff members of the state statutes and school district policy, (c) reminding all students that no one has the right to touch them in a sexual manner, (d) reminding all students how to complain if they believe they have been touched inappropriately, and (e) reminding all students that if they have any concerns or questions, they are strongly encouraged to talk to the principal

Suggested Risk Management Guideline (Compliance)

- School principals have an affirmative duty to ensure and enforce compliance in accord with school district policy and procedures. To ensure that your procedures are prompt and equitable, the school district should be sure that
  - One employee is delegated to coordinate the school district's efforts to comply with and carry out its Title IX responsibilities
  - One district office employee is designated to be responsible for coordinating the compliance activities at each school
  - The policy and procedures are widely publicized to all students, parents, and employees (also see Shoop, 2004)
  - The policy and procedures are written in language appropriate to the age of the school's students
  - All students and employees are notified of the name, office address, and telephone number of the employee responsible for receiving complaints
  - All complaints are taken seriously and are promptly investigated
  - The investigation is conducted by an impartial investigator
  - The investigation is conducted by a trained investigator
  - The due process rights of students and employees charged with sexual harassment are protected
  - The investigation is completed in a timely manner
  - All parties are told of the outcome of the investigation
  - Accurate records are kept to ensure that the school can and will identify and resolve recurring problems and the problem of repeat offenders
  - Training is instituted to prevent recurrence of any harassment

Suggested Risk Management Guidelines (Additional Considerations)

Note: The following guidelines are based on Justice O'Connor's explanation of the Supreme Court's decision in *Davis v. Monroe County Board of Education* (1999), as reported by Schimmel (2000). It should be remembered that the following are guidelines of legal liability, *not necessarily guidelines for best education practice*. Even though there may not be legal liability for some actions, it is hoped that school administrators will work to eliminate all forms of sexual harassment. The "operative statements" included in the guidelines below (based on Justice O'Connor's explanation) should provide administrators with the tools to set policy in the areas of (a) "deliberate indifference," (b) accusations that an administrator's "response is clearly unreasonable," and (c) "denying victims equal access to education."

- Administrators are not required to purge their schools of peer harassment.
- Schools are not required to suspend or expel a student accused of harassment, nor are administrators required to take any particular disciplinary action in response to harassment charges.

- Victims of peer harassment do not have a right under Title IX to make any particular remedial demands.
- Courts should not second-guess the disciplinary decisions made by administrators.
- Schools are not liable for the sexual harassment of their students (but only for their own acts of deliberate indifference).
- Administrators should not be considered deliberately indifferent to peer harassment unless their response is "clearly unreasonable."
- Schools are not required to take disciplinary action that would expose them to constitutional or statutory claims.
- Damages are not available simply by showing that a student has been teased or called offensive names—even if gender specific.
- Damages are not available unless the harassment is severe, pervasive, and objectively offensive and denies its victim equal access to education.
- Schools are not likely to be held liable for any single act of harassment.

CHAPTER RESOURCES

American Association of University Women. (1992). *Hostile hallways: The AAUW survey on sexual harassment in America's schools.* Washington, DC: Author.

Bethel School District No. 403 v. Fraser, 478 U.S. 675 (1986).

Black's Law Dictionary. (1979). St. Paul, MN: West.

Board of Education of Westside Community Schools v. Mergens, 496 U.S. 226 (1990).

Boroff v. Van Wert City Board of Education, 220 F.3d 465 (6th Cir. 2000).

Boyd County High School Gay Straight Alliance v. Board of Education of Boyd County, 258 F. Supp.2d 667 (E.D. Ky. 2003).

Burlington Industries, Inc. v. Ellerth, 118 S.Ct. 2257 (1998).

Chase, A. (2001) Violent reaction: What do teen killers have in common? *In these times,* quoted in *Bullying in schools: Harassment puts gay youth at risk.* Alexandria, VA, National Mental Health Association. Retrieved November 1, 2005, from www .nmha.org/pbedu/backtoschool/bullyingGayYouth.cfm

Davis v. Monroe County Board of Education, 119 S.Ct. 1661, 1673 (1999).

Faragher v. City of Boca Raton, 118 S.Ct. 2275 (1998).

Flores v. Morgan Hill Unified School District, 324 F.3d 1130 (2003).

Franklin v. Gwinnett County School Board, 503 U.S. 60 (1992). (See also *Meritor Savings Bank.*)

Gay Lesbian, Straight Education Network National School Climate Survey. (2003). Retrieved from http://www.glsen.org

Gebser v. Lago Vista Independent School District, 118 S.Ct. 1989 (1998).

Harris v. Forklift Systems, 114 S.Ct. 367 (1993). (See also *Meritor Savings Bank.*)

Kosciw, J. G. (2004). *The 2003 National School Climate Study: The school-related experiences of our nation's lesbian, gay, bisexual and transgender youth.* New York: GLSEN.

Massachusetts Governor's Commission of Gay and Lesbian Youth. (1993). *Making schools safe for gay and lesbian youth.* Boston: Author.

Megan's Law, 42 U.S.C. 14071(e) (2000).

Meritor Savings Bank v. Vinson, 477 U.S. 57 (1986).

Nabozny v. Podlesny, 92 F.3d 446 (7th Cir. 1996).

National School Boards Association (NSBA). (2004). *Dealing with legal matters surrounding students' sexual orientation and gender identity.* Alexandria, VA: Author.

Office for Civil Rights, Department of Education. (2000). *Revised sexual harassment guidance: Harassment of students by school employees, other students or third parties.* 65 Federal Register 213, 66091–66114.

Oncale v. Sundowner Offshore Services, Inc., 118 S.Ct. 998 (1998).

Protection of Pupil Rights Amendment (PPRA), 20 U.S.C. § 1232h (2004).

Schimmel, D. (2000). When schools are liable for peer harassment: An analysis of *Davis v. Monroe. Education Law Report* 141, p. 437.

Shoop, R. (2004). *Exploitation of students: How to spot it and stop it.* Thousand Oaks, CA: Corwin.

Sypniewski v. Warren Hills Regional Board of Education, 307 F.3d 243 (3d Cir. 2002).

Tinker v. Des Moines Independent Community School District, 393 U.S. 503, 508–509 (1969).

Title VII of the Civil Rights Act of 1964 (42 U.S.C. §§ 2000e et seq.)

Title IX of Education Amendments of 1972 (20 U.S.C.S. §§ 1681–1688).

Uggen, C. (2004). Males, adolescents are increasingly victims of sexual harassment. *Science of Mental Health,* April.

Walker, T. (2002). School's out. *Teaching Tolerance,* Spring.

Westside Community Schools v. Mergens, 496 U.S. 226 (88-1597) (1990).

State-Created Danger and Deliberate Indifference

W hile all acts that result in injury to a potential plaintiff generally fit into the category of negligence, the difference with state-created danger is its application under the Fourteenth Amendment and Section 1983. In this current chapter, we look at a new approach to holding school officials responsible when they knew of impending danger, were recklessly indifferent to the danger, and through the authority vested in them by the state, knowingly and affirmatively created the opportunity for the plaintiff's injury to occur—an injury that would not otherwise have occurred.

FOCUS POINT: School District Liability at the Federal Civil Level, Based on the Fourteenth Amendment's Due Process Clause and Section 1983 of Chapter 42 of the United States Code

Section 1 of the Fourteenth Amendment to the U.S. Constitution provides that "no state shall deprive any person of life, liberty, or property without due process of law." This due process clause offers constitutional safeguards to persons affected by governmental (including public schools) actions or decisions. Both procedural and substantive due process must be satisfied for a government action affecting life, liberty, or property to be constitutional.

Procedural due process generally specifies how governmental actions are to be applied and requires that specific safeguards be satisfied before a governmental action affecting life, liberty, or property can take place. In contrast, substantive due process, generally defined, is a protection requiring such governmental actions to be fair and reasonable in content as well as application. When a governmental action is both unfair or unreasonable and damaging to life, liberty, or property, it is said to violate substantive due process.

In school-based cases, plaintiffs' claims typically center on school districts' failures to take steps that would have prevented dangerous situations that, as a result, had adverse impacts on people's Fourteenth Amendment rights. Plaintiffs typically claim that they have an affirmative right to governmental protection from danger under the due process clause. Courts have recognized such an affirmative right where a "special relationship" exists between a state and the individual or where a "state-created danger" exists (*Deshaney v. Winnebago County Department of Social Services*, 1989).

As an example, the Eighth Circuit Court recognized two distinct situations in which they believe the state owes an affirmative obligation to protect its citizens. They noted that the due process clause imposes a duty on "state actors" to protect and care for citizens (a) "in custodial and other settings in which the state has limited the individuals' ability to care for themselves" and (b) "when the state affirmatively places a particular individual in a position of danger the individual otherwise would not have faced." As early as 1988, they stated in *Wells v. Walker* that "state actors have an affirmative duty to protect citizens in situations of danger creation." In 1996, in *Doe v. Wright*, they reaffirmed their 1988 statement, noting that "[t]his court has held that the due process clause imposes a duty on state actors to protect citizens . . . when the state actor creates the danger."

Plaintiffs seeking to file their complaints in a federal, rather than a state, court often allege, in addition to their claim of a violation under the Fourteenth Amendment, that the school district violated their rights under Section 1983 of Chapter 42 of the United States Code which states:

Every person who, under the color of any statute, ordinance, regulation, custom, or usage, of any State . . . subjects, or causes to be subjected, any citizen of the United States or other person within the jurisdiction thereof to the deprivation of any right, privileges, or immunities secured by the Constitution and laws, shall be liable to the party injured in an action at law, suit in equity, or other proper proceeding for redress.

This clause, commonly referred to as Section 1983, has had a huge impact on the federal court system. Included in that impact are cases that have a direct bearing on public education. Vodak (1999) noted, for example, "mistreatment of school-children, deliberate indifference to medical needs, and the seizure of property without advance notice or sufficient opportunity to be heard." Courts have held school employees to be proper "persons" subject to suit under

Section 1983 (*B.M.H. v. School Board of the City of Chesapeake*, 1993). The Supreme Court stated that "acting under the color of state law" traditionally requires that a defendant exercised power possessed by virtue of state law and made possible only because the wrongdoer is clothed with the authority of state law" (*West v. Atkins*, 1988).

While litigation based on federal violations under Section 1983 is not new, in 1989 the U.S. Supreme Court issued a decision in *Deshaney v. Winnebago County Department of Social Services*, and in one sentence of the language (dicta) of its overall opinion, generated the theory of state-created danger. The Court stated: "While the state may have been aware of the dangers that Joshua faced in the free world, it played no part in their creation, nor did it do anything to render him any more vulnerable to them." While the Court in the *Deshaney* case found no liability, other courts have taken this language and "turned it on its head to create a new theory of liability" (Levin, 2000). Since the *Deshaney* case, many federal courts have grappled with this new theory of liability, its application, and the consequences of using the due process clause of the Constitution as a conduit for state liability.

In 1996, the Third Circuit Court, in *Mark v. Borough of Hatboro*, adopted the theory of state-created danger and developed a four-part test to determine whether a claim under this theory has validity. Plaintiffs alleging state-created danger must demonstrate that the following four elements exist within a cause of action:

1. The harm to the plaintiff was ultimately foreseeable and fairly direct.

2. The state acted in willful disregard for the safety of the plaintiff.

3. There existed some relationship between the state and the plaintiff.

4. The state used their authority to create an opportunity that otherwise would not have existed for the third party's crime to occur.

Other courts have summarily added to this list of elements by including dicta that incorporate such fundamentals as a showing by the defendants of deliberate indifference to the rights of the plaintiff(s) by the conscious or reckless disregard of the consequences of their acts or omissions. For example, in *Huffman v. County of Los Angeles* (1998), the Ninth Circuit Court noted that "the danger-creation plaintiff must demonstrate, at the very least, that the state acted affirmatively and with deliberate indifference in creating a foreseeable danger to the plaintiff, leading to the deprivation of the plaintiff's constitutional rights [under the Fourteenth Amendment]."

The key to state-created danger cases lies in the defendants' culpable knowledge and conduct in affirmatively placing the plaintiffs in a position of danger, effectively stripping the plaintiffs of their ability to defend themselves, or cutting off potential sources of aid. In other words, to be held liable, the environment created by the defendants must be dangerous; they must know that it is dangerous; and they must have used their authority to create an opportunity that would not otherwise have existed in which the plaintiff suffered harm. Beyond this prevailing concern, the elements, as more simply described in

Johnson v. Dallas Independent School District (1994) and again in *Armijo v. Wagon Mound Public Schools* (1998), are as follows:

- Plaintiff was a member of a limited and specifically definable group.
- The defendant's conduct put the plaintiff at substantial risk of serious, immediate, and proximate harm.
- The risk was obvious or known.
- The defendant acted recklessly in conscious disregard of that risk.
- Such conduct when viewed in total is "conscience shocking." In *Hayes v. Faulkner County, Arkansas* (2004), for example, the Eighth Circuit Court noted, in a prison-related case, that "[d]eliberate indifference to prisoner welfare [substitute "a student's welfare"] may sufficiently *shock the conscience* to amount to a substantive due process violation" (emphasis added).

While the theory of state-created danger is unresolved and still being contested in federal courts across the United States, it is wise for educators to be aware of this particular premise of negligence and add this knowledge to their practice of risk management. Some examples provide a better idea of how all of the above might fit into a school environment. The first example is a *real* case that has been adjudicated, the second is strictly *hypothetical*.

In *Armijo*, a special education student with known suicidal tendencies was suspended from school and driven home, without parental permission or notification, to an empty house with accessible guns, and fatally shot himself. In this case, the court (10th Circuit) found that the school's conduct in suspending the student, taking him home and leaving him alone with their knowledge of his fragile mental state, had increased the risk of harm to the student. In taking such actions, the school officials acted in conscious disregard for the student's safety, and their conduct could be viewed as conscience shocking.

In a *hypothetical* case, Billy, a regular education fifth-grade student, was repeatedly sexually abused by his classroom teacher (male) during school time, in the classroom and on school premises. The principal had been contacted by Billy's mother concerning some unusual discipline problems she was having with Billy at home, including his not wanting to come to school. Furthermore, other teachers in the school had noticed peculiar behavior on the part of the teacher in question and had advised the principal of such. In spite of this information, the principal decided to do only a superficial investigation, "a CYA look-see," his teachers would later state in testimony.

The principal's investigation, as cursory as it might have been and limited to gathering personal verbal observations from other faculty members, did, however, uncover the following information: the teacher in question always had his door and outside windows completely covered with student artwork, the door to the classroom was always locked during class, and his desk was placed in an position where it couldn't be seen if the classroom door was open. In addition, many teachers had observed that quite often he would have individual male students sit on his lap during class, as well as before and after school, and that he would often keep Billy past the late bus and drive him home.

As a result of his investigation, the principal concluded that what he had been told by the parent and other teachers was very possibly true, and that under the circumstances there might even be some sexual abuse of students, especially Billy. However, instead of confronting the teacher directly or questioning students in his class, he simply posted the following note over teachers' mailboxes in the main office. The handwritten bold-lettered note, signed by the principal, said

> Attention __All__ Teachers—Just a reminder.
>
> At all costs, __DO NOT__ touch a student
>
> in any manner—friendly or otherwise,
>
> unless it is to protect the student from harm!

The principal determined that he had resolved the issue by posting a general warning to teachers and made no other effort to protect students from this particular teacher or remove the teacher from the classroom.

About six months after the principal's "investigation," Billy became incorrigible at home and at school and suffered an emotional breakdown. He was institutionalized for a time and placed under the care of a psychiatrist. During one of his sessions with the psychiatrist, he talked about his relationship with his teacher both at school and away from school. He called them "camping trips." As a result, the psychiatrist notified social services and the police department. The teacher was subsequently arrested and, as a result of evidence found in his apartment, charged with a number of counts of child sexual abuse of Billy and other students. Evidence uncovered by the police and social workers quickly confirmed that the teacher's abusive sexual relationship with Billy and others started at school, and much of the sexual interaction between Billy and others and the teacher took place at school or on the school premises.

As a result, Billy's parents filed a civil suit against the school district and named the teacher and principal as primary defendants and included as secondary defendants the superintendent of schools and the board of education. Their attorney, in examining the circumstances of the case, determined that the case fit the profile of "state-created danger" and "deliberate indifference" and could be filed and tried in a federal court. In coming to this conclusion, the plaintiff's attorney examined all the facts in the case and weighed them for validity against the four-part test in *Mark v. Borough of Hatboro* (1995). In addition, the plaintiff's attorney also examined the facts of the case under the five-part test as outlined in *Johnson v. Dallas Independent School District* (1994) and in *Armijo*. The plaintiff's attorney also examined the due process issues in *Hayes v. Faulkner County, Arkansas* (2004). While the plaintiff's attorney knew the difficulties inherent in filing and defending such a case at the federal level, she felt that her chances of success were good.

Before we provide examples of management cues and risk management guidelines, we note that as you read the next chapter (Chapter 15), it might seem to you that all negligent acts committed or caused by school personnel could fit under the conceptual tenets of state-created danger outlined in this chapter. While all acts that result in injury to a potential plaintiff generally fit into the category of negligence, the difference with state-created danger is its application under the Fourteenth Amendment and Section 1983. In the current chapter, school officials *knew* of impending danger, were *recklessly indifferent* to the danger, and through the authority vested in them by the state, *knowingly and affirmatively created* the opportunity for the plaintiff's injury to occur—an injury that would not otherwise have occurred.

Example of a Management Cue

- Signs or reports of unusual teacher behavior patterns, such as, but not limited to:
  - Disciplinary action that includes confining students in closets, storage areas, and so on or otherwise exceeds the bounds of common sense and safety
  - Unusual punishment patterns that place students in vulnerable positions, either physical or emotional
  - Locking classroom doors during class sessions
  - Covering classroom windows or other actions that obscure full view in and of the classroom environment
  - Fraternization with students after school hours, without parental knowledge and consent
  - Unusual displays of temper or drastic mood swings
  - Unusual classroom and/or homework assignments that don't relate directly to the curriculum
  - Signs of overt gender discrimination in curricular or extracurricular activities, including recess
  - Unusual behavior exhibited by students of a particular class or teacher, particularly anxiety, fear, anger, withdrawal, and so on
  - Reports from parents of unusual student behavior at home that seems to be school related

Suggested Risk Management Guidelines

- Follow up on any reports of potential trouble and thoroughly investigate and document your findings regarding any incidents that might affect students' health, safety, or welfare. Don't hesitate to share (report) your findings to appropriate superiors and/or agencies.

- Don't hesitate to investigate rumors and/or innuendo. We're not suggesting you become a "witch hunter," but rather that you keep yourself fully informed about everything that is going on regarding relationships between students, faculty, staff, administrators, and other support personnel. This is a difficult task, but a prudent step in ensuring the overall safety of children entrusted to your care.

CHAPTER RESOURCES

Armijo v. Wagon Mound Public Schools, 159 F. 3d 1253, 1263 (10th Cir. 1998).

B.M.H. v. School Board of the City of Chesapeake, 833 F. Supp. 560, 564 n.6 (E.D. Va. 1993).

Deshaney v. Winnebago County Department of Social Services, 489 U.S 189 (1989).

Doe v. Wright, 82 F.3d 265, 268 (8th Cir. 1996).

Hayes v. Faulkner County, Arkansas, 2004 WL 2414160 (8th Cir. 2004).

Huffman v. County of Los Angeles, 147 F.3d 1054 (9th Cir. 1998).

Johnson v. Dallas Independent School District, 38 F.3d 198, 201 (5th Cir. 1994).

Levin, M. L. (2000). It's the law. *PSBA Bulletin,* February, pp. 33–40.

Mark v. Borough of Hatboro, 51 EM 1137 (3rd Cir. 1995).

Vodak, K. R. (1999). *A plainly obvious need for new-fashioned municipal liability.* 48 DePaul L. Rev., 785, 790.

Wells v. Walker, 852 F.2d 368 (8th Cir. 1988).

West v. Atkins, 487 U.S. 42, 49 (1988) (quoting *United States v. Classic,* 313 U.S. 299, 326, 1941).

15

The Principal's Tort Liability for Negligence as Applied to Expected Duty and Standards of Care

The obligation of the school to provide a safe place can hardly be overemphasized. It is a legal principle with strong and widely spread roots in the ethics of our society. Adults are responsible for the care and protection of children; teachers and administrators are responsible for the care and protection of students. The courts demand a high standard of performance from educators in the area of student welfare. They also expect educators to possess a high standard of reasonable-person traits.

Changes in certain legal doctrines have modified the special status accorded to schools. For example, the doctrine of governmental immunity—protecting the public school from legal liability—has been judicially or legislatively abrogated in many states. Educators' duty has been reduced by statutes that provide

AUTHORS' NOTE: Cases cited throughout this chapter have been selected on a precedent-setting or best-example basis regardless of jurisdiction or date of adjudication. (See Introduction for more information.)

qualified immunity for employees or denote liability only for injuries resulting from willful or wanton misconduct; however, schools are still frequently given the *same* status and held, by the courts, to the *same* duty as any individual or corporation providing goods or services. *The problem facing school districts and, ultimately, teachers and principals is not whether they are immune from lawsuits, but whether they can develop solutions to minimize their legal liability.*

Tort liability laws are the primary source for the definition of the educator's basic responsibilities for duty and standard of care. Without an adequate knowledge of liability, educators cannot have a clear understanding of their status under the law. Although the major emphasis is on *student* welfare in this chapter, a principal's responsibility *not* to be negligent also pertains to the welfare of faculty, staff, parents, and visitors. The basic concepts are the same. The sections in this chapter are restricted to the tort liability of educators for negligence—that is, the personal liability for injury to students or others for which school personnel may be held accountable under the law.

SECTION A: THE LAW OF TORTS AND THE CONCEPT OF NEGLIGENCE

The law of torts is difficult to define and difficult to understand. Because tort law is essentially the result of judicial decisions—case or common law rather than statutory or legislative law—the study of torts can be inconclusive in answering specific inquiries. Court decisions are primarily of two sorts: (1) interpretation of constitutional and statutory law and (2) application of common-law principles. These principles are applied when a particular set of circumstances has not been legislated on and the rights of the parties must be decided by the court on general principles handed down over the years.

❚ FOCUS POINT: The Law of Torts

A *tort* is defined as an actionable wrong against the person, property, or reputation of another, exclusive of a breach of contract, which the law will recognize and set right. Torts are historically classified into three categories:

1. The direct invasion of someone's legal right (e.g., invasion of privacy)

2. The breach of some public duty that causes some damage to an individual (e.g., denial of constitutional rights)

3. The violation of some private obligation that causes some damage to an individual (e.g., negligence)

The underlying concept of torts involves the relationship between individuals. Under our system of law, *individuals have the right to be free from bodily injury whether intentionally or carelessly caused by others.* However, societal changes have caused the courts to define new legal responsibilities between individuals with each litigated verdict. Negligence is the main cause of tort liability suits filed against educators, and due to their more direct contact with students, teachers and principals are the class of school employees most likely to have suit brought against them. Judgments in negligence suits can be financially and emotionally crippling.

Tortious actions speak directly to the professional educator through the principle of *in loco parentis*. Although the *in loco parentis* doctrine is continuously challenged, the current interpretation assigns definite responsibility to the school for the welfare of each student it serves in the absence of the student's parent or guardian. With this assignment, society legally assumes that, during the time the student is away from home, the student's interests, welfare, and safety are directed by responsible adults trained as teachers and administrators. Because elementary and most secondary students are legally required by law to attend school, courts usually review very carefully any alleged breach of normally expected *duty and standard of care* by educators. Failure to meet such duty and standard of care is negligent, and the courts may find the educator guilty of a tort.

Within the framework of the tort of negligence, this chapter examines the standards and relationships inherent in the following areas: duty and standards of care, proper instruction, proper supervision, proper maintenance, field trips, postinjury treatment, athletic liability, and spectator safety. Both the framework of negligence and the standards and relationships inherent within this framework are examined under the following *concepts*, described and defined as follows:

The Concept of a Reasonable and Prudent Person: A reasonable and prudent person, in the eye of the court, is a person who

- Has physical capabilities comparable to the defendant's
- Is of normal intelligence, perception, and memory
- Has a minimal level of experience, and
- Possesses any superior skills that the defendant possesses or presents herself or himself as possessing

School administrators and teachers hold college degrees that denote possession of specialized skills and superior knowledge of the teaching and learning process, methods of instruction, and the education environment, and they present themselves to the community as possessing such superior knowledge and skills. School administrators and teachers are, therefore, held to a higher standard of care when fulfilling their professional roles than the average citizen would be in a similar circumstance.

To resolve the question of reasonable standard of care, courts use the model of a reasonable and prudent person. This hypothetical ideal of human behavior embodies the community's ideals and possesses all the special skills and abilities of the defendant. Court dicta provide this *generic* description:

> The defendant is not to be identified with any ordinary individual who might occasionally do unreasonable things; he or she is a prudent and careful person who is always up to standard. It is not proper to identify

him or her with any member of the jury who is to apply the standard; he or she is rather a personification of a community ideal of reasonable behavior, determined by the jury's social judgment.

This abstract being, conceived in the law's imagination, performs under the question of foreseeability.

The Concept of Foreseeability: Foreseeability is the "degree to which the defendant could have or should have reasonably been able to anticipate the risk of injury or harm to the plaintiff that might result from the action or inaction" (Alexander & Alexander, 2002, p. 329). Foreseeability regarding the risks inherent in an education setting is greater for educators, because of their superior knowledge, special skills, and professional experience in working in an education environment, than it would be for the average citizen, who is not professionally trained and experienced as an educator. *If the educator could have or should have foreseen or anticipated an accident, the failure to do so may be ruled as negligence.*

The concept of foreseeability expects the educator to perform as a reasonably prudent person of similar training and circumstances should perform. This degree of care is based on the standard equivalent of the age, training, maturity, and experience, as well as any other related characteristics of the educator. The law does not require the educator to be able to see everything that might appear in the immediate future, and the courts do not require the educator to completely ensure the safety of students. Courts do, however, expect educators to act in a reasonable and prudent manner. If the ordinary exercise of prudence and foresight could have prevented an accident, courts have ruled educators to be negligent when they have not avoided a foreseeable danger to students, personnel, and patrons.

The Concept of Standard of Care: The standard of care is the degree of care necessary to protect students from *foreseeable* risk of injury or harm, based on the particular circumstances and the age and mental and physical capabilities of the students. The standard of care required is higher when the students are young and immature. The standard of care required is also higher when the students have diminished mental, learning, or physical abilities. The illustration in Figure 15.1 demonstrates the relationship between duty and standard of care and the age of the student.

The Concept of the Age of Plaintiffs: The *Rule of Seven* is often used to determine the liability for negligence. This legal doctrine requires the court to examine a student's age in determining negligence. Children are expected to exercise a degree of care for their own safety in proportion to their age, capacity, experience, and intelligence. Historically, courts have held that children from birth to age seven cannot be considered negligent under the law. Such children do not realize or understand the degree of care that must be exercised to prevent injury to themselves. Teenagers, on the other hand, are expected to have developed a general understanding of the care required for their own safety. Again, the illustration in Figure 15.1 demonstrates the relationship between duty and standard of care and the age of the student.

Figure 15.1

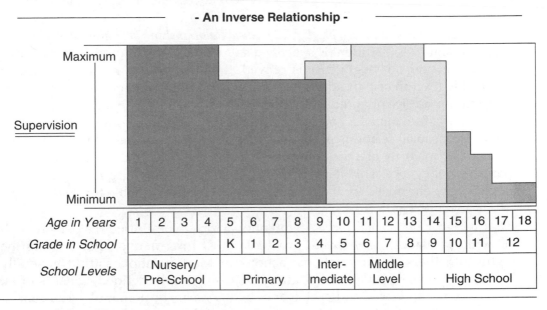

The School's Duty and Standard of Care
as Related to Student Age*

- An Inverse Relationship -

Age in Years	1	2	3	4	5	6	7	8	9	10	11	12	13	14	15	16	17	18
Grade in School					K	1	2	3	4	5	6	7	8	9	10	11	12	
School Levels	Nursery/ Pre-School				Primary				Inter-mediate		Middle Level			High School				

Students with disabilities require a higher degree of duty and standard of care at all ages and school levels.

The courts routinely differentiate the required degree of duty and standard of care at only two age levels - Ages 1 to 14 and Ages 15 to 18.

The authors believe that the required degree of duty and standard of care decreases during the elementary school years, that the onset of puberty and adolescence may require a return to maximum levels of duty and standard of care during the middle school years, and that the required level decreases progressively for senior high school students.

Note: The courts, to date, have held that children under the age of 7 may not be held responsible for their own negligence.

SOURCE: Shoop, R. J., & Dunklee, D. R. (1992). *School Law for the Principal: A Handbook for Practitioners*, p. 157. Needham Heights, MA: Allyn & Bacon.

The Concept of an Unavoidable Accident: An unavoidable accident is defined as an event that occurs without fault, carelessness, or omission on the part of the individual involved. While expecting educators to display a high level of care in the performance of their duties, the courts recognize that accidents happen when no negligence has occurred.

The Concept of Assumption of Risk: A common legal defense against negligence is based on the general legal theory of assumption of risk (no harm is done to one who consents). Although the consent may be expressed or implied, the legal theory is based on one's ability to understand and appreciate the dangers inherent in the activity. Even though the student voluntarily placed herself or himself in a position of danger, the defense must show that the student understood the danger, had foresight in regard to the consequences, and accepted the danger.

The Concepts of Contributory Negligence/Causal Relationship/Comparative Negligence: When an injury to a student is sustained as a result of the injured student's own negligence, and this negligence is proved, then the student has contributed to her or his own injury. In addition, when a student disregards the instruction, warning, or advice of an educator, the student can be held liable for her or his own injury. To counter a charge of contributory negligence, the student must establish a causal relationship between the negligence of the educator and the injury. The majority of states permit some recovery under the concept of comparative negligence. This legal doctrine prorates the damages to the degree of negligence determined by the court for each party found liable for negligence.

The Concept of Intentional Torts: An intentional tort is committed if a person, with or without malice, *intentionally* proceeds to act in a manner that impairs the rights of others. Intentional tort actions in the education setting generally involve charges of assault and battery. Assault, simply defined, consists of an overt attempt to place another in fear of bodily harm; no actual physical contact need take place. However, when an assault results in physical injury to a person, then battery has been committed.

SECTION B: THE CONCEPT OF NEGLIGENCE AND ITS APPLICATION TO DUTY AND STANDARDS OF CARE

Negligence *is a word used commonly to cover a variety of behaviors, actions, and inactions. However, in the legal world, the term is more narrowly defined as follows: the failure to take reasonable care to avoid commissions (actions) or omissions (inactions) that one can reasonably foresee would be likely to injure another. Stated a bit differently, negligence is the failure to exercise the degree or standard of care for the safety or well-being of others that a reasonable and prudent person would exercise under similar circumstances.*

The school and the personnel it employs owe a legal *duty* to protect students, employees, and visitors from unreasonable risks of injury. The duty to meet a particular standard of care stems from two primary sources:

1. *The duty may be inherent in the situation or required by statute.* Nearly every situation in which an educator engages has an inherent standard of care arising from it. These duties derive from the educator acting *in loco parentis*, acting as a professional, or acting as the administrator. Generally speaking, the school will

owe a duty of ordinary care to all personnel, children, and adults involved in educational pursuits, academic or otherwise, if sponsored under the school's authority. This standard is based on an objective test consisting of the standard of conduct demanded under the circumstances, that is, "the reasonably prudent person." The ordinary care standard takes into consideration the risk factor that may be apparent and the circumstances of the situation. The defendant's capacity—based on age, intelligence, knowledge, skill, and so forth—to handle those circumstances is also considered in certain cases.

2. *An educator may voluntarily assume a duty.* A person who does not have a legal duty to meet a particular standard of care may incur one by voluntarily creating a relationship with someone else.

❙ FOCUS POINT: The Concept of Negligence

Negligence has been defined as conduct that falls below the standard established by law for the protection of others against unreasonable risk or harm. Four elements must exist to sustain a valid claim of negligence:

1. *There must have been a duty to protect.* Duty is an obligation that derives from a special relationship between the parties involved (teacher and student, principal and teacher, principal and student, and other parties such as parents, visitors, et al.).

2. *A failure to exercise a standard of care must have occurred.* A failure to exercise a standard of care is determined by measuring the actual conduct against the conduct of a reasonable person. The standard of care is relative to the need and to the occasion. What is proper under one circumstance may be negligent under another.

3. *The conduct must have been the proximate cause of the damage.*

4. *An actual loss (injury of some kind) must result.*

There is a duty of due care that the law recognizes one person owes to another. It requires a certain standard of conduct for the protection of others against unreasonable risks. One has a legal duty to act as an ordinary, prudent, reasonable person in the circumstances. Such duty can be specified by statute or as a matter of common law. The duty and standard of care imposed on school districts demand that the responsibility for protecting the safety of students and employees be accepted and fulfilled. In our litigious society, principals need to recognize their potential liability for negligence.

Negligence may occur in one of three ways: nonfeasance, misfeasance, or malfeasance:

1. *Nonfeasance* is the failure to act when there is a *duty* to act. Nonfeasance is an act of *omission*, such as passive inaction, by which an injury occurs due to the lack of protection the law expects of a reasonable individual. In order for nonfeasance to result in liability for negligence, a duty to take positive action or to perform a specific act must be established. This duty may be established by a legal statute or by the relationship (for example, principal, teacher, student) between the parties involved. An example of nonfeasance may be found in *Gammon v. Edwardsville* (1980), in which an eighth-grade girl complained to the school guidance counselor regarding her fear of being physically harmed, based on verbal threats by another student. The other student was summoned to the counselor's office, where she was told that fighting would not be tolerated and would result in suspension. Later, in the school yard, the other student struck the complaining girl in the eye with her fist, causing a serious injury. The injured student claimed that the school's response to a given and known threat of violence on school premises was inadequate. The court ruled in favor of the injured girl.

2. *Misfeasance* is acting in an improper manner. Misfeasance is the taking of an improper action when there is a *duty* to act, and may be either an act of *omission*, or an act of *commission*. An act of *omission* is illustrated by *Libby v. West Coast Rock Co., Inc.* (1975), in which a student fell into a ditch while attempting to catch a pass in a game of football played during the school's lunch period. The principal was aware of the ditch on the school's property but had made minimal attempts to warn students and no attempt to fill the ditch. The student was injured and claimed that the school district, knowing of the hazard, did not take proper steps to protect him. The court ruled in favor of the student.

An act of *commission* can be found in *Magabgab v. Orleans Parish School Board* (1970), in which a football player passed out on the football field and was treated by school personnel for heat exhaustion instead of heat stroke. The student died as a result of the latter as well as from the amount of time that the supervisors took before contacting the parents or seeking emergency aid. The court ruled in favor of the parents of the student.

3. *Malfeasance* is acting, but guided by a bad motive. Malfeasance is an illegal act that should not be performed at all. It occurs when the individual acts *beyond the scope of duty.* A hypothetical case may illustrate the salient points best. Assume that a teacher administers corporal punishment to a student even though school district policy prohibits a teacher from administering such punishment. The student is injured as a result of the punishment and brings charges against the teacher and others. The court would likely rule for the student because the act was illegal under school district policy.

Consider the following facts:

- Educators have been found financially responsible for their professional actions when an injured student or adult proved, to the court's satisfaction, that some inappropriate action of the educator or school district led to the student's or adult's injury.

- Foreseeability of harm is a critical element in determining negligence in a given situation.
- Courts have been cognizant of the burdens placed on educators when ruling on their liability; however, these burdens have not relieved educators of the responsibility for their actions or inactions. Educators are responsible for any harmful consequences of their conduct.
- The appropriateness of an educator's conduct in a given situation is measured by whether a reasonably prudent educator, with the skill and training expected under the circumstances, would have acted in a similar fashion under similar conditions.
- The illustration in Figure 15.2 generally demonstrates the educator's risk of negligence in a school-related incident.

Examples of Management Cues

- An eight-year-old student is burned when his costume for a school play catches on fire from a lighted candle on his teacher's desk.
- A sixth-grade student is struck in the eye by a pencil eraser just prior to the start of class. The mishap is caused by a fellow student who is tapping his pencil against his desk, causing the eraser to separate and fly through the air.
- Twelve cheerleaders riding in a van owned and driven by one of the cheerleaders are injured in a collision. The accident occurs while they are "bannering" the homes of the school's football team in anticipation of the season's first game. The incident takes place during the summer when school is not in session.
- A third-grade student known for his propensity to horse around is given a pass to go to the restroom. The 8-inch plywood pass, made by the teacher, has a 20-inch nylon cord attached, and students often wear the pass around their necks as they go to the restroom. The third-grade student is discovered hanging from a stall brace with the pass around his neck. The student suffers irreversible brain damage. Earlier, the student had been joking and pretending to do this with other students in the bathroom.
- A junior high football coach, angry because one of his players misses a tackle, yells at the player, grabs his face mask, and throws the player to the ground, injuring the student's arm.

Suggested Risk Management Guidelines

- Ask the following four questions in any situation in which a person claims to have suffered an injury:

1. *Did the defendant have a duty to the plaintiff?*

   The defendant must have a duty to the plaintiff. Plaintiffs, in actions addressing the school setting, usually have little difficulty in proving that the defendant teacher or principal owes the student a duty.

Figure 15.2

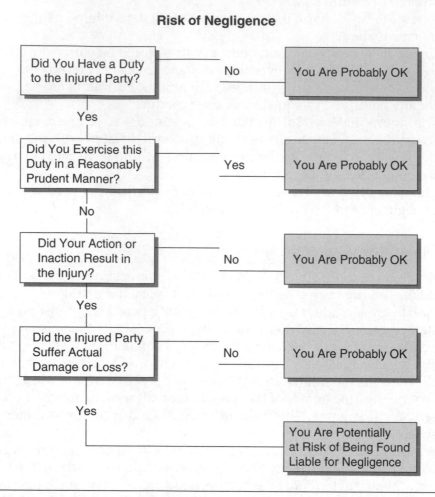

Risk of Negligence

SOURCE: Shoop, R. J., & Dunklee, D. R. (1992). *School Law for the Principal: A Handbook for Practitioners*, p. 157. Needham Heights, MA: Allyn & Bacon.

2. *Did the defendant exercise a reasonable standard of care in her or his actions?*

The defendant must have failed to exercise a reasonable standard of care in her or his actions. This area is usually the major point of contention, that is, whether or not the educator involved exercised a reasonable standard of care.

3. *Were the defendant's actions or inactions the proximate cause of injury to the plaintiff?*

The defendant's actions must be the proximate (direct) cause of the injury to the plaintiff. Even in situations in which a recognized duty is breached by the failure to exercise a proper standard of care, liability will not normally be assessed if there is not a causal connection between the actions of school personnel and the injury.

4. Did the plaintiff suffer an actual injury?

The plaintiff must prove that she or he suffered an actual injury. Actual injury and proximate cause are usually a matter of fact. For liability to be assessed under proximate cause, negligent conduct of school personnel must be the proximate or legal cause of the injury.

FOCUS POINT: The Concept of Duty and Standard of Care

There are two basic types of duty. The first type exists when the duty is inherent in the situation. *This includes nearly every situation in which an educator has the responsibility to supervise a student.* The second type of duty exists when a person voluntarily assumes or creates a relationship in which no previous relationship existed. An assumed duty exists when an educator acts in a way that leads parents or students to reasonably assume that a supervisory relationship exists.

For example, imagine a situation in which children regularly gather on school grounds long before the start of the school day. Parents have gotten into the habit of dropping their kids off in front of the school even though the building will not be open for another hour or so. Although the principal disapproves of this practice, the principal ignores it, and although aware of the need for supervision, does not provide any. The principal continues to remind parents of the fact that no one is available at the school to provide supervision and that their practice of dropping children off so early in the morning is dangerous. Such a warning appears in the school's back-to-school summer letter as well as in other principal-parent newsletters throughout the school year. If the principal acquiesces, however, and occasionally supervises the assembled group, then, if an injury occurs, the court might rule that the principal had *assumed* the duty of supervision by allowing the students to gather, and that if proper supervision had been provided, the injury might have been prevented. The court could hold the principal and school district liable for any damages.

Liability results most often when school personnel fail to meet that reasonable standard of care (breach of duty) while instructing, supplying equipment to, and supervising students. Breach of duty is determined, in part, based on the nature of the activity for which the educator is held responsible. Various school activities require different levels (standards) of care and duty. Questions normally posed by courts regarding an alleged breach of duty and standard of care are

- Whether the conduct of school personnel met the *reasonable person* standard required in a given situation
- Whether school personnel should have *foreseen* possible injury

The fact that a student is injured in a particular situation does not necessarily imply that a breach of duty has occurred. School personnel are not ensurers against all possible harm. They are, however, expected to take reasonable steps, based on inherent duty to students, to prevent harm that is reasonably foreseeable. Failure to act in this instance would constitute a breach of duty.

An examination and review of *selected* litigation related to the area of duty and standard of care provide the basis for the following summary statements:

- Educators have been found financially responsible for their professional actions when an injured student or adult proved, to the court's satisfaction, that some inappropriate action of the educator or school district led to the student's or adult's injury.
- Foreseeability of harm is a critical element in determining negligence in a given situation. Educators have been held liable for accidents that occur during their absence from the classroom or activity area if it could be anticipated that the educator's presence in the room or area would have prevented the accident.
- Educators have been found accountable for their failure to take into consideration a student's special needs or limitations, abilities, age, and preexisting medical conditions when making instructional or supervisory decisions.
- Courts have been cognizant of the burdens placed on educators when ruling on their liability; however, these burdens have not relieved educators of the responsibility for their actions or inactions. Educators are responsible for any harmful consequences of their conduct.
- The appropriateness of an educator's conduct in a given situation is measured by whether a reasonably prudent educator, with the skill and training expected under the circumstances, would have acted in a similar fashion under similar conditions.
- Educators have been found liable for their selection, maintenance, and supervision of the use of instructional equipment if the educator's action in this regard was shown to be based on poor judgment not expected of a professional educator.
- Educators have been upheld by the courts for their attempts to provide postinjury first aid to injured students; however, the courts have not afforded protection for educators who attempted to deliver medical therapy or treatment that exceeded or fell short of rudimentary first-aid procedures.
- Educators have been found accountable on field trips for the same duty and standard of care expected within the confines of the school site.
- Educators have not been found accountable for their instruction or supervision when the student was shown to have had adequate knowledge to complete the task assigned or the student knowingly assumed the risk inherent in the activity.
- Educators can be held liable for assault and battery if they use *excessive* physical force with students.

Examples of Management Cues

- A student's wrist "pops out of joint" during physical education class. The physical education (P.E.) instructor is able to manipulate the wrist until it pops back in place. When asked how he learned to do that, the P.E. instructor states that "that's what my old coach used to do to my wrist . . . never missed a game."
- The high school madrigal singers have three programs scheduled at different events across the city. All events have been approved as field trips on that date, and students are allowed to provide their own transportation. After the first performance at 10 a.m., the choir director tells the group to get lunch on their own and to meet him at the next site at 1 p.m. Three of the singers drink beer with their lunch. They are seen by a board of education member, who calls the superintendent.
- A middle school teacher has been trained in the martial arts. During lunch period, two boys get into a fight. When the teacher orders them to stop and they continue, she steps between the combatants. When one of the boys throws a punch at her, she flips him in the air and propels him head first into a locker door. The boy requires 18 stitches to close the wound to his scalp.
- Because of pressure from his students, the woodworking teacher decides not to administer the written examination required of students to work with the shop's new turbo planer. Instead, he administers a verbal question-and-answer session. Three weeks later, a student is severely injured while using the machine.
- A kindergarten teacher notices that one of the legs on the table in the art area of her classroom has a loose leg. She immediately wraps the leg to the table with gray utility tape and turns in a work order for repairs. Later in the day, the table collapses and hits a student in the knee.

Suggested Risk Management Guidelines

- Establish professional standards that take the *very basic meaning of duty and standards of care* (i.e., application to all citizens) and apply it specifically to the education arena.
- Provide guidelines that can be used both in *establishing* sound practices in the area of duty and standard of care and as definitive standards in *measuring* duty and standard of care of educators in a school setting. Such guidelines should be foundational but considered critically important, enforced, inserviced, and monitored for compliance and should serve as the *underlying structure* for any other suggested guidelines that might appear under Focus Points in subsequent sections of this chapter.
- In other words, any and all decision-making guidelines regarding duty and standard of care should be built on the following set of *affirmative* duties:

1. Duty of Building Administrator (Principal, Headmaster, Headmistress) to Students and Parents (at a minimum):

   • Ensure compliance with applicable federal, state, and local laws and regulations; enforce established school policies, procedures, and rules; and establish additional rules, as necessary and appropriate in the particular education environment, to ensure the safety and well-being of students while under the care of the school.

   • Provide effective supervision of the education program (including the development, oversight, and evaluation of appropriate curricular, intracurricular, and extracurricular activities).

   • Promote the hiring of competent administrative, teaching, and support staff appropriately trained in specific disciplines.

   • Provide effective supervision of staff (including the appropriate delegation of authority, formalization and assignment of specific responsibilities, direction of daily work activities, and observation and evaluation of performance).

   • Manage the school's physical facilities and material and financial resources to ensure the maintenance of a safe and productive learning environment.

   • Develop and maintain communication channels and media that promote effective, two-way communication about school-related issues (including student progress) between administrators and parents, administrators and teachers, administrators and students, teachers and parents, and teachers and students.

2. Duty of Education Administrator (Associate or Assistant Principal, Dean, Supervisor, Department Chair, et al.) to Students and Parents (at a minimum):

   • Adhere to applicable federal, state, and local laws and regulations; adhere to and enforce established school policies, procedures, and rules in the performance of assigned duties and responsibilities; and recommend additional policies, procedures, and rules, as appropriate, within the scope of delegated authority.

   • Provide effective supervision of the instructional activities presented by staff members of programs within the scope of delegated authority.

   • Provide effective supervision of all staff members assigned to, or working with, programs within the scope of delegated authority.

   • Facilitate effective, two-way communication about school-related issues (including student progress) in programs within the scope of delegated authority, between administrators and parents, administrators and teachers, administrators and students, teachers and parents, and teachers and students.

3. Duty of Teacher to Students and Parents (at a minimum):

   • Adhere to applicable federal, state, and local laws and regulations; adhere to and enforce established school policies, procedures, and rules in the performance of assigned duties and responsibilities.

- Develop and present instructional activities that are appropriate to, and consistent with, the approved education program and specifically designed to increase students' knowledge; facilitate the development of learning skills, life skills, and appropriate social behavior; and prepare students to interact effectively in general society.
- Provide effective supervision of students participating in instructional activities that are within the scope of assigned responsibility to ensure students' safety and general well-being.
- Facilitate effective, two-way communication about school-related issues (including student progress) in programs within the scope of assigned responsibility, between administrators and parents, administrators and teachers, administrators and students, teachers and parents, and teachers and students.

SECTION C: THE CONCEPTS OF NEGLIGENCE, DUTY, AND STANDARDS OF CARE AND THEIR APPLICATION TO PROPER INSTRUCTION, PROPER SUPERVISION, PROPER MAINTENANCE, FIELD TRIPS, POSTINJURY TREATMENT, ATHLETIC LIABILITY, AND SPECTATOR SAFETY

The wide range of activities in which educators are regularly engaged with students and the public creates multiple areas of duty and standard of care. This section looks at the principal's duty and standard of care with regard to proper instruction—ensuring that students are adequately warned of dangers inherent in an activity.

- *Proper instruction—ensuring that students are adequately warned of dangers inherent in an activity*
- *Proper supervision—ensuring that an appropriate number of capable adults are providing an adequate level of oversight to protect students and others from foreseeable danger*
- *Proper maintenance—ensuring that equipment, facilities, and grounds are kept in proper repair and pose no foreseeable safety hazards to students and others*
- *Field trips—maintaining the same duty and standard of care that would exist if students were on the school premises*
- *Postinjury treatment—taking appropriate care of a student or other person who is injured on school grounds or while engaged in a school-sponsored event*
- *School athletics and spectator safety—ensuring that participants are properly selected, instructed, and supervised; that equipment and facilities are maintained and safe; that proper medical attention is available in the event of injury to participants or spectators*

The following Focus Points address each of these areas of potential liability.

FOCUS POINT: The Application of Negligence to Proper Instruction

Cases involving various aspects of instruction frequently come before the courts. The most common complaint is that the student did not receive adequate *instruction* (how to or how not to do something), and as a result of *inadequate instruction*, the activity caused physical harm to someone. The courts tend to favor those educators who have provided adequate instruction in the proper use of equipment and methods of safety and who have warned students of the dangerous nature of any activity in which injury might occur. Failure to do either—instruct or warn—could be cause for establishing liability for negligence.

Though not nearly as common, there have also been cases in which plaintiffs have claimed harm to the intellect—commonly referred to as *education malpractice*—as a result of negligence due to improper instruction.

Authorities agree that instruction involves the teaching of a particular skill as well as instilling in the student the proper behavior for individual and class safety. In *Laveck v. City of Janesville* (1973), the court stated:

> The teacher occupies a position in relation to his [*sic*] pupils comparable to that of a parent to children. He has a duty to instruct and warn pupils in his custody of any danger which he knows or in the exercise of ordinary care ought to know . . . and to instruct them in the methods which will protect them from these dangers. A failure to warn students of such danger or to [not] instruct them in the means of avoiding such danger is negligence.

Educators are expected to select activities appropriate to the student's ability to perform and understand and to take into consideration the student's size, age, skill, condition, or special needs. When an activity entails risks to students, it is not sufficient merely to inform or warn of risks; students must also understand and appreciate the risks. Appreciation is influenced by factors such as experience, mental ability, and the obviousness of the danger. For example, in *Savers v. Ranger* (1951), a 14-year-old boy, who broke his arm when he fell from an apparatus during a gymnastics class, alleged that the teacher had failed to provide adequate instruction and warning. The facts of the case were that the boy had been given instruction in the correct method of performing the stunt and warnings about the danger of doing the activity incorrectly. Furthermore, the boy had done the stunt several times and been corrected when it was not done properly. In ruling in favor of the teacher and the school, the court determined that "sufficient instruction and warning had been provided the student."

However, in *LaValley v. Stanford* (1947), a teacher *did not* provide adequate instruction or warnings appropriate to the activity. In this case, a teacher required two high school boys to box several rounds but provided no instructions in the art of boxing or warnings of the danger involved in the activity. The court held the instructor negligent and liable when one of the boys suffered a fatal injury.

A lack of ability was alleged, in *Govel v. Board of Education in the City of Albany* (1962), when a junior high school girl was injured during a soccer game. The instructional syllabus cautioned instructors not to allow rough play and too many participants. The teacher, who provided only one 15-minute session of instruction preceding the activity, defended the short instructional period by saying that she believed that children were "naturally skilled in running and kicking and did not need an extended session on such skills." The court ruled against the teacher, asserting that "the preparation of students to participate in such an activity required more than a superficial assessment of skill in running or kicking." The court also held that "the teacher's failure to follow the syllabus was negligent and the proximate cause of the injury." In similar litigation involving the case of *Ehlinger v. Board of Education of New Hartford Center School District* (1983), negligent instruction was ruled when a teacher failed to follow *state guidelines* for instructing students to take necessary precautions during a physical fitness speed test and a student was injured.

Age and Condition of Participants

Educators have a responsibility to tailor required activities to the age and condition of students. When an 11-year-old girl was injured in a physical education class while attempting a headstand, the court, in *Gardner v. State* (1939), ruled that the stunt was inherently dangerous for any young child to attempt, and it held the instructor liable for negligence. A similar case involved a 17-year-old student who was severely injured attempting a required gymnastic exercise, although the student had previously fallen a number of times and had a "bad knee" that "went out" at times. In *Bellman v. San Francisco High School District* (1938), the court ruled that "the condition of the student should have prevented the instructor from requiring the student to participate in such an activity."

In *Luce v. Board of Education* (1956), a teacher was found negligent for failing to consider the history of a student's physical condition. The teacher had required an 11-year-old student who had previously suffered two broken arms to participate in a "rough" activity. The student fell and broke her arm again. The teacher knew of the student's history and had been asked to excuse her from "rough" activities.

Equipment and Materials

Activities that require the use of equipment often give rise to allegations of improper instruction. The following cases illustrate the thinking of the courts regarding educators' responsibilities in this area.

A 13-year-old student built a model volcano at his home, then took it to school for a demonstration in the classroom as a science project. He was injured during an encore performance for his schoolmates at the bus stop on the periphery of the school grounds. Although the boy's father had helped him build his volcano, the student claimed that the school was "negligent in supervision, instruction, and warning, since the project constituted academic homework." The court, in *Simmons v. Beauregard Parish School Board* (1975), agreed and held for the student, citing improper instruction as well as improper supervision.

In *Miles v. School District No. 138* (1979), the court ruled in favor of the school when a student severed two fingers while operating machinery in the shop class. In this case, the student had failed a safety test on the operation of the machine and had been required to look up the answers. The student claimed the teacher was "negligent in his failure to conduct a second closed-book test." The court ruled that "the instruction and warnings given by the teacher were proper under the circumstances." In *Roberts v. Robertson County Board of Education* (1985), however, a student's misuse of a drill press resulted in a serious head injury to a classmate. The teacher had *not* instructed the students in the use of a specific drill bit, had *not* warned of dangers associated with its improper use, and *was absent* from the shop during the use of the drill. The court found the teacher negligent.

Although school personnel have a duty to provide appropriate instruction to protect students from unreasonable hazards, students must also act in a reasonable manner. School personnel will generally not be found negligent if students completely disregard the instructions and warning provided.

Age, Mental Abilities, and Appreciation of Risk

When a participant is inexperienced, the teacher is required to make a greater effort to communicate any risk. If students are young but experienced, they are held to assume those risks of which they are knowledgeable. Two examples are provided below to illustrate the basic concept of appreciation of risk.

In *Chapman v. State* (1972), an 18-year-old was injured while attempting to do a stunt on a trampoline. The student lost balance and fell to the floor, suffering serious and permanent injuries. The student was experienced on the trampoline and was practicing after class. Although the teacher required four spotters to prevent such an accident in class, at the time of the injury there was only one spotter. The court ruled that a proficient 18-year-old *must* exercise the same judgment and discretion regarding trampoline safety as a person of more advanced years.

In *Brevard County v. Jacks* (1970), a student with mental retardation drowned in a swimming area that had a sudden drop-off. Although the area was normally marked by a rope-and-buoy line, the line was not in position on the day of the accident. Instead, there was a sign warning, "Swim at Own Risk." The court ruled that the student was unable to appreciate the dangers of deep water in a swimming area.

Education Malpractice

In the past, almost all cases filed against educators for inappropriate instruction that reached the appellate court level involved *physical harm to the person rather than harm to the intellect.* However, in recent years, plaintiffs have initiated litigation that tests intellectual harm. So although this chapter limits its discussion to physical harm, it is advisable for the prudent educator to be aware of this trend. The issue of education malpractice has been judicially stalled to date; however, it is likely that when a strong case appears in a more receptive judicial climate, the results may be different from those of past cases in which the courts have generally held to the dicta of the California Court of Appeals in *Peter W. v. San Francisco Unified School District* (1976), which stated:

> Unlike the activity of the highway or marketplace, classroom methodology affords no readily acceptable standards of care, of cause, or injury. The science of pedagogy itself is fraught with different and conflicting theories of how or what a child should be taught. . . . Substantial professional authority attests that the achievement of literacy in the schools, or its failure, is influenced by a host of factors which affect the student subjectively, from outside the formal teaching process, and beyond the control of its ministers. They may be physical, neurological, emotional, cultural, environmental; they may be present but not perceived, recognized, but not identified. [Holding schools accountable] . . . would expose them to the tort claims—real or imagined—of disaffected students and parents in countless numbers. They are already beset by social and financial problems which have gone to major litigation, but for which no permanent solution has yet appeared. The ultimate consequences, in terms of public time and money, would burden them—and society—beyond calculation.

Examples of Management Cues

- A local disability advocacy organization accuses some special education teachers of assigning activities beyond the skill level of students. This follows a complaint from a group of parents claiming the same is true of regular education students in middle school P.E. classes. Both groups are also concerned about teachers assigning students activities when a known physical defect exists.
- A parent threatens the school with a lawsuit, claiming that her fourth-grade child failed to achieve a passing score on a statewide standards-of-learning test because her child's teacher deviated from the required syllabus.
- A parent whose ninth-grade son was injured by a power saw in shop class is suing the district for not providing safety rules and regulations concerning the use of equipment in the industrial arts program.

Suggested Risk Management Guidelines

- Ensure that teachers consider a student's special needs or limitations, abilities, age, and preexisting medical conditions when making instructional or supervisory decisions.

- – Educators should select activities appropriate to the student's ability to perform and understand, and should take into consideration the student's size, age, skill, condition, or special needs.
- – When a student has a known physical disability or defect that restricts the child's ability to participate in certain types of activities, school personnel have a duty to ensure that the child is not required or permitted to undertake any activities that risk physical harm to the student.

- Educators have been found negligent for improper instruction when the student was shown to have had inadequate knowledge to complete the task assigned.
- Ensure that all staff members know that school personnel are expected to foresee the potential danger of an instructional situation that may result in an injury to a student or other personnel, including visitors.

- – Educators have a duty to provide students with adequate warning about the danger inherent in equipment, machinery, games, exercises, and any facility or grounds problems that the students might encounter either as part of direct instruction or as part of their experience while at school.
- – When an activity entails risks to students, it is insufficient merely to inform or warn of risks; students must also understand and appreciate the risks.

- Make sure teachers do not force students to use equipment or perform a physical activity about which they express serious apprehension. Pressure of this type could result in injury to the student and liability charges against school personnel.
- Provide a higher standard of care and instruction in laboratories, physical education classes, contact sports, and on field trips.

- – Educators have a duty to establish safety rules and regulations to ensure that student safety is maintained at all times during instructional activities.
- – School personnel are further obligated to implement and enforce such rules and regulations concerning student safety and to instruct students in following those rules and regulations.

- Provide a sound education reason for deviating from the required curriculum or published guidelines once a curriculum guide is published.

- – It is wise to view curriculum guides, published guidelines, minimum competencies, and so forth as forms of *contracts* between the school and the student.
- – Failure to follow such documents could lead to the accusation of improper instruction.

The following guidelines relate specifically to *avoiding the risk of exposure to liability for education malpractice:*

- Develop exemplary standards of practice to guide the instructional program.
- Ensure that teachers and other instructional personnel are well prepared and focused on instructional duties.
- Ensure that all required competencies and skills are taught and that curriculum objectives are translated into subject matter actually taught in the classroom.
- Provide remediation programs for students who fail to master required skills and competencies or who have difficulty learning.
- Make informed decisions regarding the appropriateness of curriculum, textbooks, and instructional policies.
- Develop flexible and varied instructional strategies and techniques to meet the individual needs of students.
- Use well-prepared promotion and retention standards as guides to decisions affecting student progress.
- Avoid inappropriate testing procedures that could result in misclassification or inappropriate placement of students.
- Develop appropriate methods to monitor instructional practices.

FOCUS POINT: The Application of Negligence to Proper Supervision

One of the most common allegations of negligence directed toward educators is that of *negligent supervision.* It is estimated that nearly one-fourth of negligence cases identify improper supervision as the primary or secondary cause of an injury. Courts recognize that it is impossible for educators to personally supervise every movement of every student every day, and that accidents will occur; no amount of supervision can completely prevent such occurrences. Educators, however, are expected to exercise a reasonable degree and quality of supervision and to be physically in the general vicinity, fulfilling the responsibilities associated with the supervision assignment.

Fact patterns for the court to examine in negligent supervision cases vary with the situations that students, teachers, and administrators create. Although these patterns differ, certain questions appear repeatedly in the case studies and seem to bear heavily on the outcome (see Figure 15.2 presented earlier in this chapter). These questions include the following:

- *Who are the defendants?*

When a classroom assignment is accepted by a teacher, or a principalship by a principal, that educator assumes the responsibility to supervise. The duty to supervise is comprehensive in scope, and some degree of supervision must be provided in all areas of the school in which students are located at any time.

- *Do they owe a duty of general or specific supervision?*

Establishing the standard of supervision is difficult. What may be adequate in one situation may not be so in another. When students are unfamiliar with an activity, or when an activity is unusually dangerous, specific supervision is required. Under normal situations, general supervision is all that is required.

- *What is the plaintiff's age?*

See Figure 15.1 presented earlier in this chapter.

- *Were the circumstances of the injury reasonably foreseeable?*

The test for determining negligent supervision is whether a reasonably prudent person, in the educator's place, should have reason to believe the situation presents the possibility of injury.

Student participation in school-related hazardous activities requires a great deal of careful supervision by school personnel. The most prevalent forms of hazardous activities involve vocational training, experiments in chemistry and physics, physical education, playground activities, and athletic or intramural activities. Educator negligence in supervising such activities is generally predicated on a failure to instruct the student properly in the correct use of a dangerous instrument or to warn of the inherent dangers associated with an activity or experiment. The standard for conduct in this area continues to be that of a reasonable person in like circumstances.

Risk Areas

Some areas in the educational setting have a greater risk of student injury associated with them than do others. These have been identified as physical education, playground and athletic areas, science classrooms, vocational shops, storage rooms, stage areas, and bus loading zones. Teachers and principals need to maintain a special awareness of the risks associated with these areas and provide such supervision as would be reasonable and prudent under the circumstances.

The Establishment of Rules

School boards have the duty to establish rules for student safety and to enforce such rules in their school districts. This duty is demonstrated by the following case in which an eight-year-old student waiting for a school bus after school became involved in a scuffle. The student was pushed to the ground and then struck in the head by another student riding a bicycle. There were no school board or district rules regarding riding a bicycle on the school grounds, even though a state statute required each school board in that particular state to establish rules and regulations regarding order and discipline. In *Selleck v. Board of Education* (1949), the court held that the school board was negligent in failing to adopt rules and regulations concerning bicycle use. In this same case, the principal of the school was found to be negligent in failing to maintain proper discipline and provide proper supervision of the bus loading area.

In the absence of board of education policy, principals have a duty to promulgate rules for their schools and, with teachers and other employees, have the duty to enforce reasonable and lawful rules established for the safety of students and others.

Lack of Proper Supervision

Schools must provide competent supervision in sufficient quantity to cover the supervisory needs of the situation. Liability arising from supervisory activities is not limited to the failure to provide competent supervision. Situations occur when competent supervision has been provided, but for various reasons, the supervisor is absent when an accident occurs. Liability in such cases usually depends on the foreseeability of an accident. If the supervisor's presence at the time of the injury would not have prevented the injury, there is likely to be no liability. However, if the accident was foreseeable and the supervisor's presence would have prevented the injury, the principal, teacher, or other school employee may be subject to litigation. In a case in which a student was injured in a physical education class while the teacher's attention was focused for an extended length of time in another area, the court ruled against the teacher in the resultant litigation. The possibility of injury in a physical education class was deemed foreseeable in *Armlin v. Board of Education* (1971).

In addition to foreseeability, courts also consider whether the supervisor's conduct was the proximate cause of the injury. Negligence is not present if proximate cause cannot be established. As an example, a principal left the playground during the lunch recess to answer the telephone. While the principal was absent, a student was hit in the eye by a stone batted by another student. In *Wilbur v. City of Binghamton* (1946), the court reasoned that the presence of a supervisor would not have prevented the accident, and that the principal's absence did not cause the accident. (See also Causal Relationship below.)

Specific Supervision

Establishing the standard of supervision is difficult. What may be adequate in one situation may not be so in another. Specific supervision is required when students are unfamiliar with an activity or when an activity is unusually dangerous. The need for specific supervision is frequently related to the age of the student. In one case, a six-year-old student was injured at a construction site next to the elementary school in which remodeling was being done. School officials knew of the potential dangers at the site, and although they reminded students daily to stay away from the area, they took no other precautions to protect students. The court found against the school, citing negligent supervision in *District of Columbia v. Royal* (1983).

General Supervision

General supervision is all that is required under normal situations. During playground time, general, rather than specific, supervision is usually adequate. In *Hampton v. Orleans Parish School Board* (1982), a 12-year-old student who was playing ball in the schoolyard during noon recess was injured by a rock thrown by another student. At the time of the incident, there were about 170 students playing in the yard and three teachers on duty to supervise. A negligence action was filed on the grounds that an unpaved area of the playground constituted an unreasonably hazardous condition. The case was dismissed on the basis that there was insufficient evidence to support the claim that the condition was hazardous and that the supervision at the time of the incident was adequate for the playground and the number of students.

However, in *Charonnatt v. San Francisco Unified School District* (1943), an assistant principal was held liable for an injury sustained by a student. In this case, a fight occurred during recess, and one student twisted the leg of another until it broke. At the time of the fight, there were over 100 students on the playground under the supervision of the assistant principal. Although the supervisor was in close proximity to the place where the student was injured, the court held that the administrator "failed to use reasonable care and diligence in supervising the conduct of the students."

Causal Relationship (Proximate Cause)

In order for negligence to be found, the supervisor's conduct must be shown to be the proximate cause of an injury. The question of whether or not a causal relationship exists can be seen in *Nester v. City of New York* (1961), in which a student was hit by a bat swung by another student. The teacher was standing 30 feet away, passing out milk, at the time of the accident. The court ruled in favor of the teacher, citing that the supervision was adequate, causal relationship was absent because the teacher was not directly responsible for the supervision of the students involved in the activity, and more supervision would not have averted the accident.

Unattended Classroom or School Area

A difficult determination of proper or improper supervision occurs when teachers leave the classrooms for which they are responsible. A primary responsibility of a teacher is to provide supervision for the classroom. After a teacher's classes have been accounted for, secondary duties, such as hall, cafeteria, or playground assignments, may be assumed. Court dicta concerning this area of supervision demonstrate the importance of classroom supervision but at the same time are somewhat ambiguous. In *Ohman v. Board of Education of City of New York* (1949), a trial court entered a judgment against a teacher for negligence in leaving a classroom in which a student injury occurred during the absence. A court of appeals reversed the verdict and found the teacher innocent of the charges; however, a dissenting justice took issue with the reversal and entered into the record the following statement, which is often noted in other cases of like nature. According to this justice, "When a large number of children are gathered together in a single classroom, without any effective control or supervision, it may reasonably be anticipated that certain of them may so act as to inflict an unintentional injury on themselves or their classmates." If there is a consensus on this issue, it appears to be that a teacher, and ultimately the principal and district, may be held liable for negligence if a teacher leaves a classroom, or other setting, unsupervised.

Examples of Management Cues

- An injured student claims that his injury was caused by the principal failing to make and enforce rules.
- A parent who feels he was verbally harassed at a football game complains to the superintendent that the principal fails to provide competent supervision and control crowds during athletic events.
- A student is injured by a rubber band shot across the classroom by an unknown student. The injured student claims that the teacher was out in the hall talking to another teacher when the incident occurred.

Suggested Risk Management Guidelines

- Ensure that a higher standard of care and supervision is evident in laboratories, physical education classes, contact sports, and on field trips.
- Develop a procedure to provide some form of supervision for students before the school day begins or after the school day ends.
- Ensure that teachers understand that foreseeability of harm is a critical element in determining negligence in a given situation. Educators have been held liable for accidents that occur during their absence from the classroom or activity area if it could be anticipated that the educator's presence in the room or area would have prevented the accident.
- Ensure that personnel take into consideration a student's special needs or limitations, abilities, age, and preexisting medical conditions when making supervisory decisions.

FOCUS POINT: The Application of Negligence to Proper Maintenance

Like other entities, school districts have an obligation and a common law duty to keep school premises, including grounds, facilities, and equipment, reasonably safe and in good repair. Courts have awarded damages to students, parents, school employees, and visitors who have been injured as a result of defective conditions in school-owned property when school employees were aware of, or should have been aware of, hazardous conditions and did not take the necessary steps to repair or correct such conditions.

Two questions arise immediately when considering proper maintenance. First, does the school district recognize that it is responsible for injuries that happen to visitors using the school's facilities or grounds at night or on weekends? Educators have been found liable for their selection, maintenance, and supervision of the use of instructional equipment if the educator's action in this regard was shown to be based on poor judgment not expected of a professional educator. School personnel have a legal duty to instruct, supervise, and provide a safe environment for students. In addition, administrators, teachers, and other school personnel have an affirmative duty to ensure that school buildings and grounds are not only safe for student use but also for visitors. Second, does the school district know how often a school's facilities and grounds should be inspected for unsafe conditions?

Nuisance Defined

Some courts draw a distinction between ordinary negligence and willful positive misconduct, and courts have held school districts liable for maintaining a nuisance. Increasingly, people injured as a result of alleged failure of schools to maintain premises in a safe condition base their suits on "safe-place" statutes that permit recovery against school districts if they maintain nuisances. Most courts hold that the fact that a public agency (i.e., school or school district) holds and manages property makes it accountable for damages that result in injury to a person or for damage to the property of others from mismanagement, willful positive conduct, or negligence.

Under common law, people cannot press for an action in tort for a nuisance unless the plaintiffs can show that they were injured due to negligence. One example is litigation concerning school roofs, which have frequently been an attraction for children to climb. In one case, the parents of a student killed in a fall from a school roof brought suit against the district for negligence, for maintaining an attractive nuisance, and for not preventing students from climbing to the roof. The student was one of three boys who, after leaving a school dance and being chased from the area, later returned to the school from a different direction and climbed up on the roof. The 13-year-old student fell from the roof and incurred injuries that resulted in his death. The court, in *Barnhizer v. Paradise Valley Unified School District No. 69* (1979), ruled in favor of the school.

However, in *Brown v. City of Oakland* (1942), the court ruled in favor of a student who sustained an injury while attending a baseball game. While playing around an abandoned long-jump pit, the student was frightened by a dog. She fell backward into the pit and cut her hand on a piece of broken glass that had been covered by sand. The girl presented evidence that the school knew of the dangerous condition because the school's janitor and school authorities had received written notification of the condition of the pit.

The legal status of one who is injured is also important in deciding claims of nuisance. The general rule is nonliability for injuries suffered by an adult trespasser. Liability has been found, however, when the trespasser is a youth who, because of his or her age, cannot perceive the danger of an attraction.

An *attractive nuisance* is seen by the courts as an unprotected, unguarded, unsafe condition that may attract a child to play. Schools can be held liable for allowing a nuisance to exist. For example, a first-grade student arrived in the school yard before school and began swinging on the monkey bars. Located adjacent to the bars was a tetherball pole about 10 feet in height. When the student reached the top of the bars, she grabbed the pole and attempted to slide to the ground. Attached to the center of the pole was a screw that protruded approximately one and one-half inches and lacerated the inside of the child's thigh when she slid over it. In *Givens v. Orleans Parish School Board* (1980), the plaintiff alleged that the location of the tetherball pole in such close proximity to the monkey bars provided an "attractive nuisance" for the student. The court agreed and ruled in favor of the child and her parents.

Proper and Improper Maintenance

The courts hold school district personnel liable for injury when they "knowingly" leave or provide a dangerous instrument exposed in a place likely to be frequented by children who, because of their age or other special condition, cannot realize or appreciate the danger. The age of the child and the child's ability to comprehend danger is always a debatable issue in court, and there are a number of interpretations of age and ability when proper maintenance is litigated. For example, in *Libby v. West Coast Rock Co., Inc.* (1975), a boy was injured when he did not see a ditch and ran into it in an attempt to catch a ball. The school was aware of the ditch and had posted a notice on the school bulletin board that the ditch was there and could present a problem. The student claimed that the school was negligent in not providing a safe place to play. The court ruled in favor of the student because the boy was deemed incapable of appreciating the danger.

In another case, a student sustained serious injuries while playing among piles of dirt and sand on the school playground after school. The area was not fenced, and prior to the incident, parents had complained to the school district concerning the dirt piles and "dirt fights" among children playing there. The court, in *Monfils v. City of Sterling Heights* (1978), concluded that the school district breached its duty to maintain the school grounds in a safe condition.

In a case that involved an older student, the student, while dressing for his physical education class, changed into his uniform and placed his clothing in an unused hallway storage area adjacent to the boys' locker room facility. Dressing and locker storage facilities were available in the locker room, but the student had no lock and chose to hide his clothing in some surplus shelving in an unused hallway. When the student returned from his physical education class and began to look for his clothing, he stepped back on a piece of plywood from which some nails protruded. One of the nails pierced his foot, causing a painful injury. The wood had been placed in the hallway by a school employee. In *Young v. Orleans Parish School Board* (1980), the court ruled against the school and for the student, citing improper maintenance caused by negligence.

Buildings and Grounds: Preventive Maintenance

Schools owe a duty to the public to take all necessary positive steps to ensure that buildings and grounds are free of any potentially hazardous conditions. The following cases illustrate the courts' expectations in this regard.

In *Mattison v. Hudson Falls* (1983), snowmobilers collided with a snow-covered bench at night on a baseball field owned by the school district. The court ruled against the plaintiffs because they could not show that the bench was a dangerous instrument or that the school district was malicious in placing the bench in that area.

The Utah Supreme Court ruled in favor of a woman who suffered injuries when she slipped and fell on an icy sidewalk leading to the side entrance of a school. In *Gurule v. Salt Lake City Board of Education* (1983), the court held that the school district had the duty to maintain buildings and grounds in a reasonably safe condition and to remove dangers and that "negligence was present."

In *Ardoin v. Evangeline Parish School Board* (1979), a Louisiana appellate court found a school district negligent in the case of a student who fell and injured his knee while running bases in a physical education class. The student claimed that the school was negligent because school personnel knew of a concrete slab that protruded about an inch above the surface of the ground on the path between two bases. The slab, the student claimed, constituted such a hazardous condition that it was a breach of the standard of care required of the school to allow it to exist on the playground. The court ruled in favor of the student.

A student in New York stepped on some glass on an outside stairway and injured his foot. The student charged that the school was negligent in allowing the glass to be present. In *Cooper v. Smith Town Central School District* (1981), the court ruled in favor of the student. Another court, however, found that a school was not negligent in a case that a nine-year-old student had brought against the district and a school bus driver for damages allegedly resulting from an illness the student suffered. The student had found a piece of unwrapped gum on the floor of the bus and chewed it. The gum was allegedly coated with phencyclidine (PCP), a dangerous and potentially lethal drug. The student claimed that the school district and the bus driver were negligent in failing to properly maintain the interior of the bus and to properly supervise infants. The court disagreed in *Hatlett v. Oswego-Appalachian School District* (1979).

Another court ruled in favor of the parents of a student who was killed when a railing came loose around a platform in the school gymnasium. The parents of the student, in *Woodring v. Board of Education of Manhasset Union Free School District* (1981), claimed that a nut and bolt were not in place to secure the railing, that the school had no program of preventive maintenance or inspection, and that such an incident was foreseeable because students were frequently seen hanging on the railing.

In *Lostumbo v. Board of Education of the City of Norwalk* (1980), a court also ruled in favor of a student who sustained injuries as a result of a fall on the school grounds. She fell while walking, at the direction of teachers, across an ice- and snow-covered sidewalk that was "uneven, slippery and defective." The student claimed that it was the school's duty to provide a safe place for students.

Proper Maintenance of Equipment

A school district has the affirmative duty to exercise reasonable care not to provide equipment that it knows or has a reason to know is dangerous for its intended use. Some jurisdictions have rephrased this standard of care, requiring an affirmative duty to supply effective equipment. Although most defective equipment suits involve playground equipment, schools have been sued, for example, for supplying defective blankets, gymnastic apparatus, football equipment, playground toys, and hockey helmets.

Occasionally, the nature of the subject matter being taught by the teacher requires students to use special apparatus. Such devices may present a hazard to student safety, especially if improper equipment is used or if the equipment is not maintained in proper working order. Teachers and others have been held responsible not only for the activities associated with a program but also for not preventing accidents caused by the unsafe condition of equipment and facilities.

The increased use of and the intricacy of equipment in today's education programs require more care on the part of educators to avoid possible injury. As a result, courts view such care as a primary responsibility of schools and generally rule that schools have a duty to provide safe equipment and comprehensive instruction to ensure its proper use. Furthermore, as the age of the school site or the size of the student population and number of activities increases, the possibility is greater that defective equipment and unsafe conditions exist. Courts tend to favor the injured student or adult in cases in which school officials know that dangerous equipment or unsafe facilities exist and fail to remedy them. In a classic case, a football player was injured when he was sent into a game with a defective helmet. The player had informed the coach before the game that his helmet was missing a face mask and had a broken chin strap. During a play, his helmet was knocked from his head and he sustained serious injuries. In *Martini v. Olyphant Borough School District* (1953), the court ruled that the injury was a result of the coach's negligence in requiring the player to participate with defective equipment.

The courts define inspection of equipment and facilities as a general *daily* responsibility. Inspections must include the building and grounds, fixed and movable equipment, floors, lighting fixtures, and seats. It is teachers' and principals' responsibility to report any dangerous condition that needs to be corrected and to modify programs to isolate hazards until proper corrections have been made.

Playground Areas

The majority of playground injuries occur when children fall from equipment and strike the underlying surface. Results of tests indicate that although they may require little maintenance or repair, surfacing materials such as asphalt do not provide injury protection from accidental fall impact and are unsuitable for use under playground equipment. The most suitable materials seem to be the more resilient surfaces such as bark, wood chips, or shredded tires.

Liability for school districts, school administrators, and teachers can and does result from improper maintenance. Courts have found teachers and principals negligent when equipment has not been kept in proper repair. School districts have an affirmative duty to exercise reasonable care not to provide or to hold equipment or property that they know or have reason to know is dangerous for its intended use.

Example of a Management Cue

- The county's risk management department, in cooperation with the county's fire and safety marshals, has cited your school for the following violations. They have given you and the school district 30 days to respond before filing formal charges. The citations note the following:
  - *Citation 1:* Maintaining a nuisance. Cause: Unused jumping pit on playgrounds—broken glass mixed in the sand
  - *Citation 2:* Failing to maintain premises in a safe condition—failing to ensure that buildings and grounds are free of any potentially hazardous conditions. Cause: Hazardous cleaning liquids stored in open closets, obsolete furniture stored in hallways, broken table in Room 32, electrical receptacle cover missing in Rooms 114 and 213
  - *Citation 3:* Causing injury to a person or damage to the property of others from mismanagement, willful positive conduct, or negligence. Cause: Lawn trimming machine caused stones to be propelled through the windows of a house adjacent to the school grounds. Flying glass may cause injury to occupant
  - *Citation 4:* Knowingly leaving or providing a dangerous instrument exposed in a place likely to be frequented by children who, because of their age or other special condition, cannot realize or appreciate the danger. Cause: Fence surrounding electrical transmitter is damaged on the west side of building
  - *Citation 5:* Failure of the school's affirmative duty to exercise reasonable care not to provide equipment that it knows or has a reason to know is dangerous for its intended use. Cause: Frayed electrical cords noted on six overhead projectors. Loose bolts on playground equipment as well as indoor physical education equipment

Suggested Risk Management Guidelines

- Ensure the maintenance of a safe and productive learning and activity environment *and* develop exemplary standards of duty and care in the maintenance of facilities, grounds, equipment, and furnishings. An educator will probably be found negligent if the educator
  - Knows or has reason to know that the equipment is, or is likely to be, dangerous for the use for which it is intended
  - Has no reason to believe that the potential users will be aware of the dangerous condition

- Fails to exercise reasonable care to inform the user of the dangerous condition or the facts that make it likely to be dangerous

- Ensure an ongoing, site-based playground inspection program and immediately remove *entrapment* hazards such as swinging exercise rings or other *open* equipment in which body parts, including the head, can be placed. Other problem areas noted are ladders, protective barriers, and handrails. All should be designed so that they will not catch a child's clothing.
  - Sharp points, corners and edges, pinch and crush points, and protrusions or projections should be covered or eliminated if possible.
  - Each piece of playground equipment should have a "use zone" and should be spaced a safe distance away from its nearest counterpart.
  - Written guidelines should be established and enforced for playground activities, and playground-related injuries should be monitored to determine if modifications are necessary to the guidelines or to playground equipment or grounds.
  - A formal inspection of playground equipment, including the breaking down of moving parts, should be conducted annually.

- Ensure that the word *inspection* is connected to positive action. Inspection should be considered an ongoing, walking-around-and-observing responsibility for all school personnel. Items of equipment, furniture, and building fixtures, as well as general conditions on the school grounds and parking lots, that are found to be defective or dangerous should be removed or isolated from students and others.

FOCUS POINT: The Application of Negligence to Field Trips

Field trips are school-related activities that take place away from school grounds. The legal obligation of educators to exercise reasonable care and supervision of students so that they will not be at risk on such trips is the same as in any other site-based supervisory situation. Field trips, including athletic events, are considered extensions of the school. Just as in the classroom and in the school, negligence on a field trip leaves the educator open to court action. Schools owe the same duty of care and supervision to take reasonable precautions to avoid foreseeable injuries to students who participate in mandatory field trips and excursions as would be owed to the students during the normal school day.

Control of Students

The assessment of liability on field trips, during which students are taken into unfamiliar situations, often turns on whether the students are on the premises solely for their own benefit or the host organization derives some benefit from the visit. In general, three legal statuses of students are recognized by law:

1. *Invitees*, when the host organization has invited the group. Invitees are due a higher standard of care from the host organization than licensees.

2. *Licensees*, when permission has been granted, on request from the educator, to visit or perform. Licensees visit the premises at their own peril, because the permission to visit does not carry with it the same standard of care as in the case of invitees.

3. *Trespassers*, when no permission has been granted to students to visit the premises. An example would be if, during a field trip, students decided on their own to visit a site without the permission or knowledge of the supervisor. Trespassers have little, if any, protection when on property without permission, unless it can be proved that the site was an attractive nuisance to the students due to their age and inexperience.

Foreseeability and Warning

School personnel have a duty to protect the health and safety of students while they are in their charge. Consequently, when students are injured, it is common to inquire whether the injury is due to a breach of this duty by a school employee. In *Williamson v. Board of Education* (1975), members of a senior class met at a city park on a Saturday to have pictures taken for the school yearbook. The school had approved the activity, and two teachers were assigned as supervisors. Two students received permission from the teachers to have their picture taken while on their motorcycles. In the course of the picture taking, a child walking nearby was hit by one of the motorcycles and injured. The court ruled in favor of the child and cited a breach of duty on the part of the teachers.

If a student is injured while on a field trip, educators may be able to prove that they took reasonable care if they can demonstrate that they visited the site prior to the trip to determine, in advance, that dangers might be involved (foreseeability) and that students were warned (proper instruction) beforehand.

In cases pertaining to breach of duty in field trips, lack of supervision is commonly demonstrated. In one case, a mentally challenged student member of a Special Olympics team was killed while walking with a group three blocks to a gymnasium. The student was accompanied by one teacher while another teacher followed in a car. The student ran into the street at a busy intersection and was struck by a car. The parents of the student claimed that the teachers were negligent by exposing the handicapped student to unreasonable and foreseeable risk of injury. The parents further claimed that the school failed to provide an adequate number of supervisory personnel and to select the safest route. The court found in favor of the parents in *Foster v. Houston General Insurance Co.* (1981).

Another example is provided in *Morris v. Douglas County School District* (1965), in which a teacher and six adults took 35 elementary and preschool children to the beach. Four of the children climbed onto a large log and posed for a picture that the teacher took. With her back to the ocean, the teacher did not see the large wave that surged onto the beach. The wave caused the log to be lifted and the children fell off. When the water receded, the log settled on top of one child and crushed him. The court cited foreseeability and a breach of the duty to properly supervise and ruled in favor of the parents of the student.

Waiver of Liability (Permission Slips)

Although requiring permission slips may provide certain public information or psychological advantages, permission slips or other forms of releases should *not* be considered a waiver of liability. Students may still sue for injuries they sustain. *School districts cannot be absolved of their obligation toward students by a parental waiver or release.* It may be that the waiver of the parent may affect only the liability arising from the act of taking the students on the trip itself. However, the above facts of law do not mean that some form of permission slip should not be used. To a certain degree, the liability may be diminished with a signed document from a legal guardian granting permission to participate in the activity.

A high school band member drowned in a hotel pool while on a trip with the band. The student dove into the water and minutes later was found at the bottom of the pool. Two chaperones who were supervising the pool activity gave immediate mouth-to-mouth resuscitation until an ambulance arrived. The parents of the student claimed negligence in failure to provide adequate supervision for their son, who did not know how to swim. The father, however, had given written permission to use the pool and did not inform anyone that his son could not swim. The court, in *Powell v. Orleans Parish School Board* (1978), ruled in favor of the school, citing the age of the student, proper supervision on the part of the field trip sponsors, and negligence on the part of the father.

Errands

Although it is common practice for educators and other school employees to send students on errands for them, there is no legal authority for educators to use students in this manner. When a student is sent on a personal or school-related errand for a school employee and the student suffers an injury while on the errand, the legal question that arises is whether the school acted reasonably in sending the student on the errand. What constitutes reasonable action depends on the circumstances of each case. Also important is the fact that, while on an errand for the school employee, the student may be classified as an agent of the school, and the liability for any damage done to, or caused by, the student may fall on the school.

Transportation

The most common area of field trip litigation relates to transportation—both that which is provided by teachers or principals and that which is contracted for, such as public or private bus service. When schools undertake to provide transportation service for students to or from any school activity, the school's duty of care regarding that transportation is at least equal to that owed on the school premises or to that owed by any public carrier, as noted by the court in *Raymond v. Paradise Unified School District* (1963). When transportation is provided by independent contractors, duty and liability rest with them rather than with the school, except when it comes to proper supervision of students, which is still the duty of the educators present.

A 12-year-old student suffered a fatal injury when she stuck her head out of the bus window and was struck by a guy wire supporting a utility pole. The court, in *Arnold v. Hayslett* (1981), ruled in favor of the school, citing the fact that the student was bright, alert, and intelligent and, as a result, contributed to her own negligence. In addition, the court noted that the supervisor and the bus driver had warned students not to place hands or other parts of the body outside windows when the bus was moving.

The issues of duty and proximate cause are not quite so clear, however, when schools play an intermediary role in organizing, arranging, or sanctioning the transportation of students by private vehicle. The issue of parental responsibility when driving on school-sponsored field trips was addressed in *Sharp v. Fairbanks North Star Borough* (1977), in which the court stated that "the duty of care, and the liability for negligence which proximately causes injury to a student, shifts from the school to a parent who undertakes to provide transportation for school children other than his own." Schools do not so easily avoid liability when supplementary transportation to school activities is provided in vehicles operated by school personnel or by students themselves and is arranged or sanctioned by school officials. Schools may be bound under the doctrine of *respondeat superior* with regard to their employees or by their duty to exercise reasonable care in the selection, approval, and supervision of student cars and drivers.

The court, in *Hanson v. Reedley Joint Union School District* (1941), held a teacher responsible for the death of a student. The teacher allowed and made arrangements for students to ride in the automobiles of other students and for the drivers of the cars to receive gasoline for such trips at the expense of his school organization. The court noted that the school assumed a duty to perform its assumed role with reasonable prudence and foresight and that the teacher negligently failed to consider the driver's reputation for recklessness or to ascertain the extraordinarily unsafe condition of the automobile in which the student was riding.

Examples of Management Cues

- A principal receives a complaint from the park service and the highway patrol that sponsors on a recent field trip failed to maintain full control of students during the time that they were away from the school, including travel to and from the site to be visited. A parent also files a complaint that, due to improper supervision of students by sponsors on the same field trip, her child was injured.
- The band director often lets clarinet, oboe, and bassoon players go to the local music store during band class if they need a new reed, and the

stagecraft teacher occasionally lets students use her car during class time, as well as before and after school, to pick up lumber and supplies from the local lumber yard.

- A debate coach allows a parent with a suspended driver's license to transport students to a meet. It is called to the debate coach's attention when the car, traveling in a caravan, is stopped by the police for having a faulty muffler.

Suggested Risk Management Guidelines

- Before approving any field trip, require that the following question be answered by the sponsors and educators: *Does the proposed field trip have an educational mission that could be defended in court?*
- Provide the same duty and standard of care on field trips, including trips to activity events (e.g., athletic, debate, clinics) with the same concern expected on school grounds.
- Instruct, supervise, and provide a safe environment for students when away from the school or school grounds while on a school-sponsored activity.
- Prohibit personnel from sending students on errands off school grounds. In addition, examine policies concerning sending students on errands *on* the school grounds, especially sending students to areas on the school grounds that might be considered dangerous (those areas that require specific supervision).
- Ensure that the trip plan outlines how sponsoring educators will have full control of students during the time they are away from the school, including during travel to and from the site or sites to be visited.

FOCUS POINT: The Application of Negligence to Postinjury Treatment, Athletic Liability, and Spectator Safety

The common use of the term *first aid* refers to the immediate and temporary care given the victim of an accident or sudden illness in order either to sustain the life of the injured person or to prevent further injury. Educators have a duty to provide the degree of assistance to injured students under their supervision commensurate with their training and experience. *Although courts do not expect educators to be physicians, they do expect people who work with children to be able to administer lifesaving first aid whenever needed, as long as the emergency care is rendered in a proper and prudent manner.*

School officials have the duty to render first aid and the duty not to render anything more than first aid. Although educators are not authorized to provide general medical treatment to students, they have a duty to administer emergency aid. Either lack of action or unwise action may lead to an allegation of negligence against the educator. In some states, Good Samaritan laws shield individuals providing treatment in emergency situations from liability. Because of the special duty of care required in the student-educator relationship, such laws often do not indemnify school personnel from liability for unreasonable action. Courts have recognized that public policy considerations dictate an obligation to ensure that medical treatment given by a school is competently rendered.

Although educators have the responsibility to implement acceptable and careful procedures, they cannot diagnose or treat injuries past the emergency state. When an emergency is indicated, educators are obligated to do the best they can relative to the amount of training and experience they possess. The range of postinjury treatment may be summed up with the generalization that educators are required to take appropriate steps in the case of an injury to a student or visitor but may be held liable if an attempt is made to help too much—or if they fail to do enough.

Millions of students engage in some type of interscholastic sport each year. Although educators may be somewhat comforted by the available defense of assumption of risk if a participant is injured, an athletic participant may generally assume the risks inherent in a particular sport but not the risks resulting from educator negligence. In applying the concept of negligence specifically to school athletics, a major consideration is the duty educators owe to the participant to

- Provide proper and adequate instruction and supervision
- Provide and maintain safe facilities and equipment
- Provide proper medical attention
- Reasonably select and match participants

When an athletic injury occurs, educators often turn to the defenses of contributory negligence and assumption of risk for protection from liability. Of the two defenses, assumption of risk appears to be the most successful. However, assumption of risk does not have universal acceptance in the courts. In some states, it has been expressly abolished on the basis that reasonableness of conduct should be the basic consideration in all negligence cases. Nevertheless, if a school district or school employee has been negligent in duty and standard of care, neither defense would probably be upheld by a court. Students assume only the *known* risks inherent in a particular athletic activity.

Express assumption of risk in which students and their guardians sign waivers of liability for claims against the school district and school personnel for their negligence are generally useless. Although these waiver forms are contracts, minors can disavow most contracts at will. Waivers signed by parents, guardians, and adult students also are generally unenforceable because they are usually contrary to public policy.

Courts have also recognized that education institutions have a duty toward spectators. Even in states that provide government immunity, dangerous facilities fall outside of most immunity provisions. Spectators must be able to have confidence that physical structures, walkways, and other facilities are safe and well maintained. In addition, crowd control procedures must be apparent, and appropriate first aid must be available.

Courts have also recognized that schools have similar duties toward spectators in terms of supervising events, providing and maintaining safe facilities and equipment, and providing first-aid assistance when needed.

Two areas of concern that can be somewhat perplexing to an educator can be seen in the following questions:

1. When an athletic injury occurs, are the defenses of contributory negligence and assumption of risk adequate for protection from liability?

2. What responsibilities, if any, does the school have in providing a safe place for spectators?

Postinjury Treatment: Failure to Act versus Proper Action

The failure of an educator to administer immediate first aid that might have prevented the death of a student resulted in litigation when a student playing hide-and-seek during lunch recess shoved her arm through a glass pane on a door. As she pulled her arm out, the student received a deep cut in her arm. The young girl panicked and ran around the playground before being stopped by an older student. The teacher had left the area, and it was several minutes before the school nurse could be located and the bleeding stopped. The girl died later at the hospital because of excessive blood loss. The court, in *Orgando v. Carquineu School District* (1938), felt that the teacher could have prevented her death by quickly stopping the flow of blood.

As long as educators administer emergency care in a proper and prudent manner, the courts appear to favor the educator. A student was hit in the stomach while playing football. The teacher took him inside the dressing room, had the student lie down, and covered him with a blanket. Later, when the student went to the restroom, he found blood in his urine. The court, in *Rickle v. Oakdale Union Grammar School District* (1953), ruled that proper and prudent care was given. The teacher had no indication of internal bleeding prior to the passing of the urine.

The court, in *Magabgab v. Orleans Parish School Board* (1970), ruled that a student's death was due to both the lack of immediate first aid after the first symptoms appeared and the improper use of first aid. This case was brought by the parents of a football player who died of profound heat exhaustion. At the end of practice, about 4:20 p.m., the boy became faint and began to vomit after running wind sprints. He was given a shower at room temperature and placed under a blanket. The coaches noticed the clamminess of his skin and his heavy breathing, but they failed to take any other action. It was not until approximately 6:45 p.m. that the boy's parents were called, and they in turn contacted a doctor. Heat stroke was diagnosed, and the boy was taken to the hospital, where he died the next day.

Unwise action may also lead to a charge of negligence against an educator. In *Welch v. Dunsmuir Joint Union High School* (1958), a football player was awarded damages when the coach failed to administer proper first aid. During a preseason scrimmage, the player was initially injured when he was tackled. A grip test was used on the playing field to test for neck injury and possible damage to the spinal cord. The boy could move his hands, so he was carried by his arms and legs from the playing field by other players under the direction of the coach. The grip test was again administered at the sideline, but the boy was then unable to move his hands, arms, or legs. The court ruled that the boy became a quadriplegic because of a spinal injury resulting from his being improperly moved from the playing field to the sideline. The standard of care in this instance required the attention of a doctor and the use of a stretcher. (See also *Czaplicki v. Gooding Joint School District No. 231*, 1989; *Barth v. Board of Education of Chicago*, 1986.)

In a classic case of improper first aid, two teachers forcibly held the injured hand of a student in scalding water for 10 minutes, as described in *Guerrieri v. Tyson* (1942). The treatment resulted in the development of blisters and permanent disfigurement of the hand. The student was hospitalized for almost a month. The court considered the treatment to be unreasonable and improper, even though the intentions of the teachers were directed toward the welfare of the student. (See also *Reed v. University of North Dakota*, 1996.)

A case of improper treatment was demonstrated when medical treatment was administered by students under the direction of the teacher. The plaintiff student had a preexisting medical condition in one of his knees. The teacher directed incompetent and untrained students to attempt medical treatment of the knee; as a result, the plaintiff's knee was further damaged. The court ruled against the teacher in *O'Brian v. Township High School District 214* (1979). (See also *Harvey v. Ouachita Parish School Board*, 1996.)

Administering Medication

Educators and school personnel regularly find themselves in the situation of being asked to give medication to students during school hours. School personnel are not medical professionals and need to restrict their administration of medication and any medical procedures to those who are trained and authorized to conduct, in accordance with school district policies and procedures. To ensure the safety of schoolchildren and minimize the administration of medications to children during the school day, each school district should develop guidelines. Suggested guidelines for administering medication are listed later in this Focus Point.

Examples of Management Cues

- Any injury to a child or adult who falls under the duty and care of the school, including visitors at the school or at school-sponsored events
- Any request from a parent or guardian for the school to administer medication or provide medical assistance or support for a student while under the duty and care of the school

Suggested Risk Management Guidelines

- Ensure that school personnel understand that they are responsible for any harmful consequences of their conduct (both their actions and their inactions) in regard to postinjury treatment, administration of medication, athletic liability, and spectator safety.
- Educators' conduct will be measured against how a reasonably prudent educator, with the skill and training expected under the circumstances, would have acted in a similar fashion under similar conditions.
- Educators have been upheld by the courts for their attempts to provide postinjury first aid to injured students; however, the courts have not afforded protection for educators who attempted to deliver medical therapy or treatment that exceeded or fell short of rudimentary first-aid procedures.
- Consider providing inservice training to adult school personnel on first-aid procedures and update such procedures as recommended by the American Red Cross.

General Guidelines for Administering Medication

These are general guidelines—more specific guidelines may be available from the state department of health in particular states.

- Require that written requests from the parent or guardian and from the physician or dentist accompany any medication to be administered, including over-the-counter drugs such as aspirin, ibuprofen, and cough medicine.
  - Require the physician request form to be dated and to identify the time of day medication is to be given and the anticipated number of days.
  - Require that any changes in the type of drug, dosage, or time of administration also be accompanied by new physician and parent permission signatures.
  - Require that the medication be provided to the school in the original prescription container.
- Require that registered nurses, physicians, or dentists be responsible for overall administration of medication in the schools. Delegate administration to a licensed practical nurse or unlicensed staff member only after an initial assessment by the school nurse.
- Limit medications to be administered by school personnel, if possible, to oral or topical medications, except in emergency situations. Exceptions might include the administration of eye drops, ear drops, and rectal suppositories.
- Prohibit school personnel from maintaining supplies of over-the-counter medications on school premises, including athletic areas, unless a prescription is provided along with written parent permission to administer.
- Keep an individual and comprehensive record of any medication administered to students and keep all medication in a locked container.

- Require that all medications be inventoried at least once a semester by a licensed health care professional.
- Have parents pick up out-of-date medications or destroy them. Seal needles and syringes in puncture-proof containers and dispose of them properly.
- Provide all local physicians and dentists with the policy approved by the school board regarding administration of medication and conduct of medical procedures at school. Make the school district's request for administration of medication forms readily available to local health care professionals.

Athletics and Spectator Safety

- Provide adequate instruction and warning to students and parents.
- Provide adequate supervision of athletic participants and all other sports-related student organizations (e.g., cheerleaders).
- Ensure that only proper equipment is used and that proper maintenance of equipment takes place.
- Practice only reasonable matching of participants.
- Hire and retain only qualified athletic personnel and trained coaches.
- Ensure that there is proper supervision, including formal evaluation, of adult personnel by administration.
- Restrict activities to proper facilities and playing fields.
- Ensure that proper health care is available to participants and that participant fitness and health are monitored. Require medical examinations prior to allowing students to participate in athletic activities.
- Ensure that all school athletics and activities are conducted in compliance with statutory guidelines, regulations, safety rules, and eligibility requirements.
- Provide proper and safe transportation to athletic and other extracurricular school activities.

ADDITIONAL CASES OF INTEREST TO EDUCATORS

Brown v. Tesack, 566 So.2d 955 (La. 1990). A *breach of a duty of reasonable care* imposes liability on a school board.

Brownell v. Los Angeles Unified School District, 4 Cal.App.4th 787, 5 Cal.Rptr.2d 756 (1992). The school district did not have reason to *foresee* the gang-related shooting of a student.

Fallon v. Indiana Trail School, 148 Ill. App.3d 931, 102 Ill. Dec. 479, 500 N.E.2d 101 (1986). A trampoline is not abnormally dangerous for the purpose of imposing *strict liability*.

Hammond v. Board of Education of Carroll County, 639 A.2d 223 (Md. App. 1994). A student (female) assumed the normal risks of injury in choosing to play tackle football.

Hutchison v. Toews, 476 P.2d 811 (Or. App. 1970). An injured student with *knowledge of risk* involved is *contributorily negligent*.

Johnson v. School District of Millard, 253 Neb. 634, 573 N.W.2d 116 (1998). A *reasonably prudent* teacher could have *foreseen* possible injury to student.

Simonetti v. School District of Philadelphia, 454 A.2d 1038 (Pa. Sup. 1982). A momentary *absence* from classroom by teacher does not constitute *negligence*.

Spears v. Jefferson Parish School Board, 646 So.2d 1104 (La. App. 1994). A school district is liable for damages for an *intentional act* by a teacher resulting in *emotional harm* to a student.

Stevens v. Chesteen, 561 So.2d 1100 (Ala. Sup. 1990). A brief *absence from class* by teacher does not constitute a breach of *duty of reasonable supervision*.

Wagonblast v. Odessa School District, 110 Wash.2d 845, 758, P.2d 968 (1988). *Releases or waivers* that parents are required to sign as a condition of a student engaging in school activities and that absolve school districts from liability for negligence *are invalid*.

CHAPTER RESOURCES

Alexander, K., & Alexander, M. (2002). *American public school law* (5th ed.). Belmont, CA: West/Thompson.

Ardoin v. Evangeline Parish School Board, 376 So.2d 372 (La. App. 1979).

Armlin v. Board of Education, 36 A.D.2d 877, 320 N.Y.S.2d 402 (1971).

Arnold v. Hayslett, 655 S.W.2d 941 (Tenn. 1981).

Barnhizer v. Paradise Valley Unified School District No. 69, 599 P.2d 209 (Ariz. 1979).

Barth v. Board of Education of Chicago, 490 N.E.2d 77 (Ill. App. 1986).

Bellman v. San Francisco High School District, 81 P.2d 894 (Cal. Sup. 1938).

Brevard County v. Jacks, 238 So.2d 156 (Fla. App. 1970).

Brown v. City of Oakland, 124 P.2d 369 (Cal. App. 1942).

Chapman v. State, 492 P.2d 607 (Wash. App. 1972).

Charonnatt v. San Francisco Unified School District, 133 P.2d 643 (Cal. App. 1943).

Cooper v. Smith Town Central School District, 441 N.Y.S.2d 553 (N.Y. App. 1981).

Czaplicki v. Gooding Joint School District No. 231, 775 P.2d 640 (Idaho 1989).

District of Columbia v. Royal, 465 A.2d (D.C. 1983).

Ehlinger v. Board of Education of New Hartford Center School District, 465 N.Y.S.2d 378 (App. Div. 1983).

Foster v. Houston General Insurance Company, 401 So.2d 759, 763 (La. App. 1981).

Gammon v. Edwardsville, 403 N.E.2d 43 (Ill. App. 1980).

Gardner v. State, 22 N.E.2d 344 (N.Y. App. 1939).

Givens v. Orleans Parish School Board, 391 So.2d 976 (La. App. 1980).

Govel v. Board of Education in the City of Albany, 235 N.Y.S.2d 300 (N.Y. Sup. 1962).

Guerrieri v. Tyson, 24 A.2d 468 (Pa. Sup. 1942).

Gurule v. Salt Lake City Board of Education, 661 P.2d 975 (Utah Sup. 1983).

Hampton v. Orleans Parish School Board, 422 So.2d 202 (La. App. 1982).

Hanson v. Reedley Joint Union School District, 43 Cal.App.2d 643, 111 P.2d 415 (Ca. App. 1941).

Harvey v. Ouachita Parish School Board, 674 So.2d 372 (110 Ed. L. Rep. 507) (La. App. 1996).

Hatlett v. Oswego-Appalachian School District, 420 N.Y.S.2d 448 (N.Y. Sup. 1979).

LaValley v. Stanford, 70 N.Y.S.2d 460 (N.Y. App. 1947).

Laveck v. City of Janesville, 204 N.W.2d 6 (Wis. Sup. 1973).

Libby v. West Coast Rock Co., Inc., 308 So.2d 602 (Fla. App. 1975).

Lostumbo v. Board of Education of the City of Norwalk, 418 A.2d 949 (Conn. Sup. 1980).

Luce v. Board of Education, 157 N.Y.S.2d 123 (N.Y. App. 1956).

Magabgab v. Orleans Parish School Board, 239 So.2d 456 (La. App. 1970).

Martini v. Olyphant Borough School District, 83 Pa. D. & C. 206 (C. Lackawana County 1953).

Mattison v. Hudson Falls, 458 N.Y.S.2d 726 (N.Y. App. 1983).

Miles v. School District No. 138, 281 N.W.2d 396 (Neb. 1979).

Monfils v. City of Sterling Heights, 269 N.W.2d 588 (Mich. App. 1978).

Morris v. Douglas County School District, 430 P.2d 775 (Ore. 1965).

Nester v. City of New York, 211 N.Y.S.2d 975 (N.Y. Sup. 1961).

O'Brian v. Township High School District 214, 73, 3d 618, 92 N.E.2d 615 (Ill. App. 1979).

Ohman v. Board of Education of City of New York, 300 N.Y.S. 306, 90 N.E.2d 474 (N.Y. 1949).

Orgando v. Carquineu School District, 71 P.2d 641 (Cal. App. 1938).

Peter W. v. San Francisco Unified School District, 60 Cal.App.3d 814 (1976).

Powell v. Orleans Parish School Board, 354 So.2d 229 (La. App. 1978).

Raymond v. Paradise Unified School District, 218 Cal.App.2d 1, 31 Cal. Rptr. 847 (1963).

Reed v. University of North Dakota, 543 N.W.2d 106 (106 Educ. L. Rep. 891) (Minn. App. 1996).

Rickle v. Oakdale Union Grammar School District, 253 P.2d 1 (Cal. Sup. 1953).

Roberts v. Robertson County Board of Education, 692 S.W.2d 863 (Tenn. App. 1985).

Savers v. Ranger, 83 A.2d 775 (N.J. App. 1951).

Selleck v. Board of Education, 276 A.D. 263, 94 N.Y.S.2d 318 (1949).

Sharp v. Fairbanks North Star Borough, 569 P.2d 178 (Alaska 1977).

Shoop, R. J., & Dunklee, D. R. (1992). *School law for the principal: A handbook for practitioners.* Needham Heights, MA: Allyn & Bacon.

Simmons v. Beauregard Parish School Board, 315 So.2d 883 (La. App. 1975).

Welch v. Dunsmuir Joint Union High School, 326 P.2d 633 (Cal. App. 1958).

Wilbur v. City of Binghamton, 66 N.Y.S.2d 250 (N.Y. App. 1946).

Williamson v. Board of Education, 375 N.Y.S.2d 221 (N.Y. App. 1975).

Woodring v. Board of Education of Manhasset Union Free School District, 435 N.Y.S.2d (N.Y. 1981).

Young v. Orleans Parish School Board, 391 So.2d 11 (La. App. 1980).

Index

**CORWIN
PRESS**

The Corwin Press logo—a raven striding across an open book—represents the union of courage and learning. Corwin Press is committed to improving education for all learners by publishing books and other professional development resources for those serving the field of PreK–12 education. By providing practical, hands-on materials, Corwin Press continues to carry out the promise of its motto: **"Helping Educators Do Their Work Better."**